D1447813

COMPONENT-BASED
SOFTWARE DEVELOPMENT:
CASE STUDIES

SERIES ON COMPONENT-BASED SOFTWARE DEVELOPMENT

Aims and Scope

Component-based software development (CBD) is concerned with software development by using independently produced components, e.g. commercial off-the-shelf (COTS) software. It is an emerging discipline that promises to take software engineering into a new era. Building on the achievements of object-oriented software construction, CBD aims to deliver software engineering from a "cottage industry" into an "industrial age for Information Technology," whereby software can be assembled in the manner that hardware systems are currently constructed from kits of parts. Although the idea of using components to build complex systems is as old as the software engineering discipline itself, it is only recently that CBD has become the focus of research for a sizeable international community.

This series aims to serve this community by publishing all kinds of material on CBD: state-of-the-art reports and surveys, conference proceedings, collected works, research monographs, as well as textbooks. It should therefore provide a key forum for CBD researchers, practitioners and students worldwide.

Call for Contributions

If you have suitable ideas or material for the series, please contact the Editor-in-Chief:

Kung-Kiu Lau
Department of Computer Science
The University of Manchester
Manchester M13 9PL
United Kingdom
kung-kiu@cs.man.ac.uk

Series on Component-Based Software Development – Vol. 1

COMPONENT–BASED SOFTWARE DEVELOPMENT:
CASE STUDIES

Kung-Kiu Lau

The University of Manchester, UK

editor

World Scientific

NEW JERSEY • LONDON • SINGAPORE • SHANGHAI • HONG KONG • TAIPEI • CHENNAI

Published by

World Scientific Publishing Co. Pte. Ltd.

5 Toh Tuck Link, Singapore 596224

USA office: Suite 202, 1060 Main Street, River Edge, NJ 07661

UK office: 57 Shelton Street, Covent Garden, London WC2H 9HE

British Library Cataloguing-in-Publication Data
A catalogue record for this book is available from the British Library.

COMPONENT-BASED SOFTWARE DEVELOPMENT
Case Studies

ISBN 981-238-828-1

Printed in Singapore.

Preface

Component-based Software Development (CBD) is an emerging discipline that promises to take Software Engineering into a new era. Building on the achievements of Object-Oriented Software Construction, CBD aims to deliver Software Engineering from a 'cottage industry' into an 'industrial age for Information Technology', whereby software can be assembled from components, in the manner that hardware systems are constructed from kits of parts nowadays.

As with any emerging discipline, there is as yet no standard terminology in CBD. No universal agreement has been reached on the very definition of what a software component is, and there is even an alternative to the acronym CBD itself, namely CBSE (Component-based Software Engineering), which is just as widely used. Even less clear is how the whole field will develop in the near future, let alone the longer term. Therefore it would seem more sensible (and feasible) to survey the current state of CBD, as reflected by activities that have been going on recently under the banner of CBD, than to predict future trends. The primary aim of this volume therefore is to attempt to provide such a snapshot. It is hoped that the survey would have the desirable side-effect of indicating pointers to future trends.

The articles in this volume report on case studies into a sample of the myriad aspects of CBD. Case studies are loosely defined as self-contained fixed-term investigations with a finite set of clearly defined objectives and measurable outcomes. In a new field, where mature theories do not yet exist, case studies provide an informative glimpse into the current concerns and issues.

The first part of the book deals with COTS (commercial off-the-shelf) components. These are the first commercially available software components. Typically they are executable binaries that come with no proper specifications, no source code and no guarantees. Chapter 1 is a survey of approaches to constructing software using COTS components. Chapter 2 describes one approach to specifying COTS components, and Chapter 3 reports on a case study on an acquisition process for third-party COTS components.

Various methodologies for CBD have been proposed. Chapter 4 describes a case study on using the KobrA method, and Chapter 5 argues for an aspect-oriented approach to the design and implementation stages of CBD life cycle.

A crucial property of CBD software is compositionality, i.e. how to calculate or predict properties of a composite from those of its constituents. Indeed, compositional or pre-dictable assembly is a pre-requisite for CBD to succeed in general. Chapter 6 presents a theory of properties of component-based systems. Chapter 7 shows an approach to mea-suring properties of embedded control systems.

Software testing is also important for component software. Chapter 8 describes a case study on testing CORBA software.

What about the role of formality in CBD? Chapter 9 describes a formal approach to using components in the requirements capture stage of the software life cycle, and Chapter 10 presents a formal approach to specifying and adapting components.

Reflecting the diverse nature of CBD, the last part of the book deals with components used in Grid Computing. Chapter 11 describes a case study on a CORBA-based architec-ture for legacy applications in Grid Computing, and Chapter 12 reports on experiments in Problem Solving Environments for numerical computations.

Finally, as editor, I would like to thank all the contributing authors. Personally I have enjoyed learning about their work. I wish them success in their CBD research, and I look forward to their future contributions. I would also like to thank the people who provided invaluable help with the reviews: Manuel Carro, Len Freeman, Bernd Fischer, Shui-Ming Ho, Tuomas Ihme, Gerald Kotonya, Rikard Land, Chang Liu, Zhiming Liu, Frank Lüders, John Penix, Judith Stafford and Anders Wall. To all the authors and the reviewers, I owe a debt of gratitude.

Manchester   Kung-Kiu Lau
September 2003

Contents

Chapter 1

A Survey of Proposals for Architecting Component Software

TUOMAS IHM

VTT Electronics, Kaitovayla 1, P.O.Box 1100
FIN-90571 Oulu, Finland
Tuomas.Ihme@vtt.fi

Abstract. This chapter is a literature survey of architecting component software. It focuses on the architectural problems, challenges and proposals faced when utilizing commercial off-the-shelf (COTS) components in COTS-intensive systems, as well as in real-time and embedded systems. It also addresses the more mature architectural area of component-based systems and product lines where the specific characteristics of COTS components have been ignored.

1.1 Introduction

There were several reuse shortcoming in early component systems (Weinreich and Sametinger, 2001). Components at the application level were too coarse-grained for widespread reuse, the component systems lacked composition support, and operating systems lacked domain-specific standards. Operating systems, relational database engines and transaction-processing monitors are among the early successful component systems (Szyperski, 1998). Applications from different vendors often adhere to the same standard defined by an operating system. Operating systems are component model implementations (Weinreich and Sametinger, 2001). An implementation of a component model standard defines the interoperation between components from independent component suppliers in a binary form.

    Component-based development has been considered a true revolution on a par with stored-program computers and high-level languages in computing technology during the past fifty years (Maurer, 2000). The consensus today is that component software is the most promising reuse approach (Messerschmitt and Szyperski, 2001). Szyperski identifies the following three sets of arguments in favor of component software (Szyperski, 2000):

- Baseline argument: Strategic components are made while non-strategic ones are bought.
- Enterprise argument: A core set of components can be configured in the products of one product line in different ways. In addition, product specific components may also be configured in the products. Product evolution can be controlled by versioning components and reconfiguring systems.
- Dynamic computing argument: Modern open systems can be dynamically extended.

The second section of this chapter discusses general COTS component related topics, such as definitions of COTS components, component models, software development processes, the maturity of COTS products, COTS components in real-time and embedded systems, and the benefits and risks of COTS components. The third section describes the more mature architectural area of component-based systems and product lines where the specific characteristics of COTS components have been ignored. The fourth section discusses the challenges created by the COTS components for the architecture of software systems. Finally, some interesting issues concerning the architecture of COTS component intensive systems will be discussed and some conclusions will be provided in the last section.

1.2 COTS Software Components

Heineman and Councill (2001) define the concept software component as "A software element that conforms to a component model and can be independently deployed and composed without modification according to a composition standard." Meyers and Oberndorf (2001, p. 13) include the roles of the vendor and consumer in their COTS product definition. IEEE Standard 1062 (1998) defines that "COTS software is defined by a market driven need, commercially available and whose fitness for use has been demonstrated by a broad spectrum of commercial users. Also, the COTS software supplier does not advertise any willingness to modify the software for a specific customer."

Variability can be achieved by plugging different components together. However, common COTS products can be tailored by the integrator in many ways to enhance a component with a functionality not provided by the supplier (Carney and Long, 2000). Tailoring does not include modifying a COTS component so that the modified component is no longer replaceable with the supplier's future releases. IEEE Standard 1062 (1998) defines that a so-called MOTS (Modified-Off-The-Shelf) software product "is already developed and available, usable either "as is" or with modification, and provided by the supplier, acquirer, or a third party. MOTS software does advertise services to tailor the software to acquirer-specific requirements."

1.2.1 *Component Models*

The most important distinction between components and objects is that software components conform to the standards defined by a component technology (Weinreich and Sametinger, 2001). The specification of a component's context dependencies must include its provided and required interfaces and the component technology (or technologies) to which it conforms (Szyperski, 1998). The most popular component technologies are Microsoft's COM+, Sun's Enterprise JavaBeans (EJB) and the Common Object Request Broker Architecture (CORBA) Component Model (CCM) (Councill and Heineman, 2001, p. 660; Volter, 2001).

These component technologies share the three important characteristics (Councill and Heineman, 2001, p. 659). A component model standard describes how to implement components that conform to the specific component model. The component model implementation is necessary for these components to execute. The well-defined component model with its robust implementations is capable of creating an entire component-based industry.

The Cat One component model (D'Souza and Wills, 1999) is itself extensible. Apperly *et al.* (2001, p. 770) anticipate that a new MQM (Message Queuing Middleware) component model will appear in the near-term future or that there will be bridges between commercial component models and MQM.

1.2.2 *COTS Components and the Software Development Process*

Several component-oriented methods such as Catalysis (D'Souza and Wills, 1999), UML components (Cheesman and Daniels, 2002) and KobrA (Atkinson *et al.*, 2001; Atkinson and Muthig, 2002) have emerged in the last few years. Component-oriented methods have roots in the first-generation object-oriented methods. One of these methods, Real-Time Object-Oriented Modeling (ROOM) (Bass *et al.*, 1998), was a precursor of run-time component models. Interface ports and protocols of UML-RT (Selic and Rumbaugh, 1998) (the successor of ROOM) capsules allow one to standardize component interfaces so that it is possible to connect different candidates or variants of commercial software in the architecture. The Rational Rose RealTime (Rose RT) tool from Rational Software Corporation supports UML-RT. The integrability of the candidates and variants can be evaluated using the tool. Object-oriented method frameworks, such as Rational Unified Process (Jacobson *et al.*, 1998) comprise many component-oriented concepts. The frameworks must be tailored to the needs of specific organizations or projects. Several product line oriented methods have emerged in recent years that focus on the development of product families. They and other architecture oriented methods prefer components to fit with software architecture, whereas current component-based software engineering prefers existing components (Lau, 2001). Lau (2001) argues that existing methods are not capable of predictable component assembly, i.e., they do not meet key pre-requisites for component-based software engineering. He believes that the key pre-requisites are the following: a standard semantics of components and component composition, good interface specifications, and a good assembly guide for selecting components.

The use of COTS components has several implications for the software development process (Boehm and Abts, 1999; Brown and Wallnau, 1988; Brownword *et al.*, 2000; Dean and Vigder, 1997; Fox *et al.*, 1997; Lau, 2001; Morisio *et al.*, 2000). A dynamic, spiral, risk-driven development process is needed. Initial software requirements must be defined at a high abstraction level, because detailed requirements can only be determined in parallel with COTS component selection. COTS-components are identified, evaluated and selected in several decision steps during the requirements analysis phase. Significant up-front and early stage effort is required for COTS components acquisition and evaluation. Over-hasty commitment to a specific architecture should be avoided. There is an overlapping definition and trade-off of the COTS marketplace, system requirements, and system architecture. COTS component integration is an act of composition. The maintenance of COTS components occurs at the level of components rather than at the level of source code. In contrast to the above implications, the components have an important role only in the final implementation and deployment phases in most software development approaches.

1.2.3 *The Maturity of COTS Products and COTS-based Systems*

Ten hypotheses (Basili and Boehm, 2001) summarize the area of COTS products and COTS-based systems (CBS). (1) More than 99 percent of all executing computer instructions come from COTS products. Every project should weigh CBS benefits, costs and risks against other options. (2) More than half the features in large COTS software products go unused. This added complexity requires expanded computer resources. (3) The average COTS software product undergoes a new release every eight to nine months, with active vendor support for only its most recent three releases. This introduces maintenance risks if the product development of a COTS integrator is inconsistent with the market's evolution. (4) CBS development and post-development efforts can scale as high as the square of the number of independently developed COTS products targeted for integration. Four such products can be too many. (5) CBS post-development costs exceed CBS development costs. The lifecycle cost distributions for CBS software and non-CBS software are similar. (6) Although glue-code development usually accounts for less than half the total CBS software development effort, the effort per line of glue code averages about three times the effort per line of developed-applications code. COTS assessment investment can reduce glue-code. (7) Non-development costs, such as licensing fees, are significant, and projects must plan for and optimize them. The technical and management processes of an organization should address CBS issues. (8) CBS assessment and tailoring efforts vary significantly by COTS product classes. There is no robust data available for the estimation of the efforts. (9) Personnel capability and experience remain the dominant factors influencing CBS-development productivity. Difficult COTS integration challenges should not be undertaken without skilled support. (10) CBS is currently a high-risk activity, with effort and schedule overruns exceeding non-CBS software overruns. Yet many systems have used COTS successfully for cost reduction and early delivery. CBS cost and schedule estimates should be validated frequently and systematically.

CBS is a relatively immature area and therefore the above list represents preliminary hypotheses, rather than results, for examining CBS project decisions against small empirical data samples. The list can be considered a starting point for the development of solid methods for coping with empirical knowledge of CBS.

Dean and Vigder (1997) believe that COTS components cannot be pre-qualified as generic components for use in related systems in their domain. Components must be re-evaluated against criteria that are valid only for each individual system. Often there is no evidence that any rigorous and disciplined process has been used for the development of COTS components (Talbert, 1998). Therefore, a lot of extra work has to be done to show that the COTS component fits its intended use. Reusable domain components are often found only within a singular domain (Williams, 2001).

Trusted components require the following three things (Councill and Heineman, 2001, p. 748): Adequate documentation of the components and the component infrastructure, component-based software management, and third-party certification. Specifications of architectural components are intrinsically incomplete and must be extensible, incremental and heterogeneous (Shaw, 1996). Structural and extra-functional properties (Shaw, 1996), as well as product line constraints, augment the conventional functional properties of components. An especially important structural property is the packaging of a component, which includes the component type and the types of supported interactions. The idea of the credential of a component (Shaw, 1996) has been incorporated in an approach for building systems from commercial components (Wallnau *et al.*, 2001). A credential includes the name of the component property, the value of this property and the means that have been used to obtain this value. Lau (2001) argues that a priori correctness will provide a basis for component certification and also form the basis of predictable component assembly.

It is useful to classify software components based on complexity, cost, productivity factors, and the skill sets needed to develop and use the components. Williams (2001) divides components into the following three categories: GUI components, service components and domain components. Applications are provided with access to common services through service components. Service components are combined with message-oriented middleware, transaction servers, data transformation engines, database access services, system integration services, infrastructure support, and workflow systems (Williams, 2001). There is no standard approach to documenting and cataloguing software components (Apperly *et al.*, 2001).

1.2.4 *COTS Components in Real-time and Embedded systems*

Applications that rank functionality, ease of use, and flexibility higher than reliability and integrity are good candidates for COTS. The more availability, integrity, reliability and safety are emphasized, the harder it becomes to make COTS use cost-effective and to make a convincing argument for using COTS (Talbert, 1998). Conventional COTS software has been incapable of guaranteeing stringent quality of service (QoS) properties or partially QoS-enabled but inflexible and non-standard, and thus is unsuitable for mission-critical distributed real-time and embedded systems (Schmidt, 2002).

Challenging requirements for those systems are identified in (Schmidt, 2002; Szyperski, 1998). It is important but difficult to describe the abstract interaction of components. How can variety and flexibility needs be covered? Multiple QoS properties must be satisfied and guaranteed in real time in the presence of third-party components. Service levels must be scalable according to different configurations, environmental conditions, and costs. The service levels in different dimensions must be co-ordinated to meet mission needs. The distributed system software must adapt to dynamic changes in mission requirements and environmental conditions.

The most frequently used COTS components in embedded real-time systems are large software components such as GUIs, middleware, operation systems, and databases. There has been not much use of small, low-level COTS components such as device drivers (Talbert, 1998). Embedded and application software components, which have not demonstrated compliance with software standards, may eventually not be permitted in the future (Flynt, 2001, p. 707). For example, the ANSI/UL 1998 Standard (Standard for Software in Programmable Components) addresses important product life cycle issues for system components that result in end products. The Underwriter Laboratories provide certification services for safety-critical software for programmable components (Flynt, 2001). Yacoub *et al.* (2000) describe a model for generating COTS certification criteria for product lines.

Middleware standards have matured considerably with respect to the requirements of distributed real-time and embedded systems (Schmidt, 2002). For example, the Minimum CORBA renders CORBA usable in memory-constrained applications. The Real-Time CORBA supports applications that reserve and manage the network, CPU, and memory resources predictably. The CORBA Messaging provides timeouts, request priorities, and queuing disciplines to applications. The Fault-Tolerant CORBA supports replication, fault detection, and failure recovery. Robust implementations of these CORBA standards are available. In addition, there are emerging standards such as the Dynamic Scheduling Real-Time CORBA, the Real-Time Specification for Java, and the Distributed Real-Time Specification for Java. However, COTS middleware technology is not yet mature enough to cover large-scale dynamically changing systems. Pree and Pasetti assess existing middleware such as CORBA and its real-time extension as being too complex for real-time control systems and propose a lean middleware concept instead of it (Pree and Pasetti, 2001).

1.2.5 *Risks and Benefits of COTS Components*

COTS components are separated from each other and from the integrator's system by evolution over time and by independent development over space. A fundamental risk issue within the use of COTS components is their interoperability across time and space (Szyperski, 1998): how can these COTS components co-operate within the integrator's system? The most difficult problems and risks are at the software architecture and system levels (Clements and Northrop, 2001). Risks associated with the use of COTS components have been reported in (Ballurio, 2002; Boehm and Abts, 1999; Carney *et al.*, 2000; Clements and Northrop, 2001; Kotonya and Rashid, 2001; Rakic and Medvidovic, 2001; Szyperski, 1998; Talbert, 1998; Wallnau *et al.*, 2001; Vigder, 1998; Vigder and Dean, 1997). The benefits of COTS components have been reported for example in (Boehm and Abts, 1999; Szyperski, 2000; Vigder, 1998).

1.3 Components and Software Architecture

Szyperski (Szyperski, 1998) argues that the architecture of component-based systems is significantly more demanding than that of traditional software systems. He writes that architectural issues are particularly urgent and challenging problems in component software. The non-functional properties of a software system are mainly determined by its architecture (Anderson and Dyson, 2000). A component system architecture is an open research problem (Szyperski, 1998). Szyperski (Szyperski, 1998) proposes a layered architecture with three tiers: components, component frameworks and a component system. He considers component frameworks, called also component infrastructures (Heineman and Councill, 2001), as one of the most powerful component engineering approaches. He defines a component framework as "A collection of rules and interfaces (contracts) that govern the interaction of components plugged into the framework."

Frameworks are like customizable components. Vendors sell them as products and integrators may integrate several frameworks into an application (Johnson, 1997). Designers must learn the complex interfaces of frameworks before they can use and customize them. Architectural patterns and frameworks are descriptions of and solutions to recurring architectural problems. Fig. 1.1 illustrates the relationships between patterns, frameworks and components (Larsen, 1999).

A pattern or a framework in Fig. 1.1 can be an architectural pattern or framework. Frameworks can be applied like patterns but only frameworks may have extension points for augmenting their behavior. Components are composed without modification. A pattern or framework is usually implemented across many components. Many patterns can be applied within a framework or component. A component can be used in many frameworks.

The distributed nature of users and information, as well as the need for scalability and robustness, have led to the adoption of multi-tier architecture in most modern systems (Longshaw, 2001; Volter, 2001). Longshaw proposes a middle-tier component architecture for the component model implementation of middle tier servers in distributed systems.

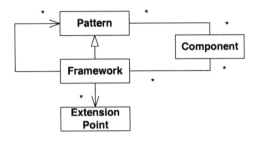

Fig. 1.1 A metamodel for the relationships between patterns, frameworks and components (Larsen, 1999).

A component composition standard supports the creation of a component infrastructure, sometimes also called a component framework, for the assembly of components (Heineman and Councill, 2001, p. 42). Components are connected with each other and inserted and substituted within a component infrastructure. The basic component interaction types are client-server and publish-subscribe.

Component infrastructures support not only component reuse but also the reuse of an entire design. For example, there are reusable component infrastructures for graphic editors, compound documents and simulation systems (Heineman and Councill, 2001).

1.3.1 *Integration of Software Components*

Most object-oriented approaches do not result in plug-in component architectures (Schneider and Nierstrasz, 2000). Software components must be integrated into the existing software architecture in such a way that the system's domain-specific services can be executed as required and the global design principles are met.

Visual or graphic application building can be successfully used when the number of components or entities in any architectural view is small. In other cases, a more spacious, economical and maintainable abstract method, such as a tabular, formula based, or textual method, is preferable (Szyperski, 1998).

System generation has been applied to software architecture descriptions and inter-component communication mechanisms to improve productivity when building system families whose architectures are well understood (Stafford and

Wolf, 2001). System generation can improve the manageability of component-based applications because changes affecting the components can be effectively managed during the generation process rather than at the component level.

The simulation and validation of executable architectural designs offer important benefits (Ihme, 2001). Simulation and validation tools can aid in analyzing the quality attributes of architecture. The tools can also aid to ensure that stated functional requirements can be achieved when a specified architecture is in use, and that a certain part of the runtime structure of a product corresponds to the related part of the reference architecture. Meanwhile, software reuse potential has proven minimal across the development tools supporting simulation, validation and code generation (Ihme, 2001).

There are scripting languages for defining connections between components (Achermann and Nierstrasz, 2002; Szyperski, 1998). Agent communication languages are used to define the overall structure of an agent system and standard patterns of interaction between agents (Griss, 2001). Glue abstractions are used to bridge components that have not been designed to work together (Achermann and Nierstrasz, 2002; Schneider, 1999).

A composition language is a high-level language for composing applications from software components. The components are implemented in conventional programming languages. Composition languages are not biased towards any one particular scripting paradigm as scripting languages are. Composition languages allow components to be posed according to different compositional styles. A composition language allows an explicit software architecture description and the flexible composition of components (Nierstrasz and Meijler, 1995). Piccola is a prototype of a pure composition language (Achermann and Nierstrasz, 2002). It allows applications to be expressed as compositions in terms of components, scripts, and glue (Schneider and Nierstrasz, 2000).

Aspect-oriented component engineering (Grundy, 2000) has been used for specifying requirements-level component aspects, categorizing component design decisions, choosing inter-component relationships, accessing high-level knowledge about a component's capabilities, performing basic configuration validity checks, and accessing run-time information about component aspects.

Object modeling notations have been used for describing component-based systems designs (Szyperski, 1998). The notations have many advantages, such as familiarity among software designers, a direct mapping to implementations, and the support of commercial tools and design methods (Garlan *et al.*, 2000). They have several deficiencies regarding the architecture of component-based systems: only the method invocation primitive for component interaction, weak support for hierarchical description, no support for the definition of product families, and no direct support for non-functional properties (Garlan *et al.*,

2000). UML 2.0 is anticipated to enhance the inadequate support of UML 1.x for component-based development (Kobryn, 2002). These problems can also be overcome by using an architecture description language (ADL) (Garlan *et al.*, 2000). There are a few commercial architecture description languages such as SDL (Specification and Description Language) and ROOM (Real-Time Object-Oriented Modeling) (Bass *et al.*, 1998).

1.3.2 *Software Components and Product line Architecture*

One lesson from the history of software architectures, components and reuse is that it is profitable to focus on a narrow domain or subdomains, and collect components which are known to be useful in that particular domain (Barroca *et al.*, 2000). These subdomains have often been a combination of application subdomains and technology subdomains. For example, large distributed telecommunication and automation systems have included operating, management and maintenance subsystems (application subdomains) on desktop and workstation computers (technology subdomains) that provide open platforms for commercial software products. Another lesson is that useful component collections in most cases have been small, e.g. only 100 components, so that library retrieval systems have not been necessary (Barroca *et al.*, 2000). It is important to understand the domain in which components are deployed and how to use domain knowledge in integrating the components. These observations have led to domain specific software architectures, product-line approaches and component frameworks (Barroca *et al.*, 2000; Szyperski, 1998). Experiences (Obbink *et al.*, 2002) show that product qualities and the life-cycle phase of products should be taken carefully into account in selecting and implementing a component platform oriented software product-line. The product qualities affect business performance, development process performance, and product performance, or are intrinsic qualities to the products. Obbink *et al.* (2002) describe how different product qualities lead to variations in component-oriented platform architecting in the mature life-cycle phase of two product families. Griss (2000) suggests that modeling a set of common and variable features is essential for building a flexible product line architecture for customized, feature-oriented components. Van Gurp *et al.* (2001) provide a conceptual framework, patterns and a method for variability in software product lines.

Component-based software methods typically emphasize the implementation of software artefacts as components and provide only some heuristics for their reusability. The augmentation of component-based software engineering approaches with product-line engineering techniques provides a notable benefit potential (Atkinson and Muthig, 2002; Heineman and Councill, 2001, p. 744). A product line architecture specifies the common components of the product line. The product line architecture and a product line production plan prescribe how the product line components must be assembled and used together. The components share assumptions about common things such as the division of responsibilities, data encoding and protocols (Shaw, 1996). Product line components are evolved and maintained in the asset base. There may be also product specific components.

1.4 COTS Components and Software Architecture

While composability (Messerschmitt and Szyperski, 2001) is the key issue for COTS-intensive systems, it is difficult to archive. Components are composable with respect to some specific opportunity if they are interoperable and complementary with respect to that opportunity (Messerschmitt and Szyperski, 2001). Components are interoperable if they can communicate in a meaningful way. They are complementary if they enable useful communication. The architecture of COTS-intensive systems should be fault-tolerant. It should allow the system to be composed of COTS components without loss of the maintainability and other key properties of the complex system. For example, the exact impact of composed COTS components on overall system performance is hard to predict precisely: a combination of separately fast components can be very slow (Messerschmitt and Szyperski, 2001).

The architecture of COTS-intensive systems is typically created in a process of coincidental piecemeal growth (Coplien, 1999), i.e. without any systematic process for the growth and changes of the architecture. This process often results in deteriorated architectures. An architectural COTS component often admits the use of whole sets of available and compatible COTS components and inhibits the use of whole sets of incompatible components.

A method of analyzing the architectures of COTS-intensive systems (Ballurio, 2002) has recently emerged. Communication protocols, data access, data synchronization, distribution of functionality, physical deployment, scalability, system performance and security often cause special difficulties in the system design of COTS-intensive systems (Ballurio, 2002). Component-based architectures have potential benefits in supporting localized refactoring, not only within components, but also in designing a hierarchical system architecture for the selective refactoring of subsystems (Szyperski, 1998). Architectural deterioration can also be avoided by integrating a product-line approach with a component-based software engineering approach.

1.4.1 *COTS Components and Product line Architecture*

It may pay to modify the product line architecture to make places for COTS components (Clements and Northrop, 2001, Ch. 4.4). Yacoub *et al.* (2000) identify four context attributes in their architecture conformance criteria for integrating COTS components in a product line: generality, interoperability, portability, and compliance with standards. Product line reference architecture defines the operation context of COTS components.

Clements and Northrop give some guidelines for integrating COTS components into a product line (Clements and Northrop, 2001). Organization-specific constraints and standards need to be written so they can be reviewed for completeness and relevancy, and be given to guide the product development. It will pay to follow middleware products, relevant COTS components, standards groups and products conforming to standards. Develop flexible requirements. Develop evaluation criteria and evaluation procedures for COTS components. Develop COTS purchasing polices. Plan COTS integration tasks, including adaptation with wrappers and middleware. Test interfaces, interactions with other components and especially their quality-attribute requirements. Manage the current product configuration and anticipate potential replacements and new products.

COTS components can populate the core assets of a product line, or they can be integrated with specific products in the product line (Clements and Northrop, 2001, Ch. 4.4.1). The COTS components of the core assets must satisfy the variability needs and requirements of the product line that cannot be compromised. A product line architecture solution including COTS components needs to be generalized to involve general-purpose integration mechanisms such as wrappers and middleware for a number of potential products instead of single-product systems. Evolution and maintenance strategies are now more complex, due to the greater range of affected products. A product line architecture solution including COTS components needs to be more flexible. It must be possible to analyze its architecture for maintainability, evolution, and group quality attributes. The concept of components must have an important role in the earlier phases of development and product line concepts should be explicitly supported in the later phases of development (Atkinson and Muthig, 2002).

Core asset COTS components need to be dependable for a long period of time and the following component issues are emphasized (Clements and Northrop, 2001, Ch. 4.4.2): maturity and stability, expected update schedules, interoperability with the components of a wide variety of products, interoperability with the component infrastructure of the product line, stability of the supplier, generality and extensibility. In addition, licensing issues are more complex, because the component may be used in multiple copies of many different products.

A product line approach proved to be urgent in the development of the Control Channel Toolkit (Clements and Northrop, 2001) for COTS-intensive product lines of ground-based spacecraft command and control systems. The development was not architecture-centric from the start.

Framelets are self-standing units, small product lines, within the product line (Pasetti and Pree, 2000). They export three types of constructs: components, interfaces and design patterns. Component constructs are configurable binary units that can be used "as they are".

1.4.2 *MOTS Frameworks and COTS Components*

Frameworks provide a reusable context for components ((Johnson, 1997). A component framework can be used to create a coarser-grain component from a set of relevant components, their connections and partial configurations (Messerschmitt and Szyperski, 2001). Middleware frameworks support the configuration and integration of multiple independently developed capabilities to meet the functional and QoS requirements of individual applications (Schmidt, 2002). Large customized MOTS frameworks, such as the Control Channel Toolkit (Clements and Northrop, 2001) and SCOS-2000 (Di Girolamo *et al.*, 2001), have proven to be successful in building ground-based spacecraft command and control systems. The frameworks, or component infrastructures, are also called product line asset bases. Open reference architecture is the key asset of the asset bases. It supports variability on the system, application and implementation levels and allows multiple contractors, varying COTS products and technology evolution. The frameworks do not provide complete solutions for integrators but they have to customize the asset bases and integrate additional self-made and COTS components into the asset base architectures.

1.4.3 *Desirable Properties for Component Software Architecture*

Desirable properties for component software architecture have been identified for example in (Talbert, 1998; Vigder and Dean, 1997; Vigder *et al.*, 1996). An appropriate architecture for the use of COTS components should allow the substitution of components and the use of redundant components. It should support the isolation of components and minimal coupling between components. It should allow unwanted functionality to be hidden or masked, and behavior to be monitored and verified during runtime, and faults in a component to be prevented from propagating through the system. It should be like a product line architecture, allowing components to be shared across projects and products. The architecture must adapt to the potentially different component integration styles, data models and formats and to the connectors and interfaces available in component models. It must adapt to the functionality available in the components by adding a desired functionality as well as hiding or masking undesired functionality. The integrator must adapt components to the desired architecture and, often simultaneously adapt the architecture to the available COTS components in order to minimize the architectural mismatch. The whole spectrum of components, in-house software, custom components, MOTS components and COTS components, is usually needed to build a commercial application. One of the greatest challenges facing software architecture is to allow these components to be integrated into the system in a consistent manner.

The integration of COTS and custom components will need specific integration components such as wrappers, glue code and tailoring (Truyen *et al.*, 2001; Vigder and Dean, 1997). The integrator may use a wrapper to isolate a COTS component from other components for example to conform to standards, e.g., a CORBA wrapper around legacy systems, and to filter the propagation of change impacts in the system. A wrapper may provide a standard interface for a range of components within a mature domain. For example, wrappers are used in (Ihme and Niemela, 1997) to isolate the impact of the variability of the real-time operating system component on other software components in the system. Standard interfaces are a precondition for substituting a component with a different supplier's COTS component that may produce different problems. A wrapper may allow multiple versions of a component to execute in parallel in the running system (Rakic and Medvidovic, 2001). Wrappers have been used to add functionality to a component, to filter or hide a certain functionality that could invoke unwanted functions, to provide a look and feel control over a component through the wrapper of the component that is not controlled by the integrator, and to provide one logical identity and access to a component.

Wrappers have also been used to implement the composition logic of components externally to COTS components (Truyen *et al.*, 2001), but the glue code seems to be more suitable for that. The glue code can be used to invoke the functionality of the underlying components when needed (control flow), to resolve interface incompatibilities between components, to isolate components, to minimize coupling between components, and to provide a consistent exception handling mechanism (Vigder and Dean, 1997).

A component supplier may provide component tailoring capabilities for the integrator to enhance a component with a functionality not provided by the supplier. Plug-in components and scripting languages are used for tailoring. A plug-in registers with the enclosing application, which gives callback to the plug-in when its functionality is required. The integrator must treat tailoring components as separate configuration items (Vigder and Dean, 1997).

1.4.4 *Patterns for the Architecture of COTS-intensive Systems*

Architectural patterns and design patterns have been used to achieve understandable, controllable and visible component dependencies and maintainable architectures in COTS component integration (Table 1.1). The patterns often play a similar role in providing a common desired interface even though their solutions are not identical. The patterns in (Schmidt *et al.*, 2000) form a pattern language that captures the design steps of the communication support involved in the component models of most middleware.

The Adapter pattern (Gamma *et al.*, 1995) helps conversion between the interface of the application and the interface of the COST component (Buschmann, 1999). It offers the application the services it needs. It performs all the necessary data transformations and programming paradigm and language conversions. It has been used to make component dependencies controllable (Vigder, 2001) and to implement the co-ordination of several COTS components that provide combined services for the application (Buschmann, 1999). Finally, it hides all unneeded services offered by COTS components.

The Blackboard pattern (Buschmann *et al.*, 1996) has been used to achieve a combined behavior pattern between independent units in the system without direct interaction between the units (Obbink *et al.*, 2002). The Decorator pattern (Gamma *et al.*, 1995) allows additional features to be attached or unneeded features to be 'removed' from the services of the COTS component (Buschmann, 1999). Its intent is to extend an object dynamically. The Extension Interface (Schmidt *et al.*, 2000) pattern and its variant Extension Object (Martin *et al.*, 1998) enable adding missing or new services to an existing COTS component (Buschmann, 1999).

The Facade pattern (Gamma *et al.*, 1995) has been used to shield the application from complex internal structures or the connection topologies of COTS components (Buschmann, 1999; Vigder, 2001). The Wrapper Facade pattern (Schmidt *et al.*, 2000) provides concise, robust, portable, maintainable and cohesive class interfaces that statically hide complex lower-level function and data structure application programming interfaces. It also provides building block components that can be plugged into higher-level components. The intention of this pattern is similar to, but more specific than the intention of the Facade pattern.

Table 1.1 Patterns help to achieve various architectural purposes in COTS component integration.

Purpose	Pattern
Conversion between the desired interface of the application and the interface of the COST component	Adapter
Shielding the application from complex internal structures of COTS components (class relationships)	Facade
Statically shielding the application from complex function and data structure API relationships	Wrapper Facade
Achieving a combined behavior pattern between independent units in the system without direct interaction between the units	Blackboard
Encapsulating complex component collaborations within an integrator-controlled component	Mediator
Adding or removing features from the services of the component	Decorator
Extending the functionality of a component by adding new extension interfaces for services that are implemented separately from the original component. Existing interfaces remain unchanged.	Extension Interface and Extension Object
Decomposing a system in a number of layers	Layers
Exchanging runtime components	PluggableComponent

The Layers pattern (Buschmann *et al.*, 1996) has been used to decompose a system in a number of layers (Clements *et al.*, 2002; Hofmeister *et al.*, 1999; Ihme, 2001; Obbink *et al.*, 2002; Schmidt, 2002; Schwanke, 2001). The Mediator pattern (Gamma *et al.*, 1995) has been used to encapsulate complex component collaborations within a single object. A management interface glue code as part of the mediator may be used to make component collaborations visible (Vigder, 2001). The PluggableComponent pattern (Volter, 1999) has been designed for runtime component exchange. It allows parts of a software system to be changed and lets the user configure these parts interactively. It is especially interesting for framework developers.

Pattern-specific guidelines are insufficient for applying patterns in building large-scale and complex real-world software architectures, where the integration of combinations of patterns is an important issue (Buschmann, 1999). Guidelines for pattern-based software development (Buschmann, 1999) help the use of design patterns to manage the growth of the architecture of COTS-intensive systems.

1.4.4.1 Middleware Layers

Schmidt (2002) uses the Layers pattern to decompose middleware into multiple layers and describes R&D efforts related to each layer. Those layers can also be considered as a structure for commercial middleware components. The layers are as follows (Schmidt, 2002): host infrastructure middleware, distribution middleware, common middleware services, and domain-specific middleware services.

The host infrastructure middleware layer encapsulates portable and reusable components that abstract away the incompatibilities of individual operating systems. Next-generation middleware should be adaptable to changes in underlying operating systems and networks and customizable to fit into devices from PDAs (Personal Digital Assistant) and sensors to powerful desktops and multicomputers (Kon *et al.*, 2002). Some host infrastructure middleware components are available for real-time and embedded systems.

Distribution middleware augments the host infrastructure by defining higher-level distribution programming models. QoS-enabled object request brokers (ORBs) are at the core of distribution middleware. Some ORBs are available for real-time and embedded systems.

Common middleware services extend distribution middleware by defining higher-level domain-independent components that focus on allocating, scheduling, and co-ordinating various end-to-end resources throughout distributed systems. Traditional middleware glues together distributed application components and its support for evolving software requirements relies only on component interfaces. The role of middleware in many mobile systems is less to glue components than to enable dynamic interaction patterns between autonomous concurrent components (Agha, 2002). Some open source services at common middleware services layer are available for real-time and embedded systems.

Domain-specific middleware services target vertical markets, unlike the previous three middleware layers, which provide horizontal services. Domain-specific middleware services are the least mature of the middleware layers from the point of view of COTS components. However, they have great potential for cost-effective COTS components.

1.4.5 *COTS Component Integration*

A carefully designed flexible architecture, where the availability of COTS components and open standards are systematically taken into account, will result in more reliable software products that can evolve over time. The Component-Oriented Legacy Integration pattern (Buschmann, 1999) provides the following solution for the integration of COTS or legacy software into the application. The application's desired view onto the COTS component should be specified. The specification should cover the part of the design in which the COTS component must be integrated, and the global design principles of the system. The component can be integrated directly as if its interface matches with the desired interface of the application. Otherwise, the Adapter pattern can be used for conversion between the two interfaces. A separate adapter is needed for every role the component implements. Missing component services can be added or unneeded component services hidden using design patterns. Finally, the specified mapping should be integrated with the base-line architecture of the system.

Vigder and Dean (1997) have defined a set of rules-of-thumb for COTS component integration. All COTS components should have wrappers placed around them. Using the wrappers, the integrator can control the interface and interactions of the component and isolate and filter the propagation of change impacts between components in the system. The glue code should interact with COTS components using standard interfaces indirectly through the wrappers. The glue code performs functionalities such as data and control flow, exception handling and data conversion. The compatibility of component versions in current component configurations should be verified. Since COTS components are black-box components, the glue and wrappers are the primary places to add run time assertions. It is important to conform to open standards whenever possible and avoid closed proprietary standards. Over-hasty commitment to specific inflexible architectures and technologies should be avoided.

Wrapper filters allow the use of COTS products that might not otherwise be usable (Talbert, 1998). There are also drawbacks to wrappers (Talbert, 1998). They may need to be made extremely complex. They must be thoroughly understood before constraints can be placed on the inputs and outputs. The specifications of COTS components are rarely good enough for writing test cases for their wrappers. The benefits of wrappers do not come free: they often increase development efforts, memory usage, and response times (Ihme and Niemela, 1997).

Yakimovich (2001) classifies the 35 COTS component incompatibility and integration problems found by himself, Gacek (1997) and Abd-Allah and Boehm (1996) as follows: functional problems, non-functional problems, architectural style problems, architectural problems and interface problems. He also suggests possible solutions to the problems. He does not address the COTS component integration problems that are specific to the development platforms of systems.

1.4.6 *Architectural Mismatch*

No complete schema is available for mediating between COTS components in various architectural styles and models (Yakimovich *et al.*, 1999). Homogenous components, e.g., the component kit in (D'Souza and Wills, 1999) can be designed into a common architecture and big components can easily be made by plugging smaller ones together in many ways. The builder of an assembly of heterogeneous components has to focus on how to glue together the given pieces to achieve set goals. There are not many opportunities to think about beautiful product line architecture.

Garlan *et al.* (1995) identify four main categories of assumptions that contribute to architectural mismatch: the nature of components, the nature of connectors, the global architectural structure, and the construction process. The nature of components category includes three main subcategories: infrastructure, control model, and data model. COTS components may either provide or expect to use additional unwanted infrastructure. Serious problems can be due to the assumptions made about what part of the software holds the main thread of control. COTS components also assume certain things about the nature of data they will be manipulating. The nature of connectors category comprises two subcategories: protocols and data model. COTS components may assume specific interaction details that are difficult to understand and construct. They also make assumptions about the data that will be communicated over connectors. A COTS component may assume a communication model for components in the system that is unacceptable for the purposes of the integrator. COTS components can make conflicting assumptions about the construction process that result time-consuming and complicated construction.

Many of developers' assumptions about components may be reasonable in isolation but may still lead to architectural mismatches in a reuse situation. Gacek (1997) describes 23 such mismatches. Yakimovich *et al.* (1999) address assumptions about how a COTS component interacts with its environment and use five variables to describe these assumptions: component packaging, type of control, type of information flow, synchronization and binding. Davis *et al.* (2003) describe and substantiate a set of architecture-based conflicts that embody the predominant interoperability problems found in COTS integration. Payton *et al.* (2002) show a composite solution for the architecture and security mismatch problem types in COTS integration.

1.4.7 *Maintainability of Component Software Architecture*

Maintaining complex COTS-intensive software systems is difficult, since the maintenance of COTS components remains under the primary control of the component suppliers and thus outside the integrators' control (Carney *et al.*, 2000). The integrator maintains the system at the level of component structures and interfaces rather than at the level of source code (Vigder, 2001). This involves substituting new components or component versions for old components.

The following maintainability requirements for component software architecture can be derived from the key maintenance activities (Vigder, 2001) of component-based software systems. It should be possible to reconfigure component configurations. Integrators must be able to manage the component configurations that are installed at each installed site. They must be able to customize and tailor components and component configurations to satisfy the evolving requirements of the product line or the specific requirements of product types or products in the product line. They can do this by tailoring glue and wrapper components at the components structure and interface level or using vendor-supported component tailoring techniques. The component structure should allow make it possible to monitor the behavior and resource usage of components at their edges, and to determine which components are causing failures or problems. It should be possible to filter or repair the functionality or behavior of components that invoked failures, problems or unwanted functions, and also to filter the propagation of failures and problems in the system. It should also allow inter-component and system monitoring capabilities to be built to observe the system's behavior.

1.4.8 *Architectural Views and COTS Components*

An architectural description of a software system identifies the stakeholders and concerns that are considered in the description (IEEE-Std-1471, 2000). It can contain many architectural views. Each view corresponds to one viewpoint that may address several stakeholders and concerns. Clements et al. (2002) call the stakeholders COTS engineers that are responsible for selecting COTS candidate components, qualifying them, selecting the winners and integrating them into the system. The acquisition process of COTS components often takes a long time. Valid COTS-related architectural decisions, constraints and knowledge must be communicated from design processes to COTS acquisition processes and business processes and vice versa. Many architectural and design decisions must be made concurrently with the COTS component selection process.

Hofmeister *et al.* (1999) identify one of the engineering concerns of the conceptual architecture view as being specification of how the COTS components are to be integrated and how they should interact with the rest of the system. Ihme discusses (2003) the selection of the conceptual structural configuration of the Component-and-Connector (C&C) viewtype for early-stage COTS component decisions.

The decomposition and layered views in the module viewtype, the shared-data, client-server and peer-to-peer views in the C&C viewtype, and the deployment and work assignment views in the allocation viewtype have proved very useful for COTS engineers in the ECS project (Clements *et al.*, 2002). The COTS engineers utilized some details from the generalization view in the module viewtype and from the communicating-processes view in the C&C viewtype. UML-RT provides a better match to document C&C views than the standard UML (Clements *et al.*, 2002; Medvidovic *et al.*, 2002).

Achievement of certain quality attributes, build-versus-buy decisions and product line implementation are important architectural drivers for decomposing software modules (Clements *et al.*, 2002). Modules are elements of the module decomposition, uses and generalization views from the module viewtype (Clements *et al.*, 2002). Hofmeister *et al.* (1999) stipulate that the module architecture view should describe what techniques can be used to insulate the product from changes in COTS software. Many modern architecture design approaches partition the software into the two highest level modules: application software into the applications module and infrastructure software into the infrastructure module (Fig. 1.2). The rationale for this is that application software and infrastructure software will often change independently and they have distinct supplier value chains in the software industry (Messerschmitt and Szyperski, 2001). A software system may also be partitioned according to the most-important quality attributes, for example into a high-reliable part for high-reliable components, and into a high-performance part for high-performance components. A system or software architecture may allow redundant or replaceable components or partially redundant subsystems during run-time.

The allocation viewtype presents a mapping of the elements of the module and C&C viewtypes onto the elements of a hardware environment (e.g. processors in Fig. 1.2), a configuration management system and a development organization (Clements *et al.*, 2002). A layered diagram has been used to depict the partition of the software into layers that represent virtual machines (Clements *et al.*, 2002). Each virtual machine provides a cohesive set of services with a public interface. The interface should be independent of a particular platform. The layers should be independent of each other as much as possible. The layer structure may remain stable even though the content of the layers may change if the system's hardware topology from the deployment view, e.g., processors in Fig. 1.2 changes. The allowed-to-use relation associates layers with each other. The Layers pattern (Buschmann *et al.*, 1996) helps organize software into layers.

The layered view of architecture seems to be the most suitable for refining the needs, possibilities and location of potential COTS components in architecture. The mappings between the layered view and the other viewtypes such as the module decomposition view and the deployment view should be taken into account in the progress of COTS component decisions. Generally, there may be a many-to-many relationship between modules and run-time structures and components.

The examples of layers in an air traffic control system, an Earth observation system, and an avionics software system (Clements *et al.*, 2002) show the tendency of layers in different domains to be very different. The software of the air traffic control system was divided into the Subsystem, Application Support, Communications and Platform (Operating System) layers. Schwanke (2001) proposes the following layers for real-time event processing systems: Application, Product Line Component Bus, Distributed Communication, Operating System, Device Driver and Hardware. Wallnau et al. (2001) enumerate that the following classes of interfaces exist between component boundaries: network services, operating system services, hardware services (device drivers), runtime services and the component's own application programming interface.

Common software architecture for the family of Measurement subsystems (Ihme 2001) is shown in Fig. 1.2. The software is partitioned into six layers in which a higher layer is allowed to use any lower layer. Specific software implementations can make exceptions to this general rule. There is a one-to-one mapping between the architecture layer and the application module. The software parts of the other layers in Fig. 1.2 correspond to parts of the infrastructure module.

The Communication and Operating Systems layers are common to all four examples above including the layers in Fig. 1.2. The Application and Device Drivers layers are common to three of the examples because the Subsystem layer of the air traffic control system corresponds to the Application layer. The Hardware Interface layer has been explicitly mentioned in two examples. The Code Generator Services layer is only in Fig. 1.2, but this layer includes thread management and event management services that Wallnau et al. (2001) classify as runtime services.

1.4.9 *UML-RT and COTS Component Integration*

The Rose RT tool supports the integration of classes defined outside the toolset, either in third-party libraries or in reusable code, in the UML-RT model. The tool also supports several commercial target operating systems. In addition, the toolset supports the use of location services and explicit connections for the communication between executable components on different hosts and between components on the same host. These components can be UML-RT applications or other applications and COTS components.

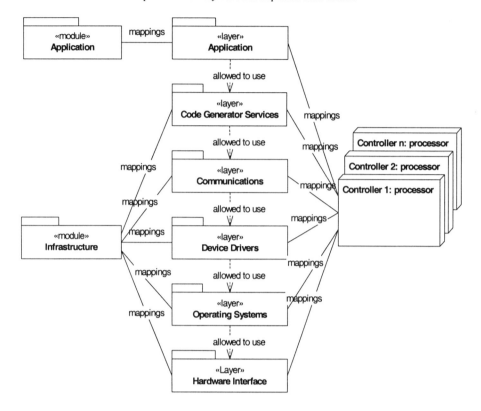

Fig. 1.2 The software of Measurement subsystems is partitioned into six layers and two high level modules and allocated to several processors.

The model in Fig. 1.3 has been derived from the conceptual configuration in (Ihme, 2003) and inserted as a segment in the Application layer in Fig. 1.2. This UML-RT collaboration diagram has been modeled using the Rose RT tool that supports executable UML-RT designs and target code generation from the UML-RT designs. UML-RT provides a seamless modeling paradigm for components and connectors from conceptual models to executable designs and target code generation.

The structure of the Measurement subsystem in Fig. 1.3 follows the Measurement Control pattern (Ihme, 1998) that is similar to the Mediator pattern (Gamma *et al.*, 1995) with the exception of allowing the Data Acquisition Control component to send data chunks to the Data Management component. The Measurement Control component controls the Data Acquisition Control and Data Management components in a predefined sequence. The Data Acquisition Control component provides interfaces for controlling the data acquisition and hides data acquisition details. The Data Management component provides interfaces for storing data chunks and hides data storage details. It transmits the stored data to the system that controls the Measurement subsystem.

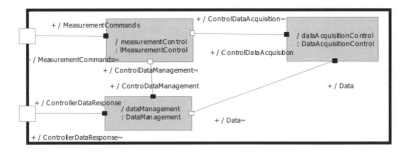

Fig. 1.3 The UML-RT collaboration diagram of the Rose RT tool shows the component structure of the Measurement subsystem (Ihme, 2001).

The capsule is a central architectural entity in UML-RT design providing interfaces that encapsulate the capsule internals from other capsules or external entities. A capsule never references any other capsules or external entities directly but only through interface ports. This makes it easy to connect different variants of capsules in the architecture.

UML-RT capsules are design elements that are allocated to executable components in a deployment view (Fig. 1.4). A set of capsules that form only a subset of the whole system may be allocated to an executable component. Domain-specific performance requirements may constrain the sets of capsules to be allocated. For example, the science data acquisition of the Measurement subsystem is time-critical and this may require that the Data Acquisition Control and Data Management components have to be allocated to the same executable component, e.g., to the Data Process in Fig. 1.4. The Measurement Control component can be allocated to the separate Control Process. The configuration and execution settings of these executable components are created according to the requirements of processes in a target platform and in order to fulfil the requirements of the design elements to be allocated. Any particular allocation must fit the requirements of the executable components to the constraints of available execution platforms.

This forward-directed process supported by the Rose RT toolset can be converted into a component integration process. Existing executable components may fit the executable components specified by the UML-RT capsules. It is possible to integrate or connect different candidates or variants of commercial software in the UML-RT model for evaluating their integrability using the simulation and validation features of the Rose RT tool. The tool can also observe components on a target platform that is not running the toolset.

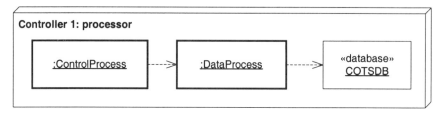

Fig. 1.4 Dashed arrows indicate the use of services between executable components on the Controller 1 processor.

The UML-RT model of the Measurement subsystem combined with the support of the Rose RT tool specifies the component interfaces of the Measurement subsystem. A potential COTS component may implement one or several component roles in the Measurement subsystem or the whole subsystem. The UML-RT model of the Measurement subsystem has to be modified for different alternatives. The recommended approach is to isolate the interface to the external COTS application in a wrapper capsule. The wrapper capsule provides the architecture line's, product line's or application's desired interface for representing the external COTS application to the rest of the model. For example, the Data Management capsule in Fig. 1.3 may be the wrapper capsule of the COTSDB component in Fig. 1.4. Other components and capsules in the UML-RT model, e.g., the Measurement Control and Data Acquisition Control capsules in Fig. 1.3 are allowed to communicate with the external COTSDB application through this interface only. The wrapper performs the necessary translation of a sent message into a form that is usable in accessing the COTS application. The wrapper translates the response from the COTS application into a message that is sent back to the original requesting capsule. This approach will allow you to test your application using a wrapper stub capsule in place of the COTS component wrapper while the COTS component is being acquired. This stub would respond to requests from model capsules with "canned" responses.

1.4.10 *COTS Components in the Layers Associated with the Infrastructure Module*

There is significant potential for COTS components in the layers associated with the infrastructure module in Fig. 1.2. Wrappers can be used to implement the mapping between the desired interface of the application, architecture line or product line and the specific interfaces of COTS and MOTS components as shown in Fig. 1.5. Design patterns such as the Adapter pattern in Fig. 1.5 help in designing wrappers.

Fig. 1.5 provides useful architectural information about the variation points of communication protocols. The {MOTS} protocol component must implement the desired protocol interface. The component has interfaces both in the Communications layer (the {MOTS} Protocol Application interface) and in the Hardware Interface layer (the {MOTS} Protocol HW Interface). The braces { } in Fig. 1.5 have been used to delimit optional and anticipated parts of the architecture. {MOTS} Protocol Application Interface and {COTS} Communication Protocol Kernel mean that the components might be MOTS or COTS components or might be developed in-house. The Middleware component is anticipated to be acquired or implemented in future.

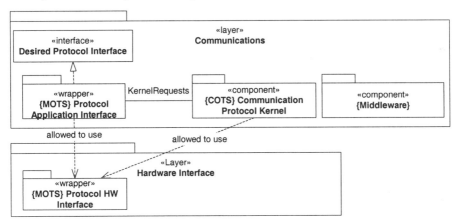

Fig. 1.5 The Communications layer constitutes communication services for applications.

1.5 Discussion and Conclusions

System architecture is of utmost importance, but difficult for COTS intensive software systems while architecting must accommodate changes in the evolving component market (Szyperski, 1998; Wallnau *et al.*, 2001). Current method proposals typically describe experiences with component frameworks and research results classify COTS component composition problems and COTS challenges for software architecture. They may suggest possible solutions to some specific problems, but they do not describe any solutions as to how software architecture should rise to the COTS challenge comprehensively. Particularly, they do not describe solutions that ensure the reliability and run time performance requirements of real-time control systems.

Many modern architecture design approaches separate software into software layers, which helps to manage the impact of change and evolution in component market and technology on software architecture. Szyperski (Szyperski, 1998) proposes a layered architecture with three tiers: components, component frameworks and a component system. Longshaw (2001) proposes a middle-tier component architecture for the component model implementation of middle tier servers in distributed systems. Schmidt (2002) proposes a layered hierarchy for middleware services and commercial middleware components, particularly for distributed real-time and embedded systems.

There are composition language prototypes and scripting languages for composing applications from software components. Visual or graphic application building can be successfully used when the number of components or entities in any architectural view is small. Aspect-oriented component engineering supports the identification, description and reasoning of high-level component requirements, the refinement of these requirements into design-level component aspects, the implementation of better component interfaces and the encoding of knowledge of a component's capabilities. The OMG's new Model Driven Architecture approach will make it possible to delay making a commitment to a specific component model, by providing a UML standard for platform independent models that can be mapped to specific component models to generate the specific code of an application.

The architecture of COTS component intensive systems is often created in a process of piecemeal growth, where architecture continuously grows and accommodates changes in the component market. Guidelines for pattern-based software development (Buschmann, 1999) help the use of design patterns to manage the growth of the architecture. Lessons from the history of software architectures, components and reuse have led to domain specific software architectures, product-line approaches and component frameworks and platforms (Barroca *et al.*, 2000; Clements and Northrop, 2001; Di Girolamo *et al.*, 2001; Obbink *et al.*, 2002; Szyperski, 1998). The integration of product-line and component-based software engineering approaches and design patterns help to achieve architectures that can be managed even when accommodating changes in the component market. However, the architectural ideas behind component-based software engineering approaches and product-line engineering techniques need to be evolved, because COTS components differ from in-house components. COTS components are black box components that intentionally hide the details of their internal state. The integrator has minimal influence over the evolution of COTS components. The integrator must maintain COTS components and handle their problems at the level of architecture and interfaces. Complete specifications of architectural COTS components will not be available. A priori correct COTS components could be composed into larger systems in a hybrid approach that is both top-down and bottom-up (Lau, 2001). No complete schema is available for mediating between COTS components in various architectural styles and models as well as in interfaces. An architectural standard, component model or architectural COTS component often admits the use of whole sets of available and compatible COTS components, and inhibits the use of whole sets of incompatible components.

Architecture-based software often approaches separate components (data and processing elements) from connectors (interaction elements). This key architectural property seems to be promising for the future prospects of managing the architecture of COTS intensive systems. System generation has been applied to software architecture descriptions and inter-component communication mechanisms, to improve productivity when building system families whose architectures are well understood (Stafford and Wolf, 2001). Carrying out system generation from designs in an architecture description language can improve the manageability of component-based applications, because changes affecting components can be effectively managed at the architectural design level rather than at component level. A generator tool may provide communication mechanisms for the communication between components on different hosts and between components on the same host. An architecture description language may allow one to standardize component interfaces so that it is possible to connect different candidates or variants of commercial software in the architecture for evaluating their integrability using simulation and validation tools that support the language.

Many great challenges are facing the architecture of COTS component intensive systems (Medvidovic, 1999; Vigder and Dean, 1997) and it is difficult to imagine that they will be solved by a particular architectural approach in the near future. The architecture should be manageable, fault-tolerant, tailorable, and able to be reconfigured. It should allow for troubleshooting, repairing and monitoring the system. It must adapt to the functionality available in the components being used and to the interfaces and data models used by the diverse components. It should also allow desired inconsistencies, incompleteness and technology independence in early stage architectures. Over-hasty commitment to a specific architecture with inadequate background information about the related component market should be avoided. The architecture should ensure specified architectural properties are present in the latter stages of the life cycle. The architectural descriptions of COTS component intensive systems should support new COTS component related stakeholders and concerns. There should be a strategic balance in the design of product-line architecture between the core competence of the product line owner and the purchasing of COTS and MOTS components. Today this balance in embedded software systems is often maintained so that business domain software is in the core competence and is built using in-house components. COTS component related efforts have focused on software infrastructures, platforms and development tools.

References

Abd-Allah, A. and Boehm, B. (1996). Models for Composing Heterogeneous Software Architectures, Los Angeles, California, University of Southern California. USC-CSE-96-505.

Achermann, F. and Nierstrasz, O. (2002). Applications = Components + Scripts - A Tour of Piccola, In: Aksit, M. (eds.). *Software Architectures and Component Technology*, Boston, USA, Kluwer Academic Publishers, pp. 261-292.

Agha, G. (2002). Adaptive Middleware, *Communications of the ACM*, 45, 6, pp. 31-32.

Anderson, B. and Dyson, P. (2000). Reuse Requires Architecture, In: Barroca, L., Hall, J. and Hall, P. (eds.). *Software Architectures: Advances and Applications*, Springer Verlag, pp. 87-99.

Apperly, H., Booch, G., Councill, B., Griss, M., Heineman, G., Jacobson, I., Latchem, S., McGibbon, B., Norris, D. and Poulin, J. (2001). The Near-Term Future of Component-Based Software Engineering, In: Heineman, G. and Councill, W. (eds.). *Component-Based Software Engineering*, New York, Addison-Wesley, pp. 753-774.

Atkinson, C., Bayer, J., Bunse, C., Kamsties, E., Laitenberger, O., Laqua, R., Muthig, D., Paech, B., Wust, J. and Zettel, J. (2001). *Component-based Product Line Engineering with UML*, Addison-Wesley.

Atkinson, C. and Muthig, D. (2002). Enhancing Component Reusability through Product Line Technology, *Proc. 7th International Conference, ICSR-7*, Berlin, Germany, Springer-Verlag, pp. 93-108.

Ballurio, K. (2002). COTS Architectural Analysis Method: Overview with Example, Herndon, Virginia, Software Productivity Consortium. SPC-2002002-CMC.

Barroca, L., Hall, J. and Hall, P. (2000). An Introduction and History of Software Architectures, Components, In: Barroca, L., Hall, J. and Hall, P. (eds.). *Software Architectures: Advances and Applications*, Springer Verlag, pp. 1-11.

Basili, V. and Boehm, B (2001). COTS-Based Systems Top 10 List, *IEEE Computer*, 34, 5, pp. 91-93.

Bass, L., Clement, P. and Kazman, R. (1998). *Software Architecture in Practice*, Reading, Massachusetts, Addison-Wesley.

Boehm, B. and Abts, C. (1999). COTS Integration: Plug and Pray?, *IEEE Computer*, 32, 1, pp. 135-138.

Brown, A. and Wallnau, K. (1988). The Current State of CBSE, *IEEE Software*, 15, 5, pp. 37-46.

Brownword, L., Oberndorf, T. and Siedge, C. (2000). Developing New Processes for COTS-Based Systems, *IEEE Software*, July/August 2000, pp. 48-55.

Buschmann, F. (1999). Building Software with Patterns, *Proc. Fourth European Conference on Pattern Languages of Programming and Computing*, Bad Irsee, Germany.

Buschmann, F., Meunier, R., Rohnert, H., Sommerlad, P. and Stal, M. (1996). *Pattern-Oriented Software Architecture, a System of Patterns*, Chichester, England, John Wiley & Sons.

Carney, D., Hissam, S. and Plakosh, D. (2000). Complex COTS-based software systems: practical steps for their maintenance, *Journal of Software Maintenance: Research and Practice*, 12, 6, pp. 357-376.

Carney, D. and Long, F. (2000). What Do You Mean by COTS?, *IEEE Software*, March/April 2000, pp. 83-86.

Cheesman, J. and Daniels, J. (2002). *UML Components (Custom Version): A Simple Process for Specifying Component-Based Software*, Addison Wesley.

Clements, P., Bachmann, F., Bass, L., Garlan, D., Ivers, J., Little, R., Nord, R. and Stafford, J. (2002). *Documenting Software Architectures, Views and Beyond,* Boston, MA, Pearson Education, Inc.

Clements, P. and Northrop, L. (2001). *Software Product Lines: Practices and Patterns*, New York, Addison-Wesley.

Coplien, J. (1999). Reevaluating the Architectural metaphor: Toward Piecemeal Growth, *IEEE Software*, September/October 1999, pp. 40-44.

Councill, B. and Heineman, G. (2001). Summary, In: Heineman, G. and Councill, W. (eds.). *Component-Based Software Engineering*, New York, Addison-Wesley, pp. 741-752.

Davis, L., Flagg, D., Gamble, R. and Karatas, C. (2003). Classifying Interoperability Conflicts, In: Erdogmus, H. and Weng, T. (eds.). *COTS-Based Software Systems. Second International Conference, ICCBSS 2003. Ottawa, Canada, February 2003. Proceedings*, Berlin, Springer-Verlag, pp. 62-71.

Dean, J. and Vigder, M. (1997). System implementation using commercial off-the-shelf software, Canada, National Research Council of Canada. NRC Report No. 40173.

Di Girolamo, G., Maldari, P., Croce, F. and Albeti, M. (2001). INTEGRAL Mission Control System (IMCS): Technology and Integrated Solutions for Supporting a Complex Scientific Mission, *Proc. 27th EUROMICRO Conference*, Warsaw, Poland, IEEE Computer Society, pp. 154-161.

D'Souza, D. and Wills, A. (1999). *Objects, Components, and Frameworks with UML: The Catalysis Approach*, Reading, Massachusetts, Addison Wesley.

Flynt, J., Desai, M. (2001). The future of software components: standards and certification, In: Heineman, G. and Councill, W. (eds.). *Component-Based Software Engineering*, New York, Addison-Wesley, pp. 693-708.

Fox, G., Marcom, S. and Lantner, K. (1997). A Software Development Process for COTS-Based Information System Infrastructure, Part 2: Lessons Learned, *Proc. the IEEE/SEI-sponsored Fifth International Symposium on Assessment of Software Tools and Technologies*, Pittsburgh, Pa, pp. 8-10.

Gacek, C. (1997). Detecting architectural mismatches during systems composition, Los Angeles, CA, University of Southern California. USC/CSE-97-TR-506.

Gamma, E., Helm, R., Johnson, R. and Vlissides, J. (1995). *Design patterns: Elements of Reusable Object-Oriented Software*, New York, Addison-Wesley.

Garlan, D., Allen, R. and Ockerbloom, J. (1995). Architectural Mismatch: Why Reuse Is So Hard, *IEEE Software*, 12, 6, pp. 17-26.

Garlan, D., Monroe, R. and Wile, D. (2000). Acme: Architectural Description of Component-Based Systems, In: Leavens, G. and Sitaraman, M. (eds.). *Foundations of Component-Based Systems*, New York, Cambridge University Press, pp. 47-67.

Griss, M. (2000). Implementing Product-Line Features with Component Reuse, *Proc. 6th International Conference on Software Reuse*, Vienna, Austria, Springer-Verlag, 17p.

Griss, M.. (2001). Software Agents as Next Generation Software Components, In: Heineman, G. and Councill, W. (eds.). *Component-Based Software Engineering*, New York, Addison-Wesley, pp. 641-657.

Grundy, J. (2000). Multi-perspective specification, design and implementation of software components using aspects, *International Journal of Software Engineering and Knowledge Engineering*, 20, 6.

Heineman, G. and Councill, W. (2001). *Component-Based Software Engineering*, New York, Addison-Wesley.

Hofmeister, C., Nord, R. and Soni, D. (1999). *Applied Software Architecture*, Reading,

Massachusetts, Addison Wesley.

IEEE-Std-1062 (1998). IEEE Recommended Practice for Software Acquisition, New York, IEEE, The Institute of Electrical and Electronics Engineers, Inc., 43p. IEEE Std-1062, 1998 Edition.

IEEE-Std-1471 (2000). IEEE Recommended Practice for Architectural Descriptions of Software-Intensive Systems, New York, IEEE, The Institute of Electrical and Electronics Engineers.

Ihme, T. (1998). An SDL Framework for X-ray Spectrometer Software, *Proc. the 1st Workshop of the SDL Forum Society on SDL and MSC*, Berlin, Germany, Humboldt University Berlin, pp. 125-134.

Ihme, T. (2001). An architecture line structure for command and control software, *Proc. 27th EUROMICRO Conference*, Warsaw, Poland, IEEE Computer Society Press, pp. 90-96.

Ihme, T. (2003). A Model for Recording Early-Stage Proposals and Decisions on Using COTS Components in Architecture, In: Erdogmus, H. and Weng, T. (eds.). *COTS-Based Software Systems. Second International Conference, ICCBSS 2003. Ottawa, Canada, February 2003. Proceedings*, Berlin, Springer-Verlag, pp. 101-111.

Ihme, T. and Niemela, E. (1997). Adaptability in object-oriented embedded and distributed software, In special issues in object-oriented programming: workshop reader of 10th European Conference on Object-Oriented Programming ECOOP '96, Linz, Austria, July 1996, Heidelberg, dpunkt, pp. 29-36.

Jacobson, I., Booch, G. and Rumbaugh, J. (1998). *The Unified Software Development Process*, Addison-Wesley.

Johnson, R. (1997). Frameworks = (patterns + components), *Communications of the ACM*, 40, 10, pp. 39-42.

Kobryn, C. (2002). Will UML 2.0 be agile or awkward?, *Communications of the ACM*, 45, 1, pp. 107-110.

Kon, F., Costa, F., Blair, G. and Campbell, R. (2002). The Case for Reflective Middleware, *Communications of the ACM*, 45, 6, pp. 33-38.

Kotonya, G. and Rashid, A. (2001). A Strategy for Managing Risk in Component-Based Software Development, In *Proceedings of 27th EUROMICRO Conference*, IEEE Computer Society, pp. 12-21.

Larsen, G. (1999). Designing component-based frameworks using patterns in the UML, *Communications of the ACM*, 42, 10, pp. 38-45.

Lau, K.-K. (2001). Component Certification and System Prediction: Is there a Role for Formality?, In: Crnkovic, I., Schmidt, H., Stafford, J. and Wallnau, K. (eds.). *Proceedings of the Fourth ICSE Workshop on Component-based Software Engineering*, IEEE Computer Society Press, pp. 80-83.

Longshaw, A. (2001). Choosing Between COM+, EJB, and CCM, In: Heineman, G. and Councill, W. (eds.). *Component-Based Software Engineering*, New York, Addison-Wesley, pp. 621-640.

Martin, R., Riehle, D. and Buschmann, F. (1998). *Pattern Languages of Program Design 3*, Addison-Wesley.

Maurer, P. (2000). What If They Gave a Revolution and Nobody Came?, *IEEE Computer*, 33, 6, pp. 28-34.

Medvidovic, N., Rosenblum, D. and Redmiles, D. (2002). Modeling Software Architectures in the Unified Modeling Language, *ACM Transactions on Software Engineering and Methodology*, 11, 1, pp. 2-57.

Medvidovic, N., Rosenblum, D., Taylor, R. (1999). A Language and Environment for Architecture-Based Software Development and Evolution, *Proc. 21st International Conference on Software Engineering, ICSE'99*, Los Angeles, CA, ACM, pp. 44-53.

Messerschmitt, D. and Szyperski, C. (2001). Industrial and Economic Properties of Software: Technology, Processes, and Value, Berkeley, California, University of California at Berkeley, Computer Science Division. UCB//CSD-01-1130.

Meyers, B. C. and Oberndorf, P. (2001). *Managing Software Acquisition: Open Systems and COTS*

Products, New York, Addison Wesley.

Morisio, M., Seaman, C., Parra, A., Basili, V., Kraft, S. and Condon, S. (2000). Investigating and improving a COTS-based software development., *Proc. 22nd international conference on software engineering*, Limerick, Ireland, ACM Press, pp. 32-41.

Nierstrasz, O. and Meijler, T.D. (1995). Requirements for a Composition Language, In: Ciancarini, P., Nierstrasz, O. and Yonezawa, A. (eds.). *Object-Based Models and Languages for Concurrent Systems*, Springer-Verlag, pp. 147-161.

Obbink, H., van Ommering, R., Wijnstra, J. and America, P. (2002). Component Oriented Platform Architecting for Software Intensive Product Families, In: Aksit, M. (eds.). *Software Architectures and Component Technology*, Boston, USA, Kluwer Academic Publishers, pp. 99-141.

Pasetti, A. and Pree, W. (2000). Two Novel Concepts for Systematic Product Line Development, In: Donohoe, P. (eds.). *Software Product Lines, Experience and Research Directions*, Proceeding of the First Software Product Lines Conference (SPLC1), Denver, Colorado, USA, August 28-31, 2000, Boston, USA, Kluwer Academic Publishers, pp. 249-270.

Payton, J., Jonsdottir, G., Flagg, D. and Gamble, R. (2002). Merging Integration Solutions for Architecture and Security Mismatch, In: Dean, J. and Gravel, A. (eds.). *COTS-Based Software Systems. First International Conference, ICCBSS 2002. Orlando, FL, USA, February 4-6, 2002. Proceedings*, Berlin, Springer-Verlag, pp. 199-208.

Pree, W. and Pasetti, A. (2001). Embedded Software Market Transformation Through Reusable Frameworks, In: Henzinger, T. and Kirsch, C. (eds.). *Embedded Software, First International Workshop, EMSOFT 2001, Tahoe City, CA, USA, October 8-10, 2001, Proceedings*, Berlin, Germany, Springer-Verlag, pp. 274 - 286.

Rakic, M. and Medvidovic, N. (2001). Increasing the confidence in off-the-self components: a software connector-based approach, *Proc. SSR'01*, Toronto, Canada, pp. 11-18.

Schmidt, D. (2002). Middleware for real-time and embedded systems, *Communications of the ACM*, 45, 6, pp. 43-48.

Schmidt, D., Stal, M., Rohnert, H. and Buschmann, F. (2000). *Pattern-Oriented Software Architecture, Volume 2: Patterns for Concurrent and Networked Objects*, John Wiley & Sons.

Schneider, J. (1999). Components, Scripts, and Glue: A conceptual framework for software composition, Bern, Switzerland, University of Bern.

Schneider, J. and Nierstrasz, O. (2000). Components, Scripts and Glue, In: Barroca, L., Hall, J. and Hall, P. (eds.). *Software Architectures - Advances and Applications*, Springer-Verlag, pp. 13-25.

Schwanke, R. (2001). Toward a Real-Time Event Flow Architecture Style, Proc. the Eighth Annual IEEE International Conference and Workshop on Engineering of Computer Based Systems, pp. 94 - 102.

Selic, B. and Rumbaugh, J. (1998). Using UML for Modeling Complex Real-Time Systems, Cupertino, CA, Rational Software.

Shaw, M. (1996). Truth vs. knowledge: the difference between what a component does and what we know it does, *Proc. 8th International Workshop on Software Specification and Design*, IEEE Computer Society Press, pp. 181-185.

Stafford, J. and Wolf, A. (2001). Software Architecture, In: Heineman, G. and Councill, W. (eds.). *Component-Based Software Engineering*, New York, Addison-Wesley, pp. 371-387.

Szyperski, C. (1998). Component software: beyond object-oriented programming, Harlow, England, Addison Wesley.

Szyperski, C. (2000). Component Software and the Way Ahead, In: Leavens, G. and Sitaraman, M. (eds.). *Foundations of Component-Based Systems*, New York, Cambridge University Press, pp. 1-20.

Talbert, N. (1998). The Cost of COTS, *IEEE Computer*, 31, 6, pp. 46-52.

Truyen, E., Vanhaute, B., Joosen, W., Verbaeten, P. and Jorgensen, B. (2001). Dynamic and

Selective Combination of Extensions in Component-Based Applications, *Proc. 23rd International Conference on Software Engineering, ICSE 2001)*, Toronto, Canada, pp. 233-242.

Van Gurp, J., Bosch, J. and Svahnberg, M. (2001). On the Notion of Variability in Software Product Lines, *Proc. The Working IEEE/IFIP Conference on Software Architecture (WICSA 2001)*, pp. 45-55.

Vigder, M. (1998). An architecture for COTS based software systems, National Research Council of Canada, 22p. NRC Report No. 41603.

Vigder, M. (2001). The Evolution, Maintenance, and Management of Component-Based Systems, In: Heineman, G. and Councill, W. (eds.). *Component-Based Software Engineering*, New York, Addison-Wesley, pp. 527-539.

Vigder, M. and Dean, J. (1997). An architectural approach to building systems from COTS software components, *Proc. 22nd Annual Software Engineering Workshop*, Greenbelt, Maryland, pp. 99-113.

Vigder, M., Gentleman, W.M. and Dean, J. (1996). COTS Software Integration: State of the Art, National Research Council of Canada, 19p. NRC Report No. 39198.

Volter, M. (1999). PluggableComponent - A Pattern for Interactive System Configuration, *Proc. The EuroPLOP 99 conference*, Irsee, Germany.

Volter, M. (2001). Server-Side Components - A Pattern Language, *Proc. The EuroPLOP '2001 conference*, Irsee, Germany, 53p.

Wallnau, K., Hissam, S. and Seacord, R. (2001). *Building Systems from Commercial Components, New York*, Addison-Wesley.

Weinreich, R. and Sametinger, J. (2001). Component Models and Component Services: Concepts and Principles, In: Heineman, G. and Councill, W. (eds.). *Component-Based Software Engineering*, New York, Addison-Wesley, pp. 33-48.

Williams, J. (2001). The Business Case for Components, In: Heineman, G. and Councill, W. (eds.). *Component-Based Software Engineering*, New York, Addison-Wesley, pp. 79-97.

Yacoub, S., Mili, A., Kaveri, C. and Dehlin, M. (2000). A Hierarchy of COTS Certification Criteria, In: Donohoe, P. (eds.). *Software Product Lines, Experience and Research Directions*, Proceeding of the First Software Product Lines Conference (SPLC1), Denver, Colorado, USA, August 28-31, 2000, Boston, USA, Kluwer Academic Publishers, pp. 397-412.

Yakimovich, D. (2001). A comprehensive reuse model for COTS software products, College Park, Maryland, University of Maryland.

Yakimovich, D., Bieman, J. and Basili, V. (1999). Software architecture classification for estimating the cost of COTS integration, *Proc. 21st International Conference on Software Engineering (ICSE'99)*, ACM, pp. 296-302.

Chapter 2

Describing Specifications and Architectural Requirements of COTS Components[*]

LUIS IRIBARNE

Department of Lenguajes y Computación, University of Almería
Ctra Sacramento s/n, 04120 Almería, Spain
liribarne@ual.es

JOSÉ M. TROYA and ANTONIO VALLECILLO

Department of Lenguajes y Ciencias de la Computación, University of Málaga
Campus de Teatinos, Málaga, Spain
{troya,av}@lcc.uma.es

Abstract. Currently there is an increasing interest in the use of COTS components for building software applications. One of the key aspects in the construction of COTS-based applications is the definition of software architecture prototypes from visual notations and reusable components (commercial components). These specifications must comply with some related aspects of COTS components, such as the quality of service (QoS), or the non-functional and functional information of the component. However, the possible benefits of COTS software architecture development, such as low cost, low risk, and high quality, cannot be satisfactorily achieved due to inadequate and/or incomplete proposals for commercial component, specification and architecture definition. This chapter discusses an approach for describing specifications and architectural requirements of COTS components. It uses an extended UML-RT notation by means of notes, tagged values and restrictions to accommodate component information. A small GIS system example of a COTS-based software application is also used to illustrate the approach.

2.1 Introduction

In Component-based Software Engineering (CBSE) a common practice known as "buy, don't build", promoted by Fred Brooks [Brooks (1987)], discusses the use of prefabricated components without having to develop them again. This common practice has provided us with the use of some specific *bottom-up* development processes to component-based systems [Mili *et al.* (1995); Robertson and Robertson (1999)], such as: (a) searching for

---

[*]This work has been partially supported by the projects: "WEST: Web-oriented Software Technology" (CYTED subproject VII, code VII.18) and Indalog (CICYT project, Ref. TIC2002-03968).

35

components available in software repositories that may fulfil the requirements imposed by both the user and the application's software architecture; (b) evaluating the components according to some criteria; (c) adapting or extending the selected components to fit into the system architecture; and (d) gluing and integrating these components together.

Accordingly, in COTS-based systems the system designer needs to produce quickly prototypes of the system architecture, making use of visual notations and taking into account the third-party components available in software repositories, by using a bottom-up approach. In a more realistic approach, these results are more adapted in order to achieve the reuse in a component mass market, moving organizations from application *development* to application *assembly*. Furthermore, the specification of these components must comply with some related aspects to produce quickly prototypes of a software architecture. Such aspects deal for instance with the quality of service (QoS), or the non-functional and functional information of the component.

In the existing literature, there are several proposals to produce software architectures, which are available as architecture definition languages (ADL), such as ACME [Garlan *et al.* (2000)], Rapide [Luckham *et al.* (1995)], Wright [Allen and Garlan (1997)] or LEDA [Canal *et al.* (2001)], among others. However, there are a few of them that can work with COTS components, and a graphical, quick and easy way to construct *COTS-based software architectures* is necessary. UML-RT [Selic and Rumbaugh (1998)] is a visual modelling language that lets developers write basic architectural constructs, such as protocols, connectors or ports, among others. For our proposal, we have used the UML-RT notation to describe the software architecture. We will justify this decision later in Section 2.4.

This chapter discusses an approach for describing specifications and architectural requirements of COTS components by using the UML-RT notation. It uses a small example of a simple spatial image translator system (GTS) to illustrate the approach. In accordance with this, the UML-RT capsules — referring to components — are extended by means of notes, tagged values and restrictions to accommodate component information.

The rest of the chapter will be organized as follows. Section 2.2 describes how a COTS document can specify commercial components, and how they can help to describe software architectures. Then, Section 2.3 introduces a simple example to illustrate the approach. Sections 2.4 and 2.5 deal with software architectures and the use of the UML-RT notation. Section 2.6 discusses how the software architecture can be described by using UML-RT. Section 2.7 shows how the architectural requirements can be integrated into others spiral methodologies to build COTS-based systems. Finally, Section 2.8 discusses some concluding remarks.

2.2 Definition of Commercial Components

Firstly, and before explaining some architectural issues for COTS components, let us define what we mean by a *component*. We will adopt the Clemens Szyperski's definition [Szyperski (1998)]: *"A software component is a unit of composition with contractually specified interfaces and explicit context dependencies only. A software component can be deployed independently and is subject to composition by third parties"*. In addition, the "COTS" qualifier refers to a particular kind of component [Brown and Wallnau (1999); Ncube and Maiden (2000)]: *"A commercial entity (i.e., that can be sold or licensed) that allows for packaging, distribution, storage, retrieval and customization by users, which is usually coarse-grained, and lives in software repositories"*.

In this section we describe the traditional software component information — i.e., interfaces and semantic information, such as pre/post, and protocols — and some other important information — i.e., non functional information, or deployment, implementation, and marketing information — which is used to set the requirements of commercial components (COTS) to build software architectures — i.e., architectural requirements. Then, we will describe this information by using *COTS documents* [Iribarne *et al.* (2001b)].

2.2.1 *Component Interfaces*

Component capabilities and usages are specified by *interfaces*. In our proposal, an interface is *"a service abstraction that defines the operations that the service supports, independently from any particular implementation"*.

Interfaces can be described using many different notations, depending on the information that we want to include, and the level of detail of the specification. For instance, CORBA interfaces consist of the supported object public attributes, types, and methods. COM follows a similar approach, but components may have several interfaces, each one describing the signature of the supported operations. CORBA Component Model (CCM) also considers that component interfaces may describe not only the services they support, but also the services they require from other components during their execution.

However, this kind of interface information, also known as information at the *signature level* or *syntactic level*, has proved to be insufficient to develop applications in open systems [Yellin and Strom (1997)].

2.2.2 *Semantic and Protocol Levels*

Besides signatures, the *semantic level* deals with the "meaning" of operations — i.e., the behaviour [Leavens and Sitaraman, 2000] — though much more powerful than mere signature descriptions. Behavioural semantics of components present serious difficulties when they are applied to large applications: the complexity of proving behavioural properties of the components and applications hinders its practical utility.

The *signature level* deals with the *"plumbing"* issues, whereas the semantic one covers the *"behavioural"* aspects of component interoperation. Furthermore, Konstantas also refers to them as the *"static"* and *"dynamic"* levels [Konstantas (1995)], and Bastide and Sy talk about components that *"plug"* and *"play"* when referring to those two levels [Bastide and Sy (2000)].

Finally, the *protocol level* deals just with the components' service access protocols — i.e., the partial order in which components expect their methods to be called, and the order in which they invoke other methods [Vallecillo *et al.* (2000)]. This level, firstly identified by Yellin and Strom [Yellin and Strom (1997)], provides us with more powerful interoperability checks than those offered by the basic signature level. Of course, it does not cover all the semantic aspects of components, but then it is not weighed down with the heavy burden of semantic checks. At the protocol level, the problems can be more easily identified and managed, and practical (tool-based) solutions can be proposed to solve them.

2.2.3 *Interface Notation*

The notation to describe component interfaces will depend on the level we want to cover, and it will also influence the sort of results that can be obtained when reasoning about the application's properties right from the specifications of the components' interfaces.

Current approaches at the *signature level* use an IDL (*Interface Definition Languages*) to describe interfaces. They guarantee interoperability at this level among heterogeneous components — written in different languages. They use different object models, live in different machines, and use different execution environments. The IDLs defined by CORBA, COM and CCM are examples of those.

At the *protocol level*, most of the current approaches enrich the IDL description of the components interfaces with information about protocol interactions, using many different notations, for instance finite-state machines [Yellin and Strom (1997)], Petri nets [Bastide *et al.* (1999)], temporal logic [Han (1999)], or π-calculus [Canal *et al.* (2001)].

Finally, interfaces at the *semantic level* usually describe the operational semantics of components. Formal notations used range from the Larch family of languages [Dhara and Leavens (1996)] that use pre/post-conditions and invariants, to algebraic equations [Goguen *et al.* (1996)], or the refinement calculus [Mikhajlova (1999)].

2.2.4 *COTS Documents*

A commercial component document is an identity credential used by developers to describe particular issues of the component being build. Some system architects, to describe the components architectural requirements when they defining the software architecture can also use this kind of information, which is recovered in a commercial component document.

In previous works [Iribarne *et al.* (2001a); Iribarne *et al.* (2001b)] we studied the kind of information that a COTS document could contain. To this effect, we developed a DTD template to document COTS components. It is based on the W3C's XML Schema language. Table 2.1 shows an example of an XML-based COTS document for a simple component called `Translator`. It will be used later to describe the software architecture. This COTS document template concerns with a software component that translates several formats of spatial images. This component is a part of the GTS subsystem example that will be introduced later in Section 2.3.

As we can see, a "COTS document" begins with the `COTScomponent` tag, which has at least one attribute: the `name` of the component embedded in the COTS document. In addition to the name of the component, more than one "namespace" can be indicated.

Table 2.1   A COTS document example.

```
<COTScomponent name="Translator"
               xmlns="http://www.cotstrader.com/COTS-XMLSchema.xsd" ...>
  <functional>
    <providedInterfaces>
      <interface name="Translator">
        <description notation="CORBA-IDL">...</description>
        <behavior notation="JavaLarch"><description>...</description></behavior>
      </interface>
    </providedInterfaces>
    <requiredInterfaces>
      <interface name="FileCompressor">...</interface>
      <interface name="ImageTranslator">...</interface>
      <interface name="XDR">...</interface>
      <interface name="XMLBuffer">...</interface>
    </requiredInterfaces>
    <serviceAccessProtocol>
        <description notation="pi-protocols" href=".../trans.pi"/>
    </serviceAccessProtocol>
  </functional>
  <properties notation="W3C">
    <property name="capacity"> <type>int</type> <value>20</value> </property>
    <property name="formatConversion" composition="AND">
      <property name="compress"><type>string</type><value>ZIP,TAR</value></property>
      <property name="image"><type>string</type><value>DWG,DXF</value></property>
    </property>
  </properties>
  <packaging><description notation="CCM-softpkg" href=".../trans.csd"/></packaging>
  <marketing>
    <license href="..."/> <expirydate>...</expirydate> <certificate href="..."/>
    <vendor> <companyname>Geographic Features corp.</companyname>
      <webpage>http://www.gtranslator.es</webpage> <mailto>sales@gt.es</mailto>
    </vendor> <description>Geographic Translator Component</description>
  </marketing>
</COTScomponent>
```

A name space is used to allocate the grammar that establishes the way in which a COTS document must be written. By default, the name space for a COTS document is http://www.cotstrader.com/COTS-XMLSchema.xsd.

A COTS document also deals with four kinds of information: functional, non-functional, packaging and marketing. This kind of information then can help us to set the requirements of the components when we describe the software architecture.

Functional aspects of the component are considered including both syntactic and semantic information. In a similar way to CCM components (such as we have seen in Section 2.2.1), functional information of a COTS document deals with provided and required interfaces of the component. For example, Translator component offers one interface and requires four interfaces. Here, the syntactic information is described by using a "CORBA-IDL" notation. Semantic information is described by using "JavaLarch" notation [Leavens *et al.* (1999)]. In general, we use dots to simplify several parts of the Translator component document.

Non-functional aspects of the component — e.g., QoS, NFRs — are included in the document in a similar way to ODP *properties* [ISO/IEC (1997)]: a name of property, a type, and a value. Composed properties can be described by using AND/OR operators. For example, the `Translator` document has an "AND" composed property called `format-Conversion`, which accepts ".`zip`" or ".`tar`" compressed DWG/DXF spatial image formats.

A component document also contains *packaging* information about how to download, deploy and install the COTS component, including implementation details, context and architectural constraints, and so on. In this respect, the packaging information can be described by means of CCM softpackage notation (see e.g., [OMG (1999)]). In a similar way to other parts in a COTS document (see Table 2.1 again), this kind of information can be described in a separate file by using a `href` attribute. Table 2.2 shows a valid content for a packaging file that uses CCM softpackage notation to describe deployment information of a translator component. This information deals with for example: (a) the name of such operating systems and processors where the component can work (e.g., WinNT or AIX); (b) the name of the programming language used to develop the component (e.g., Java); (c) the way in which the component is offered (e.g., as a "jar" package); (d) or its dependencies with other programs (e.g., an ORB dependency), among other information.

Table 2.2   A soft package document using the CCM softpackage notation.

```
<?xml version="1.0"?>
<softpkg name="TranslatorService" version="1.0">
  <pkgtype>CORBA Component</pkgtype>
  <idl id="IDL:vendor1/Trans:1.0"> <link href="http://.../Trans.idl"/> </idl>
  <implementation>
    <os name="WinNT" version="4.0"/> <os name="AIX"/>
    <processor name="x86"/> <processor name="sparc"/>
    <runtime name="JRE" version="1.3"/>
    <programminglanguage name="Java"/>
    <code type="jar">
      <fileinarchive name="Translator.jar"/>
      <entrypoint>TranslatorService.translator</entrypoint>
    </code>
    <dependency type="ORB"> <name>ORBacus</name> </dependency>
  </implementation>
</softpkg>
```

Finally, *marketing* information deals with the rest of the non-technical issues of the component document, such as licensing and pricing information, vendor details, special offers, and some other information.

Once we have described the kind of information for a COTS document, we will discuss in the following sections how this document information helps to set the requirements of the software architecture's components. However, we will present first an example of COTS-based application to illustrate the software architecture discussion mentioned before.

2.3   A COTS-based Application Example

The present example concerns with a simple converter service of spatial images known as *Geographic Translator Service* (GTS). This type of service is very usual in distributed Geographic Information Systems (GIS), where the whole of the information is distributed and interconnected by using object-oriented techniques.

In a GIS system, it is very usual to have several kinds of information, such as alphanumeric information (i.e., stored in standard databases), digitalized cartographical information, aerial photographies (i.e., captured by plain), and spatial images (i.e., captured by satellite). This information, and in particular the satellite images, can be used for decision making in risk-analysis evaluations (e.g., firing forests, or area inundation, among others). Generally, these analysis processes require inputs satellite image that must be stored in a particular format. In this respect, it is very useful the use of conversion services, also known as GTS services.

Briefly, as we can see in Fig. 2.1, a component `Sender` needs to offer an image in a particular format to another component called `Receiver`; probably the last one is related to an analysis process.

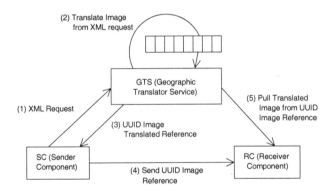

Fig. 2.1   A viewpoint of the GTS example.

Using an XML message, the `Sender` component delegates the conversion process to the GTS component (step 1 in Fig. 2.1). The XML message contains the conversion information, as Table 2.3 shows.

Table 2.3   The XML message used in the GTS subsystem.

```
<image url="http://...aplace/download/">
      <name input="RiverImage" output="RiverImage" />
      <format input="DWG" output="DXF" />
      <compression input=".zip" output=".tar" />
</image>
```

The XML message can be considered by the GTS component as follows (see step 2 in Fig. 2.1, and see Table 2.3). In the first place, following a pull model the GTS component extracts a DWG image called RiverImage — compressed in a ".zip" format — from the http site. After that, the GTS component generates a DXF file with the same name, which is compressed in a ".tar" format.

The translated and compressed image is stored in a buffer. Each cell is a register with two fields <UUID, href>, where UUID is a unique identifier of the converted image, and href is a reference to the converted image. In this example, we will suppose that the buffer also works in an XML way, that is, the buffer's registers are kept by using XML markups.

When the translated image has been stored in the buffer, the GTS component then returns the UUID item to the Sender component (step 3 in Fig. 2.1). After that, this UUID is sent to the Receiver component (step 4), which uses it as a code to extract the converted file from the buffer (step 5).

For our discussion on COTS-based software architectures, we will focus on developing a software subsystem considering the internal behaviour of the GTS component, without taking into account the Sender and Receiver components. Therefore, let us suppose that our GTS subsystem example is composed of a set of five abstract components: Translator, XMLBuffer, ImageTranslator, FileCompressor, and XDR. Table 2.4 shows the interfaces of these abstract components that we will use in the next section to describe the software architecture. Figure 2.2 also helps us to outline the methods' interaction sequence in the GTS subsystem.

Table 2.4   The IDL descriptions of the GTS components.

```
//Translator Component        //XMLBuffer Component         //ImageTranslator Component
interface Translator {        interface XMLBuffer {         interface imageTranslator {
    boolean translate            boolean pull                 boolean translate
        (in  string request,         (in  string location,        (in string source,
        out long uddi);              out string uddi);            in string iformat,
    boolean get                  boolean get                      in string target,
        (in  long uddi,              (in  string uddi,            in string oformat);
        out string url);            out string href);        };//end ImageTranslator
};//end Translator            };//end XMLBuffer


            //FileCompressor Component       //XDR Component
            interface fileCompressor {     interface XDR {
                boolean zip                    boolean unpack
                    (in string source,            (in  string template,
                    in string target,            out string iname,
                    in string format);           out string oname,
                boolean unzip                    out string oformat,
                    (in string source,            out string icompress,
                    in string format);           out string ocompress,
            };//end FileCompressor              out string url);
                                           };//end XDR
```

The Translator component's interface accepts two methods, translate and get. The translate method accepts XML requests from the Sender component to translate image files. The get method accepts UUID requests from the Receiver component to extract converted images from the associated XML buffer.

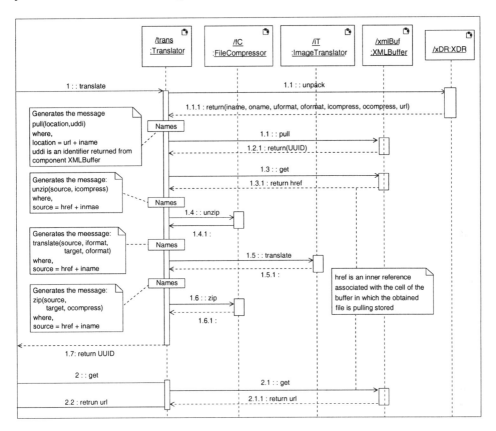

Fig. 2.2   The sequence of methods in the GTS subsystem.

The GTS component subsystem also uses a file compressor component called fileCompressor in a similar way to zip/unzip tools (e.g., *Winzip* or *pkunzip* programs). As we can see in Table 2.4, this component interface has two methods, those for compressing and uncompressing files. For example, a zip message could be zip("RiverImage","RiverImageCompressed","ZIP"). In this case, we directly put the parameter values inside the message.

On the other hand, the GTS component subsystem uses a spatial image converter component called ImageTranslator, such as commercial *Geographic Translator* or *MapObjects* programs. This component interface can translate formats such as DWG, DXF, DNF, and so on. For example, a translate message could be translate("RiverImage","DXF","RiverImage","DWG").

Considering a component called XDR, unpacking special XML requests from the Sender component are also used in the GTS component subsystem. In this case, an XML request — as shown in Table 2.3 and Fig. 2.2 — can be specified inside the parameter `template` of the `unpack` method. After the call, this method returns seven parameters, those extracted from the XML template request. Afterwards, the value of these parameters will be used by the components of the GTS subsystem.

An XML buffer called `XMLBuffer` maintains spatial image files. The interface of this component has two methods, `pull` and `get`. The `pull` method extracts a compressed spatial image file from a pointed location. This image is uncompressed, translated, and compressed again by `Translator` component, calling the methods in `FileCompressor` and `ImageTranslator` interfaces. Finally, the spatial image is stored in the buffer, assigning an identifier (UUID) to it that is returned by the `pull` method. On the other hand, using the reference code (UUID), the `get` method returns the `href` location where the translated spatial image file is stored. This location is the one that the caller component uses to pull the spatial image.

2.4 Software Architecture

In a similar way to the component concept, let us define now what we mean by a *software architecture*. Here, we will adopt the definition offered in [Bass *et al.* (1997)]: *"The software architecture of a program or computing system is the structure or structures of the system, which comprise software components, the externally visible properties of those components, and the relationships among them"*. By "externally visible" properties, they are referring to *"... those assumptions other components can make of a component, such as its provided services, performance characteristics, fault handling, shared resource usage, and so on"*.

Complex software systems require expressive notations to represent their architectures. In general, the software architecture defines its high-level structure, exposing its organization as a set of interacting components.

Traditionally, specialized Architecture Description Languages (ADLs) have been used, which allow the formal description of the structure and behaviour of the application structure being represented [Medvidovc and Taylor (2000)]. However, the formality and the lack of visual support of most ADLs have encouraged the quest for more user-friendly notations. In this respect, the general-purpose modelling notation UML is clearly the most promising candidate, since it is familiar to developers, it is easy to learn and use by non-technical people, it offers a close mapping to implementations, and has commercial tool support.

The problem is that the current definition of UML does not offer a clear way of encoding and modelling the architectural elements typically found in architectural description languages as discussed for instance in [Garlan *et al.* (2000); Medvidovic *et al.* (2002)]. And right until the new UML 2.0 is released (which is expected to support component-based development and run-time architectures of applications), the only widely accepted proposal for documenting software architectures available now is probably UML-RT [Selic and Rumbaugh (1998)]. It defines UML extensions for modelling real time systems.

We think UML-RT can be a valid notation to describe software architectures, mainly due to three reasons:

(1) The general-purpose modelling notation UML is clearly the most promising candidate, since it is familiar to developers, easy to learn and use by non-technical people, offers a close mapping to implementations, and has commercial tool support. In this respect, UML-RT is one of those proposals that make use of UML to represent software architectures.
(2) UML-RT, which adopts the original notation ROOM *Real-Time Object-Oriented Modelling* [Selic *et al.* (1994)], uses a short collection of graphical notations that can be used to describe easily software architectures.
(3) Finally, COTS-based systems usually require a quick way to produce a system architecture prototype. The UML-RT notation can be used to describe software architectures in a visual, quick and easy way to this effect.

Finally, to describe a software architecture with COTS components we suggest the use of the UML-RT notation. In particular, we have used in the present work the Rational Rose RealTime package to write the GTS architectural requirements in a graphical way (http://www.rational.com/support). It includes the original Selic and Rumbaugh's UML-RT notation [Selic and Rumbaugh (1998)]. Figure 2.3 shows an overview of the GTS project's windows-viewpoint by using the Rational Rose RealTime tool and the UML-RT notation.

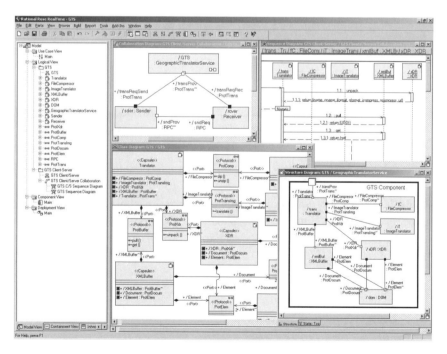

Fig. 2.3   A development view of the GTS experiment in Rational Rose RealTime tool.

We will develop this GTS example later, in Section 2.6. Let us see first some features about the UML-RT notation.

2.5   UML Real-Time

The UML notation is the standard language to specify, visualize, construct, and document the artefacts of software systems.

UML-RT is a language to model complex real-time systems (e.g., telecommunications, automatic control and aerospace applications, among others). It combines three concepts: UML, *role modelling*, and ROOM. *Role modelling* captures the structural communication patterns between software components. ROOM means *Real-Time Object-Oriented Modelling* [Selic *et al.* (1994)]. It is a visual modelling language with formal semantics to specify, visualize, document and automate the construction of complex, event-driven, and distributed real-time systems.

In our example we use three main UML-RT constructs to model the software architecture: capsules, ports and connectors. Figure 2.4 shows an example of these graphical constructs, which describe the roles of the GTS experiment.

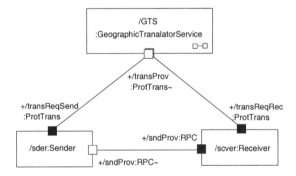

Fig. 2.4   A UML-RT example using the roles of the GTS experiment.

A **capsule** represents a graphical notation to refer to the whole component. The component specification — i.e., interfaces, behaviour, non-functional information, and so on — is described inside the capsule. This information, however, is not shown at the top level of the software architecture (*architectural view*), as it occurs in Fig. 2.4. At this level, only the name of the component is shown inside a capsule. For example, `/sder:Sender` means that `sder` is an instance of the base component `Sender`.

A **port** mediates the interaction of the capsule with the outside world. Ports realize protocols, which indicate the order in which the messages are sent between connected ports. In Fig. 2.4, the `+transReqSend:ProtTrans` notation is a port called `transReqSend` and a protocol called `ProtTrans`. The `ProtTrans~` notation represents the dual protocol.

Ports provide with a mechanism for a capsule to specify the input and output interfaces. In our approach, the output interface notation — the small black box — is used to describe the component's provided interfaces, and we use the input interface notation — the small white box — to describe those component's required interfaces. As we have seen before in Section 2.2.4, the provided and required interfaces are functional issues of a COTS component specification. Those are indicated in `providedInterfaces` and `requiredInterfaces` sections in a "COTS document". For instance, Fig. 2.5 shows the interfaces of the `Translator` component as UML-RT ports. This component was shown in Table 2.1, when we described the Translator COTS document. Please, notice how the `providedInterfaces` and `requiredInterfaces` sections in the COTS document are translated to ports in Fig. 2.5. Here, only the name of the ports is indicated.

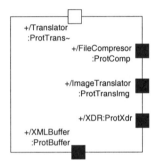

Fig. 2.5   Provided/required interfaces as UML-RT capsule's ports.

Finally, **connectors** capture the key communication relationships between capsules. They are represented by means of lines that unite two ports. If a connector unites more than one port, it must be duplicated in the capsule that requires it, shown as a double small box (see for example port `transProv` in GTS component).

2.6   Composing the Software Architecture

In the present section, we will discuss how the software architecture of the GTS subsystem can be described by using the UML-RT notation. As we advanced before, we will only concentrate on the GTS component of the experiment, without considering external components.

2.6.1   *The GTS Software Architecture*

Figure 2.6 shows an "architectural view" of the GTS subsystem using UML-RT, which contains all the components of the system and their interconnections. An architectural view can also contains global requirements associated with several components of the software architecture. As we will see later, a component requirement is described by using UML notes and tagged values.

Please notice how a capsule is used to describe the whole software architecture. A UML-RT capsule can be composed by using one or more capsules (i.e., components in our example). Please notice also that the GTS software architecture capsule represents the GTS component capsule in Fig. 2.4.

The +/transProv:ProtTrans~ port (the white box shown in GTS component) represents the boundary that communicates both sender and receiver components with the inner part of the GTS capsule. This port connects directly with +/transla-tor:ProtTrans~ dual port, which is a part of the /trans:Translator component.

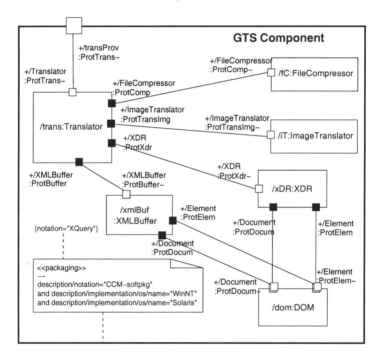

Fig. 2.6   The GTS software architecture in UML-RT.

As Fig. 2.6 shows, the GTS software architecture is composed of six components (i.e., capsules). The main component is /trans:Translator, which requires four additional components:

(a) a file compressor called /fC:FileCompressor;
(b) a translator of spatial images called /iT:ImageTranslator;
(c) a component for intermediate representation of data called /xDR:XDR;
(d) an XML buffer called /xmlBuf:XMLBuffer.

In addition to this, our GTS subsystem requires two DOM interfaces called Document and Element, which are used by XDR and XMLBuffer components to support XML formats. These interfaces are available in software packages such as IBM XML4J or Sun JAXP. In the GTS software architecture only an instance of the base component DOM is used, but `Document` and `Element` ports are duplicated to handle both `/xDR:XDR` and `/xmlBuf:XMLBuffer` components.

2.6.2 *Mapping the UML-RT GTS Example to UML Standard*

The UML-RT elements of the GTS software architecture can also be mapped to traditional UML elements. Figure 2.7 shows the UML class diagram that contains all the elements provided by the UML-RT software architecture, shown in Fig. 2.6. Please notice how the UML-RT architectural elements (i.e., capsules, ports or protocols) are represented as UML extensions by using <<capsule>>, <<port>> and <<protocol>> stereotypes. The diagram consists of twelve stereotyped classes (six capsules and six ports).

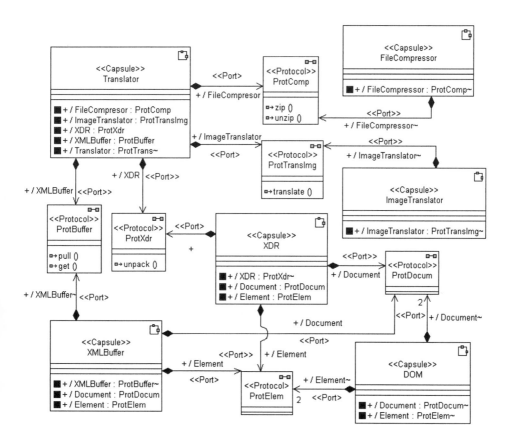

Fig. 2.7   The GTS software architecture using UML standard.

The classes are decorated with particular symbols on the top-right corner, identifying the type of architectural element. Apart from the traditional sections, attributes and operations, a *capsule* class contains a new section to show the provided and required interfaces. This section is decorated by using small black boxes. In a similar way, a *protocol* class shows the messages (i.e., operations) supported by the associated port (and its dual port). For example, the `ProtComp` protocol class has two messages, `zip()` and `unzip()`, both used by `Translator` capsule class and `FileCompressor` capsule class.

In addition to this, ports use *composition relations* to connect protocol and capsule classes. Please notice how a multiplicity 2 is indicated at the end of dual ports, `+/Document~` and `+/Element~`.

2.6.3 *Including Information into Capsules*

Up to this point, we have defined the UML-RT software architecture of our GTS experiment. However, there is some important information that must be recovered inside a capsule. This information is related to that included in a *COTS document* to specify COTS components (e.g., the COTS document in Table 2.1 (Section 2.2.4). Therefore, the following kind of information — referred to a COTS document — could be considered in order to describe component requirements in a software architecture:

(a) Functional information (i.e., interfaces, behaviour and protocols);
(b) Non-functional information, which is represented as properties;
(c) Deployment and implementation information;
(d) Marketing information.

In accordance with the component requirements, we will use UML notes and tagged values inside a capsule (i.e., the component) to represent the above kind of information. The requirement notes can be included directly in the architectural view or even inside a particular capsule. A global requirement note can be considered whether it affects to the whole software architecture. In this case, a global note is directly connected with the boundary of the architectural capsule. Particular and shared requirement notes can also be directly connected with the capsules.

In the GTS architecture example (shown in Fig. 2.6), every component has a common UML note to refer to some "packaging" requirements. Please notice how an additional tagged value is also used to indicate the notation in which the requirements are described, for example by using the XQuery notation (`http://www.w3.org/TR/query-algebra`). The packaging requirements are discussed later, when we are mentioning this example.

A third possibility of representing a requirement note is to include it inside a particular capsule. In this respect, an inner note is useful to capture those requirements that are characteristic to the capsule. For example, Fig. 2.8 shows the internal requirements imposed to the `ImageTranlator` capsule. Specifically, the interface description is directly included inside a UML note and connected with the corresponding port, since a UML-RT port refers to interfaces. In addition to this, an external tagged value {`notation="CORBA IDL"`} is connected with the IDL note to identify the type of notation used to describe the interface's signature level.

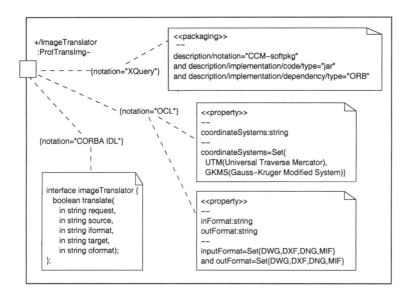

Fig. 2.8   UML-RT description of ImageTranslator capsule.

Furthermore, the properties (i.e., non-functional information) are also described in a separate note. A property description begins with the name of the stereotype <<property>>. Next, using a particular notation indicates the property description. As the interface notes, using an external tagged value denotes the description notation. For example, notice how ImageTranslator capsule describes two properties in separate notes, by using an external tagged value {notation="OCL"} connected with each note of property. Please notice also that a "--" symbol is used to separate several parts in a property note: (a) the stereotype header <<property>>, (b) the declaration of those types used in the OCL property description, and (c) the body of the property description.

Finally, packaging requirements such as deployment information can be represented as the properties. In this respect, a particular UML note starts with the <<packaging>> stereotype name. Then using a particular notation indicates the packaging information description. Like every requirement note, a packaging note can be established either at the "architectural view" — whether it is a global requirement to every component (as Fig. 2.6 shows) — or even at the "capsule view" — whether the note is a particular requirement (as Fig. 2.8 shows). Both at the architectural view and at the capsule view, the packaging note's restrictions are described in the XQuery notation by using the external tagged value {notation="XQuery"}.

Please notice that, as we discussed in Section 2.2.4, a COTS document uses the CCM softpackage notation to describe some packaging information (e.g., see Table 2.2 again).

In a packaging note, the XQuery notation is used to set those CCM softpackage constraints that a COTS document could have. It could also be possible to include the CCM notation directly in the UML note, together with an external tagged value {`notation="CCM-softpkg"`} instead of the XQuery notation. However, although it is possible, we prefer to use the XQuery notation as a constraint language — similar to OCL — for XML templates. Please notice that a CCM softpackage description is written in XML format, and currently the XQuery notation is one of the more extended W3C's XML query languages (`http://www.w3.org/TR/query-algebra`).

As a simple example, Fig. 2.8 showed an `ImageTranslator` capsule that contained a packaging note written in XQuery notation. Accordingly, this note means that we need a particular component whose associated COTS document had the following packaging requirements: (a) the packaging section must be described in the "CCM-softpkg" notation, (b) the required component must be offered and deployed in a ".jar" package, (c) the deployed and required component must support to work with some "ORB" tools (e.g., IONA's Orbacus).

2.7   Integrating the Architecture into other CBD Methodologies

COTS-based systems are usually based on spiral methodologies (see e.g. [Nuseibeh (2001)]), which progressively produce more detailed requirements, architectural specifications, and system designs by repeated iterations. Thus, a preliminary software architecture of the system is firstly defined from the user's requirements. It describes the specification of *abstract* components and their relationships. These components are then matched against the list of *particular* COTS components available in software repositories. This matching process produces a list of the candidate components that could form a part of the application. With this list, the system architecture is re-examined in order to accommodate as many candidates from the list as possible, and the software architecture's requirements are revised if needed. The process starts again until a software architecture meets the user's requirements and it is "implementable" from COTS components available in repositories.

The use of the UML-RT notation to describe architectural requirements is currently a very important-early technical stage of the TBDM method, *Trading-Based Development Method* [Iribarne *et al.* (2001a); Iribarne *et al.* (2002)]. TBDM is an automated development method based on a spiral methodology that uses a collection of processes and tools to build software applications with COTS components. It is mainly supported with three stages: (a) the description of the software architecture by using COTS components and the UML-RT notation; (b) a trading service that searches for COTS components by fulfilling the architectural requirements; and (c) a process that produces software architecture's solutions from those components found by the trading service.

Briefly, in TBDM the software architecture as an assembly of those required application's abstract components, is defined by using the UML-RT notation (as we discussed before for the GTS example). Then, TBDM uses a trading service to look for those commercial components that fulfil the requirements imposed in the software architecture.

Therefore, a previous process extracts and translates the component information from the software architecture (i.e., capsule information, as we have discussed) and produces a list of "COTS documents", one for each capsule that was defined in the UML-RT software architecture. This kind of document is that shown in Table 2.1. Then, as we have advanced before, the trading process uses these documents to search for similar commercial components into a COTS repository, which contains COTS documents. As a result, the searching process generates a list of the possible software architecture's configurations (i.e., solutions) from the selected commercial components.

In accordance with the above discussion, we underline the benefit of the suggested early approach of the TBDM method that translates the software architecture's component specifications (i.e., architectural information) into XML templates, allowing an easy integration with some methods and tools for automated construction of COTS-based systems (e.g., the TBDM method).

2.8   Concluding Remarks

A COTS-based software architecture — also called as component architecture — describes how component specifications interact with each other. The architecture shows how the building blocks fit together to form a system that meets the requirements. Therefore, component information is a very important key for building software architectures, regarding the way to describe them.

In TBDM, the definition stage of the software architecture plays an important role on building COTS-based applications because the remaining stages entirely depend on its description. This chapter reveals what kind of component information can be considered as requirements on building COTS-based software architectures. Besides, we think that the UML-RT notation can be a useful solution to build software architectures with COTS components. In this respect, we have extended the UML-RT capsules (i.e., COTS components specifications in the software architecture) with notes and tagged values to accommodate component information. A simple spatial image translator system is discussed as an example to illustrate the approach.

Finally, we also reveal how the components' architectural requirements can be translated into XML component specification templates (i.e., COTS documents), and their importance for searching and selecting processes of components to build COTS-based software applications using the TBDM spiral method.

References

Allen, R. and Garlan, D. (1997). A Formal Basis for Architectural Connection, *ACM Transactions on Software and Methodology*, **6**, 3, pages 213–249.
Bass, L., Clements, P. and Kazman, R. (1997). Software Architecture in Practice, *Addison-Wesley*.
Bastide, R. and Sy, O. (2000). Towards components that plug AND play. *Proc. of the ECOOP'2000*

Workshop on Object Interoperability (WOI'00), Vallecillo, A., Hernández, J., and Troya, J. M. (*eds.*), pages 3–12.

Bastide, R., Sy, O., and Palanque, P. (1999). Formal specification and prototyping of CORBA systems, *Proc. of ECOOP'99*, LNCS **1628**, pages 474–494.

Brooks, F. (1987). No Silver Bullet: Essence and Accidents of Software Engineering, *IEEE Computer*, **20**, 4, pages 10–19.

Brown, A. W. and Wallnau, K. (1999). The current state of CBSE, *IEEE Software*, **15**, 5, pages 37–46.

Canal, C., Fuentes, L., Pimentel, E., Troya, J. M. and Vallecillo, A. (2001). Extending CORBA interfaces with protocols, *Computer Journal*, **44**, 5, pages 448–462.

Dhara, K. K. and Leavens, G. T. (1996). Forcing behavioral subtyping through specification inheritance, *Proc. of the 18th International Conference on Software Engineering (ICSE-18)*, Berlin, Germany. IEEE Press, pages 258–267.

Garlan, D. and Kompanek, A. J. (2000). Reconciling the needs of architectural descriptions with object-modeling notations, *UML 2000 – The Unified Modeling Language. Advancing the Standard.* Proc. of the Third International Conference, October 2000. LNCS, **1939**, pages 498–512.

Garlan, D., Monroe, R. and Wile D. (2000). Acme: Architectural Description of Component-Based Systems, Chapter 3 in *Foundations of Component-Based Systems*, Leavens, G.T. and Sitaraman, M., (*eds.*), Cambridge University Press, pages 47–68.

Goguen, J., Nguyen, D., Meseguer *et al.* (1996). Software component search, *Journal of Systems Integration*, **6**, pages 93–134.

Han, J. (1999). Semantic and usage packaging for software components, *Proc. of the ECOOP'99 Workshop on Object Interoperability (WOI'99)*, Vallecillo, A., Hernández, J. and Troya, J. M. (*eds.*), pages 25–34.

Iribarne, L., Troya, J. M. and Vallecillo, A. (2001). Trading for COTS components in open environments, *Proc. of the 27th Euromicro Conference*, Warsaw, Poland, IEEE Computer Society Press, pages 30–37.

Iribarne, L., Vallecillo, A., Alves, C. and Castro, J. (2001). A non-functional approach for COTS components trading, *Proc. of the Fourth Workshop on Requirements Engineering*, Buenos Aires, Argentina, pages 124–137.

Iribarne, L., Troya, J. M. and Vallecillo, A. (2002). Selecting software components with multiple interfaces, *Proc. of the 28th Euromicro Conference*, Dortmund, Germany, IEEE Computer Society Press, pages 27–33.

ISO/IEC. (1997). RM-ODP. Reference Model for Open Distributed Processing, ISO/IEC 10746-1 to 10746-4, ITU-T X.901 to X.904.

Konstantas, D. (1995). Interoperation of object oriented applications, *Object-Oriented Software Composition*, Nierstrasz, O. and Tsichritzis, D. (*eds.*), Prentice-Hall, pages 69–95.

Leavens, G.T., Baker, L. and Ruby, C. (1999). JML: A Notation for Detail Desing, *Behavioral Specifications of Businesses and Systems*, Kilov, H., Rumpe, B., and Simmonds, I. (*eds.*), Kluwer Academic. http://www.cs.iastate.edu/~leavens/JML.html.

Leavens, G. T. and Sitaraman, M., editors. (2000). Foundations of Component-Based Systems, Cambridge University Press.

Luckham, D.C., Augustin, L.M., Kenny, J.J., Veera J., Bryan, D. and Mann, W. (1995). Specification and analysis of system architecture using Rapide, *IEEE Transactions on Software Engineering*, **21**, 4, pages 336–355.

Medvidovc, N. and Taylor, R. N. (2000). A classification and comparison framework for software architecture description languages, *IEEE Transactions on Software Engineering*, **26**, 1, pages 70–93.

Medvidovic, N., Rosenblum, D. S., Robins, J. E. and Redmiles, D. F. (2002). Modeling software architectures in the unified modeling language, *ACM Transactions on Software Engineering and Methodology*, **11**, 1, pages 2–57.

Mikhajlova, A. (1999). Ensuring Correctness of Object and Component Systems, PhD thesis, Åbo Akademi University.

Mili, H., Mili, F. and Mili, A. (1995). Reusing software: Issues and research directions, *IEEE Transactions on Software Engineering*, **21**, 6, pages 528–562.

Ncube, C. and Maiden, N. (2000). COTS software selection: The need to make tradeoffs between system requirements, architectures and COTS components, *COTS workshop: Continuing Collaborations for Successful COTS Development*. http://wwwsel.iit.nrc.ca/projects/cots/icse2000wkshp/Papers/22.pdf.

Nuseibeh, B. (2001). Weaving together requirements and architectures, *IEEE Computer*, **34**, 3, pages 115–117.

OMG. (1999). The CORBA Component Model, *Object Management Group*.

Robertson, S. and Robertson, J. (1999). Mastering the Requirement Process, *Addison-Wesley*.

Selic, B., Gullekson, G. and Ward, P. (1994). Real-Time Object-Oriented Modeling, *John Wiley & Sons*.

Selic, B. and Rumbaugh, J. (1998). Using UML for modeling complex real-time systems, http://www.rational.com/media/whitepapers/umlrt.pdf.

Stanford, J.A. and Wolf A.L. (2001). Software Architecture, *Component-Based Software Engineering. Putting the Pieces Together*, Heineman, G.T. and Councill, W.T. (*eds.*), Addison-Wesley, pages 371–387.

Szyperski, C. (1998). Component Software. Beyond Object-Oriented Programming, *Addison-Wesley*.

Vallecillo, A., Hernández, J. and Troya, J. M. (2000). New issues in object interoperability, *Object-Oriented Technology: ECOOP'2000 Workshop Reader*, LNCS **1964**, pages 256–269.

Wallnau, K. C., Carney, D. and Pollack, B. (1998). How COTS software affects the design of COTS-intensive systems, *SEIInteractive*, June 1998. http://interactive.sei.cmu.edu/Features/1998/June/COTS_Software/Cots_Software.pdf.

Yellin, D. M. and Strom, R. E. (1997). Protocol specifications and components adaptors, *ACM Transactions on Programming Languages and Systems*, **19**, 2, pages 292–333.

Chapter 3

Definition of a COTS Software Component Acquisition Process — The Case of a Telecommunication Company

PAULIINA ULKUNIEMI

Faculty of Economics and Industrial Management, University of Oulu
P.O.Box 4600, FIN-90014 Finland
Pauliina.Ulkuniemi@Oulu.fi

VEIKKO SEPPÄNEN

Department of Information Processing Science, University of Oulu,
P.O. Box 3000, FIN-90014 Finland
Veikko.Seppanen@Oulu.fi

Abstract. Several reference models for software acquisition have been presented in the literature and used by IT professionals to support the purchasing of software products and information processing systems. However, none of these models is specifically meant for supporting the acquisition of commercial off-the-shelf (COTS) software components – independent pieces of software with explicit interfaces that are being used to put together whole products for further sales. This chapter discusses hands-on experiences from an industrial case study that was conducted to define a CSCA process framework for a telecommunication company. The existing reference models were used in the initial phase of the work as a starting point, but the process framework needed, after all, to be defined based mostly on the strategic needs of the case company, taking also the specific characteristics of the intended COTS software components into account.

3.1 Introduction

Several reference models for software acquisition have been presented in the literature and   used by IT professionals to support the purchasing of software products and information processing systems. The models, such as the IEEE Recommended Practice for Software Acquisition (IEEE, 1998) and the IT

57

Purchasing Guidebook for Small Enterprises (Hansen, Dorlig, Schweigert and Lovett, 1999) provide step-by-step descriptions of software acquisition processes. Furthermore, such capability maturity models as the Software Acquisition Capability Maturity Model (SA-CMM) by SEI (Cooper, Fisher and Sherer, 1999) the Software Process Improvement and Capability dEtermination (SPICE) model (ISO/IEC, 1998) and the BOOTSTRAP Acquisition Process (Bicego and Ceccolini, 1997) can be and have been used both means to assess the present maturity level of software acquisition, and to define improvement goals to achieve.

However, none of these models is specifically meant for supporting the acquisition of commercial off-the-shelf (COTS) software components – independent pieces of software with explicit interfaces that are being used to put together whole products for further sales. Rather, they are intended for end-users to help to make investments in stand-alone software packages for factory and office automation and many other professional information processing needs.

Yet, the models can be used as a starting point to define a COTS software component acquisition (CSCA) process for system integrators that wish to make use of commercial software components. This chapter discusses hands-on experiences from an industrial case study that was conducted from Spring 2000 to Winter 2002, to define a CSCA process framework for a telecommunication company. The above mentioned models were used in the initial phase of the work, but the process framework needed, after all, to be defined based mostly on the strategic needs of the case company, taking also the specific characteristics of the intended COTS software components into account.

This chapter is organised as follows. The context of the case study is first presented, including a summary of the focal company's view to COTS software components, its motivation to address the component acquisition problem, and its state in the use of component-based software engineering (CBSE) practices in more general terms. Then, the activities carried out to define the CSCA process framework are described, starting from the analysis of the reference and capability maturity models, but focusing on the particular needs of the company, and resulting in an initial framework for the acquisition process. The main requirements and elements of the CSCA process framework are illustrated and discussed, and the results of an evaluation of the framework in a product development project outlined. In closing, general conclusions are drawn from the experiences gained during the case study.

3.2   Overview of the Case

Over the past twenty years or so, increasing use of software products has been one of the most significant changes in many industries – in addition to that software has affected the lives of hundreds of millions of individual consumers. However, there still exist many products – for example in automation, electronics and telecommunication industries – that incorporate tailored software that is embedded into product cores and is invisible to end-users. Due to the increasing standardisation of technologies, computing platforms and application software interfaces, even many of the developers of these products have become potential exploiters of COTS software. Since the companies do not, however, usually give up their own software development for good, integration of external COTS components into self-developed software becomes an option. This is the situation in the case study that we have conducted, too.

Keeping this point of view in mind, the key characteristics of COTS software components can be defined, from the viewpoint of an system integrator type purchaser, as follows:
1. the source code is not available, and the further development of the COTS software is therefore not under the control of the buyer; and
2. the purchased software must be integrated into a larger software system as individual operational parts. The rest of the software can consist of other COTS components, or software developed by the purchaser or by subcontractors controlled by the purchaser.

The case company has produced telecommunication equipment for many years, based much on embedded software. The company has used its own software engineering experts and several software subcontractors to design the required solutions. However, the use of COTS software components has gradually become quite an interesting question. One important reason behind the interest is the fact that the company has recently taken in use a component-based software engineering process based on a product line architecture, "a set of software-intensive systems sharing a common, managed set of features that satisfy the specific needs of a particular market segment or mission" (Clements and Northrop, 1999). Thereby, possibilities to reuse externally developed software components have become – in principle – much similar to internally developed component software.

However, the CBSE process taken in use neither includes, in practice, advice for purchasing COTS software components, nor guidelines for the reuse and maintenance of such components. Moreover, the roles of the company's general purchasing organisation and its software development department are rather unclear with respect to buying COTS software components to be integrated into the company's own products. The former possesses considerable expertise in contracting and buying, but only the latter has the necessary technical skills to identify and choose potential components and suppliers, as well as to collaborate with the suppliers in ongoing product development projects. Another driving force behind the use of COTS software components, from the viewpoint of the case company, is the increasing opening and standardisation of interfaces in telecommunication equipment. This concerns, for example, all-IP (Internet Protocol) type telecommunication equipment.

New firms are expected to enter the formerly more or less closed equipment markets, relying heavily on standard platforms, open IP-based interfaces and commercial hardware and software components. Some of the competitors are likely to seek benefits from extensive use of open source and other more freely available software, not only from COTS software solutions. This poses a yet another challenge for the traditionally strong actors in the field that have trusted much on their internal resources and on the use of specialised software subcontractors. One way to characterise the latter would be that in addition to the traditional *build* (own software development) and *buy* (acquisition of COTS solutions) choices, there is a third alternative, to *share* (acting as a member of a "free" software community).

Referring to the emerging changes in the markets and products, the case company was looking forward to direct business advantages from the use of COTS – or open source - software components, especially with regard to shorter time to market and higher quality of new products. However, many risks and problems were expected to be encountered. One of them is related to the fact that the company already employs several hundred software engineers and has established extensive software subcontractor relationships. Increasing use of external software components would affect this software development setting considerably both in organisational terms and with respect to the earning logic of the involved parties. Simplifying, some of the fixed product development costs would most likely turn into variable product sales costs. The change would affect the company's earning logic, depending on the volume of products and the prices of the acquired software components.

The very first business-related issues to tackle would, however, be even more practical: where to find software component suppliers – a majority of the present subcontractors would most likely be not willing or capable of producing components?, how to make explicit the process of acquiring components - the present CBSE process is targeted more towards identifying and allocating human software development resources than towards purchasing pieces of software?, and how to revise the company's CBSE strategy, if the acquisition of COTS software components – or the use of open source software – would emerge, in practice? The last question needed to be answered already in the very early phase of the CSCA process framework definition, by harmonising the framework with the internal CBSE process.

For these reasons, one of the main purposes of the work was to develop a comprehensive enough CSCA process framework for the case organisation starting from screening potential suppliers and ending with reuse and maintenance of the acquired components as an integral part of the company's CBSE-based software development approach. In other words, the focus of the work was on outlining the software component acquisition and management process so that it could be taken in use and support the internal CBSE process. Regarding the software supply, the initial interest of the case company was directed towards highly productised segments of the software industry that offer fully commercial solutions to several customers (cf. e.g. Hoch, Roeding, Purkert, Lindner and Mueller, 2000). This was seen as an insurance policy against the purchaser's dependency on very specialised suppliers, as well as a practical means to ensure second sources for the purchased software components, if needed.

Despite interest in well-packaged COTS software solutions, close and long-term collaborative relationships were wished to be established with key suppliers. Therefore, the case company did not look forward to buying from heavily competitive software component market places. Moreover, it aimed at having the two earlier ways of fulfilling its software needs still available, to make the required piece of software in house, and to use subcontractors that develop the needed software according to the purchaser's specifications. The third and newest form of software acquisition, purchasing of COTS software components, would be associated with the two earlier ways to operate, and possibly also with the use of open source software (Figure 3.1). The benefits of the different types of activities needed to be combined and should provide competitive advantage as a whole – not alone.

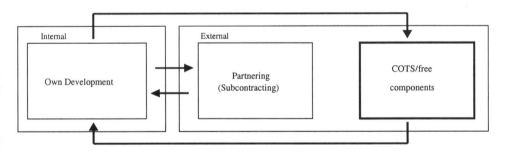

Figure 3.1. The case company's alternatives for fulfilling its software needs.

3.3 Towards the CSCA Process – Analysis of Existing Models

Several descriptions of the software acquisition process have been presented in the literature related to information systems purchasing, software management and software process improvement. These models provide rather detailed descriptions of the actions that are recommended to be taken when acquiring software. The models, such as the IEEE Recommended Practice for Software Acquisition (IEEE, 1998) and the IT Purchasing Guidebook for Small Enterprises (Hansen, Dorling, Schweigert and Lovett, 1999) provide step-by-step descriptions of a successful software acquisition process.

They do not, however, determine how well each step in the software acquisition process is conducted, although they illustrate the tasks and points that are to be taken into consideration. For the purpose, there exist software acquisition capability maturity models, such as the Software Acquisition Capability Maturity Model (SA-CMM) (Cooper, Fisher and Sherer, 1999), the BOOTSTRAP Acquisition Process (Bicego and Ceccolini, 1997) and the Software Process Improvement and Capability dEtermination (SPICE) model (ISO/IEC; 1998). These models propose different sophistication states, maturity levels, for acquisition related processes. The purpose of the models is to help to determine the current capability level of the acquisition process and to provide insights for improvements needed in order the organisation to achieve a higher maturity level in its software acquisition capability.

According to the IEEE process model, the life cycle of a software acquisition process represents the period of time that begins with the decision to acquire a piece of software. The life cycle ends when the acquired software is no longer in use. For example the BOOTSTRAP model, on the other hand, regards the process as starting from the identification of the acquirer's needs and ending with the acceptance of the software (including possibly some associated service) that has been acquired. Therefore, the IEEE model involves a somewhat more comprehensive approach to the acquisition process, taking also the management and use of the acquired software into account. The BOOTSTRAP model addresses the actual purchasing process.

3.3.1   *Overview of the Reference Models*

First of all, it is important to point out that none of the software acquisition models is specifically targeted to COTS software component purchasing, but rather, they describe the purchasing of software at a more general level. Therefore, only those aspects that were considered most relevant in the COTS software component context were considered in our case study and will be discussed below. Moreover, it was necessary to make some simplifications in order to concentrate on the essence of each model in the analysis, so that a unifying view to the models could be presented as a starting point for the CSCA process framework development. However, because the models are both overlapping and dealing with different aspects of the software acquisition process, it was also important to avoid unnecessary simplifications.

One of the main questions relevant in the development of the CSCA process framework for the case company was *how the process should proceed, in practice?* Therefore, this viewpoint was emphasised, when the models shown in Table 3.1 were analysed.

Table 3.1. Reference models for software acquisition.

Model	Type	Similarity with other models	IMPORTANCE
BOOTSTRAP 3.0 Acquisition Process and Supply Process	Process model describing the acquisition process through eight base practices.	IEEE	High, concrete
IEEE Recommended Practice for Software Acquisition	Process model describing the acquisition process through nine steps and key inputs and outputs	BOOTSTRAP	High, concrete
IT Purchasing Guidebook for Small Enterprises	The purpose of the model is to help managers and staff in SMEs to improve their businesses by establishing a more sound and advantageous approach to purchasing IT systems.	--	Low, implicit
SA-CMM Software Acquisition Capability Maturity Model 1.02	Capability maturity model including five levels of maturity of the acquisition process.	SPICE (is based on SA-CMM)	Medium
SPICE: Software Process Improvement and Capability dEtermination	Collection of international standards that define an assessment model for software development processes.	Based on SA-CMM	Medium
Trillium Model	Used by Bell Canada to assess the product development and support capability of prospective and existing suppliers of telecommunications or information-based products. Includes Capability areas, Roadmaps and Practices.		Medium

The importance of each model in terms of serving as a basis of the CSCA process framework definition, as it was judged during the early phase of the work, is indicated in the table. As can be seen, the most relevant for our needs were the IEEE and BOOTSTRAP models, because they include together explicit and comprehensive enough descriptions of the software acquisition process.

In the following, the outcome of the analysis of these models is presented and, as a conclusion, an illustration of the software acquisition process based on a union of the models – including especially the IEEE and BOOTSTRAP models - is presented.

3.3.2   *Acquisition Process Framework based on the Existing Models*

Because "pure" process models and process maturity models take a somewhat different view to the description of software acquisition, some limits had to be drawn on how the models would be analysed as a whole. This was done through concentrating on the second level of maturity in the maturity models. The basis for the choice was the fact that no defined software acquisition practices were yet used in the case company, and therefore the second maturity level would be the first target to reach. For this reason, the elements included in the second levels of the maturity models were considered as relevant in the analysis.

To summarise, the flow of actions to take in COTS software component acquisition, according to the existing models, would be as follows.

1. Planning

  a) *Identify the needs*
  - Identify the organisation's strategic objectives
  - Identify the software component acquisition objectives
  - Identify the needs from the operational/functional perspective

  b) *Specify the requirements*
  - Define software component requirements that meet the needs
  - Identify technical and functional perspectives
  - Pay attention also to the other organisational objectives
  - Establish the acquisition process

  c) *Prepare the RFP (Request For Proposal)*
  - Prepare the acquisition strategy: carry out a make-or-buy risk analysis
  - Identify supplier selection criteria
  - Identify relevant processes and supporting tasks among the own software and other processes
  - Identify the terms, conditions and control of contracts
  - Release the RFP

2. Contracting

a) *Identify Potential Suppliers*
- Gather information about the potential suppliers: use earlier experiences, references, customer surveys, etc.
- Evaluate all the potential suppliers on the basis of their financial state, experience and capabilities, software development and business processes, technical assistance, quality practices, maintenance services, warranty, costs and contracting forms.

b) *Select the Best Two or Three Candidates*
- Evaluate the received proposals
- Evaluate the suppliers more thoroughly, based on the potential suppliers' business processes
- Prepare contract requirements
- Evaluate which supplier would best meet the requirements

c) *Select the Best Supplier*
- Carry out contract negotiations
- Sign the contract (or observe failure of negotiations and approach the second best alternative)

3. Delivery and Use of the Component

a) *Implement the contract*
- Monitor the supplier's performance and progress
- Ensure open communication
- Ensure documentation

b) *Receive the Component*
- Carry out delivery inspection
- Evaluate and test the received component
- Accept the component

c) *Use the Component*
- Manufacture the product(s) where the component is used
- Evaluate contracting practices
- Monitoring the business relationship, using joint reviews, audits, and other V&V processes

d) *Make Use of the Guarantee Period*

- Monitor the performance of the component: observe and evaluate user satisfaction

e)   Monitor Performance After the Guarantee Period

f)   Remove the Component from Use

Although maturity models are not process models, the key process areas at the maturity level 2 can be illustrated as a process-like schema. Consider the key process areas of the CMM-SA maturity model as an example. Many of the key process areas are, in practice, partly overlapping and linked in different ways, but they were yet separated into a few CSCA process areas in the case study, in order to extend the simple Planning – Contracting – Delivery & Use type acquisition phase model illustrated above.

The first process area of the acquisition process would be (1) *Software Acquisition Planning,* which should take the whole life cycle of the software into account. Secondly, in the (2) *Requirements Development and Management* process area software-related contractual requirements would be developed, managed and maintained. After the requirements are established, the (3) *Solicitation* process area would ensure that a solicitation package is released and the most qualified supplier is identified on the basis of documented solicitation plans and requirements. The (4) *Evaluation* process area would be relevant during the entire lifetime of software acquisition, in order to provide an integrated approach that satisfies evaluation requirements and takes advantages of all evaluation results.

After the solicitation processes would had been conducted, (5) activities conducted in the *Contract Tracking and Oversight* process area would ensure that the software acquisition team has sufficient insights into the supplier's software engineering process, so that it can be sure that the supplier's process is managed and controlled to comply with the contract requirements. The *Project Management* process area (6) would be vital during the whole acquisition process, too, because the purpose of the project management process is be to control the performance, cost and schedule objectives from the viewpoint of the purchaser, as well as to identify and solve any possible problems encountered in the acquisition process. In the process area (7) *Transition to Support,* the acquisition team would ensure that the supplier has the capacity and capability to provide the required support for the use of the software.

In Table 2, the main phases of the generic software acquisition process, derived both from the reference and maturity models, are listed side by side. Based on the reference models (cf. the discussion above), the main phases of acquisition would be Planning, Contracting and Delivery & Use of the software.

Based on the second level of the maturity models, the key process areas would be Software Acquisition Planning, Requirements Development and Management, Solicitation, Contract Tracking and Oversight, and Transition to Support. Evaluation and Project Management would also be needed.

Table 3.2. Juxtaposition of the software acquisition process and maturity models.

Process Model	Maturity Model	Evaluation	Project Management
The Planning Phase of the Software Acquisition Process Identifying the needs Specify the requirements Prepare the RFP	Software Acquisition Planning		
	Requirements Development and Management		
The Contracting Phase of the Software Acquisition Process Identify Potential Suppliers Select Best Two or Three Candidates Select the Best Supplier	Solicitation		
The Delivery Process and the Using of the Component The Implementation phase of the contract Receiving the Component Using the software Component Guarantee Period Monitoring the Performance After Guarantee Product/Component is no Longer in Use	Contract Tracking and Oversight		
	Transition to support		

To conclude, the analysis of the existing models, including the proposed reference process and maturity models, provided quite important insights for the definition of the CSCA process framework. However, a combination of the models (cf. Table 3.2) could not simply be taken in use as such. The key aspects of the COTS software component context needed to be addressed, as well as the specific requirements of the case company. These were approached through interviewing the representatives of the company – altogether some twenty persons – who had been somehow involved in the use of externally developed or purchased software.

3.4   Requirements for the CSCA Process – the Purchaser's Perspective

In addition to the interviews, several group rehearsals and internal workshops were organised, and a few selected potential software suppliers (involving a database and an operating system supplier, i.e. "classical" COTS software components) contacted. Data gathering was done in a semi-structured way, so that only some basic themes for the interviews were prepared in advance. In particular, the analysed reference and maturity models were not used as a basis of the interviews.

However, most interview data was tape recorded and all the data was transcripted. An interview data review report was written and contrasted to the analysis report of the reference and maturity models. This appeared to be very useful, the key similarities and differences between the "literature" and the "needs for everyday practice" could be explicitly identified.

The data gathering formed not only a basis for the definition of the CSCA process framework, but it also brought up much information concerning the future of the use of COTS software in the case company in more general terms. In particular, one of the recurring themes in the interviews was what advantages and disadvantages the use of COTS software would cause, after all – and which of the two would be greater. These concerns were, in practice, tried to be taken into account by following a value creation perspective (cf. Anderson and Narus, 1999; Parolini, 1999) in the definition of the CSCA process. This required fitting together the value-creating activities of the COTS purchaser and suppliers, keeping in mind the three alternative ways of the purchaser to acquire software shown in Figure 1.

3.4.1   *Main concerns Revealed by the Interviews*

According to the interviews, COTS software components would ideally be "large" and standard pieces of software that can be incorporated into several different types of other products. The suppliers should preferably sell the same component to several different customers, and thereby lower development costs and prices. This would require the availability of market-related information concerning the supply of certain types of software components. As the markets of some component would develop, the purchasers would be able to choose from a variety of potential suppliers. The shortage of purchasers' resources in screening and following market development especially in the early stages of COTS software acquisition initiatives were, however, seen as a considerable hindrance for this. Therefore, purchasers should gain "easy access" to the offerings of potential suppliers.

Speaking of the case company itself, it would be beneficial, if several different software development projects would use the very same software component. This would both simplify the acquisition task, in practice, and help to share experiences from the use of the purchased software components. In other words, the scope of the use of a component was seen as a very important aspect – the larger, the better.

Difficulties and uncertainties in the time schedules of software component deliveries were seen as one of the major risks in the use of COTS solutions. Typically, the purchaser's software projects that would need external components have very tight time schedules. On the other hand, the purchaser may have rather limited possibilities to influence on the component releasing schedules of the suppliers. Although penalties can be included in contracts, they may not help – after the contract has been signed, or even earlier if there is only one or very few potential supplier, the purchaser's power was seen to decrease, compared to the supplier screening and evaluation phase. Great losses could result, if deliveries and corrections would drag on, and if projects could not carry on without component deliveries.

One of the most critical points in the use of COTS software components was considered to be the quality issue, how can the customer be sure of the quality of the component and the time schedules of possible repairs? Although higher quality of acquired software based on large-scale use of the same component was one of the benefits sought from COTS, the opposite concern is also understandable when thinking of the case company's two alternative software acquisition means. As a rather big and well-established product manufacturer, it had developed strict quality assurance and management procedures both for its internal software process and for the use of software development subcontractors. Most of the latter are much smaller than the case company and dependent on its subcontracting contracting volumes.

Independent COTS software sellers would most likely be less controllable in this regard, even small companies that may have plenty of customers to choose from. Said in another way, the size of the purchaser as a company would matter less, only the volume of its purchasing would result in some influence on the suppliers' present practices and future roadmaps.

A special concern that came out from the interviews was the threat of the bankruptcy of the suppliers. Although Escrow paragraphs would be included into contracts to ensure the use of the source code of the component, the possible bankruptcy would cause a very difficult situation compared to the two other forms of software acquisition, where the change of internal software engineering experts or subcontractors' resources is rather common and can be managed by hiring new persons.

Especially if the COTS supplier were a small company, there would also the possibility that a competitor would buy out the supplier. Evidently, this could lead even to the loss of important business secrets, or at least a sudden end of the supply relationship, and thereby support and further development of the component would also finish.

Another possible disadvantage that came up in the interviews was the fact that as new releases of some software component would come into markets, adequate component evaluation and testing procedures would need to be prepared so that the quality of the component's new version can be verified. Several other concerns related to the responsibilities and guarantees with regard to purchased components were also brought up, too.

Based on the interviews, the main challenges for the definition of the CSCA process framework can be summarised as follows:

Contracting and negotiation:
- Purchasing expertise is needed for the execution of the acquisition process (e.g. negotiations).
- Importance that the case company would have among the other customers of the potential supplier.
- Developing a general contract outline so that the time needed for the contract negotiations would be shortened as much as possible.
- Taking the ESCROW procedure into account to ensure that the component can be used and further developed in case of bankruptcy or the like.
- Determining the responsibilities between the contract parties (responsibilities, guarantees etc.)
- Managing the different kinds of maintenance contracts for the management of the purchased components.
- Making sure that the willingness of the suppliers to fix the identified bugs as soon as possible is ensured through contract paragraphs.
- The suppliers need to be made committed to the processes of the customer (e.g. through using royalties as pricing strategy) so that it is in its interest to support the customer.
- Ensuring that excessive payments are not required until the component is received and proven to function.

Evaluation of components and suppliers:
- Specifying the right kind of technical evaluation criteria so that all the different environments in which the component could be used are taken into account.

- In addition to the technical criteria, also other, more business related criteria are needed (future of the supplier; its business and technical road maps, ownership relations; financial status; links to competitors).
- Determining the cost analysis for the components (e.g. what kind of pricing is accepted, how the acceptable price is determined, fixing the principles for the cost-benefit analysis etc.)
- Determining the criteria for making the decision of using the component (instead of making the component or having it tailor-made by a subcontractor). Justifying also the decision to not use a component although these are preferred from the management level.
- Ensuring that the acquired component "is what it is said to be" (thorough technical evaluation).
- As COTS components always require resources (managing the interface with the supplier etc.), criteria for a kind of component that is worth these resources should be determined. In case of very small components resources required for the acquisition may not be worthy of it.
- Determining who should conduct the evaluations. Who inside the organisation and/or what kind of external professional organisation could be used?

Management of components and supplier relationships:
- Managing the purchased component throughout the component's life cycle, even though the project originally needing it is finished.
- Ending the management of the component.
- Enabling the effective information flow inside the organisation concerning the component (which components are already acquired, whether new releases are taken into use, what kinds of debugs are made to the components in use, etc).
- Managing the new releases of the component so that the needs of every project using the component are taken into account. Informing every party involved and making also sure, that the older version is available in case some project would prefer using it.
- Developing a kind of database of the potential suppliers and their components or determining the information sources, that should be used as the potential suppliers are being identified.
- Finding ways of influence on the suppliers and on the future development of the acquired components.
- Only few COTS SW component suppliers should be used as the more suppliers are used the more interfaces are needed to be under control.

- Finding ways to influence the third parties that are suppliers of the additional components that are related to the purchased component.
- Finding ways of identifying the component needs earlier in the SW development processes.
- Determining the criteria for making the decision of changing the component into another if the selected component turns out to be unsatisfactory after the purchase.

These challenges are related to several different areas of the acquisition process framework, as it was initially outlined, based on the reference and maturity models. This results in an important conclusion that all responsible parties involved in the acquisition process need to be clearly identified. According to the interviews, the roles of at least three different parties should be addressed. Firstly, *someone would need to carry out the process*, in practice. This could naturally be the project personnel needing some specific component.

Secondly, a *party responsible for guiding the project personnel* in following the systematic acquisition process would be needed. Such a party could, for example, be a team of specialised software subcontracting managers. Thirdly, *someone must be responsible for the continuous development of the acquisition process*, e.g. the company's software quality team.

3.5   Illustration of the Defined CSCA Process Framework

On the basis of the analysis of the reference and maturity models and, more importantly, of the empirical data, the four phased process framework for COTS software component acquisition and management shown in Figure 3.2 was defined. The actual process model based on the framework was documented following the notations of the intranet-based software process support environment of the case company.

In addition to the process description, the model includes training material and a variety of different kinds of suggestions and notes to consider when starting COTS software component acquisition. Document templates, checklists, etc. are also included in the process description to guide acquisition. The process was harmonised with the case company's CBSE model by the use of cross-references in task descriptions, by making sure that the overlapping phrases used in the two models are the same, and by defining COTS-related software reuse responsibilities in the CBSE model.

As can be seen from Figure 3.2, the CSCA process revolves around the underlying value creating business processes to which the purchasing and use of COTS software components is related. The main phases of the reference models form the centre of the acquisition process schema, and the outer circle of the framework represents the processes through which value is created for the purchaser, when associating with software component suppliers.

The Value Creation Process of a Company Buying Software Components

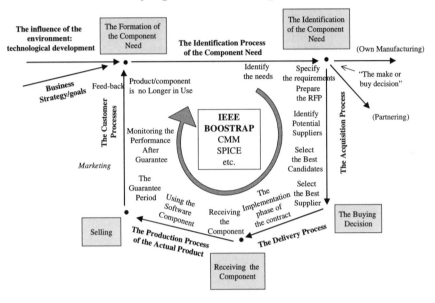

Figure 3.2. COTS software component acquisition process framework

The process framework was used as a foundation for the definition of the key process areas of the actual CSCA process. The framework was named "COTS Software Component Acquisition and Management Processes" to emphasise the holistic nature of the entire process setting. In other words, it was understood that the actual buying procedures such as identifying potential suppliers and evaluating alternative components was not enough. A more comprehensive view was needed, and therefore rather much attention was paid to such processes as identifying own software needs and using COTS components, managing the future versions of components, co-operating with the suppliers, and finally ending the management of some specific component.

The process framework includes four key process areas: *1. Planning, 2. Analysing and Evaluating, 3. Negotiating,* and *4. Managing and Reusing* (Figure 3). Each of the four process areas are composed of base practices that describe the phases and issues of each process area in more details.

It is important to notice that the four process areas do not represent only different phases of the software component acquisition and management processes, but also different topics related to the phenomenon. Therefore, the process framework shown in Figure 3.3 does not consist of successively ordered phases (cf. the reference models), but rather of several parallel and overlapping processes. Some tasks should certainly be taken before another, but many of the tasks would need to be conducted in parallel and continuously. Also, the process framework should ensure that the acquisition could be aborted at any stage of the process, if so would be decided by the purchaser.

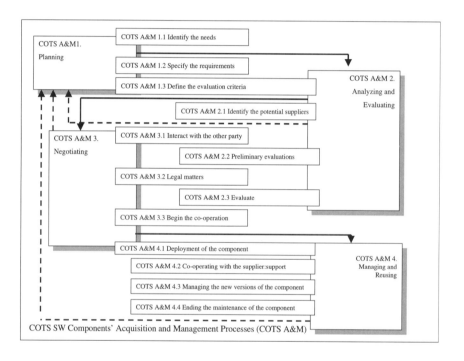

Figure 3.3. CSCA processes and base practices.

The Planning process includes tasks that the COTS software component acquirer should conduct internally, before actively interacting with suppliers. The software component needs should be identified as early as possible in the software development process. Furthermore, when identifying the needs, a variety of aspects should be taken into account: strategic, operational, functional, technical and business-related needs should be acknowledged.

After identifying the needs, the actual requirements for the component as well as for the supplier candidate that meet the identified needs should be defined. Finally, evaluation criteria should be defined on the basis of the needs and requirements. The criteria should include technical, business and legal elements to ensure that all of the necessary aspects of a business transaction – and preferably a continuing business relationship – would be addressed during the whole acquisition process. The criteria should be ranked in order according to their relative importance.

The Analysing and evaluating process is more related to interacting with the suppliers. Its purpose is to ensure that the evaluation of alternative software components and suppliers is conducted as effectively and thoroughly as possible. The process includes identifying the potential suppliers and making both preliminary and more thorough evaluations. The idea of the two-phased evaluation is to ensure that no unnecessary resources are spent in the evaluation, the most inappropriate candidates are discarded as early as possible. This can be done during the identification of potential suppliers, but at the latest during the preliminary evaluation, emphasising business-related evaluation criteria and the suppliers' competence.

A very important point is also to pay attention to the role of the Negotiation process, which is conducted in parallel with the Analysing and evaluating process. The Negotiation process includes such issues as how to interact with the negotiation partner, which kinds of legal issues are the most important to take into account, and how to conclude the negotiations so that a constructive and valuable relationship can be started. Because the negotiations are conducted in parallel with the evaluations, a good and well-functioning information flow should be maintained between the technical, business and legal experts of the purchaser used in the evaluation, and the negotiation team members.

After the buying decision has been made, co-operation with the supplier should be started so that a beneficial business relationship is enabled. Moreover, reuse of the acquired component should be carefully planned, so that the component would be soon enough in full use. Such issues as planning for the deployment of the component, organising support inside the purchasing organisation and in relation with the supplier, and managing new versions of the component should be taken care of. Finally, maintenance of the component would end at some point, and issues related to this would also need to be considered early enough.

3.6   Evaluation of the Process Model — The Server Project

The developed CSCA process framework was evaluated in one product development project, Server, which aimed at using "as many external software components as possible" in the own words of the project team. In the project, several kinds of software components were intended to be bought, ranging from system software (computing platforms, data bases, operating system, protocol stacks, etc.) to generic application frameworks and middleware software. Without going into any details, it can be said that the uppermost application-related layers of the Server product were planned to be developed following the two earlier software acquisition means, but the entire computing and basic data transfer layers would be based on external software components.

3.6.1   *Feedback from the Evaluation*

The Server project was already ongoing during the evaluation, in "The Acquisition Process" phase in terms of Figure 3.2. At first it was thought to be a serious problem that no controlled experiment could be planned and conducted from the very beginning of the acquisition. However, it appeared that the possibility of comparing how the project had actually started to carry out software acquisition to the CSCA process framework resulted in yet another new insight. In other words, the people who were in the middle of an ongoing software acquisition case were useful evaluators of the developed process framework, although they were not yet strictly following the proposed CSCA process.

At a general level, the main finding of the evaluation was that the prepared process framework would have prevented many problems faced by the Server project already in the early phases of COTS software component acquisition. Firstly, although the requirements and evaluation criteria for components had been defined, they were not documented. This caused many problems, especially because the acquisition of some components took several months. The importance of systematically documented and updated requirements and evaluation criteria is strongly emphasised in the developed CSCA process framework.

Also, the exchange of information between technical, business and legal experts was rather poor in the Server project. In particular, the flow of information was not functioning in relation to evaluations and decision-making. The role of information sharing across the different aspects of the acquisition, as well as the roles and responsibilities of the parties involved in the acquisition process are an integral part of the developed CSCA process description, and would possibly have prevented at least some of the problems already encountered in the Server project.

Some of the most important findings with regard to developing the CSCA process framework further, on the basis of the experiences gained from the Server project, can be outlined as follows. Firstly, *the definition of a product strategy* would be important as a starting point and foundation for any software acquisition. Whether the use of COTS is preferred over internal or subcontracted software development should be strategically evaluated, because the comparison of these alternatives may become difficult or even impossible later.

Furthermore, *criteria for the kinds of suppliers that are preferred, as well as the risk levels* that are accepted in relation to software components and suppliers *should be made clearly explicit.* To support a product development project's decision making in relation to these issues, the developed CSCA process framework would need to be extended with new base practices. However, these strategies should not restrict the effectiveness of projects, product developers should still have the possibility to diverge from the strategy, if necessary.

Thirdly, yet another very important finding from the Server evaluation was the importance of even more detailed definition of the *roles and responsibilities* related to the acquisition and management of COTS components. Evidently, at least two important expertise areas are needed in the CSCA process in addition to software engineering expertise: both legal and business expertise are vital for successful software component acquisition. However, the existence of such expertise in the company or in the acquisition team does not guarantee the success. The point is to define even more clearly and in further details the roles and responsibilities related to the software acquisition than what was done.

The persons involved in the process should be named and their responsibilities should be defined. Communication between these persons should be secured and the decision making procedures made visible. The exchange of information with supplier candidates should be kept co-ordinated during the whole acquisition process, and also the internal information flow should be secured. The owners of software components as well as the owners of supplier relationships should be appointed, in order to ensure well co-ordinated information flows during the acquisition and management of the component.

Finally, one of the most difficult areas that would need better support in CSCA process is the *determination of the costs of the components.* This can be seen as a practical managerial aspect of the value creation approach around which the CSCA process framework was designed. The prices suggested by suppliers are, based on the Server experiences, very difficult to evaluate and compare, because suppliers use several different pricing strategies. Pricing of internal and subcontracted software development is, in comparison, very straightforward indeed. Moreover, COTS software component offerings entail different contents, some only a particular software code with all the additional services at additional costs, whereas other include much more comprehensive packages.

Because suppliers more and more prefer volume-based licensing, the estimated purchasing volumes and other such information becomes a critical issue in negotiations. In summary, if the strategy of the purchasing company changes considerably towards COTS software component acquisition, there are considerable pressures to analyse the costs and benefits related to the software incorporated into the purchaser's products as a whole.

3.6.2   *Conclusions – General Implications*

The case study discussed above was launched in order to make explicit co-operation between the purchasing organisation and its COTS software component suppliers. The focus was on outlining the acquisition and management processes of COTS software components, so that the acquisition process could be supported at a practical software engineering and managerial levels. During the study, information was gathered through analysing existing software acquisition reference and maturity models, as well as through interviews of selected representatives of the case company and a few COTS software suppliers.

Although the process framework uses the existing models as its basis, it is more based on the empirical material and specific needs of the case company. The framework is directed towards managing specifically COTS software component acquisition, and therefore it brings forward new aspects to the spectrum of existing models for software acquisition. The framework illustrates the issues that were raised as important considerations, both in the literature and in everyday practice. The processes and base practises in the framework are not described at identical level of accuracy, neither do they represent issues that would be of equal importance. Some of the base practices are rather straightforward instructions, whereas others are made explicit using quite general and descriptive terms. However, the process description structured around the framework inevitably outlines the most important considerations that should be taken into account when acquiring COTS software components. Moreover, it gives many guidelines and points to consider, from a very practical viewpoint.

Use of COTS software components clearly requires a change in the thinking and attitudes of software engineers in the case company. Moreover, a variety of new competencies and skills are required in COTS-based software development. The attitudes of the technical people towards buying and using COTS software components can be rather critical, even negative, because of the new tasks, competencies and people involved in software acquisition. The role of training and support is apparently much more important than what it was in the case study.

The very next task to carry out in the case company, in order to start actively using the new process, would therefore be to help the process roll-out by training and support. This would require much more extensive forms of information exchange, feedback and experimentation than what has been done this far. Also, because COTS software component markets are still at their early developing stage, it is likely that the developed software acquisition processes would need to be constantly adapted to market changes. As an example, the use of open source and other kinds of freely available software would most likely need to be addressed. Some of the case company's present software subcontractors may become providers of modified-off-the-shelf (MOTS) components, and their new role as the company's suppliers should be made visible, and so on. In short, it would be important that the developed process framework and description is constantly developed further, so that it is consistent with the changes of both the environment and the internal operations of the case company.

References

Anderson, J., Narus, J. (1999) Business market management: understanding, creating and delivering value, Upper Saddle River, NJ: Prentice Hall.

Bicego, A. and Ceccolini, S. (1997) BOOTSTRAP 3.0 Acquisition Process, BOOTSTRAP Institute.

Clements, P. and Northrop, L. (1999) A Framework for Software Product Line Practice - Version 2.0, CMU/SEI.

Cooper, J., Fisher, M., and Sherer, S.W. (eds.) (1999). Software Acquisition Capability Maturity Model (SA-CMM) Version 1.02. Technical Report, CMU/SEI-99-TR002, ESC-TR99-002

Hansen, S., Dorling, A., Schweigert, T., and Lovett, J. (1999). IT Purchasing Guidebook for Small Entreprises. A guide for getting more value from your IT purchases. QAI Europe, United Kingdom.

Hoch, D.J., Roeding, C.R., Purkert, G., Lindner, S.K. and Mueller, R. (2000). Secrets of Software Success: Management Insights from 100 Software Firms around the World. Harvard Business School Press, Boston, MA. 312 p.

IEEE Std 106 (1998). The Institute of Electrical and Electronics Engineers, Inc. United States of America

ISO/IEC TR 15504-2 (1998). Information Technology - Software Process Assessment - Part 2: A Reference Model for Processes and Process Capability. Technical Report type 2, International Organisation for Standardisation (Ed.), Case Postale 56, CH-1211 Geneva, Switzerland.

Parolini, C. (1999). The Value Net. A Tool for Competitive Strategy. John Wiley Books, Chichester, UK.

Chapter 4

The Library Systems Product Line: A Case Study Demonstrating the KobrA Method

JOACHIM BAYER and DIRK MUTHIG

Fraunhofer Institute for Experimental Software Engineering (IESE)
Sauerwiesen 6, D-67661 Kaiserslautern, Germany
{bayer,muthig}@iese.fraunhofer.de

Abstract. The KobrA method, which has been developed at the Fraunhofer Institute for Experimental Software Engineering (IESE), combines and integrates several software engineering competencies under the umbrella of a systematic method for component-based product line engineering. In this chapter, an application of the KobrA method in constructing and using a generic component framework for a family of library systems is demonstrated. The case study serves two major purposes. On the one hand, it allowed us to play around with new ideas and to experiment with alternative approaches for realizing diverse concepts in the method. On the other hand, it is a comprehensive example that illustrates all aspects and features of the method.

4.1 Introduction

The KobrA[1] method, which has been developed at the Fraunhofer Institute for Experimental Software Engineering (IESE), combines and integrates several software engineering competencies under the umbrella of a systematic method for component-based product line engineering [Atkinson *et al.* (2001)]. It, therefore, represents a synthesis of several advanced software engineering technologies. Besides product line development, it includes component-based development, frameworks, architecture-centric inspections, quality modeling, and process modeling. These have been integrated with the basic goal of providing a systematic approach to the development of high-quality, component-based application frameworks. One of the key characteristics of the KobrA approach is its introduction of the notion of components as early in the life cycle as possible, that is, during analysis and design. The logical components developed there can then be implemented from scratch or realized by reusing pre-existing components. Numerous methods claim to sup-

---

[1] KobrA stands for "Komponenten-basierte Anwendungsentwicklung", German for component-based application development

81

port component-based development, but these invariably tend to be rather vague and non-prescriptive in nature. They define a lot of possibilities, but provide little if any help in resolving the resulting choices between them. The KobrA method, in contrast, aims to be as concrete and prescriptive as possible.

The library systems product line case study described here was performed to serve two major purposes. On the one hand, a case study was needed to play around with new ideas and to experiment with alternative approaches for realizing diverse concepts in the method. For this purpose, material from an industrial context is not suitable for two reasons. First, researchers are typically no experts in the particular application domain and they also have no access to the experts in the industrial organization. Hence, it is difficult to work with such material. Second, industry material is typically large and thus it costs much effort to realize a conceptual change consistently.

On the other hand, the case study was planned as an example that illustrates all aspects and features of the KobrA method. Also for this purpose, material from an industrial context is not suitable for several reasons. First, most parts of industry material is concerned with details of an application domain that is not understood by everybody. Second, such a material is not fully owned by the researchers and thus they are usually not permitted to publish it completely and in all details. Third, industry material is large and voluminous and thus many aspects of it do not concern method features but simply add complexity to the example.

For the given reasons, we decided to do an academic case study that is small enough to enable our experimental research approach. That is, the effort needed to propagate changes to all models and thus to keep the entire case study consistent was realistic. Additionally, the academic case study was large and complex enough to illustrate all features and concepts of the KobrA method. Especially the illustration of product line variabilities, their complexity, and the need for special mechanisms for managing them require an appropriate level of complexity.

For our case study it was essential to find a suitable domain with a sufficient spectrum of variability, which is easily understandable. As a customer-oriented example the domain of library systems seems to be a good choice, because nearly everyone is familiar with some features as a user of a modern city library for private purposes or has used a university library during his or her study.

However, beside the above mentioned two types of library, libraries can be classified into far more different library types—each with specific mission, target groups, and tasks. The library types common in Germany can be classified into the following main categories [Hacker (1992)]:

- National Libraries
- Central Subject Libraries
- Regional Libraries
- Academic Libraries
- Special Libraries

Each category includes a large variety of library types [Paul *et al.* (1996)].

The domain of library systems offers a sufficient spectrum of variability for a small, but yet non-trivial case study. We selected three libraries as being members of the library system product line: a city library, a university library, and a research library.

In the following section, the component model of the KobrA method applied is introduced. Section 4.3 then describes the application of the method itself to create a framework for a set of library systems. Section 4.4 illustrates how this framework is used to construct concrete library systems. Finally, Section 4.5 summarizes the case study and draws some conclusions.

4.2 KobrA Components

One of the main practical challenges faced by software developers today is finding an effective way of combining the vast array of implementation technologies, middleware platforms, and development paradigms currently available on the market. Many development organizations would like to adopt the latest development approaches, such as component-based development and product line engineering, but are deterred by the shear number of solutions on offer and the lack of guidelines on how they can be used together.

One of the most prominent attempts to address this problem is the OMG's recent Model Driven Architecture (MDA) initiative [OMG (2002)]. It is based on the philosophy of modeling the essential application-oriented properties of a system independently of specific implementation and middleware solutions. By separating concerns for the truly application driven features of a system from the idiosyncrasies of specific realization technologies, the underlying architecture not only becomes more robust and insensitive to platform evolution, but is also more easily understood by, and communicated between, architects and developers.

Although the MDA philosophy represents a significant step forward, however, it still leaves some major questions unresolved. In particular, it does not address the problem of how competing system-organization paradigms should be reconciled. The essential features of a system can be isolated from middleware and implementation details by documenting them in the form of platform-independent models (e.g., using the UML [Rumbaugh *et al.* (1998)]), but they cannot be isolated from the underlying strategy used to organize and modularize information (e.g., component-based development, product line engineering, etc.). The practical exploitation of the MDA approach is therefore contingent on an effective strategy for reconciling the various competing system-organization paradigms.

The KobrA method addresses this problem by leveraging the MDA philosophy in tandem with the component-based development (CBD) and product line engineering (PLE) paradigms. When used in combination, these approaches tend to enhance each other's strengths and plug each others' weaknesses. The MDA approach is enhanced by explicit, systematic strategies for organizing and managing architectural information; the CBD approach [Szyperski (1998); Heineman and Councill (2001)] is enhanced by explicit and systematic strategies for its application in the early phases of development, and for making components more reusable; and the PLE approach [Clements and Northrop (2001); Donohoe (2000); Chastek (2002)] is enhanced by concrete mechanisms for capturing and manipulating the variabilities that characterize a product line. The resulting synergy provides a highly effective way of separating and organizing information in a development project, and thus provides the foundation for the systematic and rigorous exploitation of the UML in software development.

The next section describes how the KobrA method integrates the component-based development, product line, and MDA approaches by organizing development artifacts and activities in terms of three orthogonal development dimensions. The sections that follow then focus on each of these dimensions individually, describing what aspect of development the dimension addresses, and how UML models support it.

4.2.1 *Modeling Dimensions*

The UML models developed in a project based on the KobrA method are organized in terms of the three orthogonal development dimensions illustrated in Fig. 4.1 — one dealing with the level of abstraction, one dealing with the level of genericity, and one dealing with containment.

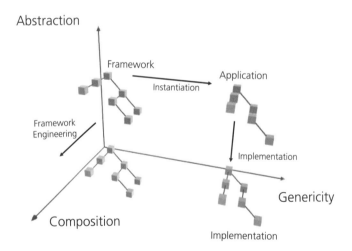

Fig. 4.1   Primary Development Dimensions

In an ideal project, development begins with the box in the top right hand corner of Fig. 4.1. This represents a generic, abstract, black-box description of the system to be developed. It is generic because it has possibly variant features (i.e., parameters), it is abstract because it is comprised mainly of UML models at a level akin to analysis and design, and it is a black box because it describes only the externally visible properties of the system when considered as a single whole. In order to create an executable version of this system it is necessary to:

(1) Decompose the system into finer grained parts to yield a containment tree of nested components (Decomposition)
(2) Remove the genericity to create an instance of the system that meets the needs of a specific application (Instantiation)
(3) Reduce the level of abstraction to create an executable representation of the system and its parts (Embodiment)

Performing all three transformations produces the system in the bottom left part of Fig. 4.1, which is represented in terms of finer grained components, lower (i.e., zero) genericity, and a concrete (i.e., an executable) representation.

All methods that aim to support reuse through component-based software development must support the same basic transformations in one way or another. However, most mix containment, genericity, and abstraction issues in ad hoc ways leading to unnecessary complexity and confusion. In the KobrA method, these three dimensions are fully orthogonal. Development concerns dealing with the genericity dimension come under the umbrella of product line engineering, development concerns dealing with the containment dimension come under the umbrella of component modeling, and development concerns dealing with abstraction dimensions come under the umbrella of component embodiment.

The separation of these concerns does not mean that they are addressed in sequential order. On the contrary, since they are genuinely orthogonal in the KobrA method, they can be tackled in various orders, and in fact arbitrarily interweaved, depending on the precise set of circumstances found in a particular project. The only requirement for strict separation is that at any point in the development process a developer knows precisely, which concern he/she is working on. Figure 4.1 shows only the canonical route of getting from the abstract, generic and course-grained (i.e., user-oriented) view of a system to a concrete, specific, and fine-grained version that can be executed.

4.2.2 Containment

The containment dimension of modeling is concerned with the description of the properties of components and the nature of the relationships between them. In particular, it describes how large components are made up of, or "composed of", smaller components. The driving principle is that all behavior-rich entities should be viewed as components and modeled in the same basic way regardless of their size, complexity, or location in the containment tree. Thus, the system to be constructed in a project is viewed as a component and treated in the same way as its constituent subsystems and abstract data types. Components are thus logical parts of a system's architecture and/or design rather than physical components of the UML kind. The closest UML concept to components in the component model used in the KobrA method is the subsystem. Like a subsystem, a component there has both a class facet, in that it exports behavior, and a package facet in that it can contain other system elements (including other components). The main difference between KobrA components and

UML subsystems is that while subsystems do not possess their own behavior (but merely encapsulate that of other elements) KobrA components do possess their own behavior.

A consequence of this approach is that there is no distinction between the activities involved in component fabrication and component application. Components are fabricated by assembling smaller components, and are applied (or used) by combining them with others to create larger components. Another consequence of this principle is that any component providing a useful standalone service to a user can be treated as a system, provided that its environmental requirements can be satisfied.

4.2.2.1 Component Specification versus Realization

The notion of viewing a system as component lies behind the KobrA method's approach to modeling components in terms of UML diagrams. As illustrated in Fig. 4.2, to support the principle of encapsulation, every Komponent (short for: *KobrA component*) has a "specification", which describes what a component does, and a "realization", which describes how it does it.

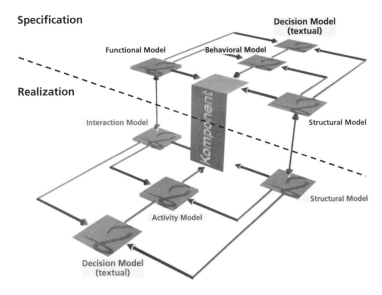

Fig. 4.2   Component Specification versus Realization

The specification of a component describes the requirements that the component is expected to fulfil, both functional and non-functional, and the expectations that the component places on its environment. It therefore describes all the properties of its instances that are visible to other component instances, including the set of services that the instances makes available to others (commonly called the supplied or server interface), and the set of server instances that the component instances need to acquire (commonly called imported, supplied or used interfaces). The specification also defines the behavior of the component over time, including the different states that they may exhibit.

The realization, in contrast, describes the design by which the component fulfil ls these requirements, partly with the help of server components. It therefore describes the private design by which its instances realize the properties defined in the specification. This includes a description of any server creations performed by the instances, and the identification of any subcomponents. The realization also describes how the various server instances (created and acquired) are linked together within the component's instances. In other words, it describes the architecture or design of the component.

4.2.2.2 *Containment Trees*

The realization of a component defines which server components are needed to realize its operations. In other words, it identifies which component instances the component in question is a client of. A component instance can gain access to a required server component instance in one of two ways—it can acquire it from outside as the parameter of an operation invocation, or it can create the component instance itself. In the latter case, if a server component instance remains a private part of the client for its entire lifetime, the server component is often viewed as subcomponent of the client. A subcomponent is regarded as being contained by its supercomponent and, as illustrated Fig. 4.3, its specification models are tightly tied to its supercomponent's realization models.

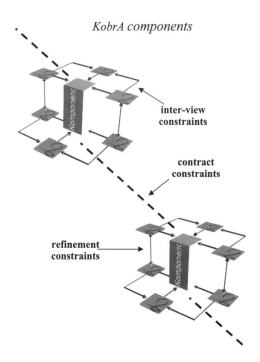

Fig. 4.3   Constraints and Relationships in a Containment Tree

When applied hierarchically, this approach of modeling some components as subcomponents of others yields a component containment tree, in which each child component is contained by its parent. The end result is a component-oriented description of the system architecture, including the definition of the containment relationships, documented almost entirely in the form of UML diagrams.

4.2.3 *Genericity*

The genericity dimension of modeling in the KobrA method handles product line aspects. Product line engineering can be added incrementally to single system development. It is basically an approach for planning and developing several similar systems concurrently in order to systematically exploit their commonalities.

Historically, it is a descendant of domain engineering, which pioneered the creation of a generic reference model for an application domain from which multiple, similar concrete applications could be derived. The essential concept of product line engineering is to take common and varying aspects of applications into account at all life cycle stages and for all kinds of products. Commonalities and variabilities are equally important: commonalities define the skeleton of systems in the product line while variabilities bound the space of required and anticipated variations of the common skeleton. The product line aspects of the KobrA method are described in more detail in [Atkinson *et al.* (2000)].

4.2.3.1 *Generic Components*

Every component in a containment tree can be regarded as representing an individual system in its own right, regardless of its position in the containment hierarchy. In a project that is not intending to exploit product lines, each component defines the properties of exactly one system. When generalized to support a product line, however, each component in the containment tree can be thought of as defining a family of systems — each member of which represents a different variant. A KobrA component that represents a family of systems (or components) as opposed to just one is referred to as generic component, and the artifacts of which it is composed are referred to as generic artifacts.

Not every component in a framework need be generic. In fact, in the extreme case, none of the components in a framework need be generic. However, such a framework represents a situation in which a product line only has one member. As soon as more members are identified, one or more of the components in the framework must be generic.

A generic component differs from a specific component in two main ways:

- The regular artifacts describing the component capture all the features for all members of the family represented by the component. In addition they use the stereotype «variant» to highlight features that are not common to all members of the family (i.e., features that represent variabilities between the family members). This enables the UML compliant modeling of generic components.
- An additional artifact, known as a decision model, is defined that relates the variabil-

ities in the family to externally visible choices that collectively identify a particular member of the family.

This applies to both the specification and realization of a component. In other words, the specification and realization of a component both have their own decision models relating the variable features captured in their respective models. This is important since it allows variabilities in component realizations to be handled separately from variabilities in component specifications. In fact, the variabilities in a component's realization should, by definition, be related to the variabilities in its non-functional requirements specification (within its specification) since different realizations should only change "how well" a realization supports non-functional requirements.

4.2.3.2 *Frameworks versus Applications*

Generic frameworks cover a set of applications. To derive a specific application from such a framework, the genericity in the framework has to be removed to make it specific. This is called application engineering. The purpose of the application engineering activity is to generate a specific set of artifacts that meet the needs of a specific system. In the context of a product line it does this by instantiating the framework created within the framework engineering activity. A KobrA component framework is instantiated by systematically resolving all decision models and turning the generic framework artifacts into concrete application artifacts.

From a practical perspective, the only thing that distinguishes a generic component in a framework from a specific component in an application is whether it possesses a decision model or a decision resolution model. Specific components have decision resolution models that record how the decisions in the decision model have been resolved for the component in question.

4.2.4 **Abstraction**

The artifacts generated in component modeling are at a high-level of abstraction akin to analysis and design. Naturally, these models are only of value if they can be transformed into an executable form in an efficient and verifiable way. In the KobrA method, the set of activities involved in developing such executable and hence deliverable forms of logical components are encompassed by the concept of embodiment. Thus, component embodiment is a separate dimension of concern from the modeling of composition at the level of analysis and design in terms of the UML. This allows the containment tree to be mapped flexibly to many different kinds of architectures, and is the basis for the support of MDA in the KobrA method.

One strategy for the embodiment of a logical component is to implement it from scratch (i.e., if a suitable predefined component cannot be found). The first stage of this process is "implementation", which is primarily concerned with developing a tool comprehensible form of a component that can be automatically transformed into an executable form. In

many implementation technologies this is known as source code. Since modeling yields an
abstract description of components and their relationship, at analysis and design levels, they
can be implemented in virtually all mainstream implementation technologies, including
physical component technologies such as .Net/COM+ or J2EE/EJB.

4.2.4.1 *Implementation*

As well as being strictly separated from the genericity and containment dimension explained previously, the implementation dimension itself applies the principle of separation
of concerns at a lower level. As illustrated in Fig. 4.4, most methods approach the problem
of transforming abstract models into tool comprehensible source code by defining a set
of guidelines specifying how each abstract modeling feature can be mapped into a set of
equivalent programming language concepts. Such guidelines therefore essentially aim to
add implementation detail and change representation form in one big step, as illustrated by
the diagonal line from the realization (i.e. design) to the source code in Fig. 4.4. However,
this not only increases the complexity of the transformation, potentially leading to reduced
quality, but also reduces the opportunities for reuse.

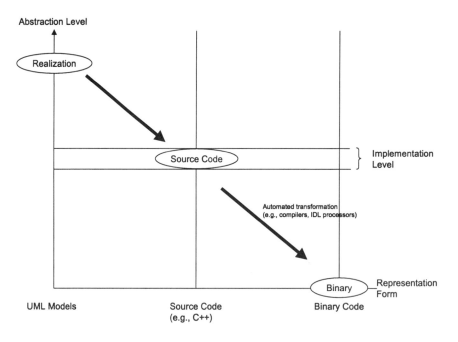

Fig. 4.4   Direct Transformation of Models

    In contrast, the KobrA method strictly separates the transformation process into dis-
tinct refinement and translation steps. As illustrated in Fig. 4.5, refinement is concerned
with describing model elements at a lower level of detail, but using the same notation,

while translation is concerned with mapping model elements into program elements. Separating these concerns not only simplifies the individual transformation steps, but also allows refinement guidelines to be reused with multiple language and implementation vehicles.

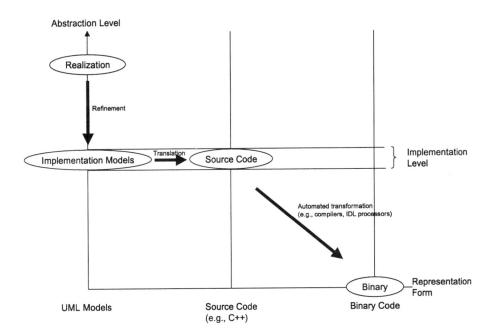

Fig. 4.5   Separating Refinement and Translation

Following this approach yields a UML representation of the source code, but in terms of implementation level model elements. Such an "implementation" model complements the source code, and is constructed using a specially defined implementation profile of the UML.

One of the key questions to be resolved during implementation is how logical components are to be mapped into physical components. A physical component represents an independently deployable and replaceable unit of software. The components of traditional component technologies therefore represent physical components, but in general any separately executable software unit, such as a main program, or an applet etc., is also viewed as physical component in the KobrA method. In general, a component in a containment tree can be "flattened" into physical components in various ways. At one extreme, the whole tree can be mapped to a single physical component, while at the other extreme every individual component can be mapped to a separate physical component. The choice depends on the nature of the target execution environment, performance requirements, and the desired level of run-time substitutability.

4.2.4.2   *Reuse*

Implementation is not the only strategy for component embodiment in the KobrA method. Once the specification of a component has been defined it is also possible to embody the component by reusing an external component already in existence. This may be another KobrA component initially developed within another containment tree, or a foreign component, such as a COTS component. In both cases the process of reusing an external component is roughly the same. The reusing component and the candidate component for reuse must somehow be brought into agreement on the nature of the contract between them. In the KobrA method, this contract is represented by a specification. In the rare case that the reuse candidate satisfies the precise needs of the reusing component, it can be incorporated without change into the containment tree. More typically, however, the reusing component and/or the reused component have to be modified in some way to arrive at a mutually agreed interface.

4.3   Framework for Library System Product Line

4.3.1   *Product Line Members*

This section characterizes the product line members which were used as the basis for defining the scope of the case study. The three types of library systems, namely a city library, a university library, and a research library, are described in the following subsections.

4.3.1.1   *Research Library*

The research library is a specialized, scientific library for the researchers, students, and employees working at a research institute. It is also responsible for different information gathering, documentation, training, and consulting tasks. The purpose of the research library is to supply people at the institute with specialized information based on their specific needs for research and project work.

4.3.1.2   *University Library*

A university library is a scientific library. Its purpose is to provide university members (i.e., students, professors, and other scientific staff) comprehensively with scientific literature. The research areas and the curriculum subjects of the university are covered by the library. In most cases, university libraries are also part of a supra-regional inter-library lending system.

4.3.1.3   *City Library*

A city library is a public library. Its purpose is to provide all citizens of a city and the surrounding areas with literature and media for personal education and training, for day-to-day management, and as a basis for forming their own opinions. Its stock includes fiction and non-fiction, poetry, juvenile literature, and periodicals. Further purposes of a city library are to teach competence in the use of media and to promote reading.

4.3.2 Framework Scope

A framework scope defines the set of features to be covered by a framework. The KobrA method defines a framework scope in the form of a product map, which is a table relating features to the systems in the product line. In order to be able to present the case study here, its originally considered scope had to be reduced. The result of this feature reduction is the product map shown in Table 4.1.

Table 4.1   Product Map for the Library System Product Line

		City Library	University Library	Research Library
Customer Management	Registration	X	X	X
	Unregistration	X	X	X
	Registration Change	X	X	X
Loan Management	Loan	X	X	X
	Return	X	X	X
	Report Loss	X	X	X
	Item Reservation		X	X
	Item Suggestion		X	X
Stock Management	Overdue Control	X	X	X
	Inventorying	X	X	X
	Statistics		X	X
	Classification Management	X	X	X
	Keyword Management		X	X
	Descriptor Management	X		
Item Management	Item Acquisition	X	X	X
	Item Registration	X	X	X
	Item Removal	X	X	X
Periodical Management	Subscription Acquisition		X	X
	Periodical Registration		X	X
	Periodical Monitoring		X	X
	Periodical Contents Registration		X	X
	Periodical Removal		X	X
	Periodical Unsubscribing		X	X
Data Exchange	Data Import		X	X
	Data Export		X	X
Accounting	Billing	X		
	OPAC		X	X

4.3.3 *Context Realization*

The framework engineering process of the KobrA method recursively specifies and re-
alizes components. Thereby, specifications of further components are derived from the
realizations of component acquiring servers in order to fulfil their specification. To start
the framework engineering process, the context of the library system is "realized" first and
then the specification of library systems is derived as intended by the process.

The process producing the context realization is the backend (or a part) of the performed
requirements engineering activities. Figure 4.6 shows the business process hierarchy to be
supported by the library system product line. The grayed processes are optional processes,
that is, they are not supported by all product line members. Only the loan management
branch is shown completely.

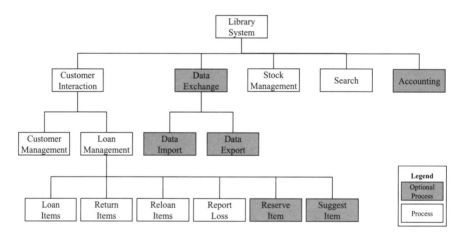

Fig. 4.6   Enterprise Process Diagram LoanManagement Branch

Each of these business processes is modeled by the means of activity diagrams. Figure 4.7 depicts two activity diagrams. The left diagram describes the process of loaning
several items at once. One of its activities, loanItem, is refined by the right diagram, that
is, the second diagram captures the process of loaning a single item.

Due to the refinement relationships between activity diagrams, the whole set of activity
diagrams defines a hierarchy of activities. Figure 4.8 depicts this hierarchy for the library
system framework.

The grayed activities in the hierarchy identify the layer of activities that is typically
seen as use cases. Use cases capture scenarios of user-system interactions, which are often
described textually. Typically there are different user roles (i.e., actors) and thus each use
case is related to the actor involved in the described scenario. Figure 4.9 shows the use
case diagram for the actor ServiceLibrarian, which are persons directly interacting
with the users of a library. The stereotype «variant» is used to depict use cases that are
not supported by all library systems (cf. the optional processes in the business hierarchy in

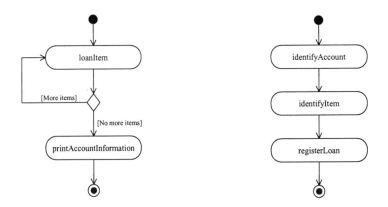

Fig. 4.7   Activity Diagrams loanitems and loanitem

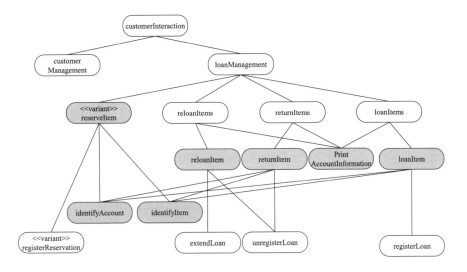

Fig. 4.8   Activity Hierarchy

Fig. 4.6).

The KobrA method refines each use case description by a sequence diagram that precisely captures the interaction in the form of messages. Figure 4.10 depicts the sequence diagram for the loanItem use case.

The message sent to a library system correspond to the system's services and thus can be directly used as the methods of the library system component. This component, all entities, and roles relevant in the system's context are shown in the class diagram of the context realization. We omit this class diagram here but show the derived class diagram that is part of the library system specification below.

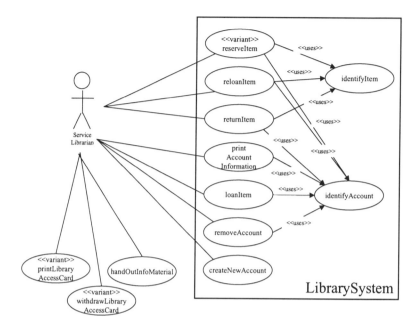

Fig. 4.9   Use case `ServiceLibrarian`

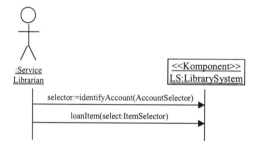

Fig. 4.10   Sequence Diagram `loanItem`

Many models describing a framework contain variant elements, meaning elements that are not part of the model for each individual system derived from the framework. In order to complete the documentation of the framework also the relationships and inter-dependencies among all variant elements must be captured. This is done in the form of a decision model. There are decision models for each individual model. Table 4.2 shows the decision model of the use case diagram depicted in Fig. 4.9.

Table 4.2   Decision Model for the Use Case Diagram

Variation	Resolution	Effect
Reservation	yes (default)	—
	no	remove use case `reserveItem`
LibraryAccessCard	yes	—
	no	remove use case `printLibraryAccessCard` remove use case `withdrawLibraryAccessCard`

4.3.4   *Framework Structure*

Before we traverse the indicated path through the library system framework, its overall structure is introduced (see Fig. 4.11). The figure shows only the parts of the framework structure relevant here. At the top of the component hierarchy there is the component representing the library system. Its specification is derived from the context realization described in the previous subsection. The library system component is described in Section 4.3.5.

The root component, however, does not realize most of the services but delegates them to subcomponents, such as the `StockManager`, the `AccountManager`, or the `LoanManager`. The latter together with its subcomponent `ReservationManager` are described in Section 4.3.6 and 4.3.7. Components, like for example the `MessageHandler`, that provide basic services and that are thus used by several components in the system are also seen as higher level components in the hierarchy due to their visibility in the overall system.

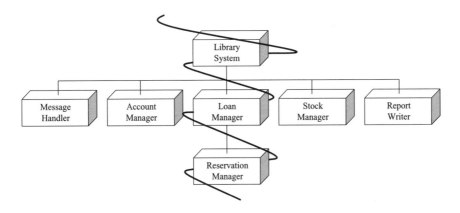

Fig. 4.11   Library System Framework Structure

4.3.5   *Library System*

In this section, the root component of the framework hierarchy is introduced: first, its specification derived from the context realization above, then the realization of the specified services.

4.3.5.1   *Specification*

The specification of the library system consists of three models: the structural, the functional, and the behavioral model. Figure 4.12 captures the structural diagram. In the class diagram there, the class representing the library system is modeled by using the stereotype «subject». The OPAC (Online Public Access Catalog) component is an externally visible part of the library system indicated by the usage of aggregation. All other classes of the stereotype «Komponent» are external components acquired by a library system in order to function in the specified way (e.g., a Printer).

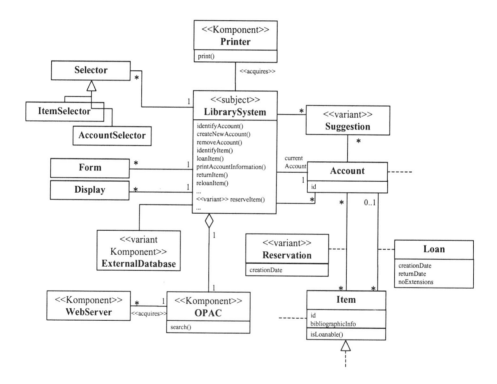

Fig. 4.12   Class Diagram

The services provided by the library systems correspond to the methods of the class LibrarySystem. Each of these operations is specified in the functional model by the means of textual specifications. Table 4.3 shows the specification of the operation loan-

Table 4.3   Operation Specification for `loanItem`

Name	loanItem()
Description	The loan of an item to currentAccount is registered
Receives	selector: ItemSelector
Sends	`MH.displayMessage()` `Item = IM.getItem(filter)`
Rules	An item is loanable if it is not an item that must always stay in the library (e.g., antique books). An item is currently loanable if it is loanable and not loaned <variant> or re-served by another user </variant>.
Changes	new Loan
Assumes	Subject is in the state `accountIdentified` Selector selects exactly one item

Result	Item selected by selector has been obtained from the `ItemManager` IM by sending the message `getItem(filter)`
	
	if item is currently loanable, a new Loan object, `loan`, has been created that relates item and account, and has the attribute values
	`creationDate = today`
	`returnDate = today + <loanPeriod>` and
	`noExtension = 0`
	and, loan has been stored.
	
	if item is currently not loanable, one of the messages has been sent to MH
	<variant>- `displayMessage("Reserved")` or </variant>
	- `displayMessage("Already Loaned")`

`Item()`.

Depending on the sequence of invoked services, the externally visible behavior of a library system may change. Figure 4.13 captures this behavior in the form of a state diagram. Besides a neutral state, the library system behaves differently depending on whether use cases are user- or item-centric.

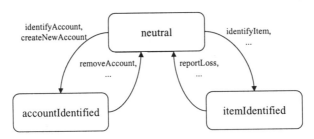

Fig. 4.13   State Diagram

Table 4.4   Decision Model for Class Diagram

Variation	Resolution	Effect
Reservation	yes (default)	—
	no	remove method `LibrarySystem.reserveItem()`
		remove association class `Reservation`
External Database	yes	—
	no (default)	remove Komponent `ExternalDatabase`
		remove method `LibrarySystem.` ...
Suggestion	yes (default)	—
	no	remove class `Suggestion`
		remove method `LibrarySystem.suggestItem()`

The introduced specification is again generic and thus its models contain variant elements. Table 4.4 shows the part of the specification decision model that references elements in the class diagram depicted by Fig. 4.12.

4.3.5.2   *Realization*

The realization of the library system consists of three models: the structural, the activity, and the interaction model. The structural model refines the specification structural diagram by adding model elements that are required to realize the specification but that are not visible outside of the component. Figure 4.14 shows the realization class diagram of the library system component. Compared to the specification class diagram in Fig. 4.12, the internal subcomponents of library systems are added (see also the first level in the framework hierarchy in Fig. 4.11).

In addition to class diagrams, a structural model may contain object diagrams to capture the possible run-time configurations of a library system. Figure 4.15 shows a run-time configuration. The grey objects are only internally visible, the white objects only correspond to the object diagram at the specification level of the library system component.

While the structural model is used throughout the modeling process to refine the data structures, the activity model is used to capture the algorithms that realize the operations of the library system. An example of activity models at an intermediate levels is given in the next subsection. The interaction model is the bridge between the data captured by the structural model and the processes/algorithms captured by the activity model. In case of the operation `loanItem()`, the collaboration (from the viewpoint of the library system component) is very simple: the request is fully delegated to the subcomponent `LoanManager` whose models are shown in the subsequent subsection. Analogously to its specification, the realization of `LibrarySystem` is generic and thus decision models captures the relationships among variant model elements, as well as between decisions at the specification and at the realization level.

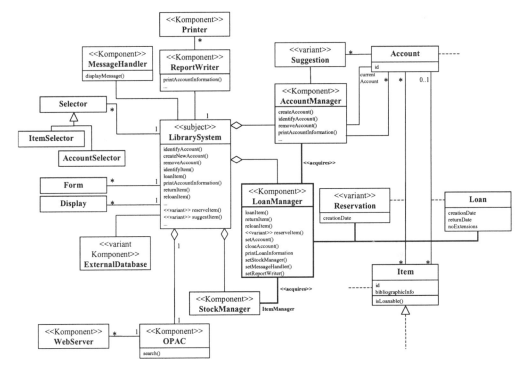

Fig. 4.14   Class Diagram

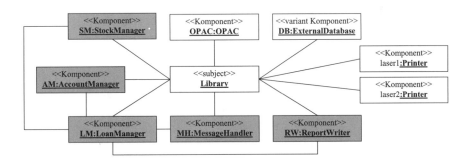

Fig. 4.15   Object Diagram

4.3.6   *Loan Manager*

4.3.6.1   *Specification*

To derive the specification class diagram of the LoanManager component, the class LoanManager and all directly related elements are cut out off the realization class diagram of `LibrarySystem` (see Fig. 4.14, elements with thickened lines). The result is depicted by Fig. 4.16.

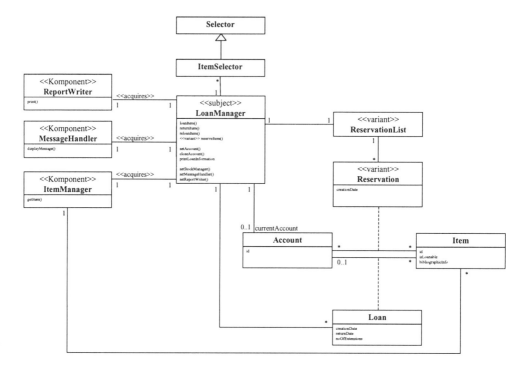

Fig. 4.16   Class Diagram

The operations provided by `LoanManager` are determined by the collaborations defined in the `LibrarySystem`'s realization. For example, `loanItem()` has been delegated to `LoanManager` and thus it is an operation that must also be specified by `Loan-Manager`. Basically, the operation specification shown above can be copied because the operation is fully delegated to `LoanManager`.

The services provided by `LoanManager` are exclusively all user-centric. That is, before any service is enabled the account of a particular user must be set by the `Library-System` (or another component if `LoanManager` is reused in a different context). Figure 4.17 shows the corresponding state diagram.

The `LoanManager` is also responsible for the optional reservation feature. Hence, all elements related to reservation are variant. The dependence between the variation points caused by the optionality of the reservation feature are captured in a decision model, which is partially shown in Table 4.5.

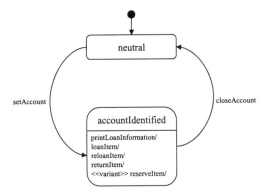

Fig. 4.17   State Diagram

Table 4.5   Decision Model

Variation	Resolution	Effect
Reservation	yes (default)	—
	no	remove method `LoanManager.reserveItem()`
		remove class `ReservationList`
		remove association class `Reservation`

4.3.6.2   *Realization*

The realization of `LoanManager` decided to encapsulate the reservation capability in a further subcomponent but to realize the loan functionality as part of the `LoanManager` component itself. The rationale behind the first decision is to allow the optional reservation functionality to be easily plugged in or out of a library system. This is not needed for the loan-related services because they are common to all library systems and they are the set of services the `LoanManager` component stands for. The realization class diagram is shown in Fig. 4.18.

The `LoanManager` itself maintains data structures that relate user accounts and items. Both accounts and items are owned by other components. That is, the `LoanManager` operates with proxy objects referencing the "real" objects. Consequently, the component must collaborate with several other components in order to realize its services. Figure 4.19 gives an example by capturing the collaborations happening while the `loanItem()` operation is performed.

Due to the optional reservation capability, a decision model (Table 4.6) is needed to capture the rationales behind variant model elements and their inter-dependencies.

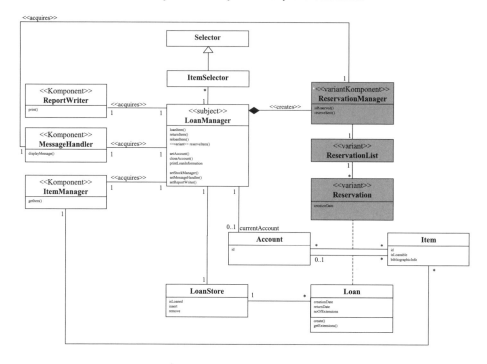

Fig. 4.18   Class Diagram

Table 4.6   Decision Model

Variation	Resolution	Effect
Reservation	yes (default)	—
	no	remove variant tags and content
loanPeriod	value [time]	replace `loanPeriod` by actual value

4.3.7   *Reservation Manager*

The `ReservationManager` is a non-generic component but it is optional as whole. This optionality is captured in the decision model of the `LoanManager` component. It is not visible in the `ReservationManager` models. The specification class diagram of the reservation manager corresponds to the grayed classes in Fig. 4.18.

4.4   A Concrete Library System

In this section, the construction of a concrete library system is illustrated. The next subsection characterizes this system, a member of the library system product line. The remaining subsections show the instances of generic components introduced the previous section with

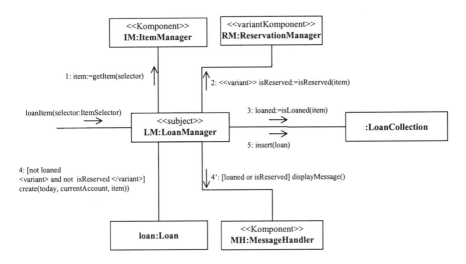

Fig. 4.19   Collaboration `loanItem`

respect to the requirements of the selected library system.

4.4.1   Concrete Product Line Member

The library system that is constructed in this section is the simplest one that can be derived from the framework introduced above. That is, all optional functionality is removed and only the commonalities are supported. For components considered here only some selected diagrams are shown in order to be not too repetitive. The instantiated diagrams can be easily derived from the diagrams shown above — the reader must follow the instructions in the decision models only.

4.4.2   Context Realization

To instantiate the framework, the questions in the decision models must be answered. In our simple case, all questions concerning the reservation capability are answered in a way that excludes the variant elements.

Figure 4.20 shows the use case diagram for the service librarian without the use case for reserving an item.

4.4.3   Library System

4.4.3.1   Specification

The exclusion of the reservation feature also means that the library system does not provide the operation reserveItem. Hence, the corresponding operation specification is not needed. For the same reason, the specification of the `loanItem` operation need not consider the

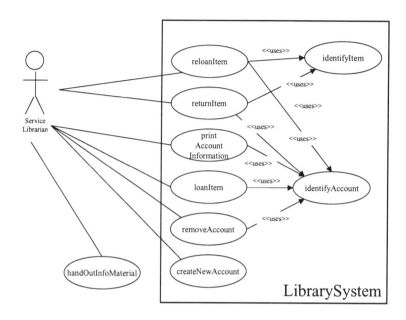

Fig. 4.20   Instantiated Use Case Diagram (cf. Fig. 4.9)

case of trying to loan a book that is reserved by another user. Hence, the case is removed from the operation specification in Table 4.3.

4.4.3.2   *Realization*

Identical decisions are made at the realization level of `LibrarySystem`. Consequently, the collaboration, for instance, that delegates the `reserveItem` operation to `LoanManager` is removed.

4.4.4   *Loan Manager*

4.4.4.1   *Specification*

The `reserveItem` operation must be removed from the class diagram, the state diagram, and the functional model. The latter means that the appropriate operation specification is removed.

4.4.4.2   *Realization*

When the specified functionality of the `LoanManager` is realized without reservation capabilities, the subcomponent `ReservationManager` is not needed. That is, all grey classes in the class diagram in Fig. 4.18 are obsolete and thus removed. This also holds for the component `ReservationManager`, which is as a whole not part of the component hierarchy for the simple library application.

4.5   Conclusions

This chapter presented a case study that has been developed using the KobrA method. A more detailed report on the library system case study can be found in [Bayer *et al.* (2001)]. The case study accompanied and supported the development of the KobrA method. It is — now that the first version of the method has been published — still a valuable resource to illustrate and communicate the ideas and principles that underly the method. We, therefore, continuously exploit it in research, training, and transfer activities because it nicely presents realistic problems and their solutions in a concise and comprehensive way.

References

Atkinson, C., Bayer, J., Muthig, D. (2000). Component-Based Product Line Development: The KobrA Approach. *Proceedings of the First Software Product Line Conference*, pp. 289–309.

Atkinson, C., Bayer, J., Bunse, C. *et al.* (2001). *Component-Based Product Line Engineering with UML*. Addison-Wesley.

Bayer, J., Muthig, D., Goepfert, B. (2001). The Library Systems Product Line: A KobrA Case Study, *Technical Report No. 024.01/E*, Fraunhofer Institute for Experimental Software Engineering (IESE).

Chastek, G. (2002). *Software Product Lines: Proceedings of the Second Software Product Line Conference* (SPLC2), San Diego, CA. Springer LNCS 2379.

Clements, P., Northrop, L. M. (2001). *Software Product Lines: Practices and Patterns*. Addison-Wesley.

Donohoe, P. (2000). *Software Product Lines: Experience and Research Directions. Proceedings of the First Software Product Line Conference*. Kluwer Academic Publishers.

Hacker, R. (1992). Bibliothekarisches Grundwissen, Saur, 6. Auflage, In German.

Heineman, G. T., Councill, W. T. (2001). *Component-Based Software Engineering: Putting the Pieces Together*. Addison-Wesley.

OMG (2002). Model-Driven Architecture Initiative. http://www.omg.org/mda/.

Paul, M., Cabtree, S., Morgenstern, E. (1996). Strategien für Spezialbibliotheken, Deutsches Bibliotheksinstitut (DBI), In German.

Rumbaugh, J., Jacobson, I., Booch, G. (1998). *The Unified Modeling Language Reference Manual* Addison-Wesley.

Szyperski, C. (1998). *Component Software: Beyond Object-Oriented Programming*. Addison-Wesley.

Chapter 5

Component-based System Design and Composition: An Aspect-oriented Approach[*]

PEDRO J. CLEMENTE, JUAN HERNÁNDEZ, JUAN M. MURILLO,
MIGUEL A. PÉREZ and FERNANDO SÁNCHEZ

Quercus Software Engineering Group
University of Extremadura, Spain
{jclemente,juanher,juanmamu,toledano,fernando}@unex.es

Abstract. Component Based Software Engineering (CBSE) and Aspect Oriented Programming (AOP) are two disciplines of software engineering, which have been generating a great deal of interest in recent years. From the CBSE point of view, the building of applications becomes a process of assembling independent and reusable software modules called components. However, the necessary dependencies description among components and its latter implementation causes the appearance of crosscutting, a problem that AOP resolves adequately. Aspect Oriented Programming allows programmers to express in a separate form the different aspects that intervene in an application. These aspects are composed later adequately. This paper analyses the problem of crosscutting that is produced during component development using one of the latest component-based development platforms, such as the Corba Component Model (CCM), and proposes one extension for this platform. This CCM extension has been named AspectCCM [Clemente *et al.* (2002a)].

5.1 Introduction

One of the disciplines of software engineering that, during recent years, has been generating wide concern is component-based software engineering (CBSE), due to CBSE's great potential for software development companies. The building of applications is transformed now into a process of assembling independent and reusable software modules called components. A component is one software composition unit with a set of interfaces and a set of requirements. A component should be able to be developed, acquired and incorporated into the system and composed with other components independently in time and space [Szyperski (1998)].

Constructing an application under this new setting involves the assembly or composi-

---

[*] This project has been financed by CICYT, project number TIC02-04309-C02-01.

tion of prefabricated pieces of software, perhaps developed at different moments, and by different people who perhaps may have imagined different scopes of usage from the way they are finally used. The objective of this perspective reduces the cost and effort of software development, while at the same time, promotes applications flexibility, reliability and reusability, due to the (re-)use of components already verified and validated. This new perspective requires a change on the part of companies in the applications building which should pass from an applications development model to a component assembly perspective.

However, component models base the assembly of their components on interface compatibility (contracts of usage) already described by Desmond D'Suoza in Catalysis [D'Souza (2000)]. In this sense, if a component A has previously described one interface that a component B requires, then a component A can be assembled with another component B. Because of the great influence that component-based development has obtained from object-oriented programming, the description of the interfaces that a component requires expresses an aggregation relationship, with consequences of code tangling well-known for years in object-oriented programming. The adaptability and reusability of components decrease due to this situation.

Aspect-Oriented Programming [Kiczales (1997)] is created with the objective of allowing programmers to express separately the different concerns of an application, in order to be composed adequately at a later stage. The main characteristics of software developed with AOP are flexibility, adaptability and reusability of the elements used to compose the system.

This chapter focuses on the study of the CCM (CORBA Component Model) [Object Management Group (2001)] and its process for software development. It will show the lack of flexibility of the systems developed, which is provoked mainly by the treatment of restrictions and attachments during the definition, implementation and assembly of components. In addition, an alternative will be proposed to the CCM specification, which incorporates additional mechanisms for the specification of dependencies between components, and uses AOP as a "glue" among independent and reusable components.

The rest of the chapter is as follows: in Section 5.2, the crosscutting problems which arise during component-based development will be identified, focusing on the CCM components implementation, where these problems are caused mainly by the dependencies declaration through the statement *uses*. In Section 5.3, our proposal is presented. In Section 5.4, an example of use is presented. Finally, we feature relations with other works and a set of conclusions and future works.

5.2 Finding Crosscutting in Component-based Systems

CBD (Component-Based Development) requires a sequence of stages to be followed until the final system is completed: interfaces description, component description, components implementation, components assembly and deployment [Cheesman and Daniels (2001)].

During these phases (interfaces specification and component specification or definition, above all) software analysts must capture on a piece of paper the necessities and services that a specific component will provide. A component specification describes the necessities of the problem domain. Let us suppose, for example, a component-based system for controlling a bank account (*ServerBank* component) in a domain where the express authorization by a competent authority is needed. Another component named *ServerCheck* provides this authorization. In the code of Figure 5.1 we can observe this components description which details the *ServerBank* component that controls the operations in a bank account, and which requires the *Authentication* interface, which *ServerCheck* provides.

```
interface AccountManager {

        void OpenAccount(in string name, in string pass);
        long Balance(in string name, in string pass);
        void AddBalance(int string name, in string pass, in long balance);
        void SubBalance(int string name, in string pass, in long balance);

};
interface Authentication {

        boolean CheckLogin(in string login, in string password);

};
component ServerBank {

        attribute string name;
        provides AccountManager for_clients;
        uses Authentication for_clients_login;

};
component ServerCheck {

        attribute string name;
        provides Authentication for_clients_check;

};
```

Fig. 5.1   IDL ServerBank and ServerCheck component description.

Experience obtained in component development allows us to ensure that the component dependencies can vary according to the evolving nature of the domains where this component is to be applied. The reusability of this component (*ServerBank*) in different domains of the problem is at stake, and this is due to the fact that from the component definition, a set of dependencies has been bound which could have been added later. In our example we can find another system with a component that needs one bank account but does not require requiring the authorization service. These dependencies become apparent during the implementation of the components. In a concrete language like Java, the use of the dependencies detailed in the description component phase is required during implementation. Now, these dependencies are transformed into invocations over the interfaces already described through the *uses* clause. This situation can be seen in the code (italic) of Figure 5.2.

This situation unmistakably supposes that any change in the component dependencies involves recoding the component. Besides, the code destined to the handling of a specific aspect of the system can appear in the form of dependencies in several components. This involves the existence of code for a specific purpose spread across several components in the system, causing the well-known problem of code tangling or crosscutting (Figures 5.2

```
public int Balance(String name, String pass){

      Authentication for_clients_login =get_connection_for_clients_login();
      if(for_clients_login == null) {

            return 0;

      }
      Permission=for_clients_login.CheckLogin(name,pass);
      if (Permission==true) {

            textArea_.append("Balance of account: +name+ "Balance: "+_balance");
            return _balance;

      }
      else {

            textArea_.append(" Balance of account: "+name +
            " non authorized"); return -1;

      }

}
```

Fig. 5.2   Implementation of Balance method in AccountManager interface

and 5.3) [Aspect Oriented Programming (2001)]. This situation of code tangling increases the dependencies among the components and introduces new opportunities for making programming mistakes; as a result, the components are less reusable, flexible and adaptable (Figure 5.3).

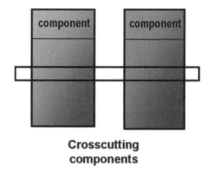

**Crosscutting
components**

Fig. 5.3   Crosscutting Components

CCM offers a set of facilities for the assembly, deployment and execution of the components that make up the final system. CCM provides for this with a set of descriptors in XML: Package descriptor, component descriptor, properties descriptor and assembly descriptor [Object Management Group (2001)]. Through these descriptors we can, for example, replace components in the system (supposing that the components have the same set of dependencies and services), deploy the components along various hosts and set up the connection dependencies during system assembly. However, we cannot re-configure the system architecture to conveniently adapt the assembly and the performance of the system to new requirements. This is due to the fact that the dependencies of each component that make up the system are established during the component specification phase, and there are no mechanisms to modify this specification. Given the evolutionary and changing nature of distributed systems, this lack would be of great concern because, on the one hand, the components can be utilized in domains different from those they were designed for, and on the other hand, the system architecture would be more flexible for supporting new requirements. The different component development platforms (like CCM) would need a mechanism allowing the establishment of new dependencies or the revocation of other dependencies that have a component, without it affecting the component implementation. This way, the components designed would be used in different contexts, that is to say, independently of the context where the components were designed. Offering a mechanism that allows designers to create generic components and guarantee that subsequently these components will be able to be adapted and assembled with others leads us to the presentation of our proposal.

5.3   AspectCCM: CCM Components through AOP

AspectCCM produces a connection between two software engineering technologies, namely CBSE & AOP. AspectCCM proposes the use of AOP as a composition mechanism for systems based on CCM components, and therefore, covers all the phases of CCM component development (definition, implementation, package and assembly). Both technologies, CBSE and AOP complement each other since the solutions provided in the scope of AOP to solve the crosscutting problem can be applied to eliminate or decrease this problem at the Component Based System (CBS). Subsequently, we will analyse the implications that the use of AOP has at each phase of CCM component development, focusing on the definition, packaging and assembly of components.

5.3.1   *Aspect CCM: Specification*

During the specification of a CCM component, the interfaces it provides (*facets*), those it requires (*receptacles*), the events it publishes (*events source*) and those it needs (*sinks*) are described. We will focus our attention on the dependencies that we declare by the *uses clause*, that is to say, the interfaces it requires to carry out the function of the component, and which are defined during this phase. However, we must ask if it is necessary to define the components dependencies during their definition, or if it is better to leave this until latter phases.

Both approaches have their advantages and their disadvantages:

- On the one hand, if the dependencies of a component are described during the specification, they belong to that component and, therefore, they must be maintained by all implementations of that component specification [Cheesman and Daniels (2001)]. With this alternative, the component provides a clear and concise idea of its behavior. However, the use of this component is quite limited. For example it is possible that in a specific framework the handling of some of the dependencies may be unnecessary or, even worse, the introduction of new dependencies may become a difficult task.

- On the other hand, if during the component specification its dependencies are not represented, they are relegated to be studied and applied later. From this approach, we are able to search for mechanisms that permit us to apply the dependencies in a phase subsequent to the specification, and thereby the components can adapt to the requirements of each context.

The final objective of component specification is to offer a useful mechanism to decide which component to use at each moment during the design of a software system. AspectCCM describes the specification of dependencies in the CCM components in such a way that they are not coupled in the implementation; in other words, the diverse implementations of a component specification are not forced to implement or support those dependencies.

To do this, we classify the component dependencies as *intrinsic* and *non-intrinsic*, since not all the dependencies have the same degree of dependency with the component. Returning to the proposed example, (*ServerBank* component), this component may be required, in specific contexts, to control the authentication of the client (*ServerCheck* component) before carrying out an operation. This dependency is *non-intrinsic*, because it depends on the context or on the functional requisites that we want to give to the system. However, in the current models of component development (like CCM) all the dependencies are treated equally (through the *uses* clause). With the objective of distinguishing both dependencies types (*intrinsic* and *non-intrinsic*), we add the *uses_aspect* sentence to the CCM component description that it carries out through IDL3, so that, for *intrinsic* dependencies the uses clause is applied, and for *non-intrinsic* dependencies the *uses_aspect* clause is used (Figures 5.4 and 5.5).

This *uses_aspect* sentence describes a new type of interconnection between components. This treats the interconnections between the components in a similar way that the *uses* clause does, that is to say, it allows for the sending of messages between components. However, this dependency is not used in the implementation as occurs at present with the created dependencies through *uses*, and they provoke crosscutting as we have seen in the previous sections.

The *uses_aspect* clause indicates that we are able to increase the components' functionality by adding a specific aspect. The addition of this aspect during subsequent phases of development allows the interconnection of components among themselves, without the need to use this type of dependencies in the implementation of the component. It is later, during the packaging and assembly phases, that the usage restrictions of these dependencies are defined and implemented.

The description of the *non-intrinsic* dependencies like *uses_aspect* does not require any generation of a subsequent code; it simply must be taken into account from the viewpoint of the systems design of component-based software as a vehicle to connect components in

```
interface AccountManager {

        void OpenAccount(in string name, in string pass);
        long Balance(in string name, in string pass);
        void AddBalance(int string name, in string pass, in long balance);
        void SubBalance(int string name, in string pass, in long balance);

};
interface Authentication {

        boolean CheckLogin(in string login, in string password);

};
component ServerBank {

        attribute string name;
        provides AccountManager for_clients;
        uses_aspect Authentication;

};
component ServerCheck {

        attribute string name;
        provides Authentication for_clients_check;

};
```

Fig. 5.4   ServerBank component description with their not intrinsic dependencies of authentication

subsequent stages of the CBD.

5.3.2   *Aspect CCM: Components Implementation*

Throughout the implementation phase of the CCM components, each component implements the interfaces it provides, as well as all the methods needed to carry out its functionality. During the implementation of these methods, dependencies can be used in the component implementation through the *uses* clause (component *intrinsic* dependencies). However, all those dependencies defined through the *uses_aspect* clause are applied throughout the package phase of software components. Therefore, *crosscutting* is not being introduced in the implementation of the component due to *non-intrinsic* dependencies (Figure 5.5).

5.3.3   *Aspect CCM: Package*

The CORBA component package includes the creation of the XML descriptors corresponding to the package software description (Package Software Descriptor), the description of the components (Component Descriptor) and the property file descriptor (Property File Descriptor).

The Component Descriptor describes a component in itself, and also embodies the characteristics described for IDL as well as CIDL. However, new characteristics have been added to the description of the CCM components (Figure 5.6) due to the fact that during the CCM component specification in IDL, a set of *non-intrinsic* dependencies was defined through the *uses_aspect*, and it is now, during component packaging phase, that we are able to specify when and where these dependencies must be applied. These new characteristics

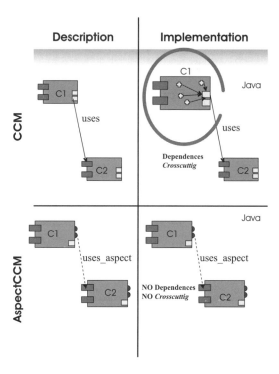

Fig. 5.5   Description and implementation comparative CCM vs. AspectCCM

are defined using a XML Descriptor[*].

Why is the packaging phase the most suitable one for describing when and where the dependencies should be applied? One of the principal advantages of our proposal is the flexibility that is obtained in the component design, precisely due to the fact that the dependencies with other components are not apparent in the component implementation, but become so once the component has been implemented according to the necessities of the context.

The description of all the dependencies is added as part of the Component Descriptor (Figure 5.7).

The information that a specific component describes in its Component descriptor is preprocessed in order to recompile the component code, and add the restrictions and dependencies that are specified in this Component Descriptor. These dependencies are expressed as aspect implementations through a generic aspect oriented programming language, such as AspectJ [kiczales:ecoop01]. This process has been illustrated in the Figure 5.8.

Using this Component-based development (CBD) structure provides a wide set of advantages:

- Adaptability. Programmers are offered the possibility of modifying the component

---

[*]The following section offers an example of this XML Descriptor.

```
¡!-SECTION FOR THE ASPECT –¿
¡!ELEMENT usesaspects (nameaplication, aspectconnector*)¿
¡!ELEMENT nameaplication (#PCDATA)¿
¡!ELEMENT aspectconnector (name, pointcut*, advice*)¿
¡!ELEMENT pointcut (name, arguments*, element_pointcut*)¿
¡!ELEMENT arguments (type, name)¿
¡!ELEMENT argumentsjoinpoint (type)¿
¡!ELEMENT element_pointcut (type_element)¿
¡!ATTLIST element_pointcut operator (and — or — not) #IMPLIED¿
¡!ELEMENT type_element (target — args — call)¿
¡!ELEMENT call (returntype, name, argumentsjoinpoint*)¿
¡!ELEMENT target (argumentselement*)¿
¡!ELEMENT args (argumentselement*)¿
¡!ELEMENT argumentselement (name)¿
¡!ELEMENT returntype (#PCDATA)¿
¡!ELEMENT type (#PCDATA)¿
¡!ELEMENT name (#PCDATA)¿
¡!ELEMENT advice (type_aspect, connectcomponent*)¿
¡!ATTLIST advice name_pointcut CDATA #REQUIRED¿
¡!ELEMENT type_aspect (type_invocation — type_exception)¿
¡!ELEMENT type_exception EMPTY¿
¡!ATTLIST type_exception name_exception CDATA #REQUIRED¿
¡!ELEMENT type_invocation EMPTY¿
¡!ATTLIST type_invocation where_as (after — before) #REQUIRED¿
¡!ELEMENT connectcomponent (nameserver, fileior, componentserver, execute)¿
¡!ELEMENT nameserver (#PCDATA)¿
¡!ELEMENT fileior (#PCDATA)¿
¡!ELEMENT componentserver (#PCDATA)¿
¡!ELEMENT execute (apply_interface+, varprovide+, provide+, attribute*, invocationmethod+)¿
¡!ELEMENT apply_interface (#PCDATA)¿
¡!ELEMENT varprovide (#PCDATA)¿
¡!ELEMENT provide (#PCDATA)¿
¡!ELEMENT attribute (#PCDATA)¿
¡!ELEMENT invocationmethod (name, argumentsexecute*)¿
¡!ELEMENT argumentsexecute (name)¿
```

Fig. 5.6   Description through XML of the dependencies to include in the component

```
¡!ELEMENT componentfeatures (inheritscomponent?,
supportsinterface*, ports, operationpolicies?, extension*)¿
¡!ATTLIST componentfeatures name CDATA #REQUIRED repid CDATA #REQUIRED ¿ . . .
¡!ELEMENT ports (uses — provides — emits — publishes — usesaspects — consumes)*¿ . . .
```

Fig. 5.7   Incorporation of the dependencies specification to the Component Descriptor

descriptor by altering the final component functionality.

- Reusability. At no time is it necessary to re-code the component, but simply to modify the component descriptor.
- Reusability and Adaptability. To exchange the *non-intrinsic* component dependencies it is necessary to return to the component definition phase and modify it. This change of dependencies does not suppose component re-coding; it simply signifies a change of requisites. Once the dependencies are adjusted to the framework or context, the component descriptor can be rewritten and the new dependencies of use can be added.

Starting from the defined dependencies, the aspect code necessary to link the component

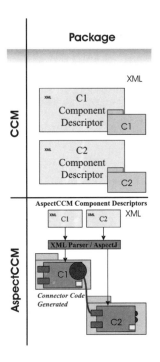

Fig. 5.8   Component obtaining scheme from their XML descriptions.

with all the dependencies described (Figure 5.8) is automatically generated. The generated code describes the interface on which the petitions are carried out, but it does not describe where to locate the component that offers that interface. This task is carried out during the assembly phase. Component packaging is not a routine task, but it is closely linked to the final design of the created component, since the *non-intrinsic* dependencies of each component are applied at this phase.

5.3.4   *Aspect CCM: Assembly*

The assembling descriptor permits us to connect the component implementations, which are part of our application. It is made up of a set of component descriptors and property descriptors; that is to say, it allows for the description of components and component instances which make up a final application. This descriptor allows us to specify the location of the components or instances.

The components can be assembled along various machines, through the use of assembly partitioning (partitioning) [Object Management Group (2001)]. Once the components are instantiated the appropriate connections between the components of the final system are established.

To carry out the assembly with in components that implement *non-intrinsic* dependencies, that is to say, the dependencies being dealt with this chapter, it is necessary to define or extend the Assembly Descriptor with the new directive *connectaspects* (Figure 5.9), which is similar in form to *connections* (like CCM), but in fact has considerable differences.

¡!ELEMENT connections (connectinterface — connectevent — connecthomes — extension — *connec-*
taspects)*¿ . . .
¡!ELEMENT *connectaspects* (aspect+)¿
¡!ATTLIST *aspect name* ID #REQUIRED ¿
¡!ELEMENT *aspect* (componentinstantiationref — findby)¿

Fig. 5.9   Description in XML of connect_aspect syntax

From this specification, a property file is created which allows for the location of those components that must offer the services at execution time, that is to say, the placement of the components that implement the dependencies. Therefore, all the necessary guidelines are established in order for the components to later be located and set in motion correctly (Figure 5.10).

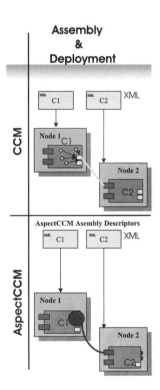

Fig. 5.10   Assembly and deployment schema comparative between CCM and AspectCCM

5.4   Example of Use

In this section, the methodology presented above is used to develop an example of a component based system (specification, implementation, package, assembly and deployment). The aim of the section is to show the reader the advantages of using Aspect Oriented Programming to build Component Based Software Systems.

For this example, let us suppose the components are stored in a component repository, and a system using these components needs to be built. The components stored are the following: *ServerBank, ServerAuthorization and ServerRegistration.* The system allows authorized clients to carry out the typical operations with a bank. These operations are registered using the services which are provided by the *ServerRegistration* component. It must be remembered that each component was built for a specific problem domain. However, we are interested in using these components in a new context.

The steps are the following: first, each component using a UML extension (Section 5.4.1) is specified. Then, each component is implemented or retrieved from a component repository (Section 5.4.2). Next, the interconnections among components to build the system is described (Section 5.4.3). These descriptions will be written in an XML Descriptor. Finally, an XML Assembly Descriptor will be used to specify when, how and where to find the components to assemble the system (Section 5.4.4).

5.4.1   *Example Specification*

The system development begins with the System Specification. In Figure 5.11, the UML representation of the components is shown. The UML representation of a component based system using this approach requires an extension of UML through *stereotypes* and *tag values*. In this specification, designers and programmers should specify *intrinsic* and *non-intrinsic* dependencies for each component [Clemente *et al.* (2002b)]. From Figure 5.11 one can infer that:

ServerBank offers the *AccountManager* interface and needs a *non-intrinsic* dependency called *Authentication* interface. *ServerAuthentication* offers the *Authentication* interface, and requires a *non-intrinsic* dependency called *Registration* interface. *The Registration* interface is needed in this component (*ServerAuthentication)* to register, for example, the incorrect and correct authentications on the system in a data base. Finally, *ServerRegistration* offers *the Registration* interface while *ClientBank* must have an *intrinsic* dependency called *Authentication*. From this specification an IDL3 components specification is obtained (see an example in Figure 5.4).

5.4.2   *Example Implementation*

The next step is focuses on the implementation of these components. These components should implement all the characteristics for providing their services, and should use their *intrinsic* dependencies for it. That is to say, each component only needs to implement its general functionality.

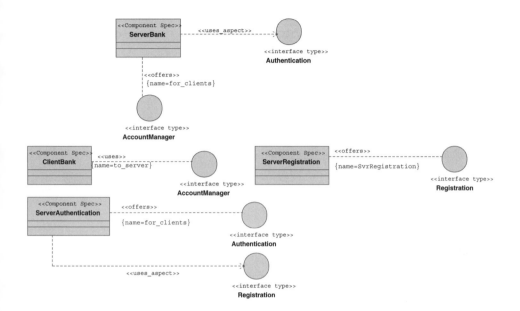

Fig. 5.11   UML Component Specification

The implementation of each component is carried out using a specific programming language. In our case, the components are implemented using the Java language. Later, in the *Package Phase,* the AspectJ language is used to include *non-intrinsic* dependencies in the system. The implementation language is not a restriction for this purpose, because we can find similar projects to *AspectJ* like ASpectC++ [Gal *et al.* (2002)]. Therefore we could apply aspects to other programming languages different from Java.

But, sometimes it is possible for the components to be already implemented and stored in a component repository. In these cases we should retrieve the component implementation necessary to build the final system.

As we can see (Figure 5.11), for this example the following components have to be implemented or retrieved:

- *ServerBank.java*
- *ServerAuthentication.java*
- *ServerRegistration.java*
- *ClientBank.java*

Each component implementation describes the services that each component provides. In this phase, we can see how *ClientBank* invokes methods on *ServerBank* (*intrinsic* dependency). However, in this phase, we can not see the appearance of *non-intrinsic* dependencies, that is to say, *ServerBank* does not invoke methods on *ServerAuthentication*, or *ServerAuthentication* does not invoke methods on *ServerRegistration* because these invo-

cations respond to *non-intrinsic* dependencies and they are not treated. Consequently, this
situation avoids the appearance of *crosscutting*. In the next phase *(Package phase)* the
non-intrinsic dependencies are included in the system software.

5.4.3   *Example Package*

The *package phase* is the most important in the development of the current system (see
Section 5.3.3), because in this phase the components that form the final system are composed. We start from the components implementation and the UML diagrams obtained in
the design phase (Figures 5.12 and 5.13).

Let us split the *Package phase* into three different parts: *Extension of XML Component
Descriptor, Generation of AspectJ code* and *Composition of all the code.*

5.4.3.1   *Extension of XML Component Descriptor*

This part is based on the specification of the interconnection among components in XML
(See XML Descriptor in Figure 5.6). For example, Figure 5.12 represents the interactions
among components when a specific *ServerBank* service is required (e.g. *Balance method*).
The UML diagram has been extended to specify how an aspect can be applied. Therefore, this diagram shows the interconnection among components expressed by *intrinsic* and
non-intrinsic dependencies. The interconnection among components describes the system
architecture. In Figure 5.13 the system architecture of the example can be observed. This
figure presents the services that each component provides (*offers*) and the requirements
that each component has (intrinsic dependencies — *uses* and non-intrinsic dependencies
— *uses_aspect*).

Using the information provided by these Figures (5.12 and 5.13), the *CCM Component
Descriptor* must be built and extended in the way described in Section 5.3.3, that is, using
the schema described in the Figure 5.6.

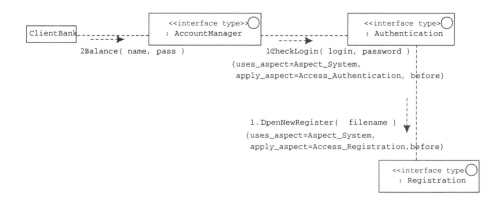

Fig. 5.12   Interaction between interfaces of the components

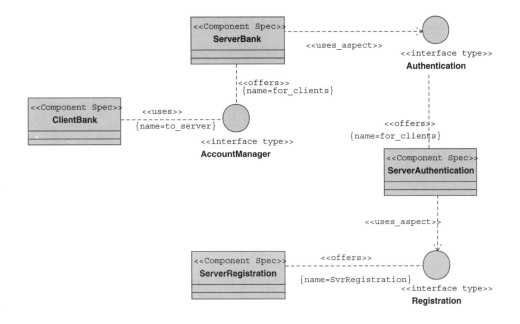

Fig. 5.13   UML Component-based Architecture

As a result of this phase, an XML file describes the interconnection among components. The XML specification of components interconnection is needed to adapt the components implementation to their interconnection specification. For example, each invocation on *Balance* method in the *ServerBank* component causes the execution of *CheckLogin* method in *ServerAuthentication* component (Figure 5.12).

In Figure 5.14 and Figure 5.15, this XML specification can be seen. In Figure 5.14 the joinpoints [Kiczales (1997)] of our example are represented, and in Figure 5.15 the code that is necessary for interconnecting the components is described. This XML file gives the same information that Figures 5.12 and 5.13, but now using XML instead of UML .

5.4.3.2   *Generation of AspectJ code*

The following process allows us to obtain the representation of components interconnections in AspectJ (Java files). AspectJ is an extension of Java for Aspect Oriented Programming. A specific tool which receives an XML file and returns the appropriate AspectJ code is being used.

In Figure 5.16 the reader can observe an extract of the AspectJ code generated. The *Authorization Aspect* is described: an *Access_Authentication Pointcut* is described. An *AspectJ Pointcut* defines a set of joinpoints. In our example (Figure 5.16), the *Access_Authentication Pointcut* is described by the *Balance* method invocation , that is to say, all invocations to *Balance method* on *ServerBank* will be captured .

```
-¡usesaspects¿                           -¡usesaspects¿
 ¡nameaplication¿BankAccount¡/nameaplication¿   ¡nameaplication¿BankAccount¡/nameaplication¿
-¡aspectconnector¿                       -¡aspectconnector¿
 ¡name¿Aspects_System¡/name¿             ¡name¿Aspects_System¡/name¿
-¡pointcut¿                              +¡pointcut¿
 ¡name¿Access_Authentication¡/name¿      -¡pointcut¿
-¡arguments¿                              ¡name¿Access_Registration¡/name¿
 ¡type¿ServerBankImpl¡/type¿            -¡arguments¿
 ¡name¿Srv¡/name¿                        ¡type¿ServerCheckImpl¡/type¿
 ¡/arguments¿                            ¡name¿Srv¡/name¿
-¡element_pointcut¿                       ¡/arguments¿
 ¡type_element¿                         -¡element_pointcut¿
 -¡call¿                                 -¡type_element¿
  ¡returntype¿int¡/returntype¿            -¡call¿
  ¡name¿Balance¡/name¿                     ¡returntype¿boolean¡/returntype¿
 -¡argumentsjoinpoint¿                     ¡name¿CheckLogin¡/name¿
  ¡type¿String¡/type¿                    -¡argumentsjoinpoint¿
  ¡/argumentsjoinpoint¿                   ¡type¿String¡/type¿
  ¡/call¿                                 ¡/argumentsjoinpoint¿
 ¡/type_element¿                         -¡argumentsjoinpoint¿
 ¡/element_pointcut¿                      ¡type¿String¡/type¿
 ¡/pointcut¿                              ¡/argumentsjoinpoint¿
+¡pointcut¿                               ¡/call¿
+¡advice name_pointcut=                  ¡/type_element¿
  "Access_Authentication"¿               ¡/element_pointcut¿
+¡advice name_pointcut= "Access_Registration"¿   ¡/pointcut¿
 ¡/aspectconnector¿                     +¡advice name_pointcut=
                                          "Access_Authentication"¿
¡/usesaspects¿                          +¡advice name_pointcut= "Access_Registration"¿
                                         ¡/aspectconnector¿

                                        ¡/usesaspects¿
```

Fig. 5.14   XML Example

```
-¡usesaspects¿                           -¡usesaspects¿
 ¡nameaplication¿BankAccount¡/nameaplication¿   ¡nameaplication¿BankAccount¡/nameaplication¿
-¡aspectconnector¿                       -¡aspectconnector¿
 ¡name¿Aspects_System¡/name¿             ¡name¿Aspects_System¡/name¿
+¡pointcut¿                              +¡pointcut¿
+¡pointcut¿                              +¡pointcut¿
-¡advice name_pointcut=                  +¡advice name_pointcut=
  "Access_Authentication"¿               "Access_Authentication"¿
-¡type_aspect¿                          +¡advice name_pointcut= "Access_Registration"¿
 ¡type_invocation where_as="before"/¿   -¡type_aspect¿
 ¡/type_aspect¿                          ¡type_invocation where_as="before"/¿
-¡connectcomponent¿                      ¡/type_aspect¿
 ¡nameserver¿ServerCheck¡/nameserver¿   -¡connectcomponent¿
 ¡fileior¿CompAutentica.ior¡/fileior¿    ¡nameserver¿ServerRegistration¡/nameserver¿
 ¡componentserver¿ComponentServer3       ¡fileior¿CompRegistra.ior¡/fileior¿
 ¡/componentserver¿                      ¡componentserver¿ComponentServer4
 -¡execute¿                              ¡/componentserver¿
  ¡apply_interface¿Authentication        -¡execute¿
  ¡/apply_interface¿                      ¡apply_interface¿Registration
  ¡varprovide¿for_clients¡/varprovide¿    ¡/apply_interface¿
  ¡provide¿for_clients¡/provide¿          ¡varprovide¿for_clients¡/varprovide¿
  -¡invocationmethod¿                     ¡provide¿SvrRegistration¡/provide¿
   ¡name¿CheckLogin¡/name¿               -¡invocationmethod¿
   ¡/invocationmethod¿                    ¡name¿OpenNewRegister¡/name¿
  ¡/execute¿                              ¡/invocationmethod¿
 ¡/connectcomponent¿                     ¡/execute¿
 ¡/advice¿                              ¡/connectcomponent¿
+¡advice name_pointcut= "Access_Registration"¿   ¡/advice¿
 ¡/aspectconnector¿                     ¡/aspectconnector¿

¡/usesaspects¿                          ¡/usesaspects¿
```

Fig. 5.15   Advice XML Example

Up to now, we have obtained a non-intrusive way to capture the invocation methods (there are more types of joinpoints). Now, we need a way to inject code to interconnect components when a *Pointcut* is to be activated: the *advices* in AspectJ. An *advice* is an AspectJ structure that allows us to associate code with a specific *Pointcut*. In this proposal,

```
aspect Aspect_Authorization {

        pointcut Access_Authentication (ServerBankImpl Srv, String name, String pass:target
        (Srv) && args (name,pass) && call (int Balance (String,String));
        before (ServerBankImpl Srv , String name, String pass) : Access_Authentication(Srv ,
        name, pass) { //Advice description

                CCMConnect Con;
                ServerCheck s;
                Con = new CCMConnect("ServerCheck"); //Obtained the component ref-
                erence
                if ((Target=Con.GetReferenceObject()))

                        s = ServerCheckHelper.narrow(Target);

                else
                {
                        Con.GetNameContext();
                        Con.GetComponentServer("ComponentServer3");
                        Con.FactoryAndInstall("BankAccount","./archives/BankAccount.jar");
                        ServerCheckHome sh = ServerCheckHomeHelper.narrow(
                        Con.GetCCMHome("fr.lifl.goal.OpenCCM.BankAccount.ServerCheckHomeImpl",
                        "sh"));
                        s = sh.create();
                        Authentication for_clients = s.provide_for_clients();
                        for_clients.CheckLogin(name , pass);

                }

        }

}
```

Fig. 5.16   Example of AspectJ Generated Code

the code in an *advice* is used to locate components[*] and to invoke methods in the way described in the design phase (see Figure 5.12). The generated AspectJ code can be seen in Figure 5.16. This code allows us to apply new functionalities to components in the system. For example, the *CheckLogin* method of *ServerCheck* component has been invoked from *ServerBank*. It allows us to accept or reject requests from *ServerBank* clients.

5.4.3.3   *Composition of all the Code*

At this point of the process, the developer has all the necessary elements to compose the final system. He has the components implementation and the AspectJ code, which allow us to interconnect the components to obtain the final software. This development phase is based on the composition code among the components implementation and the generated AspectJ code.

The AspectJ code is injected in the components implementation using the AspectJ tools (using *ajc* tool). As a result of this process, new components and a new component based system have been obtained.

The new components have changed their behaviors through the addition of new dependencies and interconnections.

---

[*] A component location is completed during the assembly phase where the location type is defined.

5.4.4 *Example Assembly*

Finally, the information for components assembly is obtained through a new XML file (see section 5.3.4). In Figure 5.17 we can see the UML assembly description.

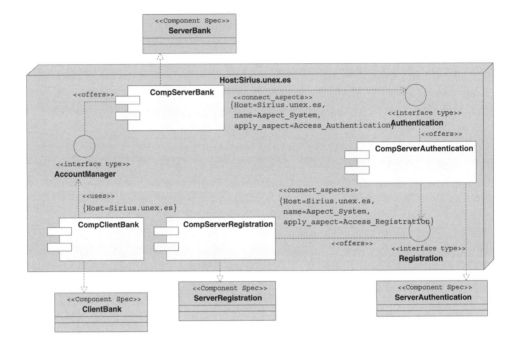

Fig. 5.17   Example of System Assembly

The XML assembly file descriptor outlines the component location as it is described in section 5.3.4. The reference for each component in the deployment phase is obtained (Figure 5.16) using a library (for this purpose a *ConnectCCM library has been implemented*) and the XML assembly file.

5.5   Related Work

The development of a component-based system is inevitably guaranteed with the appearance of software platforms like CCM, EJB, COM+. However, the inheritance that this development methodology has from Object-Orientation provokes the existence of tangled code during its composition [Brichau *et al.* (2001)]. In the same sense, Awais Rashid [Rashid and Kotonya (2001)] studies the risks that the maintenance of component-based systems will have in the future, identifying the problem of crosscutting throughout the lifecycle of the system [Brichau *et al.* (2001)].

The efforts carried out to minimize or delete crosscutting during the composition of a software system have not given the foreseen result. This is because although a set of basic characteristics for the system like persistence, transaction handling, event manipulation, and component search [Object Management Group (2001); Herrmann *et al.* (2001)] are abstracted in the different containers on the server side, the obtained components still need a greater capability to adapt themselves to different contexts and requirements, as these must be the main characteristics of the distributed systems.

Karl Lieberherr and Mira Mezini in Programming Aspectual Components [Lieberherr *et al.* (1999)] propose the use of AOP for Java component development, where the final system is composed from a decomposition of the system in aspects, and where every one of these decompositions forms an independent component to link in the system. In this way, they create the possibility of using AOP and CBSE jointly.

In this sense [Grundy (2000); Edie *et al.* (2001)] they deal with crosscutting in CBD from AOP, and they focus their work on the description of new component models (using Jview and Knit respectively) which support aspect use, mainly non-functional aspects such as persistence, security or distribution. However, AOP must integrate itself in the most popular component development models such as EJB and CCM, and thereby search the implantation of a new technology which improves the quality of the developed software.

5.6   Conclusions and Future Work

In this chapter we have presented a joined CBSE and AOP proposal in which two of the recent tendencies in software system development are united. We have expanded the life cycle of a component-based system through techniques of aspect-oriented programming with the aim of making good use of the advantages of both tendencies and obtaining more flexible, adaptable and reusable software systems.

For it we have detached every one of the stages in the CCM component development [Object Management Group (2001)]. Every one of these stages (IDL3, Component descriptor, Package descriptor, Assembly descriptor) is expanded so that a new description model of dependencies between components, which are materialized during the system composition phase, is implanted.

These interconnection descriptions in XML allow us to save time and cost, due to the fact that almost the entire necessary code is generated automatically. Finally, it should be emphasized that currently, the interconnection between components is totally transparent to the programmer.

At present, we are working on the CCM implementation carried out by the GOAL group [Merle (2002)]. Although the expected results about the adaptability and reusability of components have already been obtained, we still have a great deal of work ahead of us, above all regarding the implementation of the modifications on the XML descriptors and the AspectJ code generation.

References

Aspect Oriented Programming (2001). *Special issue of Communications of the ACM*. CACM .Vol.44.

Brichau, J., Glandrup, M., Clarke, S., and Bergmans, L. (2001). Results of Workshop on Advanced Separation of Concerns (ASoC). ECOOP. Budapest. `http://trese.cs.utwente.nl/Workshops/ecoop01/ws.pdf`.

Cheesman, J. and Daniels, J. (2001). *UML Components: A Simple Process for Specifying Component-Based Software*. Addison-Wesley.

Clemente, P. J., Hernández J., Murillo J. M., Sánchez, F. Pérez, M. A., (2002a). AspectCCM: An aspect-oriented extension of the CORBA Component Model, *Proc. of the EUROMICRO Conference. ECBSE Track*. pp: 10-17. IEEE Press.

Clemente, P. J., Sánchez, F., and Pérez, M. A. (2002b). Modelling with UML Component-based and Aspect Oriented Programming Systems. *Seventh International Workshop on Component-Oriented Programming(WCOP 2002) at European Conference on Object Oriented Programming (ECOOP)*, Málaga, Spain. `http://www.research.microsoft.com/\%7Ecszypers/events/wcop2002/`.

D'Souza, D. (2000). *Objects, Components and Frameworks with UML*. `http://www.trireme.u-net.com/catalysis/`.

Edie, E., Reid, A., Flatt, M., and Lepreau, J. (2001) Aspect weaving as component knitting: Separating concerns with Knit. In *Workshop on Advanced Separation of Concerns in Software Engineering at ICSE*.

Gal, A., Schöeder-Preikschat, W., and Spinczyk, O. (2001). AspectC++: Language Proposal and Prototype Implementation. *OOPSLA*. `http://www.cs.ubc.ca/~kdvolder/Workshops/OOPSLA2001/submissions/17-gal.pdf`.

Grundy, J. (2000). An implementation architecture for aspect-oriented component engineering. In *Proceedings of the International Conference on Parallel and Distributed Processing Techniques and Applications, Las Vegas*, pp. 249-256. CSREA Press.

Herrmann, S., Mezini, M., and Ostermann, K. (2001). Join efforts to dispel an approaching modularity crisis. DIVIDE ET IMPERA, QUO VADIS?. *Sixth International Workshop on Component-Oriented Programming. ECOOP, Budapest, Hungary*.

Kiczales, G. (1997). Aspect-Oriented Programming. *Proceedings of ECOOP*. LNCS 1241. Springer Verlag.

Kiczales, G., Hilsdale, E., Hugunin, J., Kersten, M., Palm, J., and Griswold, W. (2001). An Overview of AspectJ. *Proceedings of ECOOP*. LNCS 1241. Springer Verlag.

Lieberherr, K. J., Lorez, D., and Mezini, M. (1999). Programming with Aspectual Components. *Technical Report, NU-CCS-99-01, Northeastern University*.

Merle, P. (2002). OpenCCM, developed by the Goal Group at Lille University. `http://corbaweb.lifl.fr/OpenCCM`.

Object Management Group (OMG) (2001). Specification of Corba Component Model (CCM). `http://www.omg.org/cgi-bin/doc?orbos/99-07-01`.

Rashid, A. and Kotonya, G. (2001). Risk Management in Component-based Development: A Separation of Concerns Perspective. *Workshop on Advanced Separation of Concerns at 15th European Conference on Object Oriented Programming, Budapest, Hungary*.

Szyperski, C., (1998). *Component Software: Beyond Object-Oriented Programming*. Addison-Wesley.

Chapter 6

Properties of Software Systems Synthesized from Components

DICK HAMLET

Portland State University, Portland, OR, USA

hamlet@cs.pdx.edu

DAVE MASON and DENISE WOIT

Ryerson Polytechnic University, Toronto, Ontario, Canada

{dmason,dwoit}@sarg.ryerson.ca

Abstract. Software components are today the most promising approach to dealing with the complexity and uneven quality of software systems. The design-using-components paradigm has been extremely successful in almost every engineering field, with its benefits of rapid, routine, reliable system construction. The central dilemma of software design using components is that component developers cannot know how their components will be used and so cannot describe component properties for an unknown, arbitrary situation; but if the component customer (system designer) must determine relevant properties of each component before using it, component-based development loses much of its appeal. In technical terms, component behavior depends on the operational profile the component sees when in place in a larger system; in turn, that profile depends both on system usage and the internal structure of the system, neither of which can be known to the component developer.

A solution to the dilemma is presented in a new theory of component-based design. The component developer performs measurements and provides a component description in such a way that the component buyer can later factor in usage information without repeating the measurements. The heart of the theory is a method of calculating how an operational profile is transformed by one component to be presented to the next component in a system.

The theory originated in an investigation of system reliability to be calculated from component reliabilities. It then became apparent that similar methods applied to other system properties, such as its run time and its security properties. Each of these properties can be measured for components by conventional testing and these measurements enter into calculations of the composite system properties. The system designer does not construct or experiment with a trial system, but uses a CAD tool to make predictions of how the system will behave.

Preliminary validation experiments support the theory.

129

6.1   Components in Engineering

In many engineering disciplines, the idea of aggregating standardized components to create a complex system has allowed the creation of better systems more easily. Components are listed in a handbook, which describes what a component does, and equally important, gives constraints that allow the system designer to decide if the component is 'good enough' for the application. For example, in analog electronic systems, these constraints concern the allowable voltages for the component and performance parameters such as bandwidth. Accurate, precise handbook descriptions of components are the basis for computer-aided design (CAD) techniques. CAD tools allow the system designer to experiment with components in the abstract and predict the properties that hypothetical systems would exhibit if built from those components.

6.1.1   *Software Components?*

Any subject of current research begins with a "terminology war" in which researchers try to thrash out what they will and will not include in the subject. Historically, "component" in software is a rough synonym for "module" or "unit" or "routine." It began by referring to source code in a programming language. Some of these terms have now acquired additional precision; for example, "module" may mean an abstract data type definition, or an object-oriented class. This adds fuel to the terminology conflagration, because it raises questions like: "What's the difference between an O-O class and a component?" Clemens Szyperski has cut through much of the difficulty by removing the focus from the code source. He defines a software component as executable, with a black-box interface that allows it to be deployed by those who did not develop it [Szyperski (2002)].

In this chapter we use a restricted form of Szyperski's definition, taking a component to be an executable program with pure-functional behavior. Its interface is represented by a single parameter value for input and a single value returned as output. The restricted interface is not a theoretical limitation, since any complex input or output quantities in principle could be coded into a single value. The restriction to pure-functional behavior is a very stringent one, which is discussed in detail in Section 6.9.4.

6.1.2   *Software Component Properties*

Software components promise efficient design of quality software systems. Most research in components is devoted to functional specification, design, reuse, and cataloging of the components themselves. The complementary issue of the way in which component properties combine to appear as system properties is also important, but has received less attention. Reliability is one important system property. There are no accepted standards for the reliability of software components, largely because there is no theoretical foundation on which to base standards. Developers of safety-critical systems, and the regulatory agencies responsible for them, currently use only subjective assessments of software quality. It would be of great value to replace these with hard reliability data. Other properties of software systems emerge from the corresponding properties of their components in the same way. For example, system run time is an accumulation of components' run times and system security properties arise from secure components.

Success of the component-construction paradigm in mechanical and electrical engineering has led to calls for its adoption in software design. But the system designer who today looks for a handbook describing software component properties will be disappointed. At best a component will be described by its interface syntax and an imprecise natural-language description of its functionality. There is seldom *any* attempt to describe usage parameters. Furthermore, there is no practical candidate theory for using component properties to estimate system properties. System design using components is today done by trial and error. Properties of the system must be measured after it is implemented and tested.

Without solid handbook information and a sound way to use it in predicting system properties, software components may be no bargain. To buy off-the-shelf software with unknown properties is only to trade the difficult task of assessing your own work for the more difficult task of assessing someone else's.

6.2   Fundamental Theory for Software

'Theory' is not emphasized in software development, particularly in software engineering. Although many engineers pride themselves in going beyond 'cookbook' solutions, there are practical, pressing problems to be solved and basic understanding is a secondary concern. However, difficult problems are almost never solved by blind trial and error; researchers must have some idea how they might get where they want to go.

In the model science of physics, basic understanding begins with a microscopic theory. The physicist imagines low-level details of how a phenomenon might occur, describes those details and works out how they explain the phenomenon. The kinetic theory of gases is a textbook example. By imagining the molecules of a gas in elastic collision, in principle it is possible to calculate how the observable properties of the gas arise. The theory isn't practical in the sense that anyone uses it to calculate macroscopic properties like gas pressure, but it is essential to understanding why engineering thermodynamics (the practical theory) works. Nor is the ideal gas theory correct. Attempts to validate it for real gases show that it works only under special circumstances and then only approximately. These limitations of the kinetic theory do not cause anyone to ignore its power as a wonderful mental framework for thinking about properties of gases. Similar remarks apply to Newtonian optics and mechanics and to early models of the atom, which are important steps in developing more complex and accurate explanations.

We would like to believe that progress in software-engineering research similarly begins with basic understanding. In the case of software components, their connection into systems should be captured in as much detail as possible and the way in which their properties combine should be studied at that level. It would be wonderful if the understanding gained in this way could be directly applied to practical systems construction. But the understanding itself is worth the effort.

6.3 The Software Profile Problem

The difficulty in calculating system properties from component properties can be illustrated by a simple example. Imagine two software components used in 'series.' The first component receives the system input, does its calculation, and invokes the second component, so its output is the second component's input. The second component does its calculation on input received from the first, and its output is the system output. Consider the performance property of this composite system. To use the paradigm that has been successful in other engineering disciplines, one wants to measure the run time of each component in isolation, say T_1 and T_2, and then calculate the system run time $T = T_1 + T_2$.

Assuming each component's run time is the same for all inputs, this calculation will be correct. However, the assumption is very unlikely to hold — usually, component run times vary with input. In principle, there is no difficulty. The run times are actually functions of the input, say represented by a single variable x. Then $T(x) = T_1(x) + T_2(x')$, where x' is the output of the first component on its input x. Unfortunately, the functional values of T_1, T_2, and x' are seldom available in practice. The approach from first principles is precisely that of proving and composing functional properties of programs, an approach that has proven impractical. For practical calculations, some kind of testing and empirical measurements of component properties are needed, along with a way to make system calculations from these measurements.

For this simple example, let each of the components have a division into 'slow' and 'fast' calculations, and hence for each component there are two kinds of inputs, which lead to these run times. The system run time will then depend on two things:

(1) The distribution of system inputs over the input domain of the first component. For example, if all inputs lead to the 'slow' behavior of the first component, then the system will be slower.
(2) The way in which the first component sends its outputs into the input domain of the second component. For example, if each first-component output happens to fall on a 'slow' input point of the second component, the system will be slower.

In the example, if it happens that only the 'slow' calculations of both components are used, then the system performance is the sum of the two 'slow' times. But of course things will not be so convenient in general. The actual input distribution of the system must be taken into account.

The usage of a system can be captured by its input profile: a distribution describing how likely it is that each input will occur. Given this distribution, it would be possible to see how many system inputs invoked 'slow' or 'fast' behavior in each component and make a detailed, accurate calculation of the composite behavior. In fact, this is precisely the idea that will be proposed in Section 6.4. But setting the system designer with such a task is not at all what we originally had in mind, nor is it comparable to what happens in other disciplines when components are combined. The *component developer* was supposed to do most of the work, leaving the system designer an easy calculation of system properties in terms of component ones. Is there not some kind of "average" behavior that can be obtained for the components, which will allow easy system calculations?

Unfortunately, there is no such royal road to calculating software system properties and this is precisely the difficulty of synthesizing system properties from component properties. The behavior depends on the way in which inputs propagate through the system and *the component developer cannot know the distribution* — it is a system property, not a component property. In the example, if there is (say) a 10:1 disparity between the 'slow' and 'fast' run times then the potential system behavior could lie at either extreme, or in between, depending on the system input profile. If the components are advertised at any 'average' run time, it can badly mislead a system designer.[1]

It seems inescapable that components must be described in some way that takes profiles into account and that system calculations must be made in enough detail to use profile information. The problem is actually worse than it appears, unfortunately. In the example, the first component's behavior is determined by the system input profile. But the second component's behavior depends on the system input profile *and the behavior of the first component*. Component developers cannot know the profile and cannot know which components will be used together — those are both system properties.

The situation illustrated by this example is pervasive in software components and systems. It occurs in performance calculations (as in the example), in reliability calculations, and in dealing with complex logical properties like security. The difference between software and most other engineering components is that software behavior is intrinsically varied over an input domain and hence difficult and complex to measure and standardize. It is no wonder that engineers from other fields have thrown up their hands at including software in systems engineering calculations.[2]

Section 6.4 will present a solution to the software profile problem. The calculations required are non-trivial, as the simple example above suggests. Fortunately, most of the difficulties can be smoothed away by the work of component developers and the system-design calculations can be almost completely automated.

6.4   Outline of a Subdomain Solution

The study of software testing provides a way to deal with problems of disparate and extensive input domains: divide and conquer. So-called 'subdomain testing' divides the input domain D into a manageable number of subsets (subdomains), often but not always disjoint, and treats each in isolation. Thus the primary practical method of system testing is functional (or black-box) testing, in which system functions are gleaned from the requirements document and each such function is tested separately on its subdomain. This subdomain

---

[1] If the 'slow' time is given as a lower bound on performance, this will be correct. But then a component risks being rejected as too slow for use in a particular system, where in fact it might actually be fast in that application.

[2] Nancy Leveson tells the story that when a safety engineer needs to assign a reliability to an embedded software component, it is is usual to take the value as 1.0. She advises that probably 0.0 is a better value. And of course neither of these values is of any use to the system engineer.

is all the system inputs that should result in a particular function being performed. Similarly, structural-testing methods have subdomains defined by grouping those inputs that execute some particular program element. For example, a statement-testing subdomain for one statement comprises all those inputs that cause that statement to be executed.

Once a subdomain breakdown of the input space D has been chosen, subdomain testing proceeds by insisting that tests be selected in each subdomain. Hence all the functions, statements, etc., will necessarily be tried by such a test. There is a substantial literature on subdomain testing,[3] beginning with the work of Howden [Howden (1975); Howden (1976)] and continuing to this day [Hamlet (2000)].

In software reliability engineering (SRE), subdomains are used in a way that is close to the present purpose. In SRE, functional subdomains are assigned empirical usage probabilities, thus defining a crude kind of usage profile for a system. John Musa has been a primary advocate of obtaining and using profiles in SRE [Musa (1993)]. For example, suppose a system has seven major functions that exhaust the input space D, and thus has functional subdomains $S_1, S_2, ..., S_7$, where $D = \bigcup_{i=1}^{7} S_i$. A vector $<p_1, p_2, ..., p_7>$ with $\sum_{i=1}^{7} p_i = 1$ describes how the system will be used. The vector gives the probability p_i that input will fall in S_i; that is, the probability is p_i that the ith function will be used. This vector is often called the *operational profile*. It is an approximation to a probability distribution p (which could be called the 'true' input profile), $p : D \rightarrow [0, 1]$ assigning a usage probability to each input. The true input profile for a system is never available in practice; in fact, it may be difficult to obtain even the approximate vector [Musa (1993)]. In this paper, 'operational profile' will henceforth mean the finite vector approximation.

Leaving aside for the moment the difficult question of *which* subdomains are appropriate (see Section 6.8.1), the subdomain concept and a vector of software properties similar to the operational profile defined on subdomains can be used to attack the problem of calculating system properties from component measurements.

Going back to the example presented in Section 6.3, the appropriate subdomains for components with 'slow' and 'fast' behaviors are those inputs that cause each. For component 1, let the input domain D_1 be divided into $D_1 = S_1 \cup F_1$ with inputs in S_1 yielding slow behavior, and inputs in F_1 yielding fast behavior. Similarly divide the second component's input domain $D_2 = S_2 \cup F_2$. Now given any system operational profile, the fraction of system inputs that will fall into S_1 and F_1 can be determined. Hence the behavior of component 1 in the system is known. In order to deal with component 2, four probabilities must be determined: q_{ss}, the fraction of slow inputs in S_1 of component 1 that wind up (as component-1 output) in the slow subdomain S_2 of component 2, q_{sf}, the fraction from S_1 that wind up in F_2, and similarly q_{fs} and q_{ff} for what happens to the fast inputs to component 1. With these probabilities, the fraction of all inputs that pass through each combination of slow and fast subdomains can be determined, and hence the run time of the composite system for any given input, or an accurate average runtime for a given system operational profile, can also be determined. (For complete details of this calculation in the general case, including system structures other than series, see Sections 6.5 and 6.6 below.)

---

[3]'Subdomain testing' has in the past been called 'partition testing.'

In summary, the component development paradigm described above is as follows:

(1) The developers of the two components decide on appropriate subdomains for describing their components' behaviors. (These would be the 'fast' and 'slow' subdomains in the example.)
(2) The component developers measure the run times on each subdomain.
(3) The list of subdomains and measurements thereon constitutes the handbook entry for each component, which is provided to potential customers of the components, that is, systems designers.
(4) A systems designer now wishes to imagine two components placed in series and to calculate the system run time.
(5) The systems designer begins with an operational profile for the composite system. Using this profile, the fraction of inputs that fall in each subdomain of component 1 can be calculated, and hence the contribution of component 1 to the system runtime.
(6) (This is the crucial step.) By actually executing the first component on a set of distributed inputs, the systems designer determines how inputs in each subdomain of component 1 are carried into the input domain (and hence into the subdomain breakdown there) of component 2.
(7) By properly weighting each combination of component behaviors the complete system behavior can be calculated from the handbook values for the components.

6.5   Details of Series System Calculation

This section presents a mathematical theory to support the prediction of system properties from component values, for independent components placed in series. The issue of independence will be discussed in Section 6.8.2. Other system control structures are covered in Section 6.6. It will emerge that analysis of the series configuration is the essential part of the theory; from it the behavior of other control structures can be obtained.

The theory applies to any precise execution property of software; that is, a property whose value may depend on the software input and which is mathematically well defined. Performance (run time) and reliability are such properties with numerical (real) values; more complex security properties can also be represented. (For a discussion of these applications of the theory, see Section 6.7.) In order to be concrete, the theory will be first presented as it applies to program run time.

6.5.1   *Series Combination of Run Time Values*

A program's run time over input space D is a function T on D. Intuitively, $T(x)$ is the run time for the program when it executes on input x. For a component, the inputs are values of parameters passed to subroutine-like entities, and $T(x)$ is the run time for the subroutine when it is called with parameter value x. For a stand-alone system, x may be an input supplied by a user and read by a system i-o command, following which an execution with a certain run time ensues.

Now if two components C_1 and C_2 have run time functions T_1 and T_2, when they are placed in series so that the output of C_1 becomes the input to C_2, then for the combination the run time T is

$$T(x) = T_1(x) + T_2(x'),$$

where x' is the output of C_1 on input x.

6.5.2   *Component Developer's Measurements*

In principle, a component developer could use algorithmic analysis to derive the functional form of T from the component code, and thus provide full information for a system designer who wants to use this component. But in practice, it usually will be necessary to measure T by executing the component. By a combination of structural analysis and empirical investigation, suppose that the developer of a component C divides the input space of C into a finite number of subdomains $S_1, S_2, ..., S_n$, and approximates T as a step function that has constant value t_i on subdomain S_i, so that for all $1 \leq i \leq n$,

$$T(x) \approx t_i, \ x \in S_i.$$

Figure 6.1 indicates the approximation.[4]   The vector $<t_1, t_2, ..., t_n> = <t_i>_{i=1}^{n}$ will

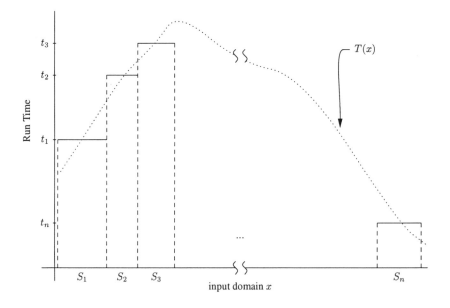

Fig. 6.1   Approximating run time by a finite vector over subdomains

---

[4]In reality, the subdomains are unlikely to be so nicely arranged in the input space as in the figure.

henceforth replace T as the run time function for C.

In obtaining the component subdomains and the run time estimates $<t_1, t_2, ..., t_n>$, the component developer must use sampling to verify that indeed the step function approximates T.[5]

6.5.3 System Designer's Calculations

Suppose that two components B and C are to be composed in a series system design with the output of B the input of C. Let the component subdomains be $S_1^B, S_2^B, ..., S_n^B$ and $S_1^C, S_2^C, ..., S_m^C$ respectively (usually $n \neq m$), and let their run time vectors be $<t_1^B, t_2^B, ..., t_n^B>$ and $<t_1^C, t_2^C, ..., t_m^C>$. It is desired to calculate a run-time step function $<t_1^{SS}, t_2^{SS}, ..., t_n^{SS}>$ for the system SS (defined on the subdomains of B, since they describe the input to S). Figure 6.2 shows the situation. The information shown in shad-

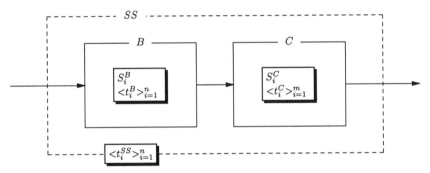

Fig. 6.2 A series-connected system of two components

owed boxes in Figure 6.2 describes the run-time property of interest, given by developers for the components B and C, and calculated for the composite system SS.

B's contribution to the system run time on subdomain S_i^B is t_i^B. The contribution of C is made up of a weighted combination of values that reach its subdomains. The fraction of inputs from S_i^B reaching S_j^C is:

$$r_{ij} = \frac{|\{z \in S_i^B | B(z) \in S_j^C\}|}{|S_i^B|}, \tag{6.1}$$

where $B(z)$ is the output of component B on input z, which is input for component C.

A system designer, having chosen B and C and decided on serial composition for SS, can estimate the fraction r_{ij} in equation (6.1) and then obtain an estimate of the run time of the composed components using the run time approximations supplied by the component

---

[5] In some cases the subdomains can be chosen so that there is no approximation, because T is actually such a step function. However, the input-output behavior on each subdomain is also involved and this is almost never a step function.

developers. Then for the run-time vector of SS, on an input in S_i^B:

$$t_i^{SS} \approx t_i^B + \sum_{j=1}^{m} t_j^C r_{ij} = t_i^B + \sum_{j=1}^{m} t_j^C \frac{\left|\{z \in S_i^B | B(z) \in S_j^C\}\right|}{|S_i^B|}. \tag{6.2}$$

Data provided by the component developers (subdomain definitions and the vectors of run time values $<t_i^B>_{i=1}^n$ and $<t_i^C>_{i=1}^m$ for the components), along with the ability to execute component B (to obtain values of $B(z)$ in equation (6.1)), allows the system designer to make a brute-force calculation of run time for a compositional system SS using equation (6.2). The calculation can be automated and supported by a design tool that allows the system designer to input component values and receive back the values of $<t_i^{SS}>_{i=1}^n$. The expensive part of this calculation is sampling each S_i^B subdomain to estimate the r_{ij} in equation (6.1).

6.6   Other System Control Structures

At the top level of a 'main' imperative program, any system can be built up inductively using the three elementary structured-programming constructions of sequence, conditional, and iteration. The standard software analysis paradigm is to:

- Obtain a general rule for analysis of each elementary construction in isolation, then
- Perform the system analysis piece by piece, using the algebra of recursive construction for a given system.

In this way, the largest system is no more difficult to analyze than the simplest – it just takes more applications of the three elementary-construction rules.

Section 6.5 gives the theory for sequences, which turns out to be the essence of the theory. The system-design constructions of conditional and iteration can be analyzed by turning them into special cases of sequences.

6.6.1   *Conditional System Control Structure*

The sequential construction of Section 6.5 can be applied to a conditional that appears following a component B:

$$B; \texttt{if } b \texttt{ then } C_T \texttt{ else } C_F \texttt{ fi.}$$

The conditional test b partitions the input domain D into:

$$D_T = \{x \in D | b(x)\} \quad \text{and} \quad D_F = \{x \in D | \neg b(x)\}.$$

First consider $B; C_T$, which can be analyzed using equation (6.1) with subdomains $S_j^{C_T}$, but in calculating the set in the numerator of equation (6.1), count a point z only if $b(B(z))$ is true. This is equivalent to intersecting the subdomains of C_T with D_T. Similarly, treat $B; C_F$ with C_F's subdomains adjusted to include only the part of each where

b is false. These two calculations determine the contribution from C_T and C_F to the run time. Equation (6.2) becomes:

$$
t_i^{SS} \approx t_i^B + \sum_{j=1}^{m} t_j^{C_T} \frac{\left|\{z \in S_i^B | B(z) \in (S_j^{C_T} \cap D_T)\}\right|}{|S_i^B|}
$$
$$
+ \sum_{j=1}^{m} t_j^{C_F} \frac{\left|\{z \in S_i^B | B(z) \in (S_j^{C_F} \cap D_F)\}\right|}{|S_i^B|}. \tag{6.3}
$$

6.6.2 *Iterative System Control Structure*

The remaining programming construction in the algebra of design is iteration. Iterative constructions are the bane of program analysis in general, because their behavior usually cannot be calculated in closed form. For this theory things are a little better than usual. Begin by unrolling the loop

while b do C od   to   if b then C fi; while b do C od.

The unrolled form could be handled as in Sections 6.5 and 6.6.1 were it not that its second part is the very loop to be analyzed. However, it could happen that $b(C(z))$ is false for all z considered in the sampling of the sequence construction, and in that case there is no contribution from the false terms in equation (6.3); that is, the residual loop construction does not contribute to the performance because the loop is exited after the first iteration. If we are not so fortunate, the loop can be unrolled a second time and perhaps now the residual loop disappears. If not, continue to unroll until the residual loop does disappear, say a total of k executions of the loop body.

   In practice, k may be too large; or, if too few samples are taken it may falsely appear that D_T in equation (6.3) is empty. However, if the loop terminates, k always exists and if it is too large the performance of the system may be unacceptable so that the design is abandoned in any case.

   One very common system design requires special consideration. Many systems are written as "one big loop" never intended to terminate and system processing is performed repeatedly within this loop. For such a program, $k \to \infty$, and there is no meaningful value of most system properties. Typically the composition operator accumulates property values in such a way that a system property approaches some limiting value that is not of interest. For example, the run time of a system diverges to ∞; system reliability goes to zero. In this case the system designer is usually interested not in the system property including the loop, but rather the per-iteration value, and the theory will be used to make that calculation.

6.7 Applications of the Paradigm

This section describes a handful of applications of the theory presented in Sections 6.5 and 6.6. In subsequent sections a number of issues are considered that affect these applications, *viz*: choosing subdomains (Section 6.8.1), component independence (Section 6.8.2), proving components correct (Section 6.8.3), and validating experiments (Section 6.10).

6.7.1 *Performance*

The run time of systems constructed from components is the most straightforward application of the theory. For this case the issues of choosing subdomains and of component independence have the best resolution, the intuitive plausibility of the theory is greatest, and validating experiments are easiest to perform.

Run time was used in Sections 6.5 and 6.6 to present the theory and it will be the subject of the first validation experiments in Section 6.10.

6.7.2 *Reliability*

Reliability is the basic quality parameter for all engineering artifacts. The inability to factor an accurate reliability for software components into the safety analysis of embedded systems is today a serious problem for agencies like the U.S. Nuclear Regulatory Commission. It was the reliability application that first suggested the subdomain solution [Hamlet (1996)] to the problem of input dependence.

For reliability, in the mathematical treatment the run-time combination operator "+" is replaced by multiplication of reliability probabilities, so equation (6.2) becomes:

$$t_i^{SS} \approx t_i^B \sum_{j=1}^{m} t_j^C r_{ij} = t_i^B \sum_{j=1}^{m} t_j^C \frac{|\{z \in S_i^B | B(z) \in S_j^C\}|}{|S_i^B|}, \qquad (6.4)$$

where the $<t_i>$ vectors now represent reliability values rather than run times.

Reference [Hamlet *et al.* (2001)] presents a detailed discussion of the reliability application.

Compared with run time, the reliability application is less satisfactory. The question of component independence is crucially important and difficult to resolve. Experiments are surprisingly difficult to perform.

In other applications, the issue of component failures is suppressed. For example, in calculating run time for a system, we assume that the components are computing correctly and that their run-time values are a given. But for reliability, failure is the basic property being investigated and when a component fails calculations of how it interacts with other components may be incorrect because of that very failure.

Furthermore, the theory of software reliability itself, on which the calculations are based in this application, is not well accepted. It is only recently that the argument: "Software is either correct or not; hence its reliability is either 1 or 0," has given way to an understanding that a statistical description based on profiles is useful. But the underlying assumptions of the statistical theory may not hold for software and it is difficult to evaluate the empirical evidence. When experiments are performed to validate reliability models, the data are always noisy, and when the curves of the model fit approximately, one wonders if this is only because they have enough parameters to fit any noisy data. Not much support can be claimed for the correctness of the underlying models.

6.7.3 Security and Safety

Testing for the purpose of validating security and safety properties may often be cast as a special case of testing for reliability. The class of failures is restricted to violations of the assertions defining security or safety, which simplifies the oracle problem for this kind of testing. Software security can be defined as the probability that a security assertion will be preserved. At the component level this probability can be estimated and a confidence assigned to the estimate when a collection of random tests have been run without violating the security assertion. The corresponding system-level probability can be calculated exactly as reliability is calculated in Section 6.7.2.

Sometimes security or safety properties only emerge at the system level, however. Neither of two components has the property, which is expected to emerge from their combination. In that case, the components must be thought of as computing intermediate 'security' values, with rules to determine the system properties from these intermediates.

Memory leaks are a good example of such a security property. A component or system is secure in this regard ("leak free") if it never gets memory that it does not later release. Components that are tested to be leak free (with some probability and confidence bound) induce similar probabilities that a system using them is leak free. However, if memory is obtained in one component and released in another, the leak-free property emerges only at the system level — it is not present at the component level. This case requires that testing a component in isolation measure as its memory-leak property the size and location of the net memory allocated, and that the systems calculation combine these allocations to show that the composite is leak free. It is evident that this calculation must take into account the variation in component behaviors across their input domains, as the theory does.

Researchers emphasize that *any* software failure is a potential breach of safety or security.[6] The point is well illustrated in this theory, because a failure unconnected with security in one component can influence security in a following component and hence the system, for example by incorrectly emphasizing a relatively insecure subdomain in the second component.

In the security application, a shift from proofs of security properties to more uncertain testing for those properties may seem inappropriate. After all, the reason to separate out security properties is their importance and the ability to deal with them using formal mathematical methods. However, the ability to test for such properties and to use a CAD tool to easily get approximate estimates of their system values in terms of component values

---

[6] And hence that safety functions should not be combined in software with any other functionality.

has merit. First, testing provides a rough check on a proof. Everyone knows of supposedly water-tight proofs that failed in practice. Second, testing quickly catches gross mistakes that occur early in system design. Even if almost every system input violates security it can be difficult to discover this by proof methods. Testing methods will find such failures immediately.

6.7.4 *Functional Behavior*

In an extreme application of the theory, it can be used to make rough system calculations of functional behavior itself. Suppose that the function approximated in Figure 6.1 is not run time, but the component's output itself — that is, the figure is an approximation to the input-output graph. Then the theory can calculate system (step-) functional values from those of its components.

In the situation described in Section 6.5 for two series components B and C, the $<t_i>$ vectors are now functional values rather than run times. When the system input falls in subdomain S_i^B, component B produces output t_i^B, which falls (say) in subdomain S_k^C, hence the system output is:

$$t_i^{SS} = t_k^C, \text{ where } t_i^B \in S_k^C. \tag{6.5}$$

There is no approximation in this version of equation (6.2); any error in the calculation comes only from approximating the component output values by discrete step functions, and most of that error occurs in the first component, which in reality may produce a range of outputs over S_i^B, leading to a potential set of outputs from C, each with a probability given by equation (6.1).[7] System calculations for the functional-behavior application have the advantage that they are more efficient than for other applications — the matrix of values r_{ij} in equation (6.1) need not be computed.

These very rough systems calculations — they amount to looking at most-likely, coarse behavior — could be useful to the system designer for:

- checking the functional behavior of the system design. Even a handful of subdomains could be enough to expose a serious flaw early in system design.
- testing partial designs. Missing components can be represented by phony handbook values created manually. This is something like testing with routine stubs, but the 'stubs' can be adjusted to mimic the required behavior more or less closely. Tools that carry out the design calculations can do almost all of the work.

---

[7]The character of a more accurate calculation is reminiscent of the way in which a probabilistic non-deterministic finite state machine calculates a set of outputs.

6.8 Theoretical Issues

6.8.1 *Choosing the Right Subdomains*

It is obvious that the accuracy of system calculations made from handbook data for components depends heavily on the subdomain breakdown chosen by the component designers. For example, if only a few subdomains are used, the properties measured for those subdomains will be averages over data that may have high variance, and the composition calculations using those averages can be inaccurate. In the extreme case of taking the entire input domain as a single subdomain, the theory reduces to combining single numbers that do not represent the components, as indicated in Section 6.3.

The insight that led testing theorists to look at subdomains in the first place was that a subdomain should group together inputs that are in some sense "the same." If this is done for one of the applications in which a property is approximated by a step function, then the approximation is perfect.[8] For example, if the run time of a component within each subdomain S is the same for all points of S, the step function *is* the actual run-time function. Evidently, the design-from-components paradigm will work better if the handbook entry for a component uses subdomains on which the property of interest does not vary much. One collection of well known subdomains has the most promise: the path subdomains.

Path subdomains represent the strongest intuitive breakdown of a program's input domain. Two inputs are in the same path subdomain if for them the program takes precisely the same path. Dave Mason has noted that the intuition behind this idea should end a path at any statement in which a run-time error could occur [Mason (2002)]. With this addition, inputs in a path subdomain invariably execute exactly the same machine instructions in a fix ed order, making them 'the same' in a strong way. Indeed, for the run-time property, the path subdomains are perfect: within one path domain, the run time is fix ed by the instruction sequence executed. For the reliability property there are no perfect subdomains, but Mason [Mason (2002)] argues that sampling over path domains may remove some of the theoretical objections to the statistical reliability theory. Unfortunately, for programs using unbounded iteration there are a potential infinity of path subdomains. Mason suggests that this infinite collection can be ordered and a most-important selection made among its members.

In conventional system testing, the most used subdomain breakdown is into the functional subdomains derived from the program specification. These subdomains are the only sensible basis for so-called black-box testing, but there is little justification for using them in a component theory. First of all, they represent what a program *should* do, not what in fact it does do. Second, 'same function' is not a strong sameness, since the actual computations may vary greatly within it. The output values for points with the same function, for example, may be quite different, as may the run times.

---

[8] It is unfortunate that testers seeking to show the absence of defects were looking for subdomains in which inputs are 'the same' with regard to *failure*. Howden [Howden (1976)] was the first to recognize that this is the desirable ideal and to show that in principle it cannot be attained.

Finally, there is a subdomain issue that cuts across all applications of the theory. The essential step in the proposed system-design paradigm is the measurement of the probabilities r_{ij} in equation (6.1) in Section 6.5. These probabilities capture the way in which a component maps its input subdomains into the subdomains of a following component. The best subdomains for this mapping are ones in which the values computed by the component are uniformly distributed in following subdomains. Section 6.9.2 below describes the problem of 'spike' behavior that can result if values are instead concentrated. But the following subdomains are known only at system-design time, so the component developer cannot know which subdomains will prove least 'spiky.'

These difficulties suggest that in practice, component developers may choose subdomains that divide the input domain more or less arbitrarily, for example, by splitting a numerical interval into equal-sized subintervals. The finer such subdivisions are, the better for accuracy of the theory, but the more expensive it makes everything, since measurements must be made for each subdomain.

6.8.2 *Component Independence*

Since the component developer measures properties of a component in isolation, it is essential to this theory that the behavior of each component be independent of any others with which it may later be combined in a system. The most far-reaching consequence of this requirement is that components may not retain implicit state. Any internal state must be explicitly represented as part of the input domain, since that is precisely what it is. The problem of component state is further discussed in Section 6.9.4.

Questions of component independence are confused by using the subroutine-call mechanism of conventional languages to invoke subroutine-like components. Parnas [Parnas (1974)] has given the reason:

> When X calls Y in a conventional language, X depends on Y to return properly and to produce correct results. If Y misbehaves in some way, X usually also misbehaves. Thus the properties of X cannot be easily separated from those of Y. Parnas calls this relationship USES(X,Y).

The confusion can be eliminated by restructuring calls so that subroutines act independently. Parnas called the necessary relationship INV(X,Y): X passes control to Y, but is indifferent to what Y does. When X is a component (or main program) calling component Y and USES(X,Y) holds, to transform the code so that INV(X,Y) holds instead:

> Separate X into fragment X1 before the call and X2 after the call. Alter X1 by ending it with an invocation of Y, passing Y its parameters, but also passing X2. Alter Y so that instead of returning, Y invokes X2, passing any result from Y.

Mason and Woit [Mason and Woit (1998)] recognized this difficulty and suggested the solution.

The theory of composing component properties tries to confine variant behavior to each component by introducing measurements on its subdomains. Unfortunately, this does not quite work. In the theory, the behavior of the second component in a series composition is influenced by the way in which its subdomains receive inputs from the first component. If the first component is incorrect, and actually sends its outputs to the wrong subdomains of the second component, this will appear to influence the behavior of the latter and the system calculations will be wrong.

For any application except reliability, to avoid bringing in the large separate issue of component correctness, we assume that incorrect component behavior does not occur. The assumption is too strong, of course. For reliability, since failure is the property of interest, something must be done, as described in Section 6.9.3.

6.8.3 *Exact Component Descriptions (Proofs)*

Although analytical functional analysis of programs is in principle a solution to the problem of calculating any system property from component properties, the methods required are those of program proving, which have been found to be impractical. If a property T is to be calculated, and component developers have been able to derive and validate mathematical formulas for T as a function of the input, then calculation is a matter of combining the component functions into a system function with the composition operator. There is one substantial additional difficulty: any component that sees the output of a previous component requires a formula for the functional values (outputs) of the previous component, since its T values arise from those outputs as inputs. In the formula for serial composition of run times, for example,

$$T(x) = T_1(x) + T_2(x'),$$

it is not enough to know the functions T_1 and T_2; one must also derive the output x' of component 1 as a function of its input x. Thus, in general, exact system calculations would require information equivalent to a correctness proof of each component [Mills *et al.* (1987)], as well as functional analysis of the property T.

However difficult this functional analysis may be, there will be cases in which it is worth performing. The best one can hope for is that in a system of many components, a few may have been analyzed mathematically; most components will have to be measured and combined using testing methods. Fortunately, it is possible to combine the two kinds of analysis. The situation is:

Let B and C be two components whose reliability is defined by testing measurements. Suppose that B is followed by a sequence of proved-correct components, which without loss of generality we take to be one correct component V. V is in turn followed by C. That is, the component sequence is B; V; C.

The details of analyzing this sequence depend on the system property of interest:

Reliability. To describe a component that has been proved correct requires no subdomains or transfer matrix; its reliability function is a constant 1.0. So long as only correct components are used in a system design, there is no need for calculation — the system reliability is 1.0. However, when correct components are used in conjunction with others whose reliability is measured by testing on subdomains, the correct components transform profiles, and the system designer must find these transformations to calculate how subsequent components will behave. Equation (6.4) can be used for a mixture of tested and proved-correct components as follows:

The composition construction described in Section 6.7.2 can be applied directly from B to C by replacing $B(z)$ in equation (6.4) with $V(B(z))$. That is, the correct component can be treated as if it simply extends the functionality of B.

Run time. If $B(z)$ is replaced by $V(B(z))$ in equation (6.2), the run times from component B (subdomain S_i^B) and component C (m subdomains S_j^C) will be included. Here again component V is just extending the functionality of B. It remains only to add the run-time contribution of component V itself. V's run time is assumed to be a known function T^V of its input. The contribution to equation (6.2) is $T^V(B(z_i))$, where z_i is any input in S_i^B.

In a more complicated case the functional behavior of component V might have been established, but its run-time behavior might have to be measured by testing. Equation (6.2) can be also adjusted for this case and for the symmetric one in which the run-time function is known but the functional behavior must be measured by testing.

Functional behavior. In equation (6.5), instead of finding k by where t_i^B falls, use $V(t_i^B)$.

Although correctness proofs are not generally accepted as a practical method of software analysis, for the serious component developer this position may need rethinking. The restricted size of components and the existence of good specifications may make proof an attractive alternative to testing. Two additional techniques can replace proof in some situations:

Exhaustive testing. A component with a finite input domain can be exhaustively tested so that its functional- and run-time behavior is determined exactly and its reliability is 1.0; Knight [Knight *et al.* (1994)] has suggested that this kind of design is possible more often than one might think.

Self-checking. Manuel Blum [Blum and Kannan (1995)] and Ammann and Knight [Ammann and Knight (1998)] have independently suggested that some programs can be made to perform random redundancy checks at run time, which are sufficient to estimate a component reliability independent of profile. Although the reliability of such a component is not 1.0, it is profile independent. There seems to be no evident application of this technique to properties other than reliability.

·6.9   Deficiencies of the Theory

6.9.1   *Problems of Scale*

Microscopic theories like this one, which give in detail an underlying model of complex behavior, best apply to components whose size corresponds to the software 'units' of 'unit testing'; that is, components roughly the size of library subroutines for a programming language like C++. The restriction arises because the component developer must measure the property of interest, and this requires the component to have a manageable set of subdomains (on the order of 100) and the use of a feasible amount of test data for each subdomain (on the order of 10^4 test points). The number of components that practically may be synthesized using the theory is also on the order of 100, because beyond that the brute-force system calculations that require sampling from subdomains become intractable.

These limits make it out of the question to use this theory on (say) a commercial word processor or operating system as a component or as a system built from components. The limitation is not surprising, since the very nature of aggregate systems changes with scale. An object-oriented library class may have a handful of methods, involve a few hundred lines of code and have a precisely defined interface. An operating system has very different parameters. This natural phenomenon of 'emergent system behaviors' is well known in many sciences and is discussed in reference [Hamlet (2001)].

6.9.2   *'Spikes' in Intermediate Profiles*

When component-composition computations are carried out, even for simple examples like the one in Section 6.3, the accuracy of the theory depends critically on the functional behavior[9] of the first component in a composition. If that first function spreads its outputs relatively evenly across input subdomains of the second, following component, then the tests done by the developer of the latter are valid, because the developer tested using a uniform profile on those subdomains. However, if the first component in the composition produces an output profile with a 'spike' in any following subdomain, then the developer's testing of the second component is called into question.[10] As an extreme example, if a component computing the constant function with value K (its output is K for any input) is first in a composition, then the subdomain S_K of the following component in which K falls has a spike at K. Any sampling procedure will assign 100% of the first-component outputs to subdomain S_K as it should, but this obscures the fact that uniformly sampling of S_K by the developer of the second component may be wildly inaccurate. Here are two special cases:

Reliability. If the second component is correct for input K then the composed failure rate should be 0; or, if it fails on input K, the composed failure rate should be 1. But the

---

[9] It is easy here to mix up the input-output behavior of the component with the property-of-interest behavior (such as the run time). The spike problem results only from the former.

[10] A similar difficulty occurs in random system testing when a uniform profile is used because user data is not available, as discussed in reference [Hamlet (2000)].

uniform sampling of S_K by the second-component developer is unlikely to have tried K at all, or if it has, the failure or success there is diluted by many other points tried in S_K.

Run time. If the second component treats K as a special case and runs very quickly there, while over most of the rest of S_K it is slow, the component developer's run-time measurement for S_K will be 'slow,' while in this particular system it should have been 'fast.'

Although uniform sampling within each subdomain seems the wrong thing to do in testing a component that may receive a profile spike, it is the only possibility. The component developer cannot know if a prior component will deliver a spike, nor if it does, where the spike will fall. The uniform test profile is the best available. What the developer can do is to shrink the size of the subdomains whose properties are measured and to avoid subdomains on which the functional outputs have a narrow distribution.

6.9.3   *Incorrect Components*

As noted in Section 6.8.2, valid system analysis depends on the first component in a series connection being functionally correct, so that it does not induce a misleading distribution of outputs over the subdomains of the following component. It is not unreasonable to assume correct component behavior in most cases. The system developer must trust the handbook values that describe components to be used; it seems not too much more to trust the component output values. The primary argument for making this assumption is that without it, the separation of concerns is lost: rather than being able to treat non-functional properties in isolation, the whole question of functional correctness is reintroduced.

The system designer can also make rough determinations of a component's correctness by treating functional correctness as a property to be calculated at the system level, as described in Section 6.7.4.

For the reliability application it is not sensible to assume correctness of components, because failure properties are the very ones of interest. This may represent only a weaker intuitive understanding of probabilistic properties (as opposed to ones like run time). However, it should be possible to study the incorrect profiles that result from erroneous component outputs, and to either estimate the error introduced in the theory, or discover ways to force the error in the direction of safety – calculating reliabilities that are worst-case values. Peter Bishop has done pioneering work [Bishop (2002)] to model what happens to reliability estimates when the profile changes.

6.9.4   *The Problem of State*

Object-oriented encapsulation is often taken as the basis for software component technology. A more general view allows a component to be any piece of software that has a black-box description and can be separately deployed [Szyperski (2002)]. In either case, persistent state is a necessary feature of useful components. The theory presented here assumes pure-functional component behavior and is thus out of step with practice.

In a way, the mismatch is not surprising, because testing itself is often at odds with information hiding and encapsulation. The very features that make for good modular design make it more difficult to test an implementation of that design. However, 'testability' of components is easily achieved by (temporarily) exposing internal state, while that trick will not work for our theory. John Musa, in his arguments for the practicality of software reliability engineering [Musa *et al.* (1990)], handles internal state by making its variables into 'hidden inputs.' He adds these variables to the input space and subjects them to the same random sampling used on the explicit inputs. The flaw in this procedure is that state variables are not independent of the other inputs — their values are created by the software itself. Any independent sampling procedure necessarily fails to emulate the behavior of real internal state.

A proper test treatment of a component in which persistent state is important is inherently *sequences* of inputs, not single test points. The actual inputs are sampled in the sequence, but state variables assume the values given them by the software. The theory presented here can be used to sample sequence behavior, but there is a combinatoric explosion in the number of test executions that must be tried. It would not be so bad if only component developers had to accept the burden of a testing explosion, since their work is done once for a given component and they have reason to do it well. But if system analysis as envisaged here in a CAD tool must employ test sequences, it will be too expensive to experiment with system configurations and component choices. Intuitively, the difficulties with state manifest themselves in capturing the functional behavior of a component, not so much in capturing its extra-functional properties.

Lacking a better way to handle state, here is advice for designing with components to minimize its problems:

- Don't use any system-wide global state.
- Select components with state early and try not to change them in the design process.
- Distinguish components that *store* state from those that only use it; use as few storing components as possible.
- Consider state-rich components as candidates for formal analysis rather than testing.

6.10 Preliminary Validation Experiments

The simplest validation experiment for this theory works like this, say for a system made from two components in series:

step 1. Each component is tested in isolation on each of its subdomains. This yields for each a measured vector of properties, one value for each subdomain.

step 2. The system property values are calculated for each subdomain of the first component using equation (6.2) and the measurements of step 1. This requires executing the first component on test data to measure the r_{ij} matrix of equation (6.1).

step 3. Measurements are made on the actual system formed from the components, for each subdomain of the first component.

step 4. The vectors obtained in steps 2 and 3 are compared. The theory is supported to the extent that they agree.[11]

6.10.1   *Validating Fundamental Theory*

The purpose of a fundamental theory is primarily understanding. It seeks to describe, with just enough detail to capture a complicated phenomenon, what is 'really' taking place. What does it mean to 'validate' such a theory? Or put another way, as Karl Popper would insist to satisfy his definition of 'science' [Popper (1959)], how could a fundamental theory be falsified, shown to be *in*valid?

The answer lies in the necessary simplifications and assumptions made in any theory, simplifications that are essential to its explanatory power. For our theory, to the extent that a component program does not behave as a step function on the subdomains chosen, the predictions will be wrong. It is expected that as subdomains grow smaller and test-sampling densities increase, the accuracy will improve. In the limit of singleton subdomains, the theory should predict run times perfectly, since it is literally calculating the exact system property from complete data. However, that a theory *should* be correct, or *should* behave in a certain way ignores the possibility of human error.

Experimental validation of basic theory then has two purposes:

(1) To check the theory's mathematics. Everything *should* work perfectly in appropriate limiting cases. But there can be a mistake in the mathematics, some important aspect of the situation improperly captured, that makes the theory fail. It is an important role of initial validation to expose such mistakes so that they can be corrected.
(2) To investigate the theory's assumptions quantitatively. Even if the theory works as it should in limiting cases, it will fail if its assumptions do not hold in "average" cases. Learning how these failures manifest themselves and how the assumptions can be quantified, moves toward a more practical theory that may better apply to unvarnished reality, or suggests another theory that better applies.

It is possible to also conduct less disciplined validation experiments. There is no reason to believe that the theory should work at all in situations that drastically violate its assumptions. For example, if components depend heavily on internal state, the theory cannot be expected to apply to them. Nevertheless, experiments could be conducted on arbitrary components and it might happen that for unknown reasons the errors are not so bad. Such 'scattergun' experiments do not seem to us productive or appropriate in the beginning. Rather, if we want to capture additional properties, we first need a theory that attempts to do so, which can then be tested in turn.

The more "real" the experimental components are, the better they can be at exposing unexpected flaws in the theory. But there is also a role for using completely "unreal"

---

[11]Except for the final two steps required to validate the calculations, the procedure is the one a system designer would use, but step 1 would have been done by the component developers.

examples. There is an exact analogy in selecting test cases for a software system. On the one hand, representative, 'real' cases are important and the most useful. But they miss many aspects that must be tested, and so they must be supplemented with contrived test cases designed to cover unusual situations, 'error' inputs, etc.

6.10.2 *First Manual Experiments*

Using the code of two simple Java methods as components, experiments were performed by hand for run-time and reliability properties with a variety of simple subdomains and different size random test sets. The number of tests (thousands) and the number of sub-domains (a handful) required to get about 1% accuracy in the calculations are reasonable justification for continuing to explore the theory.

An unexpected difficulty appeared in the reliability experiments: simple components do not fail naturally, so it was necessary to create artificial failures. There is no clearly acceptable way to seed failures, which adds a further uncertainly to these experiments. Run-time experiments do not have any similar difficulty.

It was apparent that there are so many variables that influence the outcome of composition experiments and the bookkeeping required to perform each experiment is so cumbersome, that some automation is essential. Furthermore, since the run-time property has so many advantages over reliability, we decided to begin with it.

6.10.3 *Systematic Sampling and Subdomain Experiments*

A research-prototype tool to automate run-time experiments was implemented as a Perl script. This tool is the bare bones of a CAD tool for system design. Two Java components whose run times varied widely across their input domains were used. Subdomains were taken to be contiguous intervals in the input domains. Preliminary run-time experiments [Hamlet *et al.* (2003)] using a pair of components with run times and output values increasing roughly linearly in the size of the input show that:

(1) The r_{ij} matrix of equation (6.1) can be estimated with sparse sampling, making the system calculations efficient in comparison with actually assembling the system and measuring its properties. It was only necessary to sample roughly one point in 50 to get transfer matrix elements accurate to about 4% from equation (6.1).
(2) Even subdomains chosen without regard for the detailed behavior of components can be used to capture their properties well enough to make accurate system calculations. Subdomain choice for a second component in a series configuration is more important than the choices for the first component. To get better than 5% agreement between calculations of the theory and system measurements required only five subdomains for each component, sampled at about one point in 20.
(3) The accuracy of predicted system run times was not much affected by the use of quite inaccurate transfer-matrix elements.

6.10.4 *Components Constructed to Order*

Performing run-time experiments gives an experimenter plenty of time to think while waiting for the system under test to do whatever it does. After the initial work reported above was complete, we wanted to try other component examples, with more complex run-time and functional-value behaviors. Rather than trying to create components that solve 'real' problems yet have interesting behavior as we had done previously, we hit upon the idea of creating 'phony' components to order.

A generator script was written that constructs a tailored component from a data file containing a finite collection of input-output pairs and another of input-runtime pairs. The generator script compiles a C program that stores these pairs in tables and does linear interpolation between table entries. When the program executes, it looks up the input it receives in the tables and reports its 'run time' and output value. This trick eliminates random fluctuations in run times caused by operating system timing and speeds up measurements greatly.

Our tools continue to be able to measure actual run times of arbitrary components. For the literal-minded, the components we construct can be instructed to actually waste the run time in their specifications and then measure that they did so.

6.11 Related Work

Software components have promise for making a substantial improvement in the productivity of software developers and for shortening the time to market of software products. Most of the research needed to realize this promise is properly concerned with the mechanics of creating, combining, and deploying components themselves.

Software components also offer an opportunity to attack the problem of software quality by divide and conquer. Components are less complex than systems, so if system properties can be inferred from component properties it may be possible to transfer attention to components, which should be easier to analyze than a composite system. Approaches to to this 'compositional' aspect of component-based systems are the ones we survey here.

6.11.1 *Proof-based and Analytical Theories*

In principle, excellent explanatory theories of component behavior have been available beginning in the late 1960s, in the work of Hoare [Hoare (1969); Hoare (1972)], Goguen [Goguen *et al.* (1978); Goguen (2000)], Mills [Mills *et al.* (1987); Gannon *et al.* (1987)], and many others. In these theories a component is described mathematically, by a collection of logical assertions, or by an algebra, or functionally. The mathematical descriptions have a syntactic interface part and a semantic part completely describing behavior. Component properties such a run time are described by analytical equations in its input variables. The construction of component-based systems can then be described as follows:

Components can only be used together if their interfaces match, and this match may include semantic properties. For example, one component may require that a list delivered to it by another be sorted so that binary search can be applied to the list. Once components are properly 'matched,' the functions describing their input-output behavior and their non-functional properties can be mathematically composed to obtain the system properties.

These theories are elegant and they completely solve the problem of analyzing system behavior in terms of component behavior.

The most recent incarnation of the logic-based theories of behavior is based on Bertrand Meyer's 'design by contract'. A version specifically directed at components-based system design and the possible need to modify the pre- and post-conditions of contracts, is presented by Reussner and Schmidt [Reussner and Schmidt (2002); Reussner *et al.* (2002)].

6.11.2 *Component Frameworks*

The commercial and research component frameworks, of which Enterprise Java Beans [Roman *et al.* (2001)] and the CORBA standard [Bolton (2001)] are representative,[12] are intended to make the construction of component-based systems faster and easier. Frameworks today are little concerned with predicting or even measuring system properties. Even the fact that framework overhead varies widely over different implementations and platforms is not of much interest to framework proponents.

Frameworks could be an ideal mechanism for measurement of system and component properties, however. A framework invokes and monitors its components in much the same way as our experimental tools do, but as general-purpose middleware it is not so restricted.

6.11.3 *Higher-level Models*

Most of the practical work in composing component properties to yield system properties uses Markov-chain models and most of the work is concerned with the reliability property. A system is viewed as a collection of transition probabilities for invoking each component, and when invoked the component contributes its reliability value. Littlewood's seminal paper [Littlewood (1979)] appeared long before 'component' was a popular buzzword. Cheung [Cheung (1980)] was among the first to apply a straightforward Markov model to the reliability of component systems. Mason and Woit [Mason and Woit (1998)] obtained good results from decomposing the UNIX 'grep' utility into elements that resemble functional-programming units.

Markov models of component systems must deal with two issues. First, the transition probabilities for a given system must be determined. Second, the properties of a component must be those of the context in which the model invokes it. Both of these issues involve operational profiles in disguise, the first a profile for the composite system and the second

---

[12]Heineman's book [Heineman and Councill (2001)] has chapters offering a quick tutorial introduction to these frameworks.

the profile each component sees in place. The accuracy of the model depends on how well these profiles are taken into account.

Most models begin with a fixed system architecture. The transition probabilities can then be measured from expected-usage data for the system. Yacoub et al. [Yacoub *et al.* (1999)] use UML-like use-case scenarios to obtain the model parameters. Krishnamurthy and Mathur [Krishnamurthy and Mathur (1997)] do not explicitly use a Markov model, but determine the path probabilities in a system by exercising it with a collection of tests. Singh et al. [Singh *et al.* (2001)] and Kubal, May, and Hughes [Kubal *et al.* (1999)] use a Bayesian approach, beginning with guesses for the transition probabilities and refining these as system test cases are run. Gokhale et al. [Gokhale *et al.* (1998)] use a simulation approach.

The approaches using Markov models are tied to the control flow of a program. The transition probabilities of the model come from the branches and paths a program takes in execution. But control flow is only half the story of a program's behavior. The other half is the data values that arise when the program takes a particular branch or path. The analogy to structural coverage in software testing is apt: although tests may cause each conditional, data-flow, path, etc., to be taken, they do nothing to exercise a representative variety of data used when the path, etc. is taken. To obtain more accurate Markov models, the states of the simple control-flow model must be split to account for varying transition probabilities, particularly in loop control. It is difficult to obtain plausible probabilities for the split-state transitions and there can be a state explosion.

None of these models pay much attention to the second issue above: using a proper reliability for each component. If a theory is to realize the promise of predicting system properties from component properties, the latter must be measured outside the system, in isolation. In most of the models cited, this is done with a fixed operational profile for each component. Thus component reliabilities are single numbers which are then assumed to be appropriate for use in any system in any position within the system. Some models [Krishnamurthy and Mathur (1997)] do a little better, measuring component reliabilities in place for the operational profile given to the system. With enough data and stable system behavior this can be defended, but in the limit it amounts to simply testing the composite system, without any independent component measurements. McGregor et al. [McGregor *et al.* (2003)] have tried to account for components behaving differently in different system contexts by assigning a few 'roles' to a component, measuring its reliability in each role with an appropriate profile and then assigning it one of these roles in a system.

For properties other than reliability, strong research communities exist without a 'components' emphasis. The work in performance analysis is usually analytical (with queueing theory as the mathematical basis) and concerned only with worst-case behavior to meet hard real-time constraints. Papers are just beginning to appear from within the components community [Sitaraman *et al.* (1994); Hamlet (2001)].

Memory utilization is an example of a safety property, which is more complex than either reliability or run-time. A system without memory leaks is seldom constructed from components without leaks; rather, some components get memory while others release it.

An initial approach to the problem is presented by de Jonge et al. [de Jonge *et al.* (2003)].
Most of the work cited in this section falls in two categories:

(1) Mathematical, analytical methods are entirely correct in principle, but difficult to apply in practice, where testing and measurement are the analysis methods of choice.
(2) High-level modeling of component-based systems is meant to apply to real systems. The model is chosen to work in practice, not to aid understanding.

In contrast, the approach taken here is based on testing measurements and the model is chosen to capture as much detail of the component-based system as possible, for the purpose of explaining and understanding what takes place.

A striking feature of our theory is that it applies to the composition problem for almost any property of components and systems. Other approaches use particular models and techniques peculiar to run time, reliability, etc., but our theory is essentially the same for them all.

6.11.4 *Component-based Software Engineering Workshops*

Beginning in 1997, a community interested in component-based software engineering (CBSE) has held a workshop in conjunction with the International Conference on Software Engineering (ICSE). Beginning with the fourth workshop in 2000, one concern of the community has been the so-called "compositional" aspect of systems built from components. The workshop proceedings were distributed only to participants, but the papers can be found on the web [Wallnau (1999-2001)].

6.12 **Summary and Proposed Work**

A detailed theory has been outlined that describes the calculation of system properties from component data, without constructing the system. The theory can be applied to any input-dependent system property and the system calculations can be supported by a CAD tool. Preliminary experiments support the theory.

In order to follow the paradigm suggested for component development and system design in Section 6.4, the component developer needs no new tool support. The testing required is conventional and in some cases special purpose tools are commercially available.[13] However, the system designer needs a great deal of support to carry out system-level calculations. It is proposed to develop prototype tools into a user-friendly CAD tool that will accept as input a system structure and a list of components and as output will provide system property values.

A more extensive validation effort is planned, in which a range of sample (constructed) components are used and the subdomains, profiles, and properties are varied to see the

---

[13] For example, commercial memory-leak analysis tools are precisely what's needed for the component measurements to check this safety property.

effect on the theoretical results. The application to other properties like security will be added to the run-time and reliability experiments.

Section 6.9.3 describes the way in which incorrect component behavior causes the theory to give incorrect results. Theoretical study of this situation may permit 'safe' calculations of reliability or other failure-defined parameters, in which the results never predict better system properties than actually arise.

The results of validation experiments in the trivial examples of Section 6.10 were good, but we have no way of knowing just how good they should be to support the theory. What is needed is a detailed error analysis that assigns to each experiment a confidence interval to cover known deficiencies of the theory.

Finally, we must begin to investigate component internal state, seeking both theoretical understanding and practical experience with the difficulties it causes.

Acknowledgements

Hamlet is supported by NSF ITR grant CCR-0112654. Mason and Woit are supported by NSERC grants.

Zheng Tu and Milan Andric performed many of the experiments reported in Section 6.10.

References

Ammann, P. and Knight, J. C. (1998). Data diversity: an approach to software fault tolerance. *IEEE Trans. on Computers*, pages 418–425.

Bishop, P. (2002). Rescaling reliability bounds for a new operational profile. In *Proceedings ISSTA '02*, pages 180–190, Rome.

Blum, M. and Kannan, S. (1995). Designing programs that check their work. *JACM*, pages 269–291.

Bolton, F. (2001). *Pure Corba*. Sams, 2001.

Cheung, R.C. (1980). A user-oriented software reliability model. *IEEE Trans. on Soft. Eng.*, 6(2):118–125.

de Jonge, M., Muskens, J. and Chaudron, M. (2003). Scenario-based prediction of run-time resource consumption in component-based software systems. In *Proceedings of the 6th ICSE Workshop on Component-based Software Engineering (CBSE6)*, pages 19–24. IEEE.

Gannon, J., Hamlet, D. and Mills, H. (1987). Theory of modules. *IEEE Trans. on Soft. Eng.*, pages 820–829.

J.A. Goguen, J.A., J.W. Thatcher, J.W. and E.G. Wagner,E.G. (1978). An initial algebra approach to the specification, correctness, and implementation of abstract data types. In R.T. Yeh, editor, *Current Trends in Programming Methodology*, volume 4, pages 80–149. Prentice Hall, Englewood Cliff, NJ.

Goguen, J.A. (2000). *Software Engineering with OBJ – Algebraic specification in action*. Kluwer Academic Publishers.

Gokhale, S.S., Lyu, M. and Trivedi, K.S. (1998). Reliability simulation of component-based software systems. In *Proc. of 1998 International Symposium on Software Reliability Engineering (ISSRE'98)*, pages 192–201, Paderborn, Germany.

Hamlet, D. (1996). Software component dependability, a subdomain-based theory. Technical Report RSTR-96-999-01, Reliable Software Technologies, Sterling, VA.

Hamlet, D. (2000). On subdomains: testing, profiles, and components. In *Proceedings ISSTA '00*, pages 71–76, Portland, OR.

Hamlet, D. (2001). Component synthesis theory: the problem of scale. In *Proc. 4th ICSE Workshop on Component-based Software Engineering*, pages 75–80, Toronto, Canada.

Hamlet, D., Andric, M. and Tu, Z. (2003). Experiments with composing component properties. In *Proc. 6th ICSE Workshop on Component-based Software Engineering*, Portland, OR, 2003.

Hamlet, D., Mason, D. and Woit, D. (2001). Theory of software reliability based on components. In *Proceedings ICSE '01*, pages 361–370, Toronto, Canada.

Heineman G.T., and Councill W.T. (2001). *Component-Based Software Engineering: Putting the Pieces Together*. Addison-Wesley.

C. A. R. Hoare (1969). An axiomatic basis for computer programming. *Comm. of the ACM*, pages 576–585.

C. A. R. Hoare (1972). Proof of correctness of data representations. *Acta Informatica*, 1:271–281.

Howden, W.E. (1975). Methodology for the generation of program test data. *IEEE Trans. Computers*, 24:554–559.

Howden, W.E. (1976) Reliability of the path analysis testing strategy. *IEEE Trans. on Soft. Eng.*, 2:208–215, 1976.

Knight, J., Cass, A., Fernandez, A. and Wika, K. (1994). Testing a safety-critical application. In *Proceedings ISSTA '94*, page 199, Seattle, WA.

Krishnamurthy, L. and Mathur, A. (1997). The estimation of system reliability using reliabilities of its components and their interfaces. In *Proceedings 8th Intl. Symposium on Software Reliability Engineering*, pages 146–155, Albuquerque, NM, USA.

Kubal, S., May, J. and Hughes, G. (1999). Building a system failure rate estimator by identifying component failure rates. In *Proceedings Fifth International Symposium on Software Reliability Engineering*, pages 32–41, Boca Raton, FL. IEEE.

Littlewood, B. (1979). Software reliability model for modular program structure. *IEEE Trans. on Reliability*, 28(3):241–246.

Mason, D. (2002). *Probabilistic Program Analysis for Software Component Reliability*. PhD thesis, University of Waterloo.

Mason, D. and Woit, D. (1998). Software system reliability from component reliability. In *Proc. of 1998 Workshop on Software Reliability Engineering (SRE'98)*, Ottawa, Ontario.

McGregor, J.D., Stafford, J.A. and Cho, I.-H. (2003). Measuring component reliability. In *Proceedings of the 6th ICSE Workshop on Component-based Software Engineering (CBSE6)*, pages 7–12. IEEE.

Mills, H., Basili, V., Gannon, J. and Hamlet, D. (1987). *Principles of Computer Programming: A Mathematical Approach*. Allyn and Bacon.

Musa, J.D. (1993). Operational profiles in software-reliability engineering. *IEEE Software*, pages 14–32.

Musa, J., Iannino, A. and Okumoto, K. (1990). *Software Reliability*. McGraw-Hill, New York.

Parnas, D.L. (1974). On a "Buzzword": Hierarchical structure. In *Proc. IFIP Congress*, pages 336–339. North-Holland Publishing Co.

Popper, K.R. (1959). *The Logic of Scientific Discovery*. Basic Books.

Reussner, R.H. and Schmidt, H.W. (2002). Using Parameterised Contracts to Predict Properties of Component Based Software Architectures. In Ivica Crnkovic, Stig Larsson, and Judith Stafford, editors, *Workshop On Component-Based Software Engineering (in association with 9th IEEE Conference and Workshops on Engineering of Computer-Based Systems), Lund, Sweden*.

Reussner, R.H., Schmidt, H.W. and Poernomo, I. (2002) Reliability prediction for component-based software architectures. *to appear in Journal of Systems and Software – Special Issue of Software Architecture - Engineering Quality Attributes.*

Roman, E., Ambler, S. and Jewell, T. (2001). *Mastering Enterprise JavaBeans, 2nd Ed.* John Wiley and Sons.

Singh, H., Cortellessa, V., Cukic, B., Gunel, E. and Bharadwaj, V. (2001). A bayesian approach to reliability prediction and assessment of component based systems. In *Proceedings 12th International Symposium on Software Reliability Engineering*, pages 12–21.

Sitaraman, M., Crone, J., Kulczycki, G., Ogden, W.F. and Reddy, A.L.N. (1994) Performance specification of software components. In *Proceedings of the 1994 ACM SIGSOFT Symposium on Software Reuse*, pages 19–24, May 1994.

Szyperski, C. (2002). *Component Software.* Addison-Wesley.

Wallnau, K. (1999-2001). www.sei.cmu.edu/pacc and links to CBSE4, CBSE5, CBSE6.

Yacoub, S.M., Cukic, B. and Ammar, H.H. (1999) Scenario-based reliability analysis of component-based software. In *Proceedings 10th Int. Symposium Software Reliability Engineering*, pages 22–31.

Chapter 7

Component-based Measurement and Control Software for Embedded Systems

WALTER MAYDL, BERNHARD SICK and WERNER GRASS

Institute for Computer Architectures, University of Passau

Zi. 120, Innstr. 33, D-94032 Passau, Germany

maydl@acrux.fmi.uni-passau.de

Abstract. This chapter deals — in a specific application domain — with one of the main problems of component-based software development: the derivation of properties of a component system from properties of single components and rules for their interaction. Whereas properties of components can be analyzed and described by a software engineer responsible for component construction, many properties of an overall component system cannot be guaranteed in advance. This problem arises as a consequence of the late composition of components, for example by application engineers working for third parties. In order to overcome this problem in the area of measurement, signal processing, and control in embedded systems (M&C for short), components encapsulating signal processing algorithms, signal adaptation algorithms, or control flow mechanisms are modeled by means of a hierarchy of dataflow languages: synchronous (SDF), boolean controlled (BDF), and dynamic (DDF) dataflow. If an application engineer responsible for component assembly restricts himself to the utilization of SDF components, the component system is computationally analyzable. That is, it can be decided whether the system is deadlock-free or not, the amount of memory required can be determined, and a cyclic schedule of component instances can be computed. If the application engineer uses SDF and BDF components only, the component system is still deterministic. When DDF components are used, even determinism is lost.

The objective of this chapter is to describe a novel concept of a toolset for the M&C field which can determine certain global properties of a component system automatically during component assembly, whenever possible. The application engineer benefits from these techniques without having detailed knowledge of the underlying theory.

This chapter is structured as follows: Section 7.1 provides a more detailed introduction into the afore-mentioned field. An overview of the concept for a novel M&C component toolset is given in Section 7.2. In Section 7.3, the most important SDF, BDF, and DDF component models are described. An example for an M&C component system which is based on these models is set out in Section 7.4. Finally, Section 7.5 summarizes the main findings and gives an outlook to future work. This chapter is an extended and revised version of the article "Towards a Specification Technique for Component-Based Measurement and Control Software for Embedded Systems" which appeared in the proceedings of the 28th Euromicro Conference [Maydl *et. al.* (2002)].

7.1   Introduction

In the area of measurement, signal processing, and control, various and mostly well-known parameterized algorithms (such as resampling methods, digital filters, Fourier transforms, PID controllers, fuzzy classifiers, data compactification techniques, etc.) are combined in different ways in order to solve complex application problems. Therefore, a component-based approach is a natural way to support software development in this application domain. Components (component instances, to be precise) that encapsulate algorithms interact with other components (algorithms) and with the environment of the component system (a technical process, for instance) through well-defined interfaces. Whenever a component produces data according to its algorithm, results are transmitted to the environment or to other components (multicasting is possible) that have to execute their algorithms using these results as inputs (asynchronous communication and dataflow-driven execution). The component system may, therefore, be interpreted as a dataflow graph.

In this article, we use Szyperski's notion who defines components as follows [Szyperski (1998)]: "A software component is a unit of composition with contractually specified interfaces and explicit context dependencies only. A software component can be deployed independently and is subject to composition by third parties." As a corollary of this definition, he states that "software components are 'binary' units that are composed without modification." Compared with various other definitions (see [Sametinger (1997)] or [Doucet *et. al.* (2002)] for examples and [Szyperski (1998)] for an overview), this one is quite stringent.

In the area of M&C, all the significant advantages of component-based approaches can be exploited:

- improved quality of the applications due to software reuse at the component level,
- support of rapid prototyping and rapid development (shorter time to market),
- easy adaptation to changing requirements and improved configurability (particularly important for embedded systems with changing environments),
- enhanced maintainability (e.g. due to the possibility for software updates at the component level),
- separation of tasks of application engineers (component assembly) from tasks of software engineers (component construction), and
- development of protected intellectual property (IP) libraries containing novel algorithms.

Together, these advantages lead to a multiplication of financial investment and an accelerated increase of innovation.

Component systems in the afore-mentioned application area typically contain up to several hundred component instances. Therefore, a component framework is needed that regulates the critical interoperation aspects. An important part of this framework (which may also be realized as a component) is a scheduler which transforms the partial execution order of components and communications between components given by the structure of the component system into an appropriate order (serialized in case of a one-processor system). In general, this schedule may be data-dependent (i.e. dependent on specific values).

Hence, it must be determined dynamically. The framework that has to be used here can be seen as a blackbox framework [Szyperski (1998)].

Under ideal circumstances, components support a kind of composition known as 'plug and play'. However, there are a lot of possible errors which are not apparent at the level of individual components because they are mostly a result of late composition. The question "How can critical properties of component software be guaranteed?" which will be addressed here is an important issue not only in the area of M&C. So-called *prediction enabled component technologies (PECT)* are defined to address this problem field [Hissam *et. al.* (2002); Wall *et. al.* (2002)]. A crucial point is that a component programmer faces a combinatorial explosion of possible combinations (depending on the set of compatible components, all possible structures of a dataflow graph, etc.) against which he should test his component. Moreover, the number of possible combinations continues to grow whenever new, compatible components are implemented later.

Compatibility errors can be avoided using type checking mechanisms at the wiring level. Thus, different properties can be checked at the time of component assembly, for example the consistency of data types and data block lengths of outgoing and incoming interfaces of two components that are connected. In the area of M&C, components typically use parametric polymorphism and overloading. Domain-specific properties can also be included in a static type system, e.g. sampling rates or physical units of measured or computed signals.

In order to support the development of complex component systems, design patterns can be established that describe the interaction between specific components collaborating to solve a particular problem. In our application domain, for example, a design pattern describes how while loops containing several components can be built using specific loop components and feedback connections. Loops can be used to implement an adaptive behavior of a system, for instance. Another example for a design pattern is the if-then-else construct.

Despite all these efforts, a desired behavior of the overall component system can generally not be guaranteed at wiring time. [Szyperski (1998)] (see also [Hissam *et. al.* (2002); Wall *et. al.* (2002)]) states "[...] that this area is still a focus of ongoing research." This chapter deals with the problem of modeling and specifying component-based software in the M&C field in a way that allows us to answer questions such as

- Is the overall component system deadlock-free?
- What is the overall amount of memory needed by this system?
- Does a cyclic schedule of the component instances exist and can it be calculated statically (i.e. before execution)?
- Has the overall component system a deterministic behavior?

under certain circumstances (i.e. depending on the type of components used for the construction of the component system; for a formal definition of the terms deadlock and cyclic schedule see [Buck (1993)] and [Teich (1997)]). That means, components have to be built in a way that allows for modular checking.

In order to achieve this, we split the algorithms found in typical M&C systems up into several parts: *basic signal processing algorithms, adaptation algorithms*, and *control flow mechanisms*. These algorithms are encapsulated in separate components in the sense of Szyperski which are modeled using dataflow paradigms developed at the University of Berkeley in the Ptolemy group (see [Buck (1993)] or [Bhattacharyya *et. al.* (1996)], for instance). These paradigms constitute a hierarchy of dataflow languages: SDF (synchronous dataflow), BDF (boolean controlled dataflow), and DDF (dynamic dataflow). Each language adds computational power and modeling capability to the paradigm(s) lower in the hierarchy ([Wauters *et. al.* (1996); Teich (1997)]). It must be emphasized that all the general conclusions drawn for these models can be transferred to our M&C framework. This approach makes it possible to develop specific models for each component and to deduce specific properties for each of them which can be described by a type system. Moreover, these separate components can also be regarded as different kinds of services in a layered architecture (non-strict layering).

Basic signal processing algorithms represent the actual signal processing algorithms (Fourier transform, filter algorithms, etc.). Adaptation algorithms are necessary to connect different components containing basic signal processing algorithms. Examples for adaptation algorithms are methods for splitting signals into data blocks, shifting signals in the time domain, etc. Control flow mechanisms steer the flow of data through the component system (e.g. for-next-loop).

According to the three dataflow paradigms mentioned, the components in our system can be classified as SDF, BDF, or DDF components. All the questions mentioned above can be answered if only SDF components are used to construct a component system. If SDF and BDF components are used, the last question can still be decided. If at least one DDF component is used, none of the questions can be answered. An application engineer (responsible for component assembly) decides whether he needs the computational power of BDF or DDF components accepting certain consequences regarding analyzability or whether he benefits from a restriction to SDF or SDF/BDF components. In any case, the type of the components is already specified by the component programmer.

Our work is based on experience gained earlier during the development of a popular toolset (ICONNECT) for visual, component-based programming and execution of M&C applications [Sicheneder *et. al.* (1998a); Sicheneder *et. al.* (1998b); Maydl *et. al.* (2002)]. This toolset is commercially available and used in a large number of industrial and scientific applications. However, the new modeling approach described here is not implemented in ICONNECT or any other M&C framework up to now. Examples for related M&C toolsets are Ptolemy [Buck (1993)], LabView [Mihura (2001)], Agilent Vee [Agilent Technologies (2000)], Matlab/SIMULINK [The Mathworks Inc. (2000)], Dasylab [National Instruments (2002)], DIAdem [National Instruments (2001)], and Khoros [Argiro *et. al.* (2000)].

7.2   A Novel Concept for M&C Systems

In the area of measurement, signal processing, and control for embedded systems, the structure of a typical application can be represented as set out in Figure 7.1. Signals of a technical process are measured by means of sensors. These signals are sent to a computer where the data are sampled and quantized. The digital signal is then used as input to the M&C system. The M&C system analyzes the incoming signals and computes some output signals which are transferred back to actuators which influence the technical process again. The data may be visualized for the supervisor of the overall system who can influence the execution of the M&C system. Typical application examples are [Maydl (2001)]:

- thickness control of thin metal foils and synthetic films,
- supervision of the thermal conductivity of gas concrete bricks,
- thickness control in the production of flat glass for notebook displays,
- identification of spare wheels with CCD-cameras in car assembly lines,
- control of a motor test stand with sensors for torque, temperature, pressure, etc., and
- geometry supervision in the production of beverage cans.

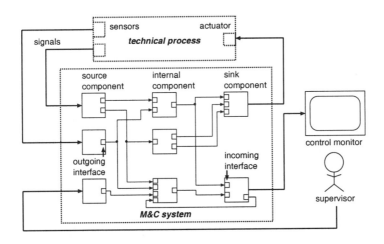

Fig. 7.1   Structure of an Embedded M&C Application

7.2.1   *Signals*

As set out in Figure 7.1, signals occur as inputs, intermediate results, and outputs of an M&C system. A very concise representation of a signal is needed in order to construct well-defined and efficient M&C applications. Here, a signal is regarded as a function $f : T \to X$ which associates a value $x \in X$ to any point in time $t \in T$ (X and T are discrete sets). Typically, T consists of a finite number of equidistant points in time. That is, the domain

T of a signal can be described by a starting point t_{start} and a sampling period t_{sample}. The range of a signal is described by a value set X and a (usually physical) unit such as Volt, Ampère, Newton, etc. X can be of any basic type such as Char, Enum, Bool, Int or Double, or of any aggregation type such as array, record, or union based on those basic types. Lumped together, a signal can be represented by a tuple

$$([x_i]_{i=0}^n, t_{start}, t_{sample}, unit)$$

with $x_i \in X$, where the corresponding points in time $t_i \in T$ can be reconstructed by $t_i = t_{start} + i \cdot t_{sample}$ (see Figure 7.2). The number $n + 1$ of signal values in this sequence is generally not known in advance as it may depend on measurement hardware in embedded systems, for instance. Moreover, each source M&C component may generate streams of signals with different lengths. From the viewpoint of the dataflow graph representing the M&C system, the lengths of signals may be different at different connections, too. The results of subsequent transformations of a signal from the time domain into another domain can also be regarded as subsequent values of a time domain signal. If, for example, subsequent intervals (value sequence of fixed length) are transformed from time domain into frequency domain, the result is a sequence of complex-valued vectors that may be associated with the starting points of the intervals in the time domain.

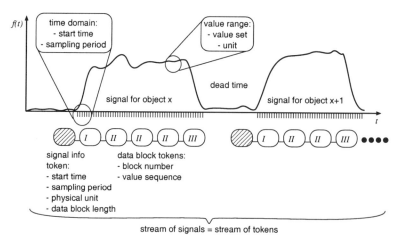

Fig. 7.2   Example for Measured Signals in an Assembly Line

However, neither single data values nor complete signals are the optimal amount of data for transportation between M&C components. On the one hand, the transport of single values results in too much computational overhead. In addition, some basic signal processing algorithms like a Fourier transform, for example, need a value sequence (data block) with a certain length for execution. On the other hand, the transport of complete signals is not possible in online signal processing applications (such as in embedded systems). Firstly, the reaction time of the overall component system has to be short in many applications. Secondly, the length of signals is not predictable in many situations. Therefore, signals are split into equally sized data blocks (If the last block of a signal is shorter, it is filled with dummy values or cut off.) and the signal info consisting of t_{start}, t_{sample}, $unit$, and the block length bl (see Figure 7.2). A data block consists of a sequence of values and a block number bnr. The block number indicates whether the data block is a starting block (I), a middle block (II), or an ending block (III) of a signal. If the signal contains just one data block, this block gets the number IIII. Data blocks and signal info are called data block tokens and signal info tokens, respectively. Therefore, a signal consists of at least two tokens (data containers). Streams of tokens representing sequences of signals are transported over a connection in the dataflow graph. A signal can be reconstructed using the signal info token and the block numbers of the data block tokens because each signal is uniquely characterized by its token sequence. As a special case, it is possible that a data block contains just a single value and that a signal consists just of one value.

7.2.2 *Communication between M&C Components*

The communication between M&C components can naturally be modeled using different layers (see Figure 7.3; the description of each layer refers to the interface between the current and the next lower layer):

(1) Value layer: Only single values and the unit of a signal are visible to the algorithm.
(2) Value sequence layer: The algorithm can access the value sequence contained in a data block token and the unit of a signal.
(3) Timed value sequence layer: The timed sequence of a data block token together with the unit of the signal is accessible.
(4) Token sequence layer: Streams of signals are represented by a stream of tokens as described above. The algorithms work on these token streams.
(5) Transport layer: Data are represented by packets which are transported via TCP/IP between different computers or via shared memory on the same computer, for instance. This layer (i.e. the communication protocols, etc.) is implemented as part of the component framework (see below).

These layers represent a hierarchy of abstraction levels. According to the classical principle of information hiding, these layers provide only the minimum of information required to execute an algorithm (see Section 7.2.3).

7.2.3 *M&C Components*

An M&C component consists of an encapsulated algorithm and interfaces to the user, to other components, and to the M&C toolset (see Section 7.2.6). These different interfaces are described by an interface description language. To allow formal analysis of different properties, types are used to specify these interfaces and the constraints between them. Especially important are the *interface types* of the access points of a component and the *architectural types* containing vital information for the scheduler.

An M&C component fits perfectly into Szyperski's definition of a component (see

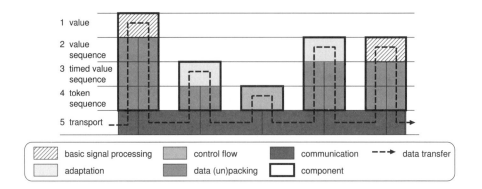

Fig. 7.3   Communication Between M&C Components (Example)

above): there are contractually specified interfaces and solely explicit context dependencies. The M&C components are provided as precompiled units in the form of shared libraries. Software engineers implement components and application engineers are responsible for component composition. The application engineers can purchase a subset of components necessary to fulfill their assignments.

In the reminder of this section the different parts of the components and the relationships between them are explained.

The *encapsulated algorithm* is the core of an M&C component. These algorithms can be classified into three sets as mentioned above (see Table 7.1). Set one contains the basic signal processing algorithms. Set two consists of adaptation algorithms. M&C components encapsulating algorithms of the first set can be found at the communication layers one, two, and three depending on whether the basic signal processing algorithms require single values, value sequences, or timed value sequences as inputs. M&C components encapsulating algorithms of the latter set are concerned with the signal domain, signal range or the token sequence and can, therefore, be found at the layers two, three, or four (see Figure 7.3). A third set of M&C components is used to control the flow of data. Examples for these so-called control flow components are switch, select, merge, and for-next-loop (see Section 7.3). Control flow components can be found at the fourth layer only.

The *interface to the M&C toolset* (see below) includes the interface to the scheduler which is based on the dataflow principle. M&C components containing basic signal processing algorithms will be modeled using the SDF dataflow paradigm. M&C components containing adaptation algorithms are modeled using the dataflow paradigms SDF, BDF, or DDF. Control flow components will be modeled using BDF or DDF. The architectural type of a component describes its membership in one of these dataflow paradigms. In order to distinguish the M&C components according to their architectural type, we use the terms SDF components, BDF components, and DDF components (which also meet Szyperski's definition of a component). The dataflow paradigms and different M&C components are explained in Section 7.3. As part of the interface specification to the M&C toolset, general information is needed such as an M&C component name, an access path to the precompiled

Table 7.1   Examples for Different M&C Component Sets

	1. value	2. value sequence	3. timed value sequence	4. token sequence
basic signal processing M&C components	PID-controller	Fourier transform	interpolation	—
	Fuzzy classifier	polynomial approximation	extrapolation	—
	arithmetic operation	smoothing	function generation	—
	Boolean operation	statistic gathering	visualization	—
	matrix operation	—	digital IO	—
	scaling	—	—	—
	filter	—	—	—
	neural network	—	—	—
adaptation M&C components	—	type casting	time shifting	collector
	—	trashcan	resampling	divider
	—	—	—	cutter
	—	—	—	filler
	—	—	—	decoupler
control flow components	—	—	—	switch
	—	—	—	select
	—	—	—	merge
	—	—	—	for-next-loop

code, and a link to an icon file (to visualize the M&C component in an editor, see below).

The *interface to other components* is provided in the form of an access point list with incoming interfaces and outgoing interfaces with the associated interface typing rules (describing the interface of the component to other components). The interface type of an access point of an M&C component has to be equal to the type of the corresponding incoming or outgoing token stream. Depending on the algorithm, it is possible to support polymorphism which may be restricted to a class of types (e.g. number types). Another possible feature is overloading. It is possible to define access point classes and to distinguish type variables which are set to the same value for all class members and type variables which are set to different values. Thus, the number of interfaces (i.e. the number of signals being processed) of an M&C component can be specified and it can be declared which type variables should have the same values for all signals and which might be different.

The *user interface* is a typed parameter list (describing the content of the parameter dialog as interface to the user) with

- structure parameters (defining the number of access points in the access point list),
- interface type system parameters (responsible for selecting interface types; for example in M&C source components),
- statistics parameters (defining the statistics which will be gathered during execution),

- scheduling parameters (the priority setting of an M&C component, for instance), and
- algorithm parameters (e.g. setting the cut-off frequencies for a filter algorithm).

All parameters can be specified during design time by the user. Some parameters can be set during runtime either by the user (statistics, scheduling, and algorithm parameters) or by the component system (algorithm parameters only). In case the parameters are set by the component system, additional incoming interfaces are needed. The user cannot set these parameters in the parameter dialog neither during design time nor runtime. The component system can, for example, calculate the cut-off frequencies of a signal and send these values as parameters to a filter algorithm (adaptive filter). This would allow the adjustment of these parameters to signals whose characteristics (e.g. dominant frequencies) alter over time.

These interfaces are described by an interface description language which also allows us to specify *constraints* between its different parts. There can be constraints concerning the types of several access points of the same M&C component (see Figure 7.4). For instance, the sampling rate of two signals at different incoming interfaces must be equal such that the operation applied to them is well-defined. Constraints can also be specified between different parts of the interface description language (parameter list and access point list with interface typing rules) and the scheduling algorithm. These constraints enable the software engineer responsible for component programming to specify meaningful cohesions which can be enforced by the editor during assembly of the component system. For example, parameters might be selected depending on the values of other parameters (e.g. depending on the selection of periodic or aperiodic functions in a function generator other parameters can be (de)selected) or types of access points (depending on the number type the number of decimal places can be set or not, for instance). It is also possible to select the types of access points (e.g. for function generators). The altering of parameters during runtime can also depend on the scheduling algorithm selected.

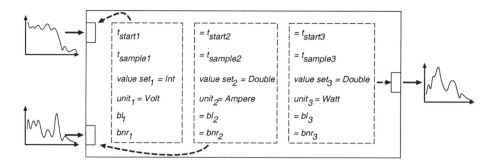

Fig. 7.4   Constraints between Interface Types of an M&C Component

7.2.4   *Component System*

The structure of a complex M&C application is very often depicted by means of a dataflow graph (so-called signal graph, see Figure 7.1). The terms dataflow graph and process network are used by researchers focussing on the analysis of such component systems whereas the term signal graph is used by engineers. Signal graphs are typically constructed using visual programming techniques. Nodes of such a graph represent M&C component instances. An M&C component encapsulates a basic signal processing algorithm, an adaptation algorithm, or a control flow algorithm, respectively. The directed edges of a signal graph describe the asynchronous flow of information (including data and control information) between access points of M&C component instances using TCP/IP or shared memory, for instance.

During the construction of a signal graph, the interface types and architectural types of the components are used in order to avoid compatibility errors and execution errors, respectively. Every time a connection between access points is drawn during the design of the component system, a type checking algorithm verifies whether the connection is allowed (equality or specialization of types) or not. If the typing rules are violated, automatic type conversion (e.g. resampling or casting from Int to Double) is carried out if there is no loss of data. If data will be lost, the user is notified. The architectural type of the signal graph is determined based on the architectural types of its components. If there are only SDF components in the signal graph, its architectural type is SDF. If there is just one BDF component, the type of the signal graph is BDF. In case there is at least one DDF component, the signal graph has the type DDF. In order to benefit from the SDF properties regarding the detection of execution errors during design, a type conversion algorithm identifies components and subgraphs violating the SDF characteristics, notifies the user and suggests alternatives, whenever possible.

The description of the component system is stored in form of a signal graph file. This file contains the description of the component system including its structure and parameter settings, the scheduling algorithm selected, static schedules for the whole component system or parts of it, predefined distribution of the M&C components in a network, and statistical requisitions.

The dataflow model implies a partial execution order for the components of a signal graph. A scheduling algorithm is necessary to get the total order in the case of a one-processor system [Buck (1993)]. Due to the inherent parallelism within a signal graph, a distributed execution in a multiprocessor system is feasible, too.

7.2.5   *Component Framework*

The component framework executes a signal graph during runtime. Important aspects are distributed execution, efficient communication (shared memory or TCP/IP), and correct scheduling.

An example for a simple dynamic scheduler is based on list scheduling [Nömmer (1997)], see Figure 7.5). A list of source M&C components SC and a list of remaining

M&C components RC is used. A more sophisticated approach uses static scheduling techniques where appropriate [Bhattacharyya *et. al.* (1996)], or tries to cluster a signal graph into statically schedulable parts and schedules the rest dynamically [Buck (1993)]. Static scheduling is used to compute a cyclic schedule testing for absence of deadlocks and calculating the amount of memory needed (see following section). If this is not possible due to the complexity of the signal graph, a totally dynamic scheduling algorithm has to be applied [Ha (1992); Shatnawi *et. al.* (2002)]. Realtime schedulers are discussed in Section 7.5.

```
WHILE SC not empty
{  WHILE not all M&C components in SC are activated DO
   {  select M&C component c with highest priority
      IF c is ready THEN
      {  execute c
         FOR ALL direct successors m of c DO
         {  IF m is ready THEN
            {  insert m into RC
            }
         }
      }
      ELSE IF c is finished THEN
      {  remove c from SC
      }
   }
   WHILE RC not empty
   {  select component d with highest priority from RC
      remove d from RC
      execute d
      FOR ALL direct successors n of d DO
      {  IF n is ready THEN
         {  insert n into RC
         }
      }
   }
}
```

Fig. 7.5   Simple List Scheduler for M&C Systems

7.2.6   *The Overall M&C Toolset*

Figure 7.6 gives an overview of the overall toolset. M&C components and scheduling components are stored as precompiled units (i.e. in binary form) in shared libraries. The M&C components can be loaded dynamically by the component framework. An interface description language is used to describe the interface of an M&C component to the user (parameter dialogs), to other M&C components (interface types), and to the M&C toolset (e.g. to the scheduler). The editor loads the files containing the interface description when started. Therefore, it is possible to add M&C components without recompiling the editor and the component framework thus providing reliability and flexibility. In the editor, the component system is constructed by visual programming techniques. The M&C components can be selected from an M&C component tree and can be placed in a canvas. The user draws lines between incoming and outgoing interfaces representing the dataflow between the M&C components. During construction, typing rules are checked (by invoking type checking functions of the analyzer component). At the end of construction, a scheduling algorithm can be selected (either static or dynamic). The description of the component system is stored in a signal graph file which is used as input to the component framework. The information regarding the execution environment (e.g. number of computers) is stored in a so-called environment file. The component framework is responsible for the execution of the signal graph by dynamically loading the M&C component instances and the scheduling algorithm selected and providing the necessary data. The most important parts of the component framework are the scheduler, the communication mechanisms and the memory management. During runtime, the signal graph is animated (i.e. the M&C components which are inactive, ready, or active are marked with different colors, respectively). It is also possible to change some M&C component parameters which do not affect the structure of the component system (i.e. the number of M&C component access points), the scheduling algorithm etc. The component system may even calculate algorithm parameters itself. During runtime, the component framework generates statistical data (to evaluate the performance for instance) and log data (for debugging purposes).

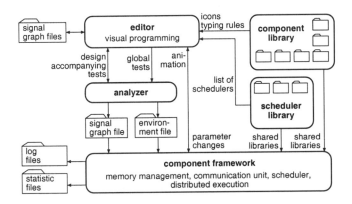

Fig. 7.6   Overview of the M&C Toolset

The presented system follows the definition of an architecture description language (ADL) for software formulated in [Medvidovic and Taylor (2000)]: "Software architecture [is a level of design that] involves the description of elements from which systems are built, interactions among their elements, patterns that guide their composition, and constraints on these patterns. An ADL is thus a language that provides features for modeling a software system's conceptual architecture, distinguished from the system's implementation."

7.3   Dataflow Model

This section gives an overview of the hierarchy of dataflow paradigms, points out its significant advantages for modeling M&C components, and introduces models for different kinds of M&C components.

7.3.1   *Dataflow Paradigms*

The basic dataflow paradigm is *synchronous dataflow (SDF)*. It consists of atomic actors and edges connecting these actors (see Figure 7.7 a). The actors have input and output edges with a fixed integer marking. An actor that has as many tokens at its input edges as the assigned numbers state is said to be enabled. An enabled actor can fire and will do so at a certain point in time depending on the scheduler. Then it will produce as many tokens at its output edges as the marking there indicates. If the marking of an edge is "1", it is usually omitted. The edges between the actors represent fifo channels. Figure 7.7 b shows an SDF actor with own memory. The memory is modeled by means of a so-called self-loop having an initialization token (shown as a black rhomb).

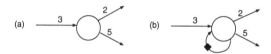

Fig. 7.7   SDF Actors Without and With Own Memory

The SDF paradigm does not model time but it includes causality. Any graph containing SDF actors only can easily be transferred into a Petri net (more precisely a place/transition net [Buck (1993); Teich (1997)]. The main property of the SDF paradigm is that its computational power is not equivalent to that of a Turing machine. Therefore, many interesting questions like presence of deadlocks, the calculation of a cyclic schedule, or the amount of memory needed can be decided or calculated for a dataflow graph containing SDF actors only [Buck (1993); Bhattacharyya *et. al.* (1996)]. This can be seen as the main advantage of the SDF paradigm compared to the following paradigms.

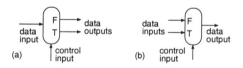

Fig. 7.8   Switch and Select Actors (BDF)

The SDF paradigm can be extended to the *boolean controlled dataflow (BDF)* paradigm by adding the actors *switch* and *select* (see Figures 7.8 a and 7.8 b). These actors are different from SDF actors in having conditional input edges or output edges. In the case of select, this means that, depending on the value of a control token at the control input edge, tokens of the input edge marked with T or with F, respectively, are passed on to the output edge. In the case of switch, the token at the input edge is passed on to the output edge marked with T or F, respectively. The BDF paradigm has the computational power of a Turing machine [Buck (1993)]. This means that the above-stated questions are not decidable any more. The advantage of the BDF paradigm in comparison to the following paradigm is that it is still deterministic since the Kahn-condition is satisfied [Kahn (1974)]: Each actor is permitted to read from its input edges in an arbitrary order, but it is not permitted to test an input edge for the presence of data; all read actions must block until the request for data (indicated by the read operation) can be met. That means, the edges in a dataflow graph containing SDF and BDF actors represent the partial order in which actors have to be executed. All valid executions of a dataflow graph containing SDF and BDF actors produce the same results for the same input data [Buck (1993)].

The modeling language *dynamic dataflow (DDF)* adds the *merge* actor (see Figure 7.9) to the BDF paradigm. If a token arrives at any of its input edges, the merge actor transmits it to its output edge. In the case that there are tokens at both of its input edges, the merge actor passes them on in a random order. The merge actor introduces nondeterminism into the modeling language [Brock and Ackermann (1981)]. Dataflow graphs can be constructed where the edges do not reflect the execution order of actors any more [Kahn (1974); Buck (1993)].

Fig. 7.9   Merge Actor (DDF)

7.3.2   *M&C Component Models*

SDF components:
SDF components directly correspond to SDF actors. Figure 7.7 shows the model of M&C components that might either contain any basic signal processing algorithm or an adaptation algorithm (which can be modeled with SDF) without (a) and with own memory (b), respectively (Control flow components are either BDF or DDF.). SDF components (like SDF actors) do not store information within themselves but in self-loops. The advantage is that it is possible to separate algorithms and data easily which might be interesting if, for example, subsequent task instances of the same M&C component instance are assigned to different processors in a multiprocessor system.

BDF components:

Typical BDF components are *switch, select, for-next-loop, collector, divider, trashcan, filler,* and *cutter.*

Switch and *select* components are used to build design patterns like if-then-else constructs and while loops, for instance. *Switch* and *select* components directly correspond to the switch and select actors discussed in the previous section (see Figures 7.8 a and b). The difference is that not only tokens but signals consisting of signal info tokens and data block tokens are switched or selected.

Another M&C component modeled with BDF actors is the *for-next-loop* (see Figure 7.10). The numbers at the actors of the *for-next-loop* component are indices which are used to reference these actors in the following description: Select 1 lets the first token of a signal (signal info token) at the input edge pass through because of the initial FALSE token at its control edge. SDF actor 2 checks whether the number of loop passes needed is already exceeded. In this case, the token will be switched to the outgoing interface of the loop in switch 3. Otherwise, the token will be sent to switch 1 via a feedback edge. In this feedback edge (represented by a dashed line) different other M&C components may be included which perform a desired computation (e.g. SDF components).

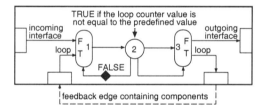

Fig. 7.10   *For-Next-Loop* Component (BDF)

The *collector* component (see Figure 7.11) collects all the data block tokens of a signal and fuses them to one data block token. Moreover, it adjusts the block length in the leading signal info token. The fusion of data block tokens is necessary, for example, if a subsequent SDF component is supposed to work not only with a single data block but with a complete signal. The behavior of the *collector* component can be described as follows: At the incoming interface, the first token of a signal (signal info token) arrives. The SDF actor 1 sends a FALSE token to switch 3 and select 5. The SDF actor 2 generates an empty list token. Switch 3 and select 5 let the list token pass through because of the two FALSE tokens. At the SDF actor 6, the list token and the first token of the signal fuse. A FALSE token is sent to switch 8, the list token remains in the M&C component, etc. As soon as the last data block token is fused with the list token, a TRUE token is sent to switch 8. The list token is passed on to SDF actor 9 which splits the list token up into the leading signal info token and the data block token.

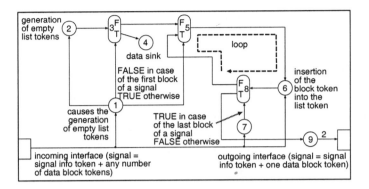

Fig. 7.11   *Collector* Component (BDF)

The *divider* component (see Figure 7.12) is – in a certain sense – the opposite of the *collector* component. It takes a data block token containing all the values of a signal and splits it up into several data block tokens. The behavior can be described as follows: At the incoming interface, a signal info token and a data block token representing a signal arrive. SDF actor 1 fuses these two tokens into one list token. The control edge of select 2 is initialized with FALSE. Therefore the token can pass through. SDF actor 3 separates a token from the list token (first the signal info token with the adjusted block size and then parts of the original data block token). The token is sent to SDF actor 4. The list token is passed on to switch 5. SDF actor 4 passes the token on to the outgoing interface and generates control tokens for switch 5 and select 2. They have the value TRUE unless the data block token is the last data block token of a signal.

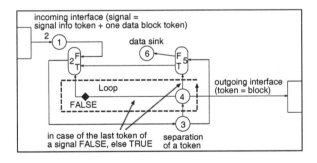

Fig. 7.12   *Divider* Component (BDF)

SDF components have the property that they produce tokens every time they are activated. The *trashcan* component (see Figure 7.13) is used to model the behavior that tokens are not always passed on. For example, error messages of SDF components are only interesting if there actually was an error. In order to maintain the notion that a signal consists of equidistant points in time, the *trashcan* component only can produce signals containing data block tokens with blocknumber IIII. The signal info token is stored in a self-loop which allows us to generate a new correct signal info token for each data block token. The *trashcan* component has the following behavior: An external token arrives at the input edge. SDF actor 1 passes on the token together with a modified leading signal info token and generates two internal control tokens for switch 2. The tokens representing the signal are discarded or passed on depending on the value (contents) of the internal control tokens.

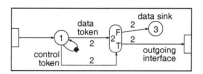

Fig. 7.13   *Trashcan* Component (BDF)

The *filler* and *cutter* components are used to adjust the lengths of two signals. This is useful if a subsequent SDF component takes tokens from signals at two (or more) different incoming interfaces. There would be no use for remaining tokens of the longer signal at one of the incoming interfaces. The *filler* component (see Figure 7.14) has the following behavior: The first token of a signal at one of the two input ports gets through switch 3 or 4, respectively. SDF actor 5 fires as soon as there are tokens at both of its incoming interfaces. If these are the first tokens of a signal they are passed on to the corresponding outgoing interface. SDF actor 5 stores the status of both input streams in the self-loop. If one of the two signals ended, the filler component puts dummy tokens at the corresponding outgoing interface.

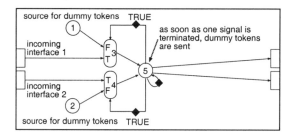

Fig. 7.14   *Filler* Component (BDF)

Compared to the *filler* component, the *cutter* component (see Figure 7.15) has a similar behavior. It shortens the length of the longer of the two signals. The first token of a signal at one of the two incoming interfaces gets through switch 3 or 4, respectively. SDF actor 5 fires as soon as there are tokens at both of its input edges. If these are the first tokens of a signal, they are passed on to the corresponding output edges. SDF actor 5 stores the status of both input streams in the self loop. If one of the two signals is finished, dummy data block tokens are passed on to the corresponding output edge. The tokens of both streams are directed to the SDF actors 8 and 9 which represent data sinks.

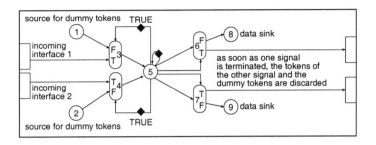

Fig. 7.15 *Cutter* Component (BDF)

DDF components:
The DDF components needed for M&C applications are *merge* and *decoupler*.

The *merge* component corresponds to the merge actor besides the fact that complete signals and not data block tokens are merged (see Figure 7.9). Therefore, a self-loop with an initialization token is added to the merge actor. This allows the *merge* component to remember whether all tokens of a signal are passed on or not. That is, the *merge* component passes on the signals which arrive at both of its incoming interfaces to its outgoing interface in the order they came in. If signals arrive at both input edges simultaneously, they are passed on in a random order.

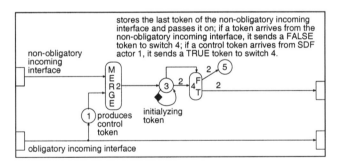

Fig. 7.16 *Decoupler* Component (1) (DDF)

The motivation for the *decoupler* component is based on the observation that there are algorithms in typical M&C systems which can be executed without having new input data. These algorithms are just provided with data if changes occur, for instance. The *decoupler* component (see Figure 7.16) uses the nondeterminism provided by the DDF paradigm to decouple its so-called non-obligatory incoming interface from the token production of the preceding M&C component connected to that interface. In order to maintain the notion of a signal, switch 4 produces signals of length one (a leading signal info token and a data block token). If an external token arrives at the obligatory incoming interface, it will be passed on to the corresponding outgoing interface. SDF actor 1 generates an internal control token for the non-obligatory edge. Merge 2 passes on external tokens and internal control tokens as well. SDF actor 3 stores the last external token and the signal info token from the non-obligatory incoming interface. Moreover, SDF actor 3 transmits the external token together with a leading signal info token to the outgoing interface if the last token which arrived was an internal control token. If the last token arrived was an external token, the external token is passed on to SDF actor 5.

If there is no obligatory incoming interface to connect the non-obligatory incoming interface with, a connection from a data source (SDF actor 1) has to take the role of the obligatory incoming interface (see Figure 7.17).

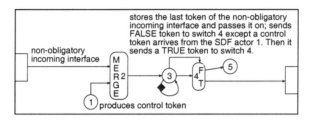

Fig. 7.17   *Decoupler* Component (2) (DDF)

Component assembly:

A software engineer responsible for M&C component construction has to assign the architectural type (SDF, BDF, or DDF) to an M&C component. This allows an application engineer responsible for M&C component assembly to decide whether he would like to use just SDF components which would make the resulting model computationally analyzable but would also restrict the computational power of a signal graph as it is not possible to construct while loops, for instance, or if he would like to construct the signal graph using BDF or DDF components accepting the afore-mentioned consequences. Algorithms to analyze SDF graphs can be found in [Bhattacharyya *et. al.* (1996)].

7.4   Application Example

In this section, an application example taken from a real-world M&C system (Iconnect) is modeled with the proposed component models. It is shown how interface types and architectural types are used to avoid compatibility errors and execution errors, respectively.

7.4.1   Iconnect *Signal Graph*

The signal graph set out in Figure 7.18 deals with quality control of cathode ray tubes (CRTs). A felt-coated sledge knocks carefully at the CRT. The resulting acoustic signal is measured and sent to the M&C system in order to detect cracks or fissures of the CRT. The soundcard component encapsulates the device driver for the soundcard where the acoustic signal is digitized. Examples of signals of a defect and a functional CRT are shown in Figure 7.18. A trashcan component (Buffer) lets the first data block token of the signal consisting of 4096 values pass through and throws away the remaining tokens. The resulting signal is transferred to two different branches of the signal graph in order to be interpreted. In the first branch, the decreasing amplitude of the signal is determined (Threshold-1). In the second branch, the signal is transformed into the frequency domain (FFT) and the highest peak in the spectrum is detected (PeakFinder). These two features are used as inputs of a fuzzy classifier consisting of two fuzzification components (Fuzzify-A and B) and a fuzzy inference component (FuzzyLogic). The threshold component (Threshold-2) determines whether the membership degree of the fuzzy output term "crack" is above a certain threshold. Correspondingly, the CRT is classified as defect (crack) or not defect (ok). This result is displayed at a monitor with a binary signal (BinaryDisplay) and also sent to an actuator (DigitalIO) which removes defect CRTs from the assembly line. The supervisor is able to change the threshold for the membership degree of the fuzzy term using a Slider component. This input has to be converted using a ParamConv component.

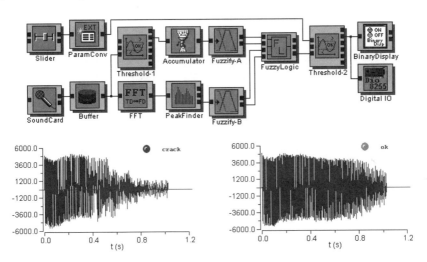

Fig. 7.18   Example of an Iconnect Signal Graph for CRT Classification

7.4.2 *Interface Types*

Figure 7.19 shows the dataflow model of the application example of Figure 7.18. The derivation of the interface types will be demonstrated on the subgraph consisting of the SoundCard, Trashcan, FFT, and Peakfinder components. Table 7.2 shows the interface types of the incoming and outgoing interfaces of the unconnected components. Some type variables are already set to fixed values. These fixed values are either predefined by the software engineer responsible for component construction or set by the user in the parameter dialog. The remaining type variables may be set to any value of their type range. The polymorphism of the Trashcan component is expressed with the type variable γ_2 as there are no further constraints about the assigned values. Constraints between different access

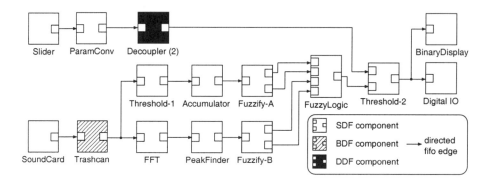

Fig. 7.19   Model of the Signal Graph for CRT Classification

Table 7.2   Interface Types (Unconnected Components)

	SoundCard	Trashcan		FFT		Peakfinder	
	out	in	out	in	out	in	out
t_{start}	α_1	α_2	α_2	α_3	α_3	α_4	α_4
t_{sample}	$10^{-6}sec$	β_2	β_2	β_3	$\beta_3 \cdot \epsilon_3$	β_4	β_4
$val.\,set$	$Double$	γ_2	γ_2	$Double$	$Double[\epsilon_3]$	$Double[\gamma_4]$	$Double$
$unit$	$none$	δ_2	δ_2	δ_3	δ_3	δ_4	δ_4
bl	ϵ_1	ϵ_2	ϵ_2	$\epsilon_3 \in \{2^i\}$	1	1	1
bnr	ζ_1	ζ_2	IIII	ζ_3	ζ_3	ζ_4	ζ_4

points of the same component or between type values of the same access point are also expressed by type variables. The use of the same type variable regarding the value set of the incoming and outgoing interface of the Trashcan component indicates that the same value set has to be assigned to both access points, for instance. The block length of the incoming interface of the FFT component must be set to values of $\{2^i : i \in \mathbb{N}\}$ so that the FFT operation is well-defined.

Everytime a connection between these components is established, the intersection of the types is calculated. Table 7.3 shows the result for the fully connected subgraph. Most of the type variables in Table 7.2 are replaced by fixed values. However, the start time of the incoming and outgoing signals is still represented by a type variable. This is correct, as the exact values for these signals will first be known during runtime. Typing rules just can enforce the equivalence of start times of signals on two different incoming interfaces, for instance. This may be achieved by inserting an adaptation component, for example.

7.4.3   *Architectural Types*

Most of the components of Figure 7.19 have the type SDF. The trashcan component is BDF (see Section 7.3) and the access point of the Threshold-2 component is non-obligatory which is made explicit in the model by use of a decoupler (2) component. The decoupler (2)

Table 7.3 Interface Types (Connected Components)

	Sound.	Trashcan		FFT		Peakfinder	
	out	in	out	in	out	in	out
t_{start}	α_1	α_1	α_1	α_1	α_1	α_1	α_1
t_{sample}	10^{-6}	10^{-6}	10^{-6}	10^{-6}	$10^{-6} \cdot 2^{12}$	$10^{-6} \cdot 2^{12}$	$10^{-6} \cdot 2^{12}$
$val.\ set$	$Doub.$	$Doub.$	$Doub.$	$Doub.$	$Doub.[2^{12}]$	$Doub.[2^{12}]$	$Double$
$unit$	$none$	$none$	$none$	$none$	$none$	$none$	$none$
bl	2^{12}	2^{12}	2^{12}	2^{12}	1	1	1
bnr	ζ_1	ζ_1	IIII	IIII	IIII	IIII	IIII

Table 7.4 Cyclic Schedule for a One-Processor System

Component	Execution Order	Component	Execution Order
Slider	1	Fuzzify-A	8
ParamConv	2	Fuzzify-B	9
SoundCard	3	FuzzyLogic	10
FFT	4	Threshold-2	11
Threshold-1	5	BinaryDisplay	12
PeakFinder	6	Digital IO	13
Accumulator	7		

component is necessary in order to maintain the SDF behavior of the Threshold component.

It can be stated that in case the signals delivered from the soundcard all have the same length no trashcan component would be needed. Moreover, the decoupler (2) component can be avoided

(1) if no user input is required,
(2) if the input is set during runtime using the parameter dialog of the component, or
(3) if the Slider component provides data even if the user does not make any changes.

In the first and third case, the whole component system would be SDF and could easily be analyzed statically (see Section 7.3). In the second case, the signal graph could be clustered into parts containing SDF components only. For these clusters, static schedules can be calculated and the decisions for the dynamic scheduler can be reduced to a minimum [Buck (1993)].

The analysis described here is performed for the third case. Using the techniques presented in [Buck (1993)], a cyclic schedule can be calculated (see Table 7.4). In order to test whether the signal graph is deadlock free or how much memory it consumes, the cyclic schedule has to be executed for one cycle. If the signal graph does not deadlock in one cycle, it will never deadlock. The maximum amount of memory needed during the entire execution is equivalent to the maximum amount of memory needed in one cycle.

The above example shows that industrial applications can be described using the component models presented in this chapter. It is possible to guarantee the mentioned correctness properties – under certain circumstances – even for large M&C systems.

7.5 Conclusion and Outlook

The starting point for the novel concept of an M&C system presented here was the observation that programming complex signal processing applications with typical M&C systems can be simplified by splitting up the algorithms in basic signal processing algorithms, adaptation algorithms, and control methods. These three kinds of algorithms may be encapsulated within M&C components described by architectural types (SDF, BDF, and DDF) and interface types (signal types). M&C components can be modeled using the well-founded dataflow paradigms SDF, BDF, and DDF. The general results derived for these paradigms can be transferred to M&C component models and the resulting component systems (described by means of signal graphs). Important questions like presence of deadlocks in such a graph, the calculation of a cyclic schedule, or the amount of memory needed can then be decided or calculated for a signal graph containing SDF components only. If the graph solely contains SDF and BDF components, the overall component system is still deterministic.

The underlying motivation of this new approach is to provide correctness by construction instead of correctness by testing. Generally, it can be stated that not only in the area of M&C systems software development processes that do not depend on exhaustive testing gain more and more importance.

Most embedded systems, and M&C systems in particular, are realtime systems. Their correctness is therefore also dependent on temporal correctness. A realtime system is one that responds to external events within a bounded interval of time [Goddard (1998)]. In the M&C application field, the realtime system is given by the signal graph. The latency time is the time between loading the sampled input data into the M&C system and outputting the processed signal. This time has to be guaranteed by the system. As can be seen in Figure 7.20 which represents the signal graph of Figure 7.1, a signal graph can be subdivided into realtime parts (subgraphs with hard realtime constraints on their latency time) and non-realtime parts (subgraphs e.g. responsible for updating control monitors, producing statistical and logging data, etc.). For guaranteeing a certain latency time, a series of preconditions has to be met:

- *Signal graph:* the execution times of the components (either as fixed execution times or as an interval between a minimum and a maximum execution time) and the time for transporting data on an edge (i.e. communication channel) have to be known in advance. This information is stored as temporal types of the M&C components and connectors. The signal graph may not contain any data dependent control structures (e.g. while loops) and M&C components with unpredictable data dependent execution times.
- *Component framework:* The component framework and especially the scheduler have

to be integrated in a realtime operating system (e.g. VxWorks or RTLinux). The communication between different computers has to be based on a realtime communication protocol (see [Krishna and Shin (1997); Liu (2000)]).

In the presented system, first the compatibility tests based on the interface types are conducted then the architectural types are used to avoid execution errors. Based on these results, temporal correctness can be deduced. If an SDF graph with a valid cyclic and distributed schedule is specified, it has to be checked whether all M&C components guarantee their execution times. If this is the case, the latency times of the signal graph can be calculated by adding the execution times of the M&C components and the communication times between the M&C components. For that, the parallel execution given by the cyclic schedule has to be considered. If the latency times do not meet the realtime requirements, M&C components which deliver less exact results but guarantee faster execution times might be selected. This is a first approach of obtaining valid realtime schedules. Realtime scheduling of dataflow graphs is an important issue in embedded system design [Balarin *et. al.* (1998)]. There are several approaches e.g. using earliest deadline first [Goddard (1998)] and rate monotonic scheduling [Parks and Lee (1995)] based on the work of [Liu and Layland (1973)]. We gained first experiences with realtime execution of signal graphs using VxWorks [Schwarzfischer (1999)].

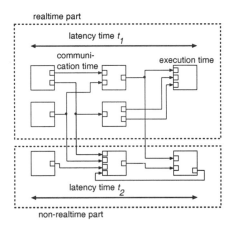

Fig. 7.20   Realtime M&C System

The implementation of an M&C system based on the proposed ideas is in progress: The implementation of the editor and the analyzer is on the way. The afore mentioned approaches regarding type system and dataflow paradigms are pessimistic as they decide about the analyzability of a signal graph depending on the presence of just one BDF or DDF component, for instance. This results from the approach to take current M&C systems, model their components with the proposed hierarchy of dataflow paradigms, and replace the components with these new models. The next step is to identify groups of M&C components in order to simplify the overall M&C component system by replacing these groups with M&C component groups having identical behavior but less complexity. That is, additional analyzing technologies based on Petri nets regarding the optimization of the structure of signal graphs (i.e. simplifying parts of the signal graph which consist of BDF and DDF components and which have an SDF behavior altogether), cyclic schedules, automatic type conversion, etc. will be investigated. Another interesting question is the influence of the (during design) unknown number $n + 1$ of values of a signal on the complexity of an M&C component system. In some cases, n is known or a maximum can be estimated. This information can be used to avoid adaptation components increasing the complexity of the signal graph, for instance. The work on the component framework is almost finished [Le (2001); Lausser (2002)]. The scheduler library and the M&C component library have to be filled with additional M&C components in order to test different scheduling strategies, for instance.

The design of the new system includes some other mutually orthogonal, modern software paradigms besides COP (component-oriented programming): OOP (object-oriented programming) for M&C component construction, visual programming techniques for M&C component assembly, and distributed execution of M&C components.

The main advantages of this combination of dataflow principles with the concept of component-based software development are:

- for the application engineer (responsible for M&C component assembly): shorter time to market because he can focus on the application problem and benefits from the implemented techniques without having detailed knowledge of the underlying theory,
- for the software engineer (responsible for M&C component construction): enhanced maintainability and easy adaptation to changing requirements.

References

Agilent Technologies (2000). *Vee OneLab User's Guide (Version 6.0).*

D. Argiro, S. Kubica, M. Young, and S. Jorgensen (2000). Khoros: An integrated Development Environment for Scientific Computing and Visualization. In E. N. Houstis, J. R. Rice, E. Gallopoulos, and R. Bramley, editors, *Enabling Technologies for Computational Science: Frameworks, Middleware and Environments*, pp. 147 – 157. Kluwer Academic Publishers.

F. Balarin, L. Lavagno, P. Murthy, A. Sangiovanni-Vincentelli (1998). Scheduling for Embedded Real-Time Systems. In *IEEE Design & Test of Computers*. pp. 71 – 82.

S. S. Bhattacharyya, P. K. Murthy, and E. A. Lee (1996). *Software Synthesis from Dataflow Graphs.* Kluwer Academic Publishers.

D. Brock and W. Ackerman (1981). Scenarios: A Model of Non-determinate Computation. In *Formalization of Programming Concepts*, pp. 252–259. Springer. LNCS 107.

J. T. Buck (1993). *Scheduling Dynamic Dataflow Graphs with Bounded Memory Using the Token Flow Model.* PhD thesis, University of Berkeley.

F. Doucet, R. Gupta, M. Otsuka, and S. Shukla (2002). An Environment for Dynamic Component Composition for Efficient Co-design. In *Design Automation and Test Conference (DATE 2002).*

S. Goddard (1998). *On the Management of Latency in the Synthesis of Real-Time Signal Processing Systems from Processing Graphs.* PhD Thesis, University of North Carolina.

S. A. Hissam, G. A. Moreno, J. A. Stafford, and K. C. Wallnau (2002). Packaging Predictable Assembly In J. Bishop, editor, *Proceedings of the IFIP/ACM Working Conference on Component
Deployment*. pp. 108 – 124. Springer. LNCS 2370.

S. Ha (1992). *Compile-Time Scheduling of Dataflow Program Graphs with Dynamic Constructs*. PhD
Thesis, University of Berkeley.

G. Kahn (1974). The Semantics of a Simple Language for Parallel Processing. *Information Processing*, 74: pp. 471 – 475.

C. M. Krishna and K. G. Shin (1997). *Real-Time Systems*. McGraw-Hill.

M. Lausser (2002). *Spezifikation und Implementierung eines Systems zur verteilten Ausführung von
Datenflussgraphen mit einfachen Kontrollstrukturen*. Diploma thesis. University of Passau.

Q. B. Le (2001). *Spezifikation und Implementierung eines modularen Tools für die Simulation der
Ausführung von Datenflussgraphen mit einfachen Kontrollstrukturen*. Diploma thesis. University of Passau.

C. L. Liu and J. W. Layland (1973). Scheduling Algorithms for Multiprogramming in a Hard-Real-
Time Environment. In *Journal of the Association for Computing Machinery*, vol. 20, number 1,
pp. 46 – 61.

J. W. S. Liu (2000). *Real-Time Systems*. Prentice Hall.

The Mathworks Inc. (2000). *MATLAB – User Manual (Version 6)*.

W. Maydl (2001). *Use of a Dataflow Paradigm with Data Dependent Control Structures for Modeling
Signal Graphs*. Internal Technical Report, University of Passau.

W. Maydl, M. Ramsauer, T. Schwarzfischer, and B. Sick (2001). Iconnect: Ein datenflußorientiertes,
visuelles Programmiersystem für die Online-Signalverarbeitung. In E. Schnieder, editor, *Engineering komplexer Automatisierungssysteme (EKA 2001)*, pp. 225 – 247.

W. Maydl, B. Sick, and W. Grass (2002). Towards a Specification Technique for Component-Based
Measurement and Control Software for Embedded Systems. In *Proc. of the 28th Euromicro
Conference (Euromicro 2002)*, Dortmund, pp. 74 – 80.

N. Medvidovic and R. N. Taylor (2000). A Classification and Comparison Framework for Software
Architecture Description Languages. In *IEEE Transactions on Software Engineering*, volume
26, number 1, pp. 70 – 93.

B. Mihura (2001). *LabVIEW for Data Acquisition*. Prentice Hall.

National Instruments (2001). *DIADem Manual (Version 8.1)*.

National Instruments (2002). *DASYLab Manual (Version 6)*.

J. Nömmer (1997). *Spezifikation und Implementierung einer Entwicklungsumgebung für Signalverar-
beitungsalgorithmen mit Ablaufsteuerung zur datenflugetriebenen Bearbeitung auf der Basis
parametrisierter Module*. Diploma thesis. University of Passau.

T. M. Parks and E. A. Lee (1995). Non-preemptive Real-Time Scheduling of Dataflow Systems In
Proceedings of the IEEE Int.Conf. on Acoustics, Speech, and Signal Processing, pp. 3225 –
3238

J. Sametinger (1997). *Software Engineering with Reusable Components*. Springer.

T. Schwarzfischer (1999). *Entwicklung einer Ablaufsteuerung für ein modulares Signalverar-
beitungssystem mit Hilfe statischer Prioritätenzuweisung auf Grundlage des Echtzeitbetrieb-
ssystems VxWorks*. Diploma thesis. University of Passau.

A. Shatnawi, M. O. Ahmad, and M. N. S. Swamy (2002). Optimal Scheduling of Digital Signal
Processing Data-flow Graphs using Shortest-path Algorithms. In *The Computer Journal*, volume 45, number 1, pp. 88 – 100.

A. Sicheneder, A. Bender, E. Fuchs, R. Mandl, M. Mendler, and B. Sick (1998). Tool-supported
Software Design and Program Execution for Signal Processing Applications Using Modular
Software Components. In T. Margaria and B. Steffen, editors, *Proc. of the Int. Workshop on
Software Tools for Technology Transfer (STTT '98)*, Aalborg, pp. 61 – 70.

A. Sicheneder, A. Bender, E. Fuchs, R. Mandl, and B. Sick (1998). A framework for the graphical specification and execution of complex signal processing applications. In *Proc. of the 1998 Int. Conf. on Acoustics, Speech, and Signal Processing (ICASSP '98)*, Seattle, volume 3, pp. 1757 – 1760.

C. Szyperski (1998). *Component Software*. Addison-Wesley.

J. Teich (1997). *Digitale Hardware/Software-Systeme*. Springer Verlag.

A. Wall, M. Larsson, and C. Norström (2002). Towards an Impact Analysis for Component Based Real-Time Product Line Architectures. In *Proc. of the 28th Euromicro Conference (Euromicro 2002)*, Dortmund, pp. 81 – 88.

P. Wauters, M. Engels, R. Lauwereins, and J. A. Peperstraete (1996). Cyclo-dynamic dataflow. In *4th EUROMICRO Workshop on Parallel and Distributed Processing*, pp. 319 – 326, Braga, Portugal.

Chapter 8

Fault-based Testing of CORBA Component Software

SUDIPTO GHOSH[1]

Computer Science Department, Colorado State University
Fort Collins, Colorado 80523, USA
ghosh@cs.colostate.edu

ADITYA P. MATHUR[2]

Department of Computer Sciences, Purdue University
West Lafayette, Indiana, 47905, USA
apm@cs.purdue.edu

Abstract. We focus on the issues related to the testing of component-based software that conforms to the CORBA 3 standard. CORBA 3 is a standard for Distributed Component Computing (DCC) middleware and is similar to Enterprise Java Beans (EJB). The specifications for DCC middleware usually offer a set of services, such as security, transaction and persistence. Testing DCC middleware and applications requires testing the services and components used to build these applications. Such testing raises several challenging issues. We report on the application of fault-based testing techniques such as interface mutation and fault injection testing to CORBA-based software and discuss their application to software conforming to other component models.

8.1 Introduction

Software enables the development of increasingly ambitious, safety-critical applications that are used in several areas. Component-based software is gaining popularity in the software industry. *Distributed Object Computing* (DOC) middleware such as Microsoft's DCOM [Lewandowski (1998)] Sun Microsystem's Java RMI [Downing (1998)] and the Object Management Group's CORBA [OMG (1995)] has now evolved into *Distributed Component Computing* (DCC). Microsoft's .NET, Sun Microsystem's Enterprise Java Beans (EJB) [Matena *et al.* (2000)] and OMG's CORBA Component Model [BEA Sys-

---

[1] All correspondence regarding this chapter may be sent to Sudipto Ghosh.
[2] Aditya P. Mathur's research was supported in part by NSF award CCR-9102331 and a grant from Telcordia Technologies and the Software Engineering Research Center.

tems *et al.* (1999)] are examples of DCC. DCC improves on DOC in several ways [Marvic *et al.* (2000)]. In DOC, connections between objects are encapsulated into objects and cannot be configured easily by external software artifacts. The use of system services, i.e. non-functional aspects, must be hard-coded into objects and mixed with the functional aspects of the application. DCC middleware provides the use of container servers that host downloadable components and manage system services implicitly. Component implementations need contain only the application business logic. With the use of DCC middleware, applications can be composed from packaged, deployable and distributed components.

Weyuker [Weyuker (1998)] emphasizes that components need to be validated, especially those that will be deployed in diverse software environments. Most of the problems that arise during the use of components stem from the fact that the components may be used in different configurations and environments than they were originally designed and tested for.

Techniques for testing have been developed in the dimensions of testing 1) object-oriented software, 2) concurrent software, and 3) distributed software. However, the combination of a pair or all the three dimensions has not been addressed satisfactorily. We address the combination of (1) and (3).

Beizer [Beizer (1990)] discusses several methods of software testing. In general terms, testing techniques can be classified into one of two kinds: 1) black-box and 2) white-box. In black-box testing, test sets are derived from the functional requirements or specifications without regard to the program structure. White-box testing techniques make use of the program structure to derive test data. Often, white-box techniques are not scalable. Large programs increase the size of the test coverage domains and hence it becomes difficult for the testers to derive adequate test sets and satisfy the criteria.

Class testing is usually employed for testing OO code [Perry and Kaiser (1990)]. Several different method sequences are applied and the resulting object states verified by the tester [Doong *et al.* (1994); Harrold *et al.* (1992); Turner and Robson (1993)]. Regression testing is required when classes are modified, and it concentrates on modified classes and their derived classes [Harrold *et al.* (1992); Perry and Kaiser (1990)].

Several aspects of testing distributed software make it a challenging task [Ghosh *et al.* (1999)]. A non-exhaustive list of these aspects appears below.

(1) Scalability of the test adequacy criteria
(2) Heterogeneity of language, platforms and architectures
(3) Need for monitoring and control mechanism in the testing of distributed software
(4) Assurance of application scalability and performance
(5) Assessment of fault tolerance

In addition, testing of concurrent programs introduces the following aspects.

(1) Reproducibility of events
(2) Deadlocks and race conditions

Testing CORBA components and middleware presents several challenges. In our approach we address the following.

(1) *Availability of source code:* Software components may be built in-house or obtained off-the-shelf. The developer of a component has access to its source code while the user usually does not. Methods for testing need to adapt to the availability of source code.

(2) *Heterogeneous platforms:* The testing methodology and tools used must be independent of the language and the platforms.

(3) *Distributed components:* A distributed monitoring and control mechanism is required. Distributed data collection and storage mechanisms need to be designed taking care of possible data buffer overflows. Often the amount of data collected for monitoring and control is large due to the large number of components and their long life-times. Care must be taken to ensure that the monitor and controller do not become bottlenecks during the data collection process.

(4) *Smaller and stronger test sets:* To address the problem of scalability we must ensure that our method requires smaller test sets, but are yet effective in detecting faults.

(5) *Assessment of fault tolerance:* Safety-critical applications have stringent fault tolerance requirements. Techniques that assess fault tolerance properties are required. This leads to a need for a systematic approach to testing such software. We need to develop fault models and derive a set of test objectives that cover all faults in the model.

Our approach is to use a two-pronged fault-based testing method. We use interface-based fault injection testing (IFIT) for assessing the fault tolerance of the application. We use interface mutation (IM) as a technique for adequacy assessment and, hence, to develop stronger test sets. These two techniques, their implementation, and results from experimental evaluation are described in subsequent sections.

The remainder of this chapter is organized as follows. Past work in mutation analysis and fault injection testing is summarized in Section 8.2. A novel approach to testing component-based applications and a prototype implementation is described in Section 8.3. The approach was evaluated experimentally. The evaluation method and results therefrom appear in Section 8.4. Strengths and weaknesses of the proposed approach are discussed in Section 8.5. A summary of the presented work and conclusions appear in Section 8.6.

8.2 Related Work

Our work is closely related to test techniques based on mutation analysis and fault injection testing. The first examines the development of mutation techniques for test adequacy assessment. The second examines the application of fault injection techniques at various levels in hardware and software.

8.2.1   Test Techniques based on Mutation

Mutation analysis aids in the assessment of adequacy of tests [Mathur (1994)]. Mutation involves the modification of programs to see if existing tests can distinguish the original program from the modified program (mutant). Traditionally, only syntactic modifications that can create programs that compile have been used. Syntactic modifications are caused by a set of *mutation operators*. This set is determined by the language of the program being tested and the mutation system used for testing. Mutation operators are created to induce simple syntax changes based on errors that programmers typically make, such as using the wrong variable name, or to force common testing goals such as executing each branch.

Various studies have reported on the application of mutation testing to actual programs [Mathur (1994)]. These studies involve compile-time or static mutation. Mutation operators have been designed for FORTRAN [Demillo *et al.* (1988)], C [Agrawal *et al.* (1989); Delamaro *et al.* (1993); Delamaro *et al.* (2001)], Ada [Offutt *et al.* (1966)] and Java [Kim *et al.* (1999); Kim *et al.* (2000)].

Interface mutation aims to identify errors that programmers may make in defining, implementing, and using interfaces. The set of errors that are likely to be made during the construction of interfaces assists with the definition of mutation operators for interface mutation.

Delamaro et al. [Delamaro *et al.* (2001)] first described the technique of using a mutation-based interprocedural criterion, named interface mutation, for the integration testing of C programs. The technique is designed to be scalable with the size of the program under test, i.e., the number of mutants generated and, therefore, the number of test cases required to kill the mutants increases in a manageable way when the size of the program increases. The size is measured in the number of sub-systems being integrated. Scalability is achieved by 1) restricting the mutation operators to model only integration errors; 2) testing only the connections between two modules, a pair at a time; and 3) applying the integration mutation operators only to module interfaces such as function calls, parameters or global variables. The underlying idea is to create mutation by inducing simple changes only to the entities belonging to the interface between modules or sub-systems.

8.2.2   Testing Techniques based on Fault Injection

Fault injection testing [Clark *et al.* (1995); Hsueh *et al.* (1997)] is a technique used to assess the fault tolerance of applications. It is often difficult to create all the erroneous conditions that cause failures in components or the interconnections. The fault injection technique is used to inject faults into the application under test and observe its behavior. Figure 8.1 shows one method for fault injection testing. In this figure the nodes $N_1, \ldots, N_k$ represent blocks in the program code. The place in the code where the fault is injected is a *fault-site*. The fault is said to *trigger* if, during the execution of the fault-injected program, control reaches the fault-site and the faulty code is executed. However, mere execution of the faulty code does not imply that the program has failed. It is possible that the observed behavior is the same as the expected behavior, for example, if the fault has been tolerated.

The behavior is observed in terms of the values of variables or other *observable* attributes.

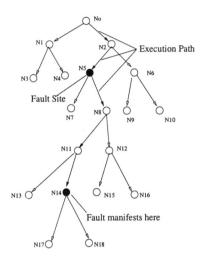

Fig. 8.1   Fault sites and failure manifestation.

An application may fail in a variety of ways. For example, an application may crash and dump its memory contents, or it may simply hang, i.e. not return control for further execution. Often several applications exhibit similar failure behaviors. Hence we classify these failure behaviors into failure modes. This classification aids in the creation of a set of generic faults that simulate the failure modes. This set of faults is used to automate the process of fault injection. The faults are made available to a tester for selection via a fault injection tool.

Several studies are reported in the area of failure mode identification. Such studies 1989, Gray 1990, Nakajo et al. 1989, Nakajo et al. 1991, and Siewiorek 1993) [Ali 1986; Barton *et al.* (1990); Chillarege *et al.* (1992); Chillarege *et al.* (1989); Gray (1990); Nakajo and Kume (1991); Nakajo *et al.* (1989); Siewiorek *et al.* (1993)] help with the long term improvement of the software development process as the recurrence of the same failures can be prevented. Failure modes can be specific to a system, or be applicable to systems in general. They can be used in testing for fault tolerance as realistic faults are needed to perform effective fault injection testing.

Fault injection testing has been used in many systems — both hardware and software. The different tools implementing fault injection testing are summarized in [Clark *et al.* (1995); Hsueh *et al.* (1997)]. The tools, namely, MESSALINE, FIAT, FERRARI, SFI and FINE rely on low-level fault injection. Faults are injected in the hardware such as the CPU pins and memory, or in the operating system. Fault injection in the hardware requires a large number of injections. Often, special purpose hardware support is required thereby making it an expensive process. None of these tools considered the underlying software architecture.

Pisces Safety Net (PSN) is an automated software analysis environment and is a module of the Whitebox Software Analysis Kit [Voas *et al.* (1997)]. It helps in identifying weaknesses in software that could cause catastrophic disasters and help pinpoint locations in the code where these weaknesses lie. PSN implements the software analysis technique called Extended Propagation Analysis (EPA). EPA injects artificial faults in both software and hardware to test the software tolerance to unusual events.

ORCHESTRA is a fault injection environment for testing fault tolerant and real-time distributed systems [Dawson *et al.* (1996)]. It is based on a framework of script-driven probing and fault injection for the evaluation and validation of the fault-tolerance and timing characteristics of distributed protocols. Fault injection techniques have been used to increase software test coverage.

Visual C-Patrol [Bieman *et al.* (1996)] was used to perform fault injection via *Assertion Violation* in C programs. It allows the tester to insert assertions regarding pre- and post-conditions in a program and recompile it. The tester is allowed to dynamically modify the state of an executing program and monitor the effect of triggered faults on control flow and assertion status. Coverage was demonstrated to have increased by using fault injection without using extra test cases.

8.2.2.1 *Interface-based Fault Injection Testing*

TAMER (Testing, Analysis and Measurement Environment for Robustness) [Li (1995)] is an interface-based fault injection testing (IFIT) tool. TAMER's test method assumes that a set of well-defined module interfaces (function calls and parameters) of the target system are available. IFIT changes the behavior of the target system by injecting a potential for error at the interface. The system behaves in a manner identical to the original one if control never reaches the interface. Failure occurs only if the control does reach the interface. TAMER allows fault injection with failure modes. It performs C source code instrumentation and keeps the tester informed about execution status. Locations for fault injection can be specified interactively by the tester.

8.3   Proposed Approach

In this chapter, a software component is a unit of composition with contractually specified interfaces. (Szyperski 1998). A software component can be deployed independently and is subject to third-party composition.

Let A be an application comprised of a set C of distinctly identifiable components where $C = \{C_1, C_2, \ldots, C_n\}, n \geq 1$. A component in C could be a client, a server, or both. We assume that each server exposes an interface. The exposed interface often consists of one or more method signatures and is specified in an Interface Description Language commonly known as IDL. These methods can be invoked on the corresponding server by clients. A method signature specifies its name, parameters passed between the server and its clients when the method is invoked, a return type, and zero or more exceptions that could be raised during its execution.

Each component is a program written in one or more programming languages. Components are assumed to be distributed over a network of machines that may not all have the same run-time environment. An application $\mathcal{A}$ is considered *dynamic* if the number of components, n, in $\mathcal{C}$ can change during its use. For a *static* application n does not change during its use. Changes in an application while it is in use might lead to altered functionality, improved performance, and improved behavior. Using the CORBA standard [OMG (1995)] it is possible to develop both static and dynamic applications.

Components in CORBA, COM, DCOM, Java-RMI and JINI have well-defined interfaces. Mathematical libraries also have well-defined interfaces. Components use the services of another component C through the interface provided by C. In CORBA, COM, DCOM, Java-RMI and JINI, there are no global variables being shared between components. However, there could be other shared resources such as databases. We treat resources such as databases as separate components too. They provide services through a well defined API. We are concerned with testing the methods that one component can invoke on another component.

8.3.1 *Interface Mutation*

Interface mutation operators are applicable to call to methods defined in some interface(s). The entities to which operators are applicable include method parameters, return values, and their types. As in traditional mutation, we do not concern ourselves with errors in type declarations. Despite this, there could be an infinite number of mutation operators because one could change the value of a parameter in a number of ways.

Parameter values may be changed according to different criteria, two of which are: 1) setting a parameter to a specific value which may be a boundary value for the domain of the parameter, and 2) increment the parameter with a fixed value. The first of the two operators models the errors in implementation where the code does not work correctly for the boundary cases. The second operator models off-by-a-constant (usually 1) error.

We have identified a set of mutation operators that can be applied to CORBA-IDL. The following operators are proposed:

(1) *Replace*: Replaces an occurrence of one of "in", "out" and "inout" with another in the list. However, based on the IDL-Java or IDL-C++ mapping, the compiler always detects if an "in" variable has been replaced with either "out" or "inout". The detection does not occur if an "out" variable has been replaced with "inout" or vice versa. This operator could be applied to the IDL itself without changing the implementation. Thus the stubs and skeletons would be mutated without a change in the implementation of the interface or the client using the interface.
(2) *Swap*: Operator for parameter swapping in the method call. Parameters of the same type could be swapped in a method call.
(3) *Twiddle*: This operator is used on a numerical (integer, long, float, etc.) or a character variable that is passed to or from a method. It replaces a variable x with succ(x) or pred(x). It also applies to the return value.

(4) *Set*: The set operator assigns a certain (fixed) value to a parameter or to the value returned from a method. This fixed value can be obtained using boundary value analysis
on the domain of the parameter. Usually the extreme values, and a few values just
inside and outside the boundaries of the domains are selected.

(5) *Nullify*: The nullify operator nullifies an object reference.

A mutant is created when an operator is applied to the interface. Usually the application
is carried out by modifying the method call of the calling component by changing the value
of the parameter at the call-location. An alternative way of applying the mutation operator
is at the server location where the method is actually implemented. The parameter values
may be changed at the point of call invocation or at the time of return.

Depending on the environment used, the application of mutation operators can be at
compile time or at run time. We implemented a prototype tool named TDS, [Ghosh *et
al.* (2000)], that inserts the index corresponding to the selected mutant inside the code in
the calling component. When execution reaches the instrumented code control is passed
to a mutant library that actually changes the value of the appropriate parameters. This is
illustrated in Figure 8.2.

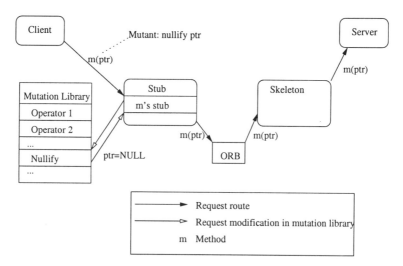

Fig. 8.2   Interface mutation using instrumented stubs.

Alternately, the operator could be applied during execution if one has capabilities for
trapping method requests and changing the values directly. This facility is provided by interceptors in CORBA. This method of interface mutation is illustrated in Figure 8.3 and is
employed in Wabash [Sridharan *et al.* (2000)]. Interception alleviates the need for instrumenting the code. Without interceptors, one needs to create and enable the application to
use components that provide additional capabilities for monitoring and control. One cannot develop a general interceptor-like mechanism without having specialized knowledge
and understanding of problems outside the application domain. With CORBA intercep-

tors one can enhance CORBA applications at runtime with components whose operation is transparent to both the application and the CORBA framework, thus modifying application behavior without modifying the application or the CORBA framework [Narasimhan *et al.* (1999)].

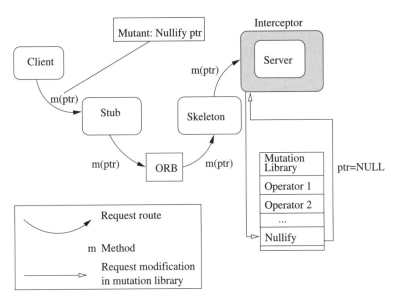

Fig. 8.3   Interface mutation using CORBA interceptors.

8.3.1.1   *Error Discovery using Interface Mutation*

Each non-mutated component and its mutants are executed once on each test input. Let the client be denoted by $Client$ and $Client_m$ for the non-mutated and mutated versions, respectively. Let the server be denoted by S and S_m for the non-mutated and mutated versions, respectively. The conditions that must be satisfied by a test input to distinguish a mutant are as follows:

(1) **Reachability**: If the method call is mutated at the client side, then the control should reach the statement containing the method call. If the method implementation has been mutated at the server, the client's method request should reach the server.
(2) **Necessity**: The state of the server component S_m should change in some way after the method is invoked when the input parameters have been mutated. This new state should be different from that of S when the same method was invoked. This should cause a value which is different from that returned to $Client$ to be returned to $Client_m$. If only the return value is mutated, that value should be different for $Client$ and $Client_m$.
(3) **Sufficiency**: Once the call to a method is completed, there should be an observable change in the behavior of the client. This observable change could be in terms of the values of variables that immediately follow the method call. A stronger condition

stipulates that the set of values of observable variables should be different from the values obtained using the original interface, once the calling component has completed execution. Many distributed applications run continuously for long periods of time, which could be days, months or years. It is up to the tester to define at what point a test is considered complete.

8.3.1.2 *Interface Mutation Adequacy Criterion*

Let P and M denote, respectively, a program under test and its mutant. Also, $P(t)$ and $M(t)$ denote, respectively, the behavior of P and M upon execution on a test input t. M is considered killed when $P(t) \neq M(t)$ for some t.

Sometimes a mutated interface may be equivalent to the original interface. If the code is available, the tester may attempt to show that the two are indeed equivalent. If the code is not available, there is no way of showing equivalence. The tester can also try to create an enhanced test set that contains a new test t which kills the mutant.

Let D be the number of mutants distinguished and N the number of non-equivalent mutants created. The interface mutation score is defined as:

$IMSCORE = \frac{D}{N}$

This score leads to a criterion for assessing test adequacy IM.

A test set is T for a program P is considered adequate with respect to interface mutation coverage if the $IMSCORE$ is 1.

8.3.2 *Interface-based Fault Injection Testing*

CORBA applications may fail from combinations of faults occurring in the server and client implementations. However, since components are distributed, there may also be failures caused by the remoteness of the components (e.g., network delays, network congestions, lost packets or network disconnections). Clients may not get the response in time and thus, time out. CORBA one-way calls make no guarantees about delivery and there may be failures in case the server never gets the call. There may be buffer overflows or exhaustion of available threads in case a server is heavily loaded. The CORBA middleware defines a number of exceptions under the group of `SystemException`. Clients need to handle these exceptions appropriately. In addition, there are user-defined exceptions that need to be handled as well.

Security and authentication are of major importance, especially with computers around the world becoming increasingly interconnected for e-business. The implementations often must deal with processes which may try to forge identities. Both clients and servers need to be aware of security issues. There could also be concurrency and synchronization related errors, but that is not inside the scope of this chapter.

The following is a proposed list of the faults that can be injected into a broker-based distributed application. It shows how a fault's effect can be simulated with the help of fault injection.

(1) • **Fault**: Overloading at server (Case 1).
    • **Effect**: Delays at client in getting responses.
    • **Injection**: Insert a delay before sending the response.

(2) • **Fault**: Overloading at server (Case 2).
    • **Effect**: Overflow of request buffers and lost request, and client never receives a reply.
    • **Injection**: Insert a delay before sending the response or never send the response back.

(3) • **Fault**: Delay in routing of requests.
    • **Effect**: Client experiences delay.
    • **Injection**: Insert a delay before sending the response.

(4) • **Fault**: Requests or responses are lost because of communication failures; especially so in the context of one way calls where the caller does not block.
    • **Effect**: Various possibilities, like client never gets a reply or computation proceeds erroneously because of inconsistencies in the client and server.
    • **Injection**: Insert a delay before sending the response.

(5) • **Fault**: Exceptions raised by servers.
    • **Effect**: Client crashes as it cannot handle the exception.
    • **Injection**: At the server side, force the server to throw an exception.

(6) • **Fault**: Intended server application crashed or malfunctioning.
    • **Effect**: Client hangs, waiting for a reply.
    • **Injection**: At the server side, force the server to throw an system exception or put an infinite delay in the response.

(7) • **Fault**: Object reference invalid.
    • **Effect**: Caller of operation receives an exception.
    • **Injection**: At the server side, force the server to throw an system exception.

8.3.3   *Mechanism for Fault Injection Testing*

Faults are injected at the interface as illustrated in Figure 8.4. Faults can be injected at the stub and skeleton. One way of implementing this is to insert extra code in the start and end of the stub or skeleton code. This code essentially is a call to an appropriate fault in a separate fault library with appropriate parameters. The library contains the actual code that will modify the value of the parameters or throw an exception or introduce delays.

Just as in interface mutation, one can use CORBA interceptors instead of instrumenting the stubs and skeletons. This is done in Wabash [Sridharan *et al.* (2000)].

The faults can be injected with the help of a tool. When tests are run, the tester must observe how the application behaves once the fault is triggered. When the application does not conform to the requirements, appropriate changes may have to be made to the fault-recovery code. The tester may need to use debugging tools to trace the execution.

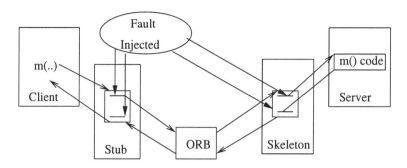

Fig. 8.4   Fault injection testing.

8.4   Experimental Evaluation

We carried out two sets of experiments for evaluation of the IM criterion. An experiment on fault injection testing was also carried out. These experiments are described below.

8.4.1 *Mutation Testing*

Experiments were conducted to compare the IM criterion with two control-flow based criteria (block coverage and decision coverage). Two sets of experiments were performed. One set, labeled APP_1 used components developed commercially. The other experiment used components developed in the SERC Laboratory; these are labeled APP_2. Details of the experiments are described in [Ghosh *et al.* (2001)].

    Consider a component C that contains one or more errors. Let T_{cf} and T_{im} be test sets adequate with respect to, the control-flow based coverage and IM respectively. Let E_{cf} and E_{im} be the number of errors revealed by T_{cf} and T_{im} respectively. We wish to investigate the relationship between E_{cf} and E_{im}.

8.4.1.1 APP_1

The architecture of APP_1 (written in C++) is shown in Figure 8.5. Some relevant characteristics of this application appear in Table 8.1. The entire application consists of 400,000 lines of code. This count includes a significant amount of code generated by the Orbix compilers. Characteristics of the implementation code considered for seeding errors are shown in Table 8.1 in the row labeled "LOC."

Table 8.1   Characteristics of APP_1.

Component	Component-1	Component-2	Component-3
LOC	1484	1268	2950
Interfaces	2	2	2
Methods	27	10	45
Exceptions	1	1	1
Mutants	69	24	127

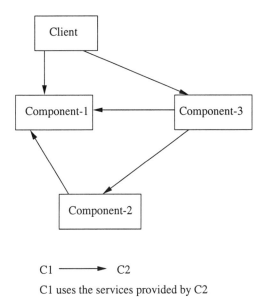

C1 ⟶ C2

C1 uses the services provided by C2

Fig. 8.5   Architecture of APP_1.

APP_1 allows clients to perform queries on Component-3 for objects stored in Component-2. The server objects register themselves with Component-1. Clients obtain the reference to these objects from Component-1. The actual objects are managed by Component-2. Component-3 implements the code for querying on these objects.

Each component was tested separately with the help of a test client. Errors that occur commonly in programs were seeded one by one in each component. The errors seeded are listed in Tables 8.2, 8.3 and 8.4. The categories used in these tables refer to the classification reported by Knuth in his study of the errors in TeX [Knuth (1989)]. These categories are explained in Table 8.5.

Table 8.2   Errors seeded in COMPONENT-1.

	Errors Seeded	Category
1	Wrong config variable used	P
2	Insufficient malloc	D
3	No malloc (using null pointer)	D
4	Forgetting to free memory	D
5	Wrong offsets in fseek, fgets	A
6	Forget string null termination	D
7	Forget strdup	D
8	Wrong variable used in search	B
9	Counts not incremented	F

Several errors belonging to each category were seeded one at a time. For each error seeded, test sets were developed such that each test set was adequate with respect to interface coverage. For each adequate test set the following was noted:

Table 8.3　Errors seeded in COMPONENT-2.

	Errors Seeded	Category
1	Wrong exception thrown	B
2	Wrong activation mode set	B
3	Transaction not removed while handling exception	A
4	Transaction id not decremented while handling exception	A
5	Transaction id not properly incremented	A

Table 8.4　Errors seeded in COMPONENT-3.

	Errors Seeded	Category
1	Wrong number returned	B
2	Error in loop exit condition	A
3	Missing increment	F
4	Not enough memory allocated	D
5	Error in using strcmp's return value	L
6	Error in string operations	L

Table 8.5　Knuth's classification of the errors of TEX.

A	Algorithm	F	Forgotten	P	Portability
B	Blunder	G	Generalization	Q	Quality
C	Cleanup	I	Interaction	R	Robustness
D	Data	L	Language	S	Surprise
E	Efficiency	M	Mismatch	T	Typo

(1) Whether or not the error was revealed while executing the code on at least one test case in the adequate test set.

(2) The block and decision coverages obtained once all tests in the adequate test set are executed.

Several errors belonging to each category were seeded one at a time. For each error seeded, test sets were developed such that each test set was adequate with respect to interface coverage. For each adequate test set the following was noted:

(1) Whether or not the error was revealed while executing the code on at least one test case in the adequate test set.

(2) The block and decision coverages obtained once all tests in the adequate test set are executed.

Each test case in a test set executes a sequence of methods with some input values. For each error, we developed 10 test-sets. The number 10 was selected so that the experiments could be completed in the limited time available. We made sure that the test inputs took care of all the different equivalence classes of inputs. When the objective was to achieve adequacy with respect to ME, the tests were chosen randomly. The test sets were developed with respect to requirements of the interface. The sequence of the method calls was also fixed and not randomized. Then, each test set was enhanced so as to be adequate with respect to IM and, subsequently, CF. For interface mutation, tests were generated with the objective of being able to kill the mutants obtained by applying the interface mutation operators to the component under test. During enhancement for adequacy with respect to CF, the test generation was driven by the additional code that was supposed to be covered.

8.4.1.2 APP_2

The second set of experiments used components from an application (APP_2) developed using C++ in the Software Engineering Research Center (SERC) at Purdue University. Figure 8.6 shows the architecture of APP_2 containing these components and Table 8.6 shows the characteristics of this application.

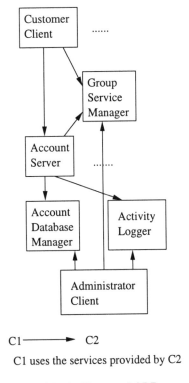

C1 ──────▶ C2

C1 uses the services provided by C2

Fig. 8.6   Architecture of APP_2.

APP_2 is a bank application. There is an Activity Logger component that records all transactions in the bank — deposits, withdrawals and transfers. The administrator starts up the Activity Logger and performs queries related to the number of total transactions, number of transactions per member and amount of money transferred. The Accounts Database Manager controls access to individual accounts. The information stored for every account

Table 8.6   Characteristics of APP_2.

Component	Activity Logger	Account Database Manager	Group Service Manager
LOC	1893	2799	5599
Interfaces	1	2	2
Methods	11	7	9
Exceptions	0	3	4
Mutants	15	6	13

consists of the name of the account holder and the available amount.

There can be one or more Account Servers that form a group of servers implementing the same code. Each Account Server connects to the Account Database Manager. The Account Servers register with the Group Service Manager. When a Customer Client needs to connect to an Account Server, the Client requests the Group Service Manager for a reference to an Account Server. In turn the Group Service Manager returns a reference according to the round-robin policy. After obtaining the reference, the Client communicates directly with the Account Server.

Each component was tested separately with the help of a test client. Errors were seeded one by one in each component. The errors seeded are shown in Table 8.7. As in the first set of experiments, the categories refer to the classification reported by Knuth in his study on the errors in TEX [Knuth (1989)].

Table 8.7   Errors seeded in components of APP_2.

	Errors Seeded	Category
1	Error in loop exit condition	A
2	Error in predicate	B
3	Wrong variable used	B
4	Wrong constant used	B
5	Uninitialized variable	D
6	Wrong initialization	D
7	Extra code, unnecessary as well as erroneous	B
8	Insufficient or no malloc	D
9	Missing statement	F
10	Wrong operator used	F

For each error seeded, test sets adequate with respect to interface coverage were developed. For each adequate test set the following was noted:

(1) Whether or not the error was revealed while by executing the code on at least one test case in the adequate test set.
(2) The block and decision coverages obtained once all tests in the adequate test set are executed.

We used the same method as before for generating test sets. However, instead of 10 test sets, we generated 100 test sets initially. A larger number was chosen to make the analysis more suitable for statistical purposes.

8.4.1.3 Summary of Experimental Results

For APP_1, the block and decision coverages obtained by tests that are adequate with respect to ME and IM are shown in Table 8.8. The number of errors revealed in each component for adequacy with respect to ME, IM and CF are shown in Table 8.9. The number of tests required for test adequacy are shown in Table 8.10.

Table 8.8 APP_1: Control flow coverage obtained with interface coverage.

Component	100% ME		100% IM	
	Block Coverage	**Decision Coverage**	**Block Coverage**	**Decision Coverage**
Component-1	74%	57%	74%	57%
Component-2	60.3%	46%	60.3%	46%
Component-3	68.5%	47%	68.5%	47%
Total	70.4%	52.4%	70.4%	52.4%

Table 8.9 APP_1: Errors revealed using different coverage criteria.

Component	ME	IM	CF
Component-1	58.5%	58.5%	58.5%
Component-2	52.0%	67.2%	75.0%
Component-3	88.1%	97.3%	90.0%
Total	66.6%	71.6%	70.4%

Table 8.10 APP_1: Number of tests required for achieving adequacy.

Component	ME	IM	CF
Component-1	1	2	29
Component-2	1	12	28
Component-3	2	29	20

For APP_2, the block and decision coverage obtained by tests that are adequate with respect to ME and IM are shown in Table 8.11. The number of errors revealed in each component for adequacy with respect to ME, IM and CF are shown in Table 8.12. The data that is shown in the interface mutation column corresponds to the mutants that are created by mutating only the parameters of the methods. It is observed that for these components, interface mutation was not any more powerful than method coverage if we mutated only parameters of the methods. However, if the contents of the attributes of the components are also mutated, then interface mutation performed a lot better. The errors revealed in the code was then 100% in all the cases. The number of tests required for test adequacy are shown in Table 8.13. Again this data corresponds to the case where interface mutation operators are only applied to the parameters of the methods, and not to the attributes themselves.

Table 8.11 APP_2: Control flow coverage obtained with interface coverage.

Component	100% ME		100% IM	
	Block Coverage	Decision Coverage	Block Coverage	Decision Coverage
Activity Logger	54.04%	44.79%	54.78%	45.31%
Account Database Manager	43.45%	30.23%	58.93%	45.35%
Group Service Manager	51.72%	42.8%	54.64%	45.34%

Table 8.12 APP_2: Errors revealed using different coverage criteria.

Component	ME	IM	CF
Activity Logger	51.5%	51.5%	100.0%
Account Database Manager	57.1%	57.1%	100.0%
Group Service Manager	72.2%	72.2%	100.0%

Table 8.13 APP_2: Number of tests required for achieving adequacy.

Component	ME	IM	CF
Activity Logger	1	2	9
Account Database Manager	1	1	5
Group Service Manager	1	2	10

In APP_1, T_{im} revealed 7.8% fewer errors than T_{cf} for Component-1. However, in Component-2 where the number of mutants was higher than those in other components, T_{im} revealed 7.3% more errors than T_{cf}. To distinguish these mutants, more tests were required. This helped in creating a stronger test set. Moreover, the kinds of mutant operators used in testing Component-3 were related to Swap and Twiddle (increment and decrement). These proved to be more effective in creating stronger test sets than the operators *Nullify* or *Set* string to empty values.

The total number of mutants created was 220, while the number of LOC considered in the implementation was 5712. Thus T_{im} needed to distinguish 220 mutants, while T_{cf} had to cover all the blocks and decisions in 5712 LOC. The sizes of the coverage domains consisting of the blocks and decisions are respectively 10 and 3 times the number of mutants. This means that the size of T_{im} was smaller than that of T_{cf}. There was less effort involved in test case development and execution when one used IM. The sizes of T_{IM} and T_{CF} were 43 and 77 respectively. Also $\frac{\#blocks}{|im|} = 10$, $\frac{\#decisions}{|im|} = 3$ and $\frac{|T_{cf}|}{|T_{im}|} = 1.79$.

For APP_2, the coverage numbers obtained using T_{ME} and T_{IM} were lower than those obtained for APP_1 although the size of code of APP_2 was smaller. APP_2 contained methods that included code with several branches based on the state of the component. For example, in a method for creating an account, there would be code that examined whether the account was the first one to be created. This would require the creation of a new structure to hold the accounts. Once an account was created, this part of the code would not be executed. However, there would be checks to see if subsequent account creation requests had duplicate member names.

This kind of code is not executed when a method is executed only once. If it were possible to mutate the attributes, the states of the objects could have been changed. Alternatively, such code can be exercised through multiple sequences of the same methods with different parameters. For example, call a method `create(m)` more than once with same and different values of m so that the code for checking duplicates and the code for handling subsequent insertions in the method gets exercised.

T_{IM} did not lead to a significant increase in the block and decision coverage obtained using T_{ME}. This is because of the kind of mutant operators that were applicable and the kind of code present. The integer increment/decrement or swap operator were not applicable. The parameters p_i's were based on strings and characters. T_{IM} increased coverage at places where the code blocks had decisions dependent on the value of p_i's. However, in the cases where there were no predicates whose outcome depended on p_i's or other variables that were functions of p_i's, T_{IM} did not help in increasing the block and decision coverage.

The percentage of errors revealed by T_{IM} and T_{ME} was the same. An explanation follows from the reasoning in the previous paragraphs. If IM was applied to the attributes of the components, the number of errors revealed would be higher. This can be seen from the number of errors revealed by using T_{CF}. It was possible to reveal 100% of the errors seeded using T_{CF}. Mutating attributes would lead to the execution of different parts of the code.

8.4.2 *Interface Fault Injection Testing*

We performed a qualitative evaluation of the the effectiveness of IFIT in testing fault tolerance properties of CORBA applications. An earlier experiment with IFIT on a distributed client-server based inventory management application (that did *not* use CORBA) in a telephone company is described in [Ghosh *et al.* (1997)].

We performed a study on similar lines using APP_2, the CORBA-based bank application. To APP_2 we added some fault handling mechanisms (e.g., checks for erroneous inputs values, duplicate account names, and remaining account balance checks). The goal of our study was to assess the effectiveness of fault injection testing at the interface level. We observed whether or not the application was able to adequately handle faults in the server. For example, we observed if there were cases where the application crashed or hung because the application did not adequately handle faults that were injected. In addition to the assessment of fault tolerant behavior, we observed if there was an increase in the code coverage of fault handling routines.

For each interface, the faults that could be injected were identified. The interface consisted of methods with input parameters and the results returned. The results were in the form of values returned by a function or as reference parameters. We then observed whether or not the server was able to take appropriate action to handle the errors in inputs from the clients. For faults in parameter values, it was the parameter type that determined which faults were selected. For example, if the parameter was a character string (char *), NULL pointers and empty strings were passed.

Application-dependent (input errors, unexpected return values and exceptions) as well as independent faults (delays, system exceptions) were considered. Once the faults were injected, the fault-handling capability of the server was observed. We observed if the methods performed as specified. Code coverage was measured in terms of block and decision coverage. Visible differences in behavior such as, system crashes, client hang-up as well as no difference from the correct behavior were recorded.

Fault injection resulted in an increase in block coverage in all the functions. Server crashes were simulated by sending to the client an error code signifying the crash. It was found that the client usually did not handle the crashes gracefully. On some occasions when null parameters were used for functions the entire application was unable to handle failures gracefully. There were occasions, however, when the application was able to issue an error message and wait for the next request to come in. When we inserted delays to server access, there was a corresponding delay in the responses sent to the client. However, no inconsistencies were observed in the responses or the client outputs.

8.5 Discussion

The basic technique employed by us could be extended to any component-based middleware because all of them utilize interface descriptions of components in the form of a language such as IDL (CORBA) or Java (RMI/EJB/Jini). The actual implementation of a tool would depend on the particular language and middleware being used. In some cases, it would utilize features provided in the middleware, such as interceptors in CORBA. Java RMI lacked interceptors until JDK 1.3, but with the arrival of RMI over IIOP, one can use interceptors in RMI as well.

There are a number of faults that can be injected independent of the application semantics. These could be faults that simulate system or network failures. One could also throw the user defined exceptions described in the IDL (CORBA) or Java (RMI/EJB/Jini) interface. Application dependent faults would require knowledge of the application domain.

Mutation operators described above mutate the data in the program directly without relying on changes in statements and operators. In our work we had the *Nullify* operator for object references. However, to introduce realistic faults in arbitrary objects and components, the mutation operators need to be able to modify the internal states of these objects and components. More work needs to be done in the area of mutation operators for arbitrary objects [Bieman *et al.* (2001)].

Another area that needs to be addressed is the application of fault-based testing to concurrent software. Concurrent software can have faults related to synchronization (race conditions and deadlocks). A possible approach (if code is available) is to build a forest of control-flow graphs of methods executed by individual threads and find all the interacting and potentially problematic interleavings of definitions and uses of shared objects. In the absence of code, one may be able to mutate shared objects based on the possibility of a race condition. This is work in progress.

8.6 Conclusion

We presented two fault-based testing techniques based on interface mutation and fault injection testing for CORBA-based systems. The significance of this work lies in the promise of systematic fault-based testing techniques that can be applied to test distributed middleware-based heterogeneous applications. Such applications are frequently encountered as embedded applications in computer systems. Developing the testing and test generation method has great promise for a large segment of the software industry which usually does not have adequate resources for software testing. Methods and tools produced as a result could have a large impact on the certification processes in industry.

References

Agrawal, H., DeMillo, R., Hathaway, R., Hsu, W. M., Hsu, W., Krauser, E., Martin, R. J., Mathur, A. P., and Spafford, E. (1989). Design of Mutant Operators for the C Programming Language. Technical Report SERC-TR-41-P, Software Engineering Research Center, Purdue University, West Lafayette, Indiana.

Ali, S. (1986) Analysis of Total Outage Data for Stored Program Control Switching Systems. *IEEE Journal on Selected Areas in Communications*, **4**, 7 pp. 1044–1046.

Barton, J., Czeck, E., Segall, Z., and Siewiorek, D. (1990). Fault Injection Experiments using FIAT. *IEEE Transactions on Computers*, **39**, 4, pp. 576–582.

BEA Systems et al. (1999). CORBA Components: Joint Revised Submission. orbos/99-02-05, OMG, Object Management Group.

Beizer, B. (1990). *Software Testing Techniques*. Van Nostrand Reinhold Company, Inc., New York.

Bieman, J. M., Dreilinger, D., and Lin, L. (1996). Using Fault Injection to Increase Software Test Coverage. *Proceedings of International Symposium on Software Reliability Engineering (IS-SRE '96)*, pp. 166–174.

Bieman, J. M., Ghosh, S., and Alexander, R. T. (2001). A Technique for Mutation of Java Objects. *Proceedings of Automated Software Engineering (ASE 2001)*, pp. 337-340.

Chillarege, R., Bhandari, I. S., Charr, J. K., Halliday, M. J., Moebus, D. S., Ray, B. K. and Wong, M. Y, (1992). Orthogonal Defect Classification — a Concept for in-process Measurements. *IEEE Transactions on Software Engineering*, **18**, 11, pp. 943–956.

Chillarege, R. and Bowen, N. (1989). Understanding Large System Failures — a Fault Injection Experiment. *Proceedings 19th International Symposium Fault-Tolerant Computing*, pp. 356–363.

Clark, J. A. and Pradhan, D. K. (1995). Fault Injection: A Method for Validating Computer-System Reliability. *IEEE Computer*, **28**, 6, pp. 47–56.

Dawson, S., Jahanian, F., and Mitton, T. (1996). ORCHESTRA: A Fault Injection Environment for Distributed Systems. Technical Report CSE-TR-318-96, EECS Deartment, University of Michigan, Ann Arbor, Michigan.

Delamaro, M. E., Maldonado, J. C., Jino, M., and Chaim, M. L. (1993). PROTEUM: Uma ferramenta de teste baseada na analise de mutantes (proteum: A test tool based on mutation analysis). *Software Tools Proceedings of the VII Brazilian Symposium on Software Engineering*, pp. 31-33.

Delamaro, M. E., Maldonado, J. C., and Mathur, A. P. (2001). Interface Mutation: An Approach for Integration Testing. *IEEE Transactions on Software Engineering*, **27**, 3, pp. 228–247.

Doong, R. K. and Frankl, P. G. (1994). The ASTOOT Approach to Testing Object-Oriented Programs. *ACM Transactions on Software Engineering and Methodology*, **3**, 2, pp. 101–130.

Downing, T. B. (1998). *Java RMI: Remote Method Invocation*. Hungry Minds, Inc, USA.

Ghosh, S. and Mathur, A. P. (2001). Interface Mutation. *Journal of Software Testing, Verification and Reliability*, **11**, 4, pp. 227–247.

Ghosh, S., Govindarajan, P. and Mathur, A. P. (2000). TDS: A Tool for Testing Distributed Component-Based Applications. *Proceedings of MUTATION 2000*, pp. 136–145.

Ghosh, S. and Mathur, A. P. (1999). Issues in Testing Distributed Component-Based Systems. *Proceedings First International Conference on Software Engineering Workshop on Testing Distributed Component-Based Systems, Los Angeles, California*.

Ghosh, S., Mathur, A.P., Horgan, J. R., Li, J. J. and Wong, W. E. (1997). Fault Injection Testing of Distributed Systems — A Case Study. *Proc. International Quality Week Europe (QWE '97), Brussels, Belgium*, pp. 348–355.

Gray, J. (1990). A Census of Tandem System Availability Between 1985 and 1990. *IEEE Transactions on Reliability*, **39**, 4, pp. 409–418.

Harrold, M. J., McGregor, J. D. and Fitzpatrick, K. J. (1992). Incremental Testing of Class Structures. *Proceedings of 14th International Conference on Software Engineering*, pp. 68–80.

Hsueh, M. C., Tsai, T. K. and Iyer, R. K. (1997). Fault Injection Techniques and Tools. *IEEE Computer*, **30**, 4, pp. 75–82.

Kim, S., Clark, J. A., and McDermid, J. A. (1999). The Rigorous Generation of Java Mutation Operators Using HAZOP. *Proceedings of the 12th International Conference on Software and Systems Engineering and their Applications (ICSSEA '99), Paris, France*.

Kim, S., Clark, J. A. and McDermid, J. A. (2000). Class Mutation: Mutation Testing for Object Oriented Programs. *Proceedings of the FMES 2000*.

Knuth, D. E. (1989). The Errors of TEX. *Software — Practice and Experience*, **19**, 7, pp. 607–685.

Lewandowski, S. M. (1998). Frameworks for Component-Based Client/server Computing. *ACM Computing Surveys*, **30**, 1, pp. 3–27.

Li, T. (1995). Adequacy Assessment of Tests for Fault Tolerance. Technical Report SERC-TR-166-P, Department of Computer Sciences, Purdue University, West Lafayette, Indiana.

Marvic, R., Merle, P. and Geib, J. M. (2000). Towards a Dynamic CORBA Component Platform. *Proceedings of International Symposium on Distributed Object Architectures 2000*, pp. 305–314.

Matena, V. and Stearns, B. (2000) *Applying Enterprise JavaBeans — Component-Based Development for the J2EE Platform*. The Java Series Enterprise Edition. Addison-Wesley Publishing Company, USA.

Mathur, A. P. (1994). Mutation Testing. In J. Marciniak, Editor, *Encyclopedia of Software Engineering*, pp. 707–713. Wiley Interscience.

Nakajo, T. and Kume, H. (1991) A Case History Analysis of Software Error Cause-effect Relationships. *IEEE Transactions on Software Engineering*, **SE**, 17, pp. 830–838.

Nakajo, T., Sasabuchi, K. and Akiyama, T. (1989). Structure Approach to Software Defect Analysis. *Hewlett Packard Journal*, **43**, 23, pp. 50–56.

Narasimhan, P., Moser, L. E. and Melliar-Smith, P. M. (1999). Using Interceptors to Enhance

CORBA. *IEEE Computer*, **32**, 7, pp 62–68.

Offutt, A. J., Voas, J. and Payne, J. (1996). Mutation Operators for Ada. Technical Report ISSE-TR-96-09, Information and Software Systems Engineering, George Mason University, Fairfax, Virginia.

OMG — The Object Management Group. *The Common Object Request Broker: Architecture and Specification, Revision 2.0*. OMG, 1995.

Perry, D. E. and Kaiser, G. E. (1990). Adequate Testing and Object-Oriented Programming. *Journal of Object-Oriented Programming*, pp. 13–19.

DeMillo, R. A., Guindi, D., McCracken, W., Offutt, A. J. and King, K. 1998. An Extended Overview of the MOTHRA Testing Environment. *Workshop of Software Testing, Verification and Analysis*, pp. 142–151.

Siewiorek, D., Suh, J. H. B, and Segall, Z. (1993). Development of a Benchmark to Measure System Robustness. *Proceedings 23rd International Symposium Fault-Tolerant Computing*, pp. 88–97.

Sridharan, B., Mundkur, S., and Mathur, A. P. (2000). Non-intrusive Testing, Monitoring and Control of Distributed CORBA Objects. *Proceedings of the Technology of Object-Oriented Languages and Systems (TOOLS 33)*, pp. 195–206.

Szyperski, C. (1998). *Component Software: Beyond Object-Oriented Programming*. Addison-Wesley Publishing Company, USA.

Turner, C. D. and Robson, D. J. (1993). The State Based Testing of Object-Oriented Programs. *Proceedings of IEEE Conference on Software Maintenance*, pp. 302–310.

Voas, J. M. (1992). PIE: A Dynamic Failure-based Technique. *IEEE Transactions on Software Engineering*, **18**, 8, pp. 717–727.

Voas, J. M., Charron, F., McGraw, G., Miller, K. and Friedman, M. (1997). Predicting how Badly Good Software can Behave. *IEEE Software*, pp. 73–83.

Weyuker, E. J. (1998). Testing Component-Based Software: A Cautionary Tale. *IEEE Computer*, **15**, 5, pp. 54–59.

Chapter 9

ARIFS Methodology: A Case Study

REBECA P. DÍAZ REDONDO, JOSÉ J. PAZOS ARIAS and ANA FERNÁNDEZ VILAS

Departamento de Enxeñería Telemática, Universidade de Vigo, Spain

{rebeca,jose,avilas}@det.uvigo.es

Abstract. In a totally formalized, iterative and incremental software process, each iteration usually implies identifying new requirements, adding them to the current model of the system, rechecking the consistency and, in many cases, modifying the model to satisfy all the functional requirements. In this context, the ARIFS (pronounced "ah-reefs", *Approximate Retrieval of Incomplete and Formal Specifications*) methodology provides a suitable reuse environment to classify, retrieve and adapt formal and incomplete requirements specifications and to reuse the formal verification results linked to them. This chapter focuses on applying this methodology to a case study, where the main goal is developing the components involved in a communication protocol. In this example application, we are able to avoid formal proofs in the consistency checking process and synthesis tasks to model the components.

9.1 Introduction

As the complexity of specifying the requirements of large and complex systems is usually excessive for a one-step design, current software engineering practice addresses this problem by the use of iterative and incremental development techniques. Besides that, it is possible to obtain the well-known advantages of formal methods by integrating different kinds of formal techniques in this style of life cycles. Finally, including software reuse in this type of totally formalized, iterative and incremental software process approaches can increase the efficiency of developing large and complex systems, specially if software reuse is tackled at early stages, such as requirements specification. This last practice is widely accepted as a desirable aim, because of the possibility of increasing the reuse benefits [Lam *et al.* (1997)]. However, there is little evidence in the literature to suggest that software reuse at requirements specification stage is widely practised.

We propose the ARIFS methodology [Díaz Redondo and Pazos Arias (2001)] (*Approximate Retrieval of Incomplete and Formal Specifications*) which deals with both concerns allowing the reuse of formal components (incomplete requirement specifications and its verification results) obtained from transient phases of a totally formalized, iterative and incremental requirements specification stage. The main aims of the methodology are: saving specification, synthesis and formal verification efforts by reusing suitable incomplete specifications; and reducing the extensive computing resources needed to check the consistency of medium-large and large requirements specifications by reusing previously obtained formal verification results. This last goal is clearly justified because of the great amount of verification tasks needed in iterative and incremental software processes, where each iteration implies checking the consistency of the current model of the system again.

In this chapter we briefly describe the requirements capture stage (Section 9.2) where the ARIFS methodology fits in (Section 9.3) and how to apply it in a case study where the main goal is developing the components involved in a communication protocol (Section 9.4). In Section 9.5 we study the benefits and costs of reuse in this environment and in Section 9.6 we summarize previous work about managing reusable components and improving the model checking efficiency. Finally, a brief summary and future work are described in Section 9.7.

9.2   Background

In this section, we briefly describe the first phase of the SCTL-MUS methodology [Pazos Arias and García Duque (2001)] (our software development process) where the ARIFS methodology is going to be included. The main aim of this phase (*Initial goals*) is achieving a complete and consistent functional specification of the system from user's requirements (Figure 9.1(a)). This specification is transferred to a *Refinements phase* by means of translation into a process algebra, where architecture decisions are incorporated and a more detailed design is successively reached, also iterative and incrementally. When the architectural design is detailed enough, the implementation of the system in a programming language is done almost automatically. Because of this, the *Maintenance phase* turns into a new software development process whose starting point is the functional specification of the previously developed system.

At the first stage of this methodology, functional requirements are specified by using the many-valued logic SCTL [Pazos Arias and García Duque (2001)] (*Simple Causal Temporal Logic*). These requirements are specified according to the syntax:

$$premise \Rightarrow \otimes \, consequence$$

which establishes a causing condition (*premise*); a temporal operator $\Rightarrow \otimes$ determining the applicability of the cause ($\Rightarrow \otimes \, \in \, \{\Rightarrow, \Rightarrow \odot, \Rightarrow \bigcirc\}$, these operators being *simultaneously*, *previously* and *next*); and a condition which is the effect (*consequence*).

Apart from causation, SCTL adds the concept of *unspecification* which is specially useful to deal with both incomplete and inconsistent information obtained by requirements capture. Although events will be *true* or *false* at the final stage, in intermediate phases users may not have enough information about them yet, so these events are *unspecified* in

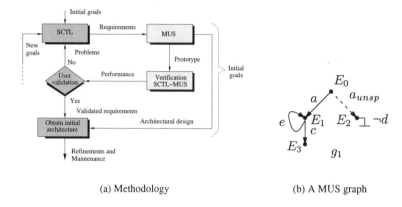

    (a) Methodology   (b) A MUS graph

Figure 9.1   SCTL-MUS Methodology

these phases. Therefore, it is possible to specify three different values: possible or *true* (1), *impossible* or *false* (0) and *unspecified* ($\frac{1}{2}$), which is the default value.

SCTL requirements are automatically synthesized to obtain a model or prototype of the system by using MUS [Pazos Arias and García Duque (2001)] (M*odel of* U*nspecified States*), which allows feedback with users. MUS graphs are based on typical labeled-transitions systems, but including another facility: unspecification of its elements. This unspecification results from the third value of the SCTL logic and is reflected in both events and states of the graph. Therefore, an event in a state of a MUS graph can be specified to be possible, to be impossible or, in its absence, to be unspecified. Consequently, a state where every event is unspecified is called an *unspecified state*. A state where no transition of the model is specified is called a *final state*, thus, both unspecified states and states where only false events have been specified are final states of a MUS graph.

An example MUS graphs is shown in Figure 9.1(b), where the model g_1 can evolve from one state into another when an event or an action of $\Lambda = \{a, b, c, d, e\}$ occurs or through the special event a_{unsp}. This special event is used whenever the user needs to specify a transition, but he does not have enough information about which event is going to be enabled. In the initial state of the graph, E_0, event a is specified as a possible one, that is, system g_1 evolves from this state into state E_1 whenever event a occurs. System g_1 evolves from E_0 into state E_2 through a_{unsp}. Since a_{unsp} is not a real event, in subsequent iterations of the requirements capture process, it will evolve to one event of Λ with the exception of event a, because MUS graphs are deterministic. In state E_2 (a final state), event d is impossible, which is denoted by $\neg d$, and, finally, state E_3 is a totally unspecified (and a final) state because every event in Λ has not been specified in this state either as a possible event or as an impossible one[1].

After the user identifies and specifies a set of new functional requirements which leads to a growth in the system functionality — the starting point of the software development

---

[1]For simplicity, unspecified events of a state are not represented, only a_{unsp} of E_0 because it implies an evolution of the model.

process is an unspecified state, it is necessary to check the consistency of the current model. Therefore, we need to know: if the model already satisfies the new requirements; if it is not able to provide these functional requirements either in the current iteration or in future (inconsistency); or, if the system does not satisfy the requirements, but it is able to do it in future (incompleteness). This formal verification is made by using a model checking algorithm which provides different levels of satisfaction of an SCTL requirement in a MUS model. These levels of satisfaction are based on causal propositions: *"an SCTL requirement is satisfied iff its premise is satisfied and its consequence is satisfied according to its temporal operator"*.

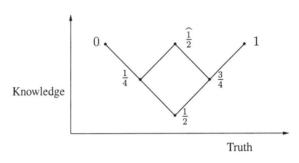

Figure 9.2   Knowledge and Truth partial orderings among levels of satisfaction.

As the SCTL-MUS methodology adds the unspecification concept, the level of satisfaction may not be *false* (nor *true*), just as the boolean logic. In fact, it must have a level of satisfaction related to its unspecification (totally or partially unspecified on the MUS model). Consequently, this methodology defines six different levels of satisfaction, $\phi \in \Phi = \{0, \frac{1}{4}, \frac{1}{2}, \widehat{\frac{1}{2}}, \frac{3}{4}, 1\}$, which can be partially ordered according to a *knowledge level* ($\leq_k$) (Figure 9.2) as follows:

- $\{1, \widehat{\frac{1}{2}}, 0\}$ are the highest knowledge levels. We know at the current stage of the model the final level of satisfaction of the property: 1 or *true* means the requirement is satisfied; 0 or *false* implies the requirement is not satisfied; and $\widehat{\frac{1}{2}}$ or *contradictory or not applicable* means the requirement cannot become *true* or *false*.
- $\{\frac{1}{4}, \frac{3}{4}\}$ are the middle knowledge levels. Although at the current stage of the model, the property is partially unspecified, we know its satisfaction tendency. That is, for the current value $\frac{1}{4}$, in a subsequent stage of specification, the level of satisfaction ($\phi \in \Phi$) cannot become 1 (*true*), it will be $\frac{1}{4} \leq_k \phi$ ($\phi \in \{\frac{1}{4}, \widehat{\frac{1}{2}}, 0\}$); and for the current value $\frac{3}{4}$, in a subsequent stage of specification, the level of satisfaction ($\phi \in \Phi$) cannot become 0 (*false*), it will be $\frac{3}{4} \leq_k \phi$ ($\phi \in \{\frac{3}{4}, \widehat{\frac{1}{2}}, 1\}$).
- $\{\frac{1}{2}\}$ is the lowest knowledge level. The property is totally unspecified at the current stage of the model and we do not know any information about its future level of satisfaction ($\phi \in \Phi$), that is, it can become $\frac{1}{2} \leq_k \phi$ ($\phi \in \{\frac{1}{2}, \frac{1}{4}, \frac{3}{4}, 0, \widehat{\frac{1}{2}}, 1\}$) in a subsequent stage of specification.

To conclude, the level of satisfaction of an SCTL requirement also varies according to its closeness to the *true* (or *false*) level of satisfaction. According to this *truth ordering* (Figure 9.2), Φ is a quasi-boolean lattice with the least upper bound operator $\vee$, the greatest lower bound operator $\wedge$, and the unary operation $\neg$ (defined by horizontal symmetry). The 4-tuple $(\Phi, \vee, \wedge, \neg)$ has the structure of the De Morgan algebra and it is called algebra of MPU [Pazos Arias and García Duque (2001)] (*Middle Point Uncertainty*).

9.3 The ARIFS Methodology: What is a Reusable Component?

Generally speaking, the ARIFS methodology [Díaz Redondo *et al.* (2002b)] enables classification, retrieval and adaptation of reusable components at the requirements specification phase of the SCTL-MUS methodology. Each reusable component (Figure 9.3) contains: the set of SCTL requirements specified by the developers; the MUS graph modeling the component's functionality; verification information (Section 9.3.3) consisting of the set of properties which have been verified on the MUS graph and their verification results — obtained by running the model checking algorithm; an interface or *functional profile* (Section 9.3.1) which is automatically obtained from its functional characteristics and used to classify and retrieve the component from the repository; and, finally, other documentation about the component (developer, data, etc.).

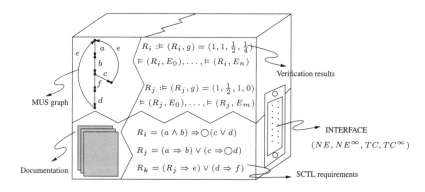

Figure 9.3 Reusable component of the ARIFS methodology

The information kept in these reusable components is reused in two different ways:

(1) Reusing the whole component at the beginning of the requirements capture stage (Figure 9.4(a)). The underlying idea is reusing already developed MUS prototypes which are functionally close to the functionality specified by the first set of SCTL requirements. Therefore, we are able to avoid synthesis tasks to translate the SCTL requirements into the MUS prototype and we are also able to reuse the verification information linked to the recovered component, saving the very probable future formal proofs.
The query, in this case, is the functional profile of the SCTL requirements, expressed in the same terms as the functional profile of reusable components (Section 9.3.1).

(2) Reusing only the verification information linked to the reusable components (Figure 9.4(b)). The underlying philosophy is reusing the formal verification results linked to those reusable components which are functionally close to the current model of the system. Therefore, we are able to reduce the amount of formal proofs needed to check the consistency of new SCTL requirements on the transient releases of the system in every iteration of the requirements capture stage.

The query, in this second case, consists of both the functional profile of the current MUS prototype of the system and the functional profile of the properties we need to verify about it.

As in both cases retrieval is done according to functional closeness between the query and the reusable components, we have decided to classify these components according to their functional similarities. These functional similarities are based on semantic and/or structural closeness (Section 9.3.1), and the retrieval is based on the quantification of the functional differences between the reusable components and the query (Section 9.3.2). Therefore, we propose a retrieval process with the following characteristics:

- It is a *totally formalized and content-oriented* retrieval which allows reusing high abstract level components.
- It is an *approximate components* retrieval based on the *unspecification* inherent to incomplete systems; instead of having an exact retrieval, which applies formal proofs.
- Finally, and because of efficiency reasons, it is a *layered retrieval process* consisting of: firstly, a rough search phase, where a little set of suitable components is retrieved; and secondly, a more refined phase, where these components are ordered depending on the adaptation efforts of each one to satisfy the functionality required by the query, that is, depending on their functional differences with the query.

9.3.1 *Static Classification of Reusable Components*

Establishing functional relationships among components enables defining component hierarchies or lattices to classify and retrieve them properly. We have defined four of them and each one is characterized in terms of a function $\mathcal{O}$ that associates with every MUS graph g a set $\mathcal{O}(g)$ which constitutes the observable behaviour of g. For every such $\mathcal{O}$, the equivalence relation $=_{\mathcal{O}} \in \mathbb{G} \times \mathbb{G}$ is given by $g =_{\mathcal{O}} g' \Leftrightarrow \mathcal{O}(g) = \mathcal{O}(g')$, and the preorder $\sqsubseteq_{\mathcal{O}} \in \mathbb{G} \times \mathbb{G}$ by $g \sqsubseteq_{\mathcal{O}} g' \Leftrightarrow \mathcal{O}(g) \sqsubseteq \mathcal{O}(g')$, that is, $\sqsubseteq_{\mathcal{O}}$ provides a partial order between equivalence classes or graph sets indistinguishable using $\mathcal{O}$-observations, so $(\mathbb{G}, \sqsubseteq_{\mathcal{O}})$ is a *partially ordered set*, or *poset*. Therefore, two graphs g and g' are $\mathcal{O}$-related iff $g \sqsubseteq_{\mathcal{O}} g'$ or $g' \sqsubseteq_{\mathcal{O}} g$.

These four functions offer four different viewpoints of a MUS graph g. Two of them, *complete traces*, denoted by $TC(g)$, and *complete and non-finite traces*, denoted by $TC^{\infty}(g)$, offer **semantic** viewpoints of the graph. Although both of them are based on traditional complete trace semantics [van Glabeek (2001)], they also take into account both *true* and *false* events in order to differentiate *false* events from *unspecified* events.

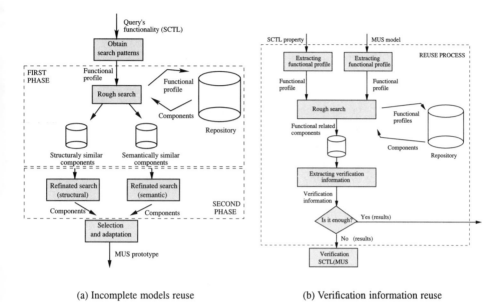

(a) Incomplete models reuse (b) Verification information reuse

Figure 9.4   Retrieval processes in the ARIFS methodology

Table 9.1   Example of applying the four functions on a MUS graph

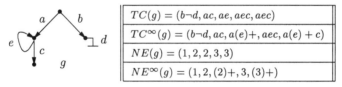

$TC(g) = (b\neg d, ac, ae, aec, aec)$
$TC^{\infty}(g) = (b\neg d, ac, a(e)+, aec, a(e) + c)$
$NE(g) = (1, 2, 2, 3, 3)$
$NE^{\infty}(g) = (1, 2, (2)+, 3, (3)+)$

Table 9.1 shows the results of applying these two functions to the MUS graph g. In this example, g has five different evolution ways, that is, it can evolve from the initial state to a final state, where event d is impossible, through event b; from the initial state to a final state through events a and c; from the initial state to a final state through events a, e and c; from the initial state to a final state through event a, an undetermined number of events e and, finally, event c; and from the initial state through event a and an infinite number of events e. These sequences of possible and impossible events are stored in $TC^{\infty}(g)$ and $TC(g)$. We have to note that although trace aec is included in $a(e) + c$,[2] both of them are explicitly included in $TC^{\infty}(g)$ and $TC(g)$ for efficiency reasons in collating tasks. Treatment of non-finite evolution ways of the graph is the main difference between the two observation criteria: non-finite traces are included in $TC^{\infty}(g)$ — contributions $a(e) + c$ and $a(e)+$, but they are considered as finite traces in $TC(g)$ — contributions aec and ae respectively.

---

[2] ()+ denotes that the set of events inside the parenthesis can be repeated an undetermined number of times.

The other two identified functions, *number of evolutions*, denoted by $NE(g)$, and *number of non-finite evolutions*, denoted by $NE^\infty(g)$, offer **structural** viewpoints of the graph. Table 9.1 also shows the results of applying these two functions to the MUS graph g. $NE(g)$ and $NE^\infty(g)$ contain the number of transitions the system have to make whenever it evolves through every evolution way. For instance, when the system evolves from the initial state to a final state through events a and c, it implies the system has to make two transitions, the corresponding number in $NE(g)$ and $NE^\infty(g)$. When the system evolves from the initial state to a final state through event a, a number undetermined of events e and, finally, event c, it implies the system has to make at least three transitions, but they could be more because of the repetition of event e, which is expressed by $(3)+$ in $NE^\infty(g)$. Treatment of non-finite evolution ways of the graph is the main difference between them: non-finite traces are included in $NE^\infty(g)$ — contributions $(3)+$ from trace $a(e) + c$ and $(2)+$ from trace $a(e)+$, but they are considered as finite traces in $NE(g)$ — contributions 3 and 2 respectively.

These four results, $TC^\infty(g)$, $TC(g)$, $NE^\infty(g)$, and $NE(g)$, are automatically obtained from the MUS graph and constitute the **functional profile** or set of characterizing attributes of a reusable component. From each of these four functions — TC^∞, TC, NE^∞, and NE — a partial order ($\sqsubseteq_{TC}^\infty$, $\sqsubseteq_{TC}$, $\sqsubseteq_{NE}^\infty$, $\sqsubseteq_{NE}$) and an equivalence relation ($=_{TC}^\infty$, $=_{TC}$, $=_{NE}^\infty$, $=_{NE}$) among MUS graph are defined. These relationships among MUS graphs are directly extrapolated to the reusable components which contain them. Therefore, two components C and C' are $\mathcal{O}$-related ($C \sqsubseteq_{\mathcal{O}} C'$ or $C' \sqsubseteq_{\mathcal{O}} C$) iff their MUS graphs g and g' are also $\mathcal{O}$-related[3]. According to these four relationships, the repository can be organized in four different lattices: one for each partial ordering. As a result of this, each reusable component (C) is classified in the repository after finding its *correct place* in each lattice, like Figure 9.5 shows. That is, it is necessary to look for those components $\mathcal{O}$-related to C such as C is $\mathcal{O}$-included on them, and those components $\mathcal{O}$-related to C such as they are $\mathcal{O}$-included on C.[4]

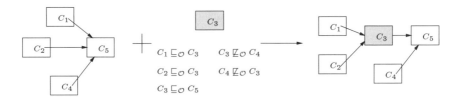

Figure 9.5   Classifying a reusable component in a lattice

Applying the four defined relationships among graphs, we are able to distinguish between semantic similarities [Díaz Redondo *et al.* (2002a)], which reflect if two reusable components have similar functional features (considering sequences of events), i.e. if they act alike, and structural similarities [Díaz Redondo *et al.* (2003a)], which reflect if two

---

[3]Where $\mathcal{O} \in \{TC^\infty, TC, NE^\infty, NE\}$.

[4]In order to eliminate superfluous reusable components connections, the anti-symmetric property of $\mathcal{O}$ is applied.

reusable components have similar representations of their MUS graph without considering events linked to each transition (only the skeleton of the graph), i.e. if they look alike. Unlike previous approaches [Jilani (1997)] which manage reusable components of code, in our case structural information is really close to semantic one.

9.3.2 *Retrieval Process*

For efficiency reasons, the retrieval process is split up into two steps. *"The closer two reusable components are classified in the repository, the more functional similarities they have"* is the underlying idea of the **first phase**. Applying this, (1) those components which are the least upper bound of the query (successor components), (2) those components which are the greater lower bound of the query (predecessor components) and (3) those components which are functionally equivalent to the query (whenever they are stored in the repository) are retrieved in this phase. The functional proximity is assessed according to structural closeness (by NE or NE^∞ criterion) and semantic closeness (by TC or TC^∞ criterion). In both cases, the selection depends on the characteristics of the query: whenever the query specifies behaviour loops, NE^∞ and TC^∞ criterion are chosen; in other case, NE and TC are applied.

Because the criterion used to recover these components from the repository only allows maintaining precedence relationships, we have probably recovered reusable components which have notable structural and semantic differences in spite of keeping the same partial ordering relationship with the query. Therefore, in the **second phase**, the search is refined by quantifying the functional differences between the recovered components and the query. Each set (the components structurally closest to the query, according to NE or NE^∞ criterion and those semantically closest to the query, according to TC or TC^∞ criterion) has a different selection process, although both of them result from a common idea: *minimizing the adaptation efforts to the query*. The formal definitions of these selection processes are included in [Díaz Redondo *et al.* (2002b)]; in this chapter, and for lack of space, we will describe them by using the case study.

9.3.3 *Reusing Verification Efforts*

After running the model checking algorithm, we achieve a set of levels of satisfaction of a SCTL property R in every state of a MUS graph g (Section 9.2). This information may be useful to future verifications of the same property — or a subset of it, over the same graph — or over a graph functionally close to it. However, and depending on the size of the graph, the management of this amount of information may be difficult, so this information must be stored under a more manageable form. Consequently, four verification results which summarize the available verification information are defined:

- $\exists \lozenge R$ expresses that *"some trace of the system satisfies eventually R"* and its level of satisfaction is denoted by $\vDash (\exists \lozenge R, g)$.
- $\exists \square R$ expresses that *"some trace of the system satisfies invariantly R"* and its level of

satisfaction is denoted by $\vDash (\exists \square R, g)$.

- $\forall \Diamond R$ expresses that *"every trace of the system satisfies eventually R"* and its level of satisfaction is denoted by $\vDash (\forall \Diamond R, g)$.
- $\forall \square R$ expresses that *"every trace of the system satisfies invariantly R"* and its level of satisfaction is denoted by $\vDash (\forall \square R, g)$.

That is, the level of satisfaction of R in g, denoted by $\vDash (R, g)$, is made up of these four results: $\vDash (R, g) = (\vDash (\exists \Diamond R, g), \vDash (\forall \Diamond R, g), \vDash (\exists \square R, g), \vDash (\forall \square R, g))$. This verification information is stored in the reusable component whose MUS graph is g, ready to be recovered (Figure 9.4(b)). We have studied how to reuse this verification information to know the level of satisfaction of one SCTL property R in a MUS graph g, $\vDash (R, g)$, knowing $\vDash (R, g')$ and $\vDash (R, g'')$, where $g' \sqsubseteq_{TC}^{\infty} g \sqsubseteq_{TC}^{\infty} g''$. As a consequence, we have obtained different tables storing these reusable verification results (deduction tables). For lack of space, these tables are not included here, but they can be found in [Díaz Redondo *et al.* (2003b)].

Whenever we need to verify the consistency of an incomplete model after adding a new set of functional requirements, we proceed as Figure 9.4(b) shows. If the recovered verification information is not enough, it is necessary to run the model checking algorithm, but this execution can be reduced. In fact, it is very probable that we only need to check some states of the graph and so we avoid exhaustive analysis. On the other hand, whenever we have new verification information of an incomplete model, we spread out this data across the lattice (according to the deduction tables [Díaz Redondo *et al.* (2003b)]) to improve the learning process of the repository. This expansion is done off-line, so it does not affect the efficiency of the reuse environment.

9.4 Applying the Methodology: A Case Study

This case study focuses on showing how to apply the ARIFS methodology to obtain a complete and consistent functional specification of each component involved in a **stop-and-wait** communication protocol [Tanenbaum (1997)]. In this case, we will see how synthesis tasks are avoided by reusing other incomplete models functionally close to the required component and how the amount of formal verifications is reduced by reusing previous verification results.

Although the set of *stop-and-wait* protocols is broad, in this case study, we focus on a protocol where data traffic is simplex and frames may be damaged, but it cannot be completely lost. We assume that only data frames can be damaged by the channel, therefore, *connect, confirm, release, ack* and *nack* frames are always error-free. To sum up, the sender starts out by fetching a packet, then it must wait until an acknowledgement frame arrives before looping back and fetching the next packet. Whenever the sender receives an nac-knowledgement frame, it sends the frame again, and this process would be repeated until the frame finally arrived intact. The set of events involved in this communication are as follows:

- Whenever the sender process is ready to send a data frame, it sends a **connect** frame as an active attempt to establish a connection.
- The receiver sends a **confirm** frame to allow the establishment of the connection.
- Once the connection is established, the sender proceeds to send the data frame (event **tx_msg**).
- Event **error** means that the channel has damaged the data frame.
- After receiving the data frame, the receiver computes the checksum. If it fails, the receiver sends an nacknowledgement frame, **tx_nack**, which is received by the sender (event **rx_nack**); otherwise, the receiver sends an acknowledgement frame, **tx_ack**, which is received by the sender (event **rx_ack**).
- After the sender has transmitted the data frame, the sender ends the connection transmitting the **release** frame.

Table 9.2   MUS graphs of the reusable components of the repository

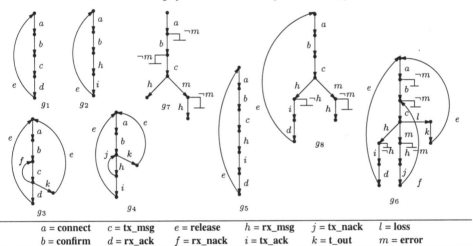

| a = connect | c = tx_msg | e = release | h = rx_msg | j = tx_nack | l = loss |
| b = confirm | d = rx_ack | f = rx_nack | i = tx_ack | k = t_out | m = error |

9.4.1   *Starting Point*

Before describing the reuse process to obtain the models of the components involved in the proposed communication protocol, we outline in this section the initial status of the repository where the retrieval is going to be done. We assume this repository consists of the eight reusable components whose MUS graphs are shown in Table 9.2, where the real name of every event has been replaced by a letter to make it more legible. These reusable components are the result of previous specification phases of parts of other kind of different communication protocols. Their classification in the repository according to NE^∞ criterion is shown by Table 9.3.(a) and according to TC^∞ criterion of Table 9.3.(b). In these tables, we have only drawn the reusable components and their precedence relationships, instead of showing the MUS graph of each component.[5] Components drawn inside dashed lines are equivalent according to the ordering criterion.

Table 9.3   Views of the repository

(a) Ordered according to NE^∞ criterion   (b) Ordered according to TC^∞ criterion

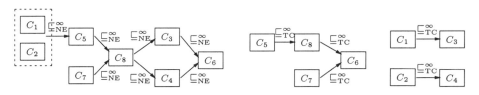

The repository grows because new incomplete models are stored at intermediate stages of the requirements capture phase.

9.4.2   *Obtaining the Sender*

In order to obtain the sender of this communication protocol, the user starts specifying its functional requirements by using the SCTL logic (Section 9.2):

$$R_1 = \text{connect} \Rightarrow \bigcirc (\text{confirm} \Rightarrow \bigcirc (\text{tx\_msg} \Rightarrow \bigcirc (\text{rx\_ack} \Rightarrow \bigcirc (\text{release} \Rightarrow \bigcirc R_1))))$$
$$R_2 = \text{connect} \Rightarrow \bigcirc (\text{confirm} \Rightarrow \bigcirc R_{21})$$
$$R_{21} = \text{tx\_msg} \Rightarrow \bigcirc (\text{rx\_nack} \Rightarrow \bigcirc R_{21})$$

Instead of translating this set into a MUS graph, we try to recover from the repository a reusable component whose functionality is as close as possible to the required by the user. In this way, we will avoid the translation tasks and, as we also recover the verification information of the reusable component, we will also save future verification efforts. To start the retrieving tasks, we need the functional profile of the SCTL requirements, that is, the query. Because of the functional loops specified in these requirements, we obtain the NE^∞ pattern: $NE^\infty(Q) = NE^\infty(R_1, R_2) = (4+, 5+, 7+, 7+)$ for the structural retrieval; and the TC^∞ one:

$$TC^\infty(Q) = TC^\infty(R_1, R_2) = ((abcde)+, ab(cf)+, (abcfcde)+, (abc(fc) + de)+)$$

for the semantic retrieval.[6] Using both patterns we can start the retrieval according to both structural and semantic criteria.

Structural Retrieval. The first step of the retrieval recovers the successor, predecessor and, if they exist, the equivalent reusable components to the functionality expressed by the structural profile of the query, $NE^\infty(Q)$. In this case, a set of successor components

---

[5] MUS graph g_i is part of the component C_i.
[6] Real names of the events have been renamed for legibility (see Table 9.2).

$\{C_3, C_4\}$, a set of predecessor components $\{C_8\}$, and any equivalent component have been recovered from the repository. The values of the NE^∞ function applied to the MUS graph of each one are as follows:

$$NE^\infty(g_8) = (5, 7+) \qquad\qquad d_{NE}^\infty(Q, g_8) = \| (5, 4+, 5+, 7+) \| = \sqrt{86}$$
$$NE^\infty(g_3) = (4+, 5+, 5+, 7+, 7+, 7+) \quad d_{NE}^\infty(Q, g_3) = \| (5+, 7+) \| = \sqrt{52}$$
$$NE^\infty(g_4) = (4+, 5+, 6+, 6+, 7+, 7+) \quad d_{NE}^\infty(Q, g_4) = \| (6+, 6+) \| = \sqrt{50}$$

The second step refines this retrieval by calculating the NE^∞ **distance** between each retrieved component and the query, denoted by $d_{NE}^\infty(Q, g_i)$. This distance, which is explained in detail in [Díaz Redondo *et al.* (2003a)], results from applying the norm to a transient vector. This vector is the result of removing those elements which are identical in both vectors $(NE^\infty(g_i)$ and $NE^\infty(Q))$ and subtracting one unit from those elements with recursivity, $()+$ (see the results above). Therefore, component C_4 is the closest one to the query, according to structural closeness.

Semantic Retrieval. Like structural retrieval, the semantic retrieval is made in two steps. In the first, a set of predecessor components $\{C_1\}$, a set of successor components $\{C_3\}$, and any equivalent reusable component to the semantic profile of the query $(TC^\infty(Q))$ are recovered from the repository. The values of the TC^∞ function applied to the MUS graphs of the previous components are as follows:

$$TC^\infty(g_1) = (\ (abcde)+)$$
$$TC^\infty(g_3) = (\ (abcde)+, ab(cf)+, (abc(cf) + de)+,$$
$$(abcfcde), (abcke)+, (abcfcke)+, (abc(fc) + ke)+)$$

Obtaining the component which needs the lowest adaptation effort to make its functionality equal to the required one is the main goal of the second step. In order to quantify this adaptation effort, we have defined several semantic refinement functions, which are explained in detail in [Díaz Redondo *et al.* (2002a)]:

- *Functional consensus* $(\rho(Q, C_i))$. This function assesses the common functionality between the query (Q) and a reusable component (C_i).
- *Functional deficit* $(\delta(Q, C_i))$. This function assesses the functional characteristics required by the current query which are not specified by the reusable component.
- *Functional excess* $(\varepsilon(Q, C_i))$. This function assesses the functional characteristics specified by the reusable component which are not required by the query.
- *Functional adaptation* $(\Delta(Q, C_i) = \delta(Q, C_i) \cup \varepsilon(Q, C_i))$. This function assesses the functionality which must be added to or removed from the reusable component C_i, to make its functionality the same as the functionality specified by the query.
- *Functional adjusting vector*. To retrieve the component C_i which maximizes the *functional consensus* and minimizes its *functional adaptation*, we define the vector $\Theta(Q, C_i) = (\rho(Q, C_i), \Delta(Q, C_i))$, which takes into account both characteristics.

The results of applying these refinement functions to the reusable components recovered in the first step are shown in Table 9.4. As this table shows, the functionality which

Table 9.4 Semantic differences

Consensus	$\rho(Q, C_1) = (abcde)+$ $\rho(Q, C_3) = ((abcde)+, ab(cf)+, (abcfcde)+, (ab(cf) + de)+)$
Deficit	$\delta(Q, C_1) = (ab(cf)+, (abcfcde)+, (abc(fc) + de)+)$ $\delta(Q, C_3) = \emptyset$
Excess	$\varepsilon(Q, C_1) = \emptyset$ $\varepsilon(Q, C_3) = ((abcke)+, (abcfcke)+, (abc(fc) + ke)+)$
Adaptation	$\Delta(Q, C_1) = (ab(cf)+, (abcfcde)+, (abc(fc) + de)+)$ $\Delta(Q, C_3) = ((abcke)+, (abcfcke)+, (abc(fc) + ke)+)$
Adjusting	$\Theta(Q, C_1) = (((abcde)+), (ab(cf)+, (abcfcde)+, (abc(fc) + de)+))$ $\Theta(Q, C_3) = (((abcde)+), ab(cf)+, (abcfcde)+, (ab(cf) + de)+,$ $((abcke)+, (abcfcke)+, (abc(fc) + ke)+))$

is necessary to add to or remove from g_1 to match the functionality required by the query, $\Delta(Q, C_1)$, is similar to $\Delta(Q, C_3)$. However, the common functionality between g_3 and the query, $\rho(Q, C_3)$, is greater than the functional consensus between g_1 and the query, $\rho(Q, C_1)$. Therefore, component C_3 is the closest one to the query, according to the semantic closeness.

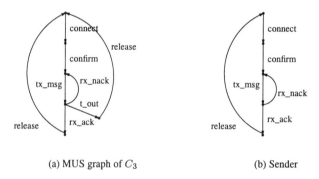

(a) MUS graph of C_3 (b) Sender

Figure 9.6   Result of adapting C_3 to obtain the sender

Adapting the Component. At this point, the user has to decide between the semantic adaptation of the component C_3 or the structural adaptation of the component C_4. As C_4 has events which do not belong to the alphabet of the query, besides the structural modifications, adapting the alphabet of events will be also necessary (semantic adaptation). Therefore, the decision seems to be clear and an experienced user will choose component C_3, which only needs to be adapted from a semantic point of view.

To adapt the functionality of C_3, it is necessary to add the functionality expressed by $\delta(g, C_3)$, and after that, to remove the extra functionality, $\varepsilon(g, C_3)$. In this case, removing the extra functionality is enough to make both functional specifications equal, and as a result we have the desired component (Figures 9.6(a) and 9.6(b)). Verification information linked to C_3 is also adapted to the new modifications — removal of evolution paths — after studying the impact of this modification in the current verification results [Díaz Redondo

(2002)].

From this new partial specification, a new component (C_9) is created and stored in the repository after finding its correct place in the lattices. Therefore, the partial orderings among the reusable components of the repository change as Table 9.5.(a) and 9.5.(b) show. This addition may be done in the background or in parallel without interfering in the requirements capture stage, so it does not affect the efficiency of the reuse environment.

Table 9.5   Views of the repository

(a) Ordered according to NE^∞ criterion   (b) Ordered according to TC^∞ criterion

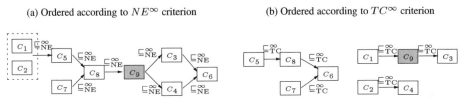

9.4.3   *Obtaining the Receiver*

As in the specification of the sender, the user starts specifying the SCTL requirements of the receiver:

$$R_1 = \text{connect} \Rightarrow\!\bigcirc (\text{confirm} \Rightarrow\!\bigcirc (\text{rx\_msg} \Rightarrow\!\bigcirc (\text{tx\_ack} \Rightarrow\!\bigcirc (\text{release} \Rightarrow\!\bigcirc R_1))))$$
$$R_2 = \text{connect} \Rightarrow\!\bigcirc (\text{confirm} \Rightarrow\!\bigcirc R_{21})$$
$$R_{21} = \text{rx\_msg} \Rightarrow\!\bigcirc (\text{tx\_nack} \Rightarrow\!\bigcirc R_{21})$$

and, after that, the functional profiles $NE^\infty(Q) = NE^\infty(R_1, R_2) = (4+, 5+, 7+, 7+)$ and $TC^\infty(Q) = TC^\infty(R_1, R_2) = ((abhie)+, ab(hj)+, (abhjhie)+, (abh(jh) + ie)+)$ are obtained to start the retrieval.[7] These profiles constitute the query of the structural and semantic retrieval respectively.

Structural Retrieval. As in Section 9.4.2, the successor, predecessor and equivalent reusable components to the query ($NE^\infty(Q)$) are retrieved from the repository. In this case, because C_9 is an NE^∞-equivalent component to the required functionality, C_9 is the result of both phases of structural retrieval.

Semantic Retrieval. After the first step of the semantic retrieval, the set $\{C_2\}$ of the predecessor components and the set $\{C_4\}$ of successor components — there is no equivalent component in the repository — are recovered from the repository, whose TC^∞ profiles are as follows:

---

[7]Real names of the events have been renamed because of legibility reasons (see Table 9.2).

$$TC^\infty(g_2) = (\ (abhie)+)$$
$$TC^\infty(g_4) = (\ (abhie)+, ab(hj)+, (abh(jh)+ie)+,$$
$$(abhjhie), (abcke)+, (abhjke)+, (ab(hj)+ke)+)$$

In the second step of the retrieval, it is necessary to obtain the functional adjusting vector as in Section 9.4.2. Therefore, in this case, we have the following values:

$$\Theta(Q, C_2) = (((abhie)+), (ab(hj)+, (abhjhie)+, (abh(jh)+ie)+))$$
$$\Theta(Q, C_4) = (((abhie)+, ab(hj)+, (abhjhie)+, (abh(jh)+ie)+),$$
$$((abke)+, (abhjke)+, (ab(hj)+ke)+))$$

Applying the same reasoning of Section 9.4.2, we conclude that C_4 is the most suitable component to satisfy the functionality required by the current query.

Adapting the Component. In this case, the user can choose between the reusable component C_9, which is NE^∞-equivalent to the one asked for, and the reusable component C_4, the closest one according to the semantic closeness criterion. As one of them is directly structurally equivalent, we assume an experienced user will choose this one. The adaptation tasks in this case are easy, because we only have to rename the events as follows:

$$rx\_msg \leftrightarrow tx\_msg \qquad tx\_ack \leftrightarrow rx\_ack \qquad tx\_nack \leftrightarrow rx\_nack$$

obtaining the model shown in Figure 9.7(a). From this new partial specification, a new component (C_{10}) is created and stored in the repository. Verification information linked to C_{10} is also adapted to the new modifications — renaming of events. After the new addition to the repository, the partial orderings among the reusable components change as Table 9.6.(a) and 9.6.(b) show.

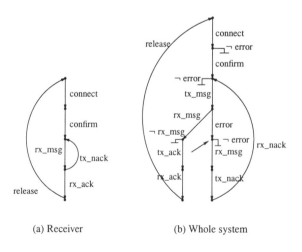

(a) Receiver   (b) Whole system

Figure 9.7   MUS graphs of the receiver process and the whole system

9.4.4 *Obtaining the Whole System*

After obtaining the synchronizer or channel, which is obtained from component C_5 and whose procedure is the same as the procedures explained before to model the sender and receiver, it is necessary to obtain the composition of these three processes, by using an over-lapping algorithm [Pazos Arias and García Duque (2001)]. Figure 9.7(b) shows the MUS model, referred to as g, obtained after this composition, to which the developer has also added, in subsequent iterations of the life cycle, the following *liveness properties* [Alpern and Schneider (1987)] to ensure the channel may make errors during the data transmission:

$$\{(\text{connect} \Rightarrow \bigcirc \neg\text{error}), \quad (\text{confirm} \Rightarrow \bigcirc \neg\text{error}),$$
$$(\text{error} \Rightarrow \bigcirc \neg\text{error}), \quad (\text{tx\_ack} \Rightarrow \neg\text{rx\_msg})\}$$

Table 9.6   Views of the repository

(a) Ordered according to NE^∞ criterion   (b) Ordered according to TC^∞ criterion

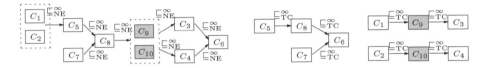

9.4.5 *Reusing Verification Information*

Once we have the MUS graph which represents the behaviour of the whole system (model g), it may be necessary to verify some properties to check the three graphs composition behaves as expected. At this intermediate stage of the requirements capture process, we assume we need to verify if the incomplete model, g, has the properties: $R_1 \equiv (\text{connect} \Rightarrow \bigcirc \text{confirm})$ and $R_2 \equiv (\text{rx\_msg} \Rightarrow \text{error})$.

Verification of R_1. Property $R_1 \equiv (\text{connect} \Rightarrow \bigcirc \text{confirm})$ expresses the following condition: *"just after a connection request occurs, an acceptance of this connection may occur"*. The main aim is that this property is verified by every possible trace of the system, that is, we are interested in this property as a *safety property* [Alpern and Schneider (1987)].

In order to retrieve any useful verification information, we retrieve from the repository (Table 9.6.(b)) those predecessor components $\{C_8, C_7\}$ and successor components $\{C_6\}$ to the given one (g). The verification information linked to them are as follows (Section 9.3.3):

$$\vDash (R_1, g_8) = \{1, 1, \tfrac{1}{2}, \tfrac{1}{2}\} \qquad \vDash (R_1, g_7) = \{1, 1, \tfrac{1}{2}, \tfrac{1}{2}\} \qquad \vDash (R_1, g_6) = \{1, 1, \tfrac{1}{2}, \tfrac{1}{2}\}$$

Besides that, we know that $\vDash (R_1, E_0|_{g_8}) = 1$ and $\vDash (R_1, E_0|_{g_7}) = 1$.[8] Starting from the information given by the predecessor components, we can deduce [Díaz Redondo *et al.*

---

[8] $\vDash (R, E_0|_g)$ denotes the level of satisfaction of R in the initial state of the MUS graph g.

(2003b)] the following levels of satisfaction of R_1 in g:

(1) As $\vDash (\exists \, \Diamond R_1, g_8) = 1$ and $\vDash (\exists \, \Diamond R_1, g_7) = 1$, therefore, $\vDash (\exists \, \Diamond R_1, g) = 1$.
(2) As $\vDash (R_1, E_0|_{g_8}) = \vDash (R_1, E_0|_{g_7}) = 1$, therefore, $\vDash (\forall \, \Diamond R_1, g) = 1$.

From the information given by the successor component, C_6, we are able to deduce that as $\vDash (\forall \, \Box R_1, g_5) = \frac{1}{2}$, therefore $\vDash (\forall \, \Box R_1, g) \leq_k 1$. Finally and as a consequence of the results obtained by applying the deduction tables, we know:

$$\vDash (R_1, g) = \{1, 1, \phi_1 \in \{\tfrac{1}{2}, \tfrac{3}{4}, 1\}, \phi_2 \in \{\tfrac{1}{2}, \tfrac{3}{4}, 1\}\}$$

To sum up, we can assure that, without running the model checking algorithm, R_1 is a *liveness property* in g [Alpern and Schneider (1987)] — this property is satisfied by every evolution path of the model — and, although it cannot be considered as a *safety property*, there is no information prohibiting that if the functional specification increases, it will became true.

Verification of R_2. Property $R_2 \equiv (\text{rx\_msg} \Rightarrow \text{error})$ expresses that "*in a state of the model where a data reception is enabled, an error must also be allowed*". This property must be satisfied by every trace of the system, because whenever a data transmission is done, an error might occur. There is one state of the model, marked by an arrow in Figure 9.7(b), where this property must not be satisfied: after an error occurs, a data reception must also occur, but in this case, an error must not be allowed, because the data frame has not been retransmitted. Therefore, we would like R_2 to be a *liveness property*, but not a *safety one*.

The retrieval of the verification information is the same as in the previous section. Therefore, we recover the predecessor components $\{C_8, C_7\}$ and the successor components $\{C_6\}$ to the given one, whose verification results are as follows:

$$\vDash (R_2, g_8) = \{1, 1, \tfrac{1}{4}, 0\} \quad \vDash (R_2, g_7) = \{1, 1, \tfrac{1}{4}, 0\} \quad \vDash (R_2, g_6) = \{1, 1, \tfrac{1}{4}, 0\}$$

Starting from the available verification information, we can deduce [Díaz Redondo *et al.* (2003b)] the following levels of satisfaction of R_2 in g:

(1) As $\vDash (\exists \, \Diamond R_2, g_8) = \vDash (\exists \, \Diamond R_2, g_7) = 1$, therefore $\vDash (\exists \, \Diamond R_2, g) = 1$.
(2) As $\vDash (\exists \, \Box R_2, g_7) = \vDash (\exists \, \Box R_2, g_8) = \frac{1}{4}$, therefore, $\vDash (\forall \, \Box R_2, g) \geq_c \frac{1}{4}$, that is, this value belongs to $\{\frac{1}{4}, \widehat{\frac{1}{2}}, 0\}$. As $\vDash (\forall \, \Box R_2, g_8) = \vDash (\forall \, \Box R_2, g_7) = 0$, therefore, $\vDash (\forall \, \Box R_2, g) = 0$.

On the other hand, the verification information linked to g_6 does not add more information. Therefore, we can obtain that $\vDash (R_2, g) = \{1, \phi_1 \in \Phi, \phi_2 \in \Phi, 0\}$, where $\Phi = \{0, \frac{1}{4}, \widehat{\frac{1}{2}}, \frac{1}{2}, \frac{3}{4}, 1\}$. According to these results, we know that R_2 it is not a *safety property* — just as we wanted — and it is satisfied at least for one of the evolution paths of g — but we need this property to be a *liveness one*, that is, it must be satisfied by every evolution path of the model. However, the information given by the deduction tables does not offer any information about $\vDash (\forall \, \Diamond R_2, g) = \phi_1 \in \Phi$, so, in this case, we would need to apply the model checking algorithm to know this result. In this kind of cases, we are working on reducing the space-state of g by reusing the verification information.

9.5 Is it Worth Reusing these Incomplete Models?

Reusing the Whole Reusable Component. Clearly, if we are able to reuse a component whose functionality is reasonably close to the required one, benefits of reuse are really high: firstly, because we are reusing at an early stage of the software process (requirements capture); and secondly, because not only current necessities are fulfilled (synthesis tasks), but also future ones may be also solved (verification tasks). Problems start if we want to quantify the benefits of software reuse. The most usual solution is quantifying the computational cost of reuse (retrieval, selection and adaptation) and comparing them with the cost of building components from scratch. We have adapted the work of [Barnes and Bollinger (1991)] to ARIFS in order to quantify the computational cost of reusing incomplete models (C_r), consequently, (1) the cost of retrieving a semantically equivalent component or (2) the cost of retrieving and adapting a component functionally close to the query:

$$C_r = B + (1 - p) \cdot (B_{approx} + q \cdot A + (1 - q) \cdot D) \qquad (9.1)$$

In this equation, B stands for the cost of retrieving a semantically equivalent component and p is the probability of finding this component; B_{approx} is the cost of retrieving a component functionally close to the required functionality and q is the probability of finding this component; A stands for the adaptation cost; and, finally, D is the cost of building the component from scratch. Unfortunately, these parameters are not easy to obtain because they not only depend on the complexity of the retrieving and adaptation algorithms and on the amount of reusable components in the repository, but also on their functional characteristics, which are more difficult to take into account. The first problem is determining the maximum functional difference which compensate reusing. It is clear that the higher this value is, the more probable finding a suitable component in the repository (q) is. The second problem is obtaining the minimum functional difference between two reusable components stored in the repository. It is also clear that the lower this value is, the more probable finding an equivalent component (p) is. In both cases, we have to come to a compromise solution between the complexity of reuse and the functional closeness among reusable components: (1) if the maximum functional difference to reuse is too high, then q is high, and so, A and C_r will be also too high; and (2) if the minimum functional differences between reusable components in the repository is too low, then p is high, and so B will be also too high because the repository could become unmanageable.

If predicting costs of reuse is not easy, estimating reusing benefits is also difficult because we must take into account factors like the possibility of reusing verification information linked to the reusable components in future iterations, so the comparison between costs and benefits is not so simple as the equation $B + (1-p) \cdot (B_{approx} + q \cdot A + (1-q) \cdot D) \leq D$ seems.

Reusing Formal Verification Knowledge. Assessing the benefits of reuse verification results in this environment shares the problems above. In this case, the computational cost of reusing verification efforts (C_{vr}) consists of (1) the cost of retrieving and deducing the verification results we exactly need and (2) the cost of retrieving and deducing a sub-set of the verification results we need:

$$C_{vr} = V_r + (1 - p) \cdot (D_f \cdot C_m) \tag{9.2}$$

In this equation, V_r stands for the cost of retrieving and deducing the verification results we exactly need, that is, in this case, we do not need to run the model checking algorithm and p is the probability of finding this information in the repository; D_f is the percentage of functional differences between the recovered reusable components and the given one which force us to verify the property in a sub-set of the state space of the current model and, finally, C_m is the cost of verifying the incomplete model (MUS graph) from scratch by using the model checking algorithm.

Because of the same reasons given above, these parameters are not easy to obtain. Obtaining the most adequate minimum functional difference between two reusable components and between two different properties linked to one reusable component is essential. It is clear that the lower these values are, the more probable finding the verification information we need (p) is. However, and like the previous situation, we have to come to a compromise solution to avoid an unmanageable repository because of the massive amount of information stored in it.

Estimating reusing benefits is also difficult because we must take into account factors like the possibility of reusing other verification results in subsequent iterations of the requirements capture process, so the comparison between costs and benefits is not so simple as the equation $C_r = V_r + (1 - p) \cdot (D_f \cdot C_m) \leq C_m$ seems.

9.6   Related Work

Organizing large collections of reusable components is one of the main issues in software reuse, because providing efficient and effective mechanisms to classify and retrieve software elements from a repository is not an easy problem. Retrieving mechanisms usually rely on establishing a *profile* or a set of component's characterizing attributes which is used to classify and retrieve them from a repository. Whenever this profile is based on formal specifications, problems derived from natural language are avoided. The typical *specification matching* process starts expressing the relation between two components by using a logical formula. Then, a theorem prover checks its validity, and only if the prover succeeds, is the component considered to be suitable. The vast number of proof tasks makes a practical implementation very hard, so in many of the following approaches this number is usually reduced by applying other techniques.

In [Zaremski and Wing (1997)] the retrieval process of code components is based on the Larch/ML specification language for component description and the associated interactive Larch prover for retrieval. Formal proofs are restricted to a small subset of the repository, which is previously selected by using preconditions and postconditions.

REBOUND (RE*use* B*ased* O*n* UND*erstanding*) tool [Penix and Alexander (1996)] is also based in Larch language, although specification matching is based on the HOL prover, this prover being almost automated. In order to reduce formal proofs, different heuristics, based on the semantics of specifications, are applied. In this first step, a dynamic classification of all the reusable components around the query is needed, which reduces the efficiency of the retrieval scheme.

In [Cheng and Jeng (1997)] a two-tiered hierarchy of the repository based on formal specifications using OSPL is proposed. The lower level is based on generality relationships; and the higher one on similarity relationships, which are assessed by a clustering algorithm. Firstly, the most suitable cluster is selected, and secondly, a theorem prover is used to finish the search; besides this, LOTOS [Chen and Cheng (1997)] is used as a supplement to the functional descriptions in order to take into account the architectural properties of components.

NORA/NAMMR tool [Schumann and Fischer (1997)] is basically a *filter pipeline* trying to ensure a *plug-in compatibility*. It uses *signature matching filters*, *rejection filters* (based on model checking techniques), and, finally, *confirmation filters* (based on Setheo theorem prover). One of its main problems is managing recursive specifications which is not supported by Setheo.

On the other hand, model checking is inherently vulnerable to the rather practical problem that the number of states may exceed the amount of computer memory available, which is known as the *state-space explosion problem*. Several effective methods have been developed to solve this problem, although the majority of them try to reduce the state-space: (a) by a symbolic representation of state spaces using BBDs (*Binary Decision Diagrams*) [Bryant (1986)]; (b) by partial-order reductions [Kurshan *et al.* (1998)] which exploits the fact that for checking many properties it is not necessary to consider all possible ways in which a state space can be traversed; (c) by using equivalence and pre-order relations [MacMillan (1995)], which transform models into equivalent, but smaller models that satisfy the same properties; and (d) by a compositional verification, that is, decomposing properties in sub-properties such that each sub-property can be checked for a part of the state space, and the combination of the sub-properties implies the required global property. Other techniques focus on efficient memory management strategies which try to optimize the use of main memory by using hashing [Holzmann (1988)], caching techniques [Holzmann (1985)], and so forth.

To sum up, current research lines focus on reusing components at later stages of the development process, like code, and on using formal descriptions to allow an exact retrieval by applying formal proofs. BY contrast, we propose reusing formal components at early stages, like requirements specification components, and avoiding formal proofs in the retrieval process, that is, providing an approximate retrieval based precisely on the incompleteness of the intermediate models. On the other hand, reusing formal verification efforts also supplements the previous techniques to reduce the great computational costs of model checking. The underlying idea is reusing formal verification results of the same property in other *functionally similar* incomplete models to the given one. The main difference with other approaches [Keidar *et al.* (2000)] is that although reusing verification results is also proposed, they focus on reusing less formalized proofs (simulation proofs) over code components (algorithms).

9.7   Summary and Future Work

The ARIFS methodology enables reusing formal and incomplete requirements specifications and the formal verification results linked to them. Reusing at such a early stage of the software development process allows increasing the reuse benefits, although the complexity is bigger than in the reuse of low level software components, like code ones. In this chapter we show how to apply this methodology to a case study whose main goal is obtaining all the components involved in a communication protocol.

The proposed classification mechanism is based on four different partial orderings among incomplete specifications. The approximate retrieval process, where formal proofs are avoided, is made in two steps. The first phase takes advantage of the static classification to recover a small set of potentially suitable reusable components. In the second phase, different metrics are used to predict structural adaptation efforts, and several semantic refinement functions are used to predict semantic adaptation efforts. By using these adaptation measures, selecting the closest reusable component to the functionality expressed by the query is possible. We have also identified what verification information can be reused and, consequently, how to reduce formal verification tasks.

In order to continue the reuse of formal verification knowledge, we are working on: (a) a *compositional verification*, that is, decomposing properties in sub-properties such that it is possible to reuse verification information about each sub-property, and the combination of the sub-properties implies the required global property; (b) how to reduce the space-state of the current model by reusing verification information of reusable components close to it according to TC^∞ criterion; and (c) the possibility of reusing verification results of *functionally similar* properties to the given one.

On the other hand, in order to continue the reuse of the whole requirement components, we are working on: (a) the selection phase to unify the way the adaptation efforts of reusable components structurally close to the query and those semantically close to the query are provided to the user; and (b) the ARIFS methodology is currently being implemented in a prototype tool (ARIFS tool) in order to provide a suitable environment which allows developers to reuse in a friendly framework. We also expect to quantify the parameters of Equations (9.1) and (9.2) by the heuristics provided by the tool.

References

Alpern, B. and Schneider, F. B. (1987). Recognizing Safety and Liveness, *Distributed Computing Journal* **2**, pp. 117–126.

Barnes, B. H. and Bollinger, T. B. (1991). Making Reuse Cost-effective, *IEEE Software*, **8**, 1, pp. 13–24.

Bryant, R. (1986). Graph-based Algorithms for Boolean Function Manipulation. *IEEE Transactions on Computers*, **35**, 8, pp. 677–691.

Chen, Y. and Cheng, B. H. C. (1997). Formally Specifying and Analyzing Architectural and Functional Properties of Components for Reuse, In *WISR 8: 8th Workshop on Institutionalizing Software Reuse*.

Cheng, B. H. C. and Jeng, J. J (1997). Reusing Analogous Components, *IEEE Trans. on Knowledge and Data Engineering*, **9**, 2.

Díaz Redondo, R. P. (2002). Reutilización de Requisitos Funcionales de Sistemas Distribuidos utilizando Técnicas de Descripción Formal, PhD Thesis, Departamento de Enxeñería Telemática–Universidade de Vigo.

Díaz Redondo, R. P. and Pazos Arias, J. J. (2001). Reuse of Verification Efforts and Incomplete Specifications in a Formalized, Iterative and Incremental Software Process. In *Proceedings of International Conference on Software Engineering (ICSE) Doctoral Symposium*, Toronto, Canada.

Díaz Redondo, R. P., Pazos Arias, J. J., Fernández Vilas, A. and Barragáns Martínez, B. (2002a). Approximate Retrieval of Incomplete and Formal Specifications applied to Vertical Reuse, In *Proc. of International Conference on Software Maintenance (ICSM)*, Montreal, Canada. IEEE Computer Society Press.

Díaz Redondo, R. P., Pazos Arias, J. J., Fernández Vilas, A. and Barragáns Martínez, B. (2002b). AR-IFS: an Environment for Incomplete and Formal Specifications Reuse, In *Proc. of Workshop on Formal Methods and Component Interaction.*, volume 66 of *Electronic Notes in Theorethical Computer Science*. Elsevier Science.

Díaz Redondo, R. P., Pazos Arias, J. J., Fernández Vilas, A. and Barragáns Martínez, B. (2003a). Approximate Retrieval of Incomplete and Formal Specifications applied to Horizontal Reuse, In *Proc. of the 28th EUROMICRO Conf. Component-based Software Engineering*, Dortmund, Germany. IEEE Computer Society Press.

Díaz Redondo, R. P., Pazos Arias, J. J. and Fernández Vilas, A. (2003b). Reuse of Formal Verification Efforts of Incomplete Models at the Requirements Specification Stage. In *Component-Based Software Quality: Methods and Techniques*, volume 2693 of *Lecture Notes in Computer Science* . Springer Verlag. (To appear).

Holzmann, G. J. (1985). Tracing Protocols, *ATT Technical Journal*, **64**, 12, pp. 2413–2434.

Holzmann, G. J. (1988). An Improved Protocol Reachability Analysis Technique, *Software-Practice and Experience*, **18**, 2, pp. 137–161.

Jilani, L. L. (1997). Retrieving Software Components that Minimize Adaptation Effort, In *Proceedings of 12th Automated Software Engineering Conference (ASE)*, pp. 255–262.

Keidar, I., Khazan, R., Lynch, N. and Shvartsman, A. (2000). An Inheritance-Based Technique for Building Simulation Proofs Incrementally, In *22nd International Conference on Software Engineering (ICSE)*, pp. 478–487, Limerick, Ireland.

Kurshan, R., Levin, V., Minea, M., Peled, D. and Yenigün, H. (1998). Static Partial Order Reduction, *Tools for the Construction and Analysis of Systems, Lecture Notes in Computer Science (LNCS)* **1394**, pp. 345–357.

Lam, W., McDermid, J. A. and Vickers, A. J. (1997). Ten Steps Towards Systematic Requirements Reuse, *Requirements Engineering*, **2**, pp. 102–113, Springer Verlag.

McMillan, K. L. (1995). A Technique of State Space Search based on Unfolding, *Formal Methods in System Design*, **6**, pp. 45–65.

Pazos Arias, J. J. and García Duque, J. (2001). SCTL-MUS: A Formal Methodology for Software Development of Distributed Systems. A Case Study, *Formal Aspects of Computing*, **13**, pp. 50–91.

Penix, J. and Alexander, P. (1996).Efficient Specification-Based Component Retrieval, *Automated Software Engineering: An International Journal*, **6**, 2, pp. 139–170.

Schumann, J. and Fischer, B. (1997). NORA/HAMMR: Making Deduction-Based Software Component Retrieval Practical, In M. Lowry and Y. Ledru, editors, *Proceedings of the 12th International Conference Automated Software Engineering (ASE)*, pp. 246–254. IEEE Computer Society Press.

Tanenbaum, A. S. (1997). *Redes de Ordenadores*. Prentice Hall.

van Glabeek, R. J. (2001). *Handbook of Process Algebra*, chapter The Linear Time - Branching Time Spectrum I: The Semantics of Concrete, Sequential Processes. Elsevier Science.

Zaremski, A. M. and Wing, J. M. (1997). Specification Matching of Software Components, *ACM Transactions on Software Engineering and Methodology*, **6**, 4, pp. 333–369.

Chapter 10

REBOUND: A Framework for Automated Component Adaptation

JOHN PENIX

NASA Ames Research Center, Moffet Field, CA 94035, USA

john.penix@nasa.gov

PERRY ALEXANDER

The University of Kansas / ITTC, Lawrence, KS 66045, USA

alex@ittc.ukans.edu

Abstract. REBOUND is a general framework for automating adaptation-based component reuse. The framework guides the selection of adaptation tactics based on the components available for reuse. Adaptation tactics are specified formally in terms of the relationship between the component to be adapted and the resulting adapted component. The tactic specifications are used to generate matching conditions for specification-based component retrieval, creating a "retrieval for adaptation" scenario. We use several examples to illustrate how the framework guides component and tactic selection and how basic tactics are composed to form more powerful tactics.

10.1 Introduction

One of the promises of component-based software is the idea that components will be pre-packaged to be pulled off the shelf as needed. However, it is well known that there are many hidden costs in software reuse and that components very often must be adapted to be used. The need for adaptation in reuse is evident in the wide spread programming language support of data-type generalization and parameterization. These methods take a specialization approach to reuse, where a component is designed abstractly and specialized at reuse time (either statically or dynamically). While these specialization techniques have permitted the development of reusable code, they focus on implementation level artifacts. Therefore, these techniques cannot avoid the limitations of concrete component reuse as described by Biggerstaff [Biggerstaff, 1994]: the reuse of small generic components does not provide enough functionality to impact the cost of a system, while the specialization required to construct a large component or framework limits its applicability. This causes a library scalability problem, where the size of the library must grow combinatorially as

235

additional features are supported [Biggerstaff, 1994].

Solving the library scalability problem requires moving from the specialization model of reuse to a generational or compositional model of reuse [Biggerstaff, 1994; Batory et al., 1994; Kiczales et al., 1997]. In this model, a library of *factors* or *aspects* that are combined together to result in a component to be used. Current technology primarily supports a layers of abstraction (LOA) approach to this solution, where factors are implemented as functions and composition is done using run-time function calls [Batory et al., 1994].

There are similar scalability issues at play when considering component integration at the architecture level. Specifically, the function of a component becomes just one factor of the component that should be independent of the style in which the component interacts. Maintaining a separate component that performs the same function for each style is not a practical approach. Therefore, the function and interface aspects of a component should be factored and then composed at reuse time to generate a component with the correct function and interface combination.

In the context of architecture description languages, module or component boundaries are not necessarily artificial, but may correspond to physical boundaries in the system. In dynamic architectures [Oreizy et al., 1998], component interactions are not known until run-time, removing the possibility of static optimization even between homogeneous localized components. It follows that an LOA-optimization approach to combining subcomponents into a larger system is inappropriate in the context of software components.

Factored reuse at the architecture level requires a solution to component composition that does not require integration of implementation level artifacts. The potential loss in efficiency is offset by the fact that architecture level compositions can be more powerful than those available from an LOA approach. The power of architecture-level abstractions can be seen in the proliferation of architectural styles, design patterns and industrial component models. Therefore, providing automated tool support for component-based software engineering requires a more general model of software adaptation and integration.

This chapter describes REBOUND (REuse Based On UNDerstanding), a framework for automated component adaptation. The REBOUND adaptation framework organizes a collection of (domain specific) adaptation tactics in a way that they can be selected based on the components available for adaptation. This is done by 1) classifying components based on their relationship to a problem specification and 2) specifying tactics based on the relationship between the component they are applied to and the component they result in.

To support architectural level abstractions, a component adaptation framework must be based on a sufficiently general model of adaptation. We distinguish between several kinds of adaptation:

(1) Type Adaptation — specialization of an abstract type or behavioral type substitution.
(2) Interface Adaptation — alters the interaction style of the component.
(3) Behavior Adaptation — changes the function of the component either by composing it with other components or replacing a subcomponent.

It is possible that a component may require a combination of these three kinds of adaptation.

This is supported by composing tactics of each kind together to make more powerful tactics.

Adaptation tactics are described in terms of formal relationships between the component to be adapted and the resulting adapted component. To retrieve *adaptable* components, the matching conditions for retrieval must state the relationship between the problem specification and the components that can be adapted to solve the problem. This is precisely the relationship that the adaptation tactics describe: the retrieved component is the component to be adapted and the problem is the resulting adapted component. Therefore, the adaptation tactic specifications are used as the matching conditions for retrieval, resulting in a "retrieval for adaptation" scenario.

The framework relies on a generalized notion of a specification-based retrieval interface to a component library. The retrieval system must simply take a collection of matching conditions and when queried, the returns a *set* of matching components for *each* match. This differs from standard specification-based retrieval interfaces where only one relationship is searched for at a time [Jeng and Cheng, 1995; Mili et al., 1997; Schumann and Fischer, 1997; Zaremski and Wing, 1997]. In addition, the interface does not need to be completely automated and formal; it can be interactive [Fischer, 2000] or combined with informal classification schemes [Penix and Alexander, 1999].

The goal of the adaptation framework is to find or construct a solution based on existing library components. This search is over the space of all possible designs that can be constructed from the components and tactics in the library. The exploration of the search space must be limited due to the potentially large number of tactic and component combinations. The framework incorporates heuristics that guide the search to avoid designs that are incorrect or require components not in the library.

To automate component adaptation, there must be heuristics for selecting adaptation tactics based on the available components and architectures. Associating various tactics with the match hierarchy provides the necessary link between specification matching and component adaptation to provide this control mechanism. The tactics are arranged based on the generality hierarchy (lattice) of their architecture specifications. Component retrieval associates components with applicable adaptation tactics. If further expanded, the hierarchy could be used to incrementally classify components [Smith, 1996] and determine the best tactic to adapt a component.

The adaptation tactics themselves are acquired via domain analysis [Prieto-Díaz and Arango, 1991]. A domain will have a collection of standard data types, component interfaces and problem decomposition strategies. These can be used to determine appropriate type, interface and behavioral adaptation tactics, respectively. This is similar to the role that architectural styles play in constructing software architectures [Abowd et al., 1995; Moriconi et al., 1995; Shaw, 1995]. However, it should be possible for the same problem decomposition strategies to be implemented using different implementation styles.

10.2   Architecture Specifications

To use software architectures models to facilitate a general framework for component adaptation, the architectures must be represented in a way that abstracts away implementation concerns while capturing the relationships between system level and component level behaviors. Existing formal models of software architecture [Allen and Garlan, 1997; Dingel et al., 1998; Gerkin, 1995; Moriconi et al., 1995; Shaw and Garlan, 1996] are mainly concerned with formalizing specific architectural styles such as pipe-filter and client-server. While architectural styles abstract away some implementation details, each still represents a highly *reduced* subset of the space of possible system designs. The fact that the space is reduced indicates that the choice of an architectural style is an important design decision that should not be made prior to adaptation.

With this in mind, we have extended Smith and Lowry's methods for specifying the structure of algorithms [Smith, 1990; Smith and Lowry, 1990] to specify the structure of architectures [Penix et al., 1997]. An *architecture specification* constrains the behavior of a system in terms of the behavior of its subcomponents via a collection of axioms. The axiomatic constraints can be used to reason in both a top-down and a bottom-up manner. Given a system specification, an architecture specification, and a subset of the components in the architecture, we can determine the functionality required in the missing components. Conversely, given a collection of components and an architecture specification, we can determine the functionality of the system constructed by plugging the components into the architecture.

A limitation of our initial work in this area was that the specification of architecture constraints was monolithic. We have extended the approach to enable architecture specifications to be constructed from parts. One benefit of using a algebraic theory-based specification notation is that large specifications can be built up from smaller specifications using extension and parameterization [Burstall and Goguen, 1977; Jüllig and Srinivas, 1993]. Specifically, we use the ability of specifications (components) to be parameters to other specifications (architectures). This allows us to define specifications for various kinds of connectors and bindings and then to combine them to create an architecture specification.

10.2.1   *Component Specifications*

Components are computational elements that provide functionality in an architecture. We use a simple component model, shown in Figure 10.1, where a Component has a Domain, Range, Input Condition and Output Relation. The Input Condition is a precondition that defined legal inputs in the Domain. Similarly, the Output Condition is a postcondition relation that defines feasible outputs for given inputs. More complex component models might support multiple functions per component, representation of component state or explicit concurrency constraints. The method of structuring specifications is independent of the specific component specification model used, or any component models used in the imple-

```
spec Component
 types D,R;
 def
  I: D → Bool;
  O: D,R → Bool;
spec DFConnector[ A:Component, B:Component]
 def
  A.R = B.D;
 axioms ∀ x,w
  A.I(x) ∧ A.O(x,w) ⇒ B.I(w);
spec BufferedConnector[ A:Component, B:Component]
 def
  A.R = Seq[B.D];
 axioms ∀ x,w
  A.I(x) ∧ A.O(x,w) ∧ z ∈ w ⇒ B.I(x);
spec InputBinding[ S:Component, A:Component]
 def
  S.D = A.D;
 axioms ∀ x:S.D
  S.I(x) ⇒ A.I(x);
spec GenericArchDF[ A:Component,B:Component,C:Component]: Component
 axioms
  DFConnector[A,B];
  DFConnector[B,C];
  InputBinding[this,A];
  ∀ w,x,y,z
  I(w) ∧ A.O(w,x) ∧ B.O(x,y) ∧ C.O(y,z) ⇒ O(w,z);
```

Fig. 10.1   Specification of a generic data flow architecture with supporting specifications

mentation technology. Therefore, this simple component model is sufficient to define and explore the adaptation framework.

10.2.2   *Connector Specifications*

A connection associates an output of one component with an input of another component. In general, the goal is to specify that the combined behavior of two components is always defined, i.e., every valid output at the source is a legal input at the destination. The specifics of this relationship depend upon the way that the components are connected.

For example, we can define a Data Flow connector as a connector relates the output of one component directly to the input of another component. The verification condition for this type of connection is:

$$\forall x, w \; I_A(x) \wedge O_A(x,w) \Rightarrow I_B(w)$$

If this condition is true, then given a legal input to A, all valid outputs of A are legal inputs to B. We use this condition to create a generic data flow connection specification. The specification is parameterized on the interface specifications of the two components being connected.

Another example connector is the buffered connector shown in Figure 10.1. This specification describes a connection where the output of the source component is a sequence of elements of the input type of the destination. Details of how the buffering is implemented are abstracted away.

10.2.3 *Interface Binding*

To view a collection of interconnected components as the architecture, it is associated with a component specification which acts as a *system interface* . This is done by mapping (or binding) the inputs and outputs of the system interface to inputs and outputs of the subcomponent interfaces. In every case, we must assure that legal inputs to the system will be legal inputs to the system components. The simplest case is when all of the system inputs are connected to all of the inputs of a single component. This is captured by the axiom:

$$\forall x\ S.I(x) \Rightarrow C.I(x)$$

where $S.I$ and $C.I$ are the input condition of the system level component and the subcomponent, respectively.

10.2.4 *Architecture Specification*

architecture specifications are constructed by combining and extending component, connector and binding specifications. For example, Figure 10.2 shows a block diagram of an architecture for a component which Finds a record in a list problem.

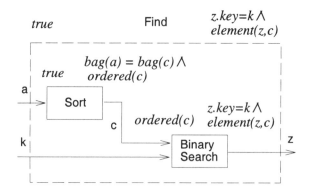

Fig. 10.2   Example Find Architecture

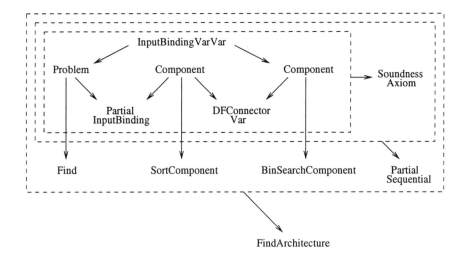

Fig. 10.3   Specification Diagram for Find Architecture

This architecture is represented by the specification diagram [Jüllig and Srinivas, 1993] in Figure 10.3. In the diagram, names represent specifications and arrows indicate conservative extensions of specifications. Extensions are use to indicate both parameterization (a specification is an extension of its parameters) and parameter instantiation (a parameter is instantiated by extending its definition with a compatible specification). When possible, we use generic names to indicate parameters (such as Component) and specific names to indicate parameter instances.

In this example, there are input bindings between a component specification and the problem specification for each of the input variables. The two components are connected by a data flow connector from the output of the first component to an input variable of the second component. The soundness axiom states the condition that must be true for the component behavior to properly implement the system level behavior. In this case, the soundness axiom has the form:

$$I(\langle a, k \rangle) \wedge O_A(a, c) \wedge O_B(\langle c, k \rangle, z)) \Rightarrow O(\langle a, k \rangle, z)$$

where I and O are the system level specification and O_A and O_B are the postconditions of the two components. The generic problem and component specifications, together with the soundness axiom, represent the generic architecture specification, labeled Partial Sequential in the diagram. By plugging in the Find problem specification and the Sort and BinSearch component specifications, the specialized Find Architecture is created.

10.3 Adaptation Tactics

We make the distinction between three types of component adaptation: type, interface and behavior. This distinction is important because each is specified differently. The effects of adaptation tactics are specified in terms of formal relationships between the component to be adapted and the resulting adapted component. It is possible that a component may require any combination of these three kinds of adaptations. This is supported by composing tactic specifications to make more powerful tactics.

In most cases, the structure of the tactics is specified as *wrappers*, an architecture containing one component. The component being wrapped corresponds to the component being adapted and the system level description corresponds to the result of adaptation. Behavior adaptation requires the use of more general architecture specifications and additional heuristic information. Tactic composition is supported using specification composition.

10.3.1 *Type Adaptation*

Type adaptation occurs when an abstract or generic type is specialized. This kind of adaptation can normally be identified and carried out by signature matching tools [Zaremski and Wing, 1995]. It must be considered separately here, because of the potential to combine type adaptation with other kinds of adaptation.

Specifically, because of the ability to adapt interfaces, components may be retrieved that do not match the signature of the problem. In addition, the ability to compose components during adaptation requires supporting partial interface matches. Therefore, type adaptation must be combined with the other kinds of adaptation so that the interface has the correct structure and types.

A type adaptation is specified using a specification morphism. For example, a Sort component in a library would likely be defined in terms of a generic list element type (E). To adapt Sort for use in a system that sorts lists of records, Rec must be substituted for E. The Sort specification is extended using a specification morphism corresponding to the proper substitution:

$$\text{SortComponent} \xrightarrow{E \mapsto Rec} \text{RecSortComponent}$$

10.3.2 *Interface Adaptation*

Interface adaptation determines how a reusable component is bound to a problem specification. Interface adaptations range from simple type conversions to *wrappers* that encapsulate sophisticated control structures. A wrapper is an architecture that contains one component. By altering a component's interface, it changes the way that it interacts with its environment.

```
TypeConvWrapper[S:Component, C:Component, f,g]
introduces
   f : S.D → C.D
   g : C.R → S.R
asserts ∀ x:D, z:Rc
   S.I(x) ⇒ C.I(f(x));
   S.I(x) ∧ C.O(f(x),z) ⇒ S.O(x,g(z))
```

Fig. 10.4   Type Conversion Wrapper

10.3.2.1   *Type Conversion*

One kind of interface adaptation is type conversion [Purtilo and Atlee, 1991]. This differs from type adaptation in that the source and destination type are not (necessarily) related by the type hierarchy. Instead, a type conversion operator is used to convert between the two types. The Type Conversion Wrapper specification, shown in Figure 10.4, defines type conversion operators between the domains ($f : S.D \rightarrow C.D$) and ranges ($g : C.R \rightarrow S.R$) of the problem and component. There are several special cases to consider, such as when the domains (or ranges) are equivalent and the further possibility that f (or g) simplifies to the identity function. The combinations of these conditions form a generality lattice of specifications, show in Figure 10.5. The bottom of the lattice is the generic Type Conversion Wrapper. At the top of the lattice is the case where the types are not changed.

To support adaptation, additional matching conditions for component retrieval can be generated by extending the Type Conversion Wrapper specification with domain specific type conversion operators defined during domain analysis. For example, the JPEG image compression standard [Wallace, 1992] specifies a multi-stage architecture for image compression. The actual core compression algorithm in JPEG operates on 8x8 grids of pixels; However, images are usually stored as a single grid corresponding to the size of the image. The conversion of the input data to grids can be specified as type conversion. A domain theory excerpt for JPEG, shown in Figure 10.6, defines types for pictures and grids and a conversion operator between them (picToGrid). Based on the domain theory definitions, the Type Conversion Wrapper can be extended with specification for the picToGrid type conversion operator substituted for f. The axioms of the extended specification correspond to the following specification matching condition that can be used to retrieve adaptable components which operate on grids:

$$P.I(x) \Rightarrow C.I(picToGrid(x)) \land (P.I(x) \land C.O(picToGrid(x), z) \Rightarrow P.O(x, z))$$

Because the extended specification carries the formal definition of picToGrid from the domain theory, a component that matches the JPEG problem specification under this condition can be correctly adapted. Figure 10.7 shows how such a component, JpegXform, can be adapted by plugging it into the specialized type conversion wrapper to create Jpeg Compress Arch.

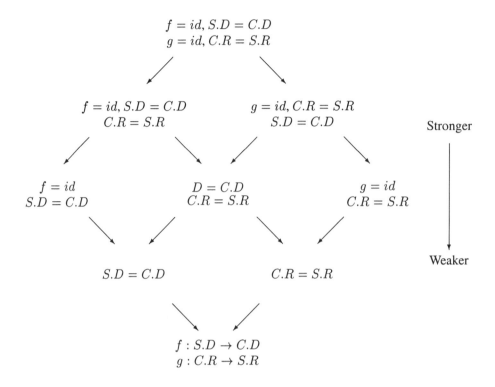

Fig. 10.5   Lattice of Type Conversion Interface Adaptations

10.3.2.2   *Generalized Wrapper Specifications*

The concept of the type conversion wrapper can be generalized to specify more powerful wrappers. If fact, any architecture specification that has all but one component instantiated can be considered a wrapper specification. However, for the purposes of component adaptation, it is important to stick to simple, intuitive tactics to: 1) increase their potential to be reused and 2) simplify the process of selecting and specifying wrappers during domain analysis.

For example, the Map Flatten Wrapper, shown in Figure 10.8, takes a component that outputs a sequence and applies it to every element of an input sequence. The results are "flattened" into one sequence. Every element in the input sequence must satisfy the precondition of the component being wrapped. For every input, a valid component output is a subsequence of the system output, in the appropriate position. For example, the JpegXform component, from the previous example, can be built using the Map Flatten Wrapper from a core algorithm component (JpegCore) that compresses a single grid. The application of the wrapper is show in the specification diagram in Figure 10.9.

```
JpegDomain : spec
 includes
  Sequence(Pixel,Pic),
  Sequence(Grid,GridSeq)
  String(BitCode,HuffStream)
introduces
  subgrid : Pic, Int → Grid
  NumGrids : → Int
  picToGrids : Pic → GridSeq
  __[__,__] : Pic,Int,Int → Pixel
  Xsize : → Int
  jpegCore : Grid, Grid, Int → HuffStream
  dctCoef: → Grid
  quantizer: → Int
asserts
  ∀ i,j,q:Int, p: Pic, g_in,g_cnst: Grid,
    rs:RunlenStream, rp:RunlenPair

  p[i,j] = p[(i * Xsize) + j];

  %% picToGrid definition
  (i < NumGrids) ⇒ ( picToGrids(p)[i]  = (subgrid(p,i)));

  %% g_in is input, g_cnst is fdct constant, q is quantify constant
  jpegCore(g_in,g_cnst,q) ==
    huffmanEncode(runlengthEncode(zigzag(quantize(
                                  FDCT(g_in,g_cnst),q)))));
```

Fig. 10.6   JPEG Domain Theory excerpt

$$\text{Component Parameter} \longrightarrow \text{PicToGridWrapper} \overset{f \mapsto picToGrid}{\longleftarrow} \text{TypeConvWrapper}$$
$$\downarrow \qquad\qquad\qquad \downarrow$$
$$\text{JpegXform} \qquad \longrightarrow \text{JpegCompressArch}$$

Fig. 10.7   Example Type Conversion

```
MapFlattenWrapper[C:Component]: Component
 def
   D = Seq[C.D];
   R = C.R;
   Rl = Seq[R];
 axioms ∀ x:D, z:R, xx:C.D, zz:Rl, n:Int
 I(x) == xx ∈ pre ⇒ C.I(xx);
 O(x,z) == ∃ zz C.O(x[n],zz[n]) ∧ z = flatten(zz);
```

Fig. 10.8   Map Flatten Wrapper

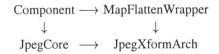

Fig. 10.9   Adaptation Using Map Flatten Wrapper

10.3.3 *Behavior Adaptation*

Behavioral adaptation tactics are applied in a incremental and constructive manner, using the architectural constraints as a guide while selecting components to plug in [Penix and Alexander, 1997]. Maintaining the validity of the constraints with each component selection, guarantees a correctly instantiated system.

In this section we describe some example architectures that can be used for behavior adaptation. The examples used are several general composition tactics that have instances in most domains. These examples are intended to be representative and not comprehensive.

- Sequential Composition — The output of one component is the input of another component. Instances of sequential composition include batch sequential architectures, pipe-filter or pipelined architectures, function composition, client-server architectures and feedback.
- Parallel Composition — Components work on independently and their results are put together to create the total result. Implementations of parallel composition are usually based on high-level abstractions of shared memory, such as black board and distributed agent architectures.
- Alternate Composition — One component is selected (possibly non-deterministically) from a set of components. This differs from parallel composition in that multiple components effect the same output. Examples of alternate composition include some black board architectures, adaptive system architectures [Hayes-Roth et al., 1995] and open implementation architectures [Kiczales, 1996].

Specifications for these architectures are show in Figure 10.10.[1]

The choice of specific architectures to use for adaptation should be driven by common problem decomposition tactics (i.e. design patterns) from the application domain. For example, sequential composition of filters is a common way to break up a digital signal processing system.

10.3.4 *Tactic Composition*

The basic adaptation tactics can be composed to form more complex tactics. This is performed by composing the architecture specification for the tactics to create a new tactic

---

[1]For parallel composition, the tuple notation $\langle P, Q \rangle$, where $P : X \rightarrow Bool$ and $Q : Y \rightarrow Bool$, indicates a new predicate over $X \times Y$ such that: $\langle P, Q \rangle (\langle x, y \rangle) \Leftrightarrow P(x) \wedge Q(y)$. Similarly for binary predicates: $\langle P, Q \rangle (\langle x, y \rangle, z) \Leftrightarrow P(x, z) \wedge Q(y, z)$.

```
SequentialComp[A:Component, B:Component] : Component
 axioms
  DFConnector[A,B];
  InputBindingTotal[this,A];
  ∀ x:D, y:A.R, z:R
  I(x) ∧ A.O(x,y) ∧ B.O(y,z) ⇒ O(x,z)


ParallelComp[A:Component, B:Component] : Component
introduces
  f : D → ⟨ A.D,B.D ⟩    %data decomposition operator
  g : ⟨ A.R,B.R ⟩ → R    %data composition operator
implies
  ∀ x:D, z:R
  I(x) ⇒ ⟨ A.I,B.I ⟩ (f(x))
  I(x) ∧ ⟨ A.O,B.O ⟩ (f(x),z) ⇒ O(x,g(z))


AlternateComp[A:Component, B:Component] : Component
axioms
  ∀ x:D, z:R
  I(x) ⇒ A.I(x) ∨ B.I(x)
  I(x) ∧ ((A.I ∧ A.O(x,y)) ∨ (B.I ∧ B.O(x,z))) ⇒ O(x,z)
```

Fig. 10.10   Example architectures for behavioral adaptation

with the properties of the originals. For example, in the JPEG example, the two interface adaptation tactics can be combined by plugging the component that results from the application of the Map Flatten Wrapper into the specialized type conversion wrapper PicToGrid Wrapper. This new tactic produces a component that satisfies the Jpeg Compress problem specification from the Jpeg Core component. The construction of this composite tactic is shown in Figure 10.11.

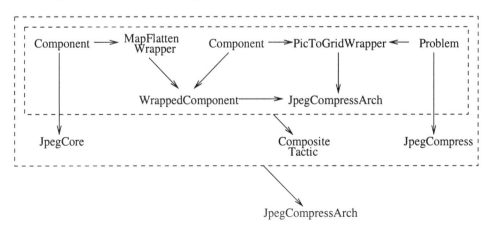

Fig. 10.11   Example Composite Tactic

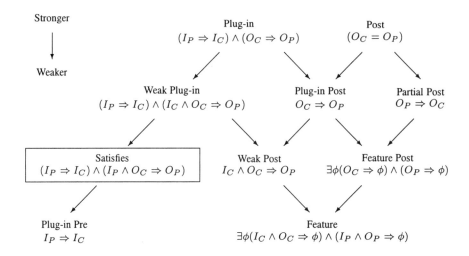

Fig. 10.12   Lattice of Specification Matches Used for Behavior Adaptation

10.3.5   *Tactic Selection*

Given this framework for specifying and combining tactics via architecture specifications, we now need a way to select architecture to adapt component. This is accomplished by associating a composition architecture and a heuristic for instantiating the architecture with the various ways that a component could match a problem specification. The partial lattice of specification matches used to guide behavior adaptation is shown in Figure 10.12.[2] The highlighted Satisfies match indicates a component that can be reused to solve a problem. The goal of behavior adaptation is to alter the behavior of a component so that it matches under a condition at least as strong as Satisfies. Therefore, an architecture should be associated with a matching condition if it can take a component with the respective match and adapt its behavior so that it matches under Satisfies.

Table 10.1 shows which matches each architectures is associated with and the instantiation rule for the match. Justification of the rules can be see by attempting to apply the architectures in the different situations [Penix, 1998]. For example, if a component matches under Plug-in Pre, it does not help to combine it with another component using the parallel or alternate architectures; the "missing" component is identical to the original problem. However, putting the component in the first position of a sequential architecture allows the derivation of a missing component specification that accepts the valid outputs of the first component and produced valid problem outputs.

---

[2] This partial lattice is extended from the one described in our previous work [Penix et al., 1997; Penix and Alexander, 1999] by including feature match relationships.

Table 10.1 Adaptation Architectures Associated with Matching Conditions

Architecture	Match	Instantiation Rule
Sequential	Plug-in Post Weak Post Feature Post	Plug component into second position and derive specification for component to satisfy missing precondition
	Plug-in Pre	Plug component into first position and derive specification for component to satisfy missing precondition
Parallel	Feature	Combine components with features that total to problem features
Alternate	Weak Post	Derive specification for component to handle missing cases
	Feature	Combine components with features that total to problem features

10.4 Case Study: KWIC

This section uses the KeyWord In Context example [Parnas, 1972; Shaw and Garlan, 1996] to demonstrate the adaptation framework. The KWIC problem as defined as follows [Parnas, 1972]:

> The KWIC index system accepts an ordered set of lines; each line is an ordered set of words, and each word is an ordered set of characters. Any line may be "circularly shifted" by repeatedly removing the first word and appending it at the end of the line. The KWIC index system outputs a listing of all circular shifts of all lines in alphabetical order.

This is formalized into the following component specification:

```
I(pre) == true;
O(pre,post) ==
  isPermutation(circshifts(lines(pre)),lines(post))
  ∧ alpha(lines(post))
```

The specification of the supporting domain theory is shown in Figure 10.13.

10.4.1 *Architecture Synthesis*

The first step of adaptation in REBOUND is to search for components that are related to the problem specification. We assume there is a component repository which contains general purpose implementations of standard sequence manipulation functions which can be applied to sequences of characters and lines of text.

Matching conditions for component retrieval are obtained by specializing the match lattices using the KWIC domain theory and problem specification. For the type conversion lattice, the domain and range of the problem specification are used to identify applicable type conversion operators. In this example, D = CharSeq and R = CharSeq so the

```
KWIC_Domain : spec

includes
  Sequence(Char,CharSeq, emptyCharSeq for empty),
  LineSeq,
  Line,
  Word,
  Sequence2(Char,Word,Line),
  Sequence2(Word,Line,LineSeq)

introduces
  circshift : Line → LineSeq
  circshifts : LineSeq → LineSeq
  alpha : LineSeq → Bool
  circshift: Line, Line → LineSeq

asserts forall c: Char, w:Word, l,l1,l2:Line,
                ls:LineSeq,   cs,cs1,cs2:CharSeq

  circshift(l) == circshift(l,emptyLine);
  circshift(emptyLine,l) == emptyLineSeq;
  circshift(w ⊣ l1,l2) ==
      (w ⊣ (l1 ‖ l2)) ⊣ circshift(l1, l2 ⊢ w);
  circshifts(emptyLineSeq) == emptyLineSeq;
  circshifts(l ⊣ ls) == circshift(l) ‖ circshifts(ls);
  alpha(emptyLineSeq);
  alpha({l});
  alpha(l ⊣ ls) == l ≤ head(ls) ∧ alpha(ls)
```

Fig. 10.13   KWIC Domain Theory

following operator substitutions apply:

$$f : D \rightarrow C.D \mapsto \text{lines} : \text{CharSeq} \rightarrow \text{LineSeq}$$

$$g : C.R \rightarrow R \mapsto \text{chars} : \text{LineSeq} \rightarrow \text{CharSeq}$$

Theses substitutions are used individually and in combination along with the problem specification to create the matching conditions shown in Figure 10.14 (after simplification). These additional matching conditions can be thought of as specifications of related problems. In this case, a generic Sort component would be retrieved as a Feature Post match (where the classification feature ϕ is ordered(z) [Penix and Alexander, 1999]) with the substitution of *Line* for the generic list element under matching condition TC3 in Figure 10.14. At this point, we have specialized a sort component (Sort[Line]) and we have selected the type conversion operator associated with TC3:

```
PartialArch1 = TypeConvWrapper[__,lines,chars];
```

The adaptation tactic for Feature Post Match uses the Sequential Composition architecture. The two alternatives are to plug the component into the first or second spot in the

$(TC1)$ $I_C(lines(x)) = true$

$\quad \wedge O_C(y,z) \Rightarrow isPermutation(circshifts(y), lines(z)) \wedge alpha(lines(z))$

$(TC2)$ $I_C(x) = true$

$\quad \wedge O_C(x,z) \Rightarrow isPermutation(circshifts(lines(x)), z) \wedge alpha(z)$

$(TC3)$ $I_C(lines(x)) = true$

$\quad \wedge O_C(y,z) \Rightarrow isPermutation(circshifts(y), z) \wedge alpha(z)$

Fig. 10.14   Matching conditions for retrieval

architecture. Because the matching part of the specification only constrains the output of the component, the Sort component is placed in the second position. At this point, we have placed a sequential composition architecture with a line sort component in the second position into the type conversion wrapper:

```
PartialArch2 = TypeConvWrapper[SequentialComp[__,Sort[Line]],
                              lines,chars];
```

The architectural constraints (the axioms) can be use to generate a specification for the missing component:

$$I_C(x) = true$$
$$O_C(x,z) = z = circshifts(x)$$

This specification is equivalent to the specification for the circular shift component used in most KWIC implementations. Therefore, the shift component will be retrieved when using this specification as a query.

A specification diagram of the system constructed from the selected adaptation tactics and retrieved components is shown in Figure 10.15. The Sort Component is specialized by substitution Line for E. The composition of the shift and sort components in the sequential architecture results in the Shift Alpha Component. This component is then wrapped using the instance of the Type Conv Wrapper associated with the TC3 matching condition, where the conversion operators *lines* and *chars* are substituted in for f and g in the general specification.

The specification of the instantiated architecture specification can be denoted as:

```
KWICArch = TypeConvWrapper[SequentialComp[Shift,Sort[Line]],
                           lines,chars];
```

which is shown elaborated in Figure 10.16. This is a complete architecture solution for KWIC. It differs slightly from the standard architecture because the functionality usually attributed to an input and output component are handled by the type conversion wrapper. However, this wrapper can be constructed from an architecture that uses two components that encapsulate the data type conversions, in this case the standard KWIC input and output

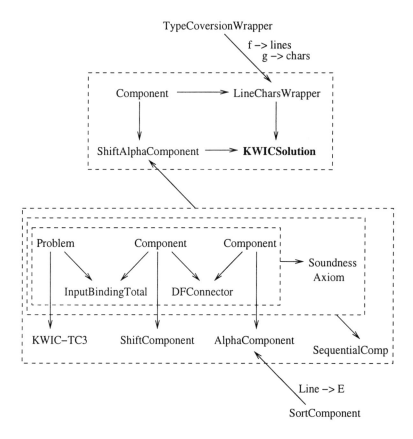

Fig. 10.15   Diagram of KWIC Adaptation Activities

components, resulting in the standard architecture with four components.

10.4.2 *Event-Driven Implementation*

This section demonstrates how an architecture specification can be mapped into an implementation component model, using the JavaBeans component model and the event-listener
pattern. The synthesis in the previous section constructs a very abstract version of the standard architecture for KWIC [Shaw and Garlan, 1996]. There are several different versions
of this architecture in the literature which are implemented in different architectural styles.
Garlan et al. describe a reactive event-driven architecture for KWIC [Garlan et al., 1992].
It this architecture, the components are connected by buffers. When a buffer is updated,
an event is sent to notify the component that is waiting for data in that buffer. In this
section we show how the architecture synthesized in previous section is mapped onto an
implementation in the event-driven architecture style.

    In the event-based implementation style, data flow connectors are implemented by re-
active buffers. Components are attached to the buffers using the event-listener [Englander,

```
spec KwicArch : KWIC
 includes
  Input : Component;
  Shift : Component;
  Sort[Line] : Component;
        Output : Component;
 axioms
  DFConnector[Input,Shift];
  DFConnector[Shift,Sort];
  DFConnector[Sort,Output];
  InputBindingTotal[this,Input];

  forall i,out:CharSeq, ls,ls_in,ls_out:LineSeq, l:Line

  I(i) ∧ Input.O(i,ls_in) ∧ Shift.O(ls_in,ls)
     ∧ Sort.O(ls,ls_out) ∧ Output.O(ls_out,out) ⇒ SystemO(i,out)
```

Fig. 10.16   Architecture Specification for KWIC

1997] (a.k.a observer [Gamma et al., 1994]) pattern. When these buffers are updated, they send buffer update events to all of the components. The Java implementation of the reactive buffer is show in Figure 10.17. It defined methods for adding data to the buffer, adding and removing event listeners (required by the listener pattern) and a local method to notify listeners of updates.

Using the event listener pattern requires that the components implement the Buffer-UpdateListener interface, so that they provide the correct method (bufferUpdate) to handle the buffer update events. To provide this interface, the special event adapter classes shown in Figure 10.18 are generated to map the event handler method to the method that provides the desired function in the component. This capability is provided in existing environments that assemble JavaBeans [Englander, 1997]. We extend the generated adapter slightly to include a target buffer to receive the component output and to account for the done message that this implementation uses to signal the end of the data stream.

The starting point for code generation is the specification representing the full instantiated KWIC architecture, shown in Figure 10.16. This specification can be translated into the Java code shown in Figure 10.19. A reactive buffer object is constructed for each of the data flow connectors. Adapted versions of the shift and sort components, as well as the Input and Output components, are instantiated and connected to the buffers as indicated by the parameters in the specification. Calling the run method on the input component executes the system.

10.5   Discussion

The goal of the adaptation framework is to guide the search for a solution based on existing library components. This search is over the space of all possible designs that can be

```
package kwic;

import java.util.Vector;

class ReactiveBuffer {

  private Vector update_listeners;

  public ReactiveBuffer() {
    update_listeners = new Vector();
  }

  public void add(Vector v) {
    notifyBufferUpdate(new BufferUpdateEvent(false,v,this));
  }

  public void done() {
    Vector v = new Vector();
    notifyBufferUpdate(new BufferUpdateEvent(true,v,this));
  }

  public void
  addBufferUpdateListener(BufferUpdateListener x){
    update_listeners.addElement(x);
  }

  public void
  removeBufferUpdateListener(BufferUpdateListener x){
    update_listeners.removeElement(x);
  }

  void notifyBufferUpdate(BufferUpdateEvent e) {
    Vector v;
    synchronized(this) {
      v = (Vector) update_listeners.clone();
    }
    for (int i = 0; i < v.size(); i++) {
      ((BufferUpdateListener)v.elementAt(i)).bufferUpdate(e);
    }
  }
}
```

Fig. 10.17 Reactive buffer implementation

```
package kwic;
import java.util.Vector;

class ShiftAdapter implements BufferUpdateListener {

  Shift wrapped;
  ReactiveBuffer target;

  public ShiftAdapter(Shift s, ReactiveBuffer t){
    wrapped = s;
    target = t;
  }

  public void bufferUpdate(BufferUpdateEvent evt) {
    if (evt.done()) {
      target.done();
    }
    else {
      target.add(Shift.shift(evt.getData()));
    }
  }
}

class SortAdapter implements BufferUpdateListener {

  Sort wrapped;
  ReactiveBuffer target;

  public SortAdapter(Sort s, ReactiveBuffer t){
    wrapped = s;
    target = t;
  }

  public void bufferUpdate(BufferUpdateEvent evt) {
    if (evt.done()) {
      System.out.println(wrapped.toString());
    }
    else {
      wrapped.merge(evt.getData());
    }
  }
}
```

Fig. 10.18 Automatically generated event adaptors

```
package kwic;

import java.util.Vector;

class Kwic {

  public static void main(String argv[]) {

    ReactiveBuffer b1 = new ReactiveBuffer();
    ReactiveBuffer b2 = new ReactiveBuffer();
    ReactiveBuffer b3 = new ReactiveBuffer();

    ShiftAdapter shift_component = new ShiftAdapter(new Shift(),b2);
    b1.addBufferUpdateListener(shift_component);

    SortAdapter sort_component = new SortAdapter(new Sort(),b3);
    b2.addBufferUpdateListener(sort_component);

    Output output_component = new Output();
    b3.addBufferUpdateListener(output_component);

    Input input_component = new Input(b1);

    input_component.run();
  }
}
```

Fig. 10.19   Java to construct Kwic architecture

constructed from the components and architectures/tactics in the library. The exploration of the search space must be limited due to the potentially large number of architecture and component combinations.

The capability of the framework to automated adaptation can be described in terms of top-down vs. bottom-up design. In top down design, a problem is repeatedly decomposed into subproblems until all subproblems are known to be solvable (or unsolvable). In bottom-up design, components are assembled into structures until the assembled system has the desired behavior, or it is determined to be an inappropriate design. Any effective design process must be a combination of both: A top-down strategy provides a goal toward which the systems is constructed from known parts. As the problem is decomposed, it is increasingly important to ensure that the problem decomposition is moving toward functionality provided in the target library or language.

The REBOUND framework combines top-down and bottom-up information in a way that allows tractable behavioral adaptation. The heuristics for behavior adaptation provide bottom-up guidance where there is a choice in the adaptation process which could lead to a combinatorial search space. The selection rules reduce this search space by identifying one alternative for instantiating an architecture. Note that the best alternative is determined by how the component matches the problem (top-down information).

The use of the type conversion architecture as an adaptation tactic is another source of branching in the state space. The type conversion lattice is instantiated using the original problem specification creating a class of related problems whose solutions can be converted to a solution to the original problem. This branching of the state space is limited by imposing additional structure on the domain theory: the type conversion operators must be predefined during domain analysis. The importance of type conversion operators in supporting black-box adaptation leads us to suggest that "converters" may need to be promoted to first-class objects just as connectors have been promoted to support architectural abstractions. Searching the domain theory to construct arbitrarily complex type conversion operators would be equivalent to deductive synthesis [Manna and Waldinger, 1992] and therefore too general and expensive to include in the framework. However, Fischer and Whittle have described an integration of deductive component retrieval into deductive synthesis which shows how retrieval based techniques like REBOUND may be described in terms of this more general framework [Fisher and Whittle, 1999].

A limitation of the framework is that the size (meaning level of abstraction or granularity) of the components in the library determines the size of the problems that can be solved by the system. The problem must be of similar size as the components in the library, because it is immediately compared to the components in the library. The adaptation tactics may allow the bridging of one or two abstraction levels (for example, the combination of a type conversion and a sequential composition might be considered two abstraction levels). However, large problems might require several levels of decomposition before reaching the abstraction level of the components. This limitation could be relaxed by allowing a few rounds of purely top-down problem decomposition before attempting the bottom-up component retrieval and adaptation. However, this would increase the search space proportional to the number of problem decomposition alternatives considered.

10.6 Related Work

The main contribution of this work is the development and evaluation the use of specification matching results to select component adaptation strategies. This builds upon the large body of research that has investigated specification-based (or deductive) component retrieval [Fischer et al., 1998; Jeng and Cheng, 1995; Mili et al., 1997; Penix and Alexander, 1999; Schumann and Fischer, 1997; Zaremski and Wing, 1997]. The REBOUND framework extends the traditional type abstraction/specialization adaptation paradigm [Goguen, 1984] by adding interface and behavior adaptation.

Behavior adaptation is an extension of the work done on Kestrel's Interactive Development System (KIDS) [Smith, 1990; Smith and Lowry, 1990; Jüllig, 1993]. In KIDS, the structure of specific algorithms such as global search or divide and conquer are represented as algorithm theories. The generalization in REBOUND is that adaptation tactics are specified in terms of subcomponent problem theories rather than operators, allowing the construction of hierarchical systems.

The Inscape [Perry, 1989] environment developed by Perry uses a formal model of software interconnection [Perry, 1987]. The Inscape semantic interconnection model has recently been integrated into the GenVoca software system generators [Batory and Geraci, 1997]. In GenVoca, the semantic constraints are used to validate compositions after they are selected, while in Rebound, the semantic constraints are used to guide component selection and integration. Also, within REBOUND the distinction is made between components and adaptors/architectures. This structure aids in the application of heuristic knowledge in guiding the construction of a system. However, GenVoca is capable of constructing larger systems than can currently be supported within REBOUND.

10.7   Conclusion

This chapter describes a framework that allows the retrieval of adaptable components based on formal specifications of component adaptation strategies. The framework is based on a formal model of components, connectors and architectures and extends the traditional type abstraction/specialization adaptation paradigm by adding interface and behavior adaptation. To demonstrate the relationship of the work to practical component models, we showed how component and architecture specifications can be mapped to a JavaBeans implementation.

The framework limits the application of automated reasoning by confining it to two situations: 1) verifying component matches and 2) generation of subproblem specifications. The search over the solution space is guided by the relationship of components to the problem, similar problems as determined by interface adaptation tactics, and the heuristics for instantiating the behavior adaptation tactics. Together, these tactics direct the search toward solutions that reuse components in library.

We are currently working on extending the system in two ways. First, we are attempting to minimize the automated reasoning required during the subproblem generation process. It is possible that for each matching condition, there is enough information to derive the subproblem specification for the general case offline, reducing the adaptation-time computation to simple substitution. This would eliminate the most expensive application of automated reasoning in the framework.

Acknowledgements

Support for this work was provided in part by the Advanced Research Projects Agency and monitored by Wright Labs under contract F33615-93-C-1316 and F33615-93-C-4304 and NASA Ames Research Center.

References

Abowd, G. D., Allen, R., and Garlan, D. (1995). Formalizing style to understand descriptions of software architecture. *ACM Transactions on Software Engineering and Methodology*, 4(4).

Allen, R. and Garlan, D. (1997). A formal basis for architectural connection. *ACM Transactions on Software Engineering and Methodology (TOSEM)*, 6(3):213–249.

Batory, D. and Geraci, B. K. (1997). Composition validation and subjectivity in GenVoca generators. *IEEE Transactions on Software Engineering*, 23(2):67–82.

Batory, D., Singhal, V., Thomas, J., Dasari, S., Geraci, B., and Sirkin, M. (1994). The GenVoca model of software-system generators. *IEEE Software*, 11(5):89–94.

Biggerstaff, T. J. (1994). The library scaling problem and the limits of concrete component reuse. In *Proceedings of The 3rd International Conference on Software Reuse*, pages 102–109, Rio de Janeiro, Brazil. IEEE Computer Society.

Biggerstaff, T. J. and Perlis, A. J., editors (1989). *Software Reusability - Concepts and Models*, volume 1. ACM Press.

Burstall, R. M. and Goguen, J. A. (1977). Putting theories together to make specifications. In *Proceedings of the Fifth International Joint Conference on Artificial Intelligence*, pages 1045–58. IJCAI.

Dingel, J., Garlan, D., Jha, S., and Notkin, D. (1998). Towards a formal treatment of implicit invocation using rely-guarantee reasoning. *Formal Aspects of Computing*, 10:193–213.

Englander, R. (1997). *Developing Java Beans*. O'Riley, first edition edition.

Fischer, B. (2000). Specification-based browsing of software component libraries. *Automated Software Engineering Journal*, 7(2):179–200.

Fischer, B., Schumann, J., and Snelting, G. (1998). Deduction-based software component retrieval. In *Automated Deduction - A basis for applications, Volume III Applications*. Kluwer.

Fisher, B. and Whittle, J. (1999). An integration of deductive retrieval into deductive synthesis. In *Proceedings of the 14th IEEE International Automated Software Engineering Conference*, pages 52–61. IEEE Computer Society Press.

Gamma, E., Helm, R., Johnson, R., and Vlissides, J. (1994). *Design Patterns: Elements of Reusable Object-Oriented Software*. Addison Wesley.

Garlan, D., Kaiser, G. E., and Notkin, D. (1992). Using tool abstraction to compose systems. *IEEE Computer*, 25(6):30–38.

Gerkin, M. J. (1995). *Formal Foundations for the Specification of Software Architecture*. PhD thesis, Air Force Institute of Technology.

Goguen, J. (1984). Parameterized Programming. *IEEE Transactions on Software Engineering*, 10(5):528–543.

Hayes-Roth, B., Pfleger, K., Lalanda, P., Morignot, P., and Balabanovic, M. (1995). A domain-specific softare architecture for adaptive intelligent systems. *IEEE Transactions on Software Engineering*, 21(4):288–301.

Jeng, J.-J. and Cheng, B. H. C. (1995). Specification matching: A foundation. In *Proceedings of the ACM Symposium on Software Reuse*, Seattle, Washington.

Jüllig, R. and Srinivas, Y. V. (1993). Diagrams for software synthesis. In *Proceedings of The Eight Knowledge-Based Software Engineering Conference*, pages 10–19. IEEE Computer Society.

Jüllig, R. K. (1993). Applying formal software synthesis. *IEEE Software*, 10(3):11–22.

Kiczales, G. (1996). Beyond the black box: open implementation. *IEEE Software*, 13(1):8–11.

Kiczales, G., Lamping, J., Mendhekar, A., Maeda, C., Lopes, C., Loingtier, J.-M., and Irwin, J. (1997). Aspect-oriented programming. Technical report, Xerox Palo Alto Research Center.

Manna, Z. and Waldinger, R. (1992). Fundamentals of deductive program synthesis. *IEEE Transactions on Software Engineering*, 18(8):674–704.

Mili, A., Mili, R., and Mittermeir, R. (1997). Storing and retrieving software components: A refinement based system. *IEEE Transactions on Software Engineering*, 23(7):445–460.

Moriconi, M., Qian, X., and Riemenschneider, B. (1995). Correct architecture refinement. *IEEE Transactions on Software Engineering*, 21(4):356–372.

Oreizy, P., Medvidovic, N., and Taylor, R. N. (1998). Architecture-based runtime software evolution. In *Proceedings of the International Conference on Software Engineering 1998 (ICSE'98)*, Kyoto, Japan.

Parnas, D. (1972). On the criteria to be used in decomposing systems into modules. *Communications of the ACM*, 15(12):1053–8.

Penix, J. (1998). *Automated Component Retrieval and Adaptation Using Formal Specifications*. PhD thesis, University of Cincinnati.

Penix, J. and Alexander, P. (1997). Toward automated component adaptation. In *Proceedings of the Ninth International Conference on Software Engineering and Knowledge Engineering*, pages 535–542. Knowledge Systems Institute.

Penix, J. and Alexander, P. (1999). Efficient specification-based component retrieval. *Automated Software Engineering*, 6:139–170.

Penix, J., Alexander, P., and Havelund, K. (1997). Declarative specification of software architectures. In *Proceedings of the 12th International Automated Software Engineering Conference*, pages 201–209. IEEE Press.

Perry, D. E. (1987). Software interconnection models. In *Procedings of the 9th International Conference on Software Engineering*. IEEE Computer Society.

Perry, D. E. (1989). The Inscape environment. In *Proceedings of the 11th International Conference on Software Engineering*. ACM Press.

Prieto-Díaz, R. and Arango, G., editors (1991). *Domain Analysis and Software Systems Modeling*. IEEE Computer Society Press tutorials. IEEE Computer Society Press.

Purtilo, J. M. and Atlee, J. M. (1991). Module reuse by interface adaptation. *Software: Practice & Experience*, 21:539–56.

Schumann, J. and Fischer, B. (1997). NORA/HAMMR: Making deduction-based software component retrieval practical. In *Proceedings of the 12th IEEE International Automated Software Engineering Conterence*, pages 246–254. IEEE Computer Society.

Shaw, M. (1995). Comparing Architectural Design Styles. *IEEE Software*, 12(6):27–41.

Shaw, M. and Garlan, D. (1996). *Software Architecture: Perspectives on an Emerging Discipline*. Prentice Hall.

Smith, D. R. (1990). KIDS: A Semiautomatic Program Development System. *IEEE Transactions on Software Engineering*, 16(9):1024–1043.

Smith, D. R. (1996). Toward a classification approach to design. In *Proceedings of the Fifth International Conference on Algebraic Methodology and Software Technology*, LCNS. Springer Verlag.

Smith, D. R. and Lowry, M. R. (1990). Algorithm Theories and Design Tactics. *Science of Computer Programming*, 14:305–321.

Wallace, G. K. (1992). The JPEG still picture compression standard. *IEEE Transactions on Consumer Electronics*, 38(1):xvii–xxxiv.

Zaremski, A. M. and Wing, J. M. (1995). Signature matching, a tool for using software libraries. *ACM Transactions on Software Engineering and Methodology (TOSEM)*, 4(2).

Zaremski, A. M. and Wing, J. M. (1997). Specification matching of software components. *ACM Transactions on Software Engineering and Methodology*, 6(4):333–369.

Chapter 11

A Web-Enabled Component-Based Architecture for Legacy Applications

GUIJUN WANG, RICHARD ROBINSON and SURYA SRIPADA
Engineering and Information Technology, The Boeing Company
Seattle, WA 98124 USA
`{guijun.wang,richard.v.robinson,surya.sripada}@boeing.com`

Abstract. Combination of component software technologies and the web technologies has brought dramatic changes in distributed systems. Traditional client-server paradigm has been replaced by web-enabled component-based multi-tier architecture paradigm. This new paradigm can benefit virtually all legacy applications from traditional enterprise applications like ERP and CRM systems to engineering applications like computational fluid dynamics and computational bio-informatics.

In this case study, we apply component software technologies and web technologies in the design and development of an "Engineering Computing Portal" based on a Web-Enabled Component-Based Architecture (WECBA) for simplifying the use and managing the runtime of scientific and engineering applications. In this architecture, a web portal manages user profiles and interacts with a user via Java Applets and Servlets. In the mid-tier of the architecture, a broker is used to locate applications and resources on the backend computation servers, manage application states, and coordinate the flow of multiple applications. Since system performance is critical for engineering applications, the broker should add as little overhead as possible to the overall system. The Engineering Computing Portal broker is implemented using lightweight high performance CORBA with a Naming service and an Event Service. The choice of CORBA is important because it enables language-independent interoperability between multiple platforms and languages. On backend host servers, a computation manager based on a lightweight high performance CORBA bridges the gap between object invocations and procedural application launches and between object-based runtime state management and process-based runtime state monitoring. The interactions between tiers are asynchronous. We discuss implementation issues and lessons learned in this case study.

11.1 Component Software Technology and Web Technology

"Component" as a concept has been utilized in all stages of software development (from modeling to deployment), albeit without consensus on a common definition. "Component" as a software artifact has also been defined in several flavors [Atkinson C., et al (2001)] [D'Sousa D., Wills A. (1998)] [Szyperski C. (2002)] [OMG (1999c)] [J2EE (2002)] [.Net (2002)]. Common characteristics of them include separation of interfaces from implementations and explicit dependencies as well as traditional object-oriented characteristics such as encapsulation and inheritance. While a number of definitions exist, Clemens Szyperski [Szyperski C. (2002)] offers a good general definition of components as software artifacts. According to Szyperski, a software component is a unit of composition with contractually specified interfaces and explicit context dependencies. In this chapter, a component is more specifically a software artifact developed and deployed based on a component model. Component model is at the center of Component Software Technology (CST) in the industry. Industry component models include JavaBeans and Enterprise JabaBeans in J2EE [J2EE (2002)], CORBA Component Model [OMG (1999c)], and Microsoft .Net [.Net (2002)].

CST defines the concepts, development time frameworks, and runtime environments for Component-Based Software Development (CBSD). Generally speaking, the CBSD approach builds software systems from well-tested, reliable, and independently developed components. This approach is analogous to component-based digital hardware development, where hardware components are designed and assembled into systems. While CBSD approach is conceptually simple, building large scale distributed systems requires the same set of concerns, namely enterprise, computation, information, technology and engineering, as any other approaches [Wang G., Ungar L., and Klawitter D. (1999)] [Wang G., Cone G. (2001)]. CBSD promises to increase system flexibility and reliability, reduce complexity for distributed systems, reduce development and deployment cost, and promote reuse.

While CST has led to new middleware products like component-based application servers (based on CORBA, J2EE, or .Net) and new component frameworks like SWING in Java for end-user client systems, it by itself is not adequate to deliver data and services from backend enterprise systems to end-users anywhere anytime. At the same time, Web Technology has gone from simple HTML and web browsers to XML and sophisticated web services. The combination of component software technology and the web technology has brought dramatic changes in distributed systems. Together with CST, web technology brings the data and services in enterprise systems to end-users anywhere in the world with a browser in a robust, secure, and timely fashion. A typical architecture of such systems is a multi-tier component-based architecture, which consists of a web portal as front-end, component-based application servers and integration brokers in the middle, and enterprise information systems at the back-end.

This kind of component-based architectures has penetrated not only in traditional enterprise applications like ERP and CRM systems, but also in engineering applications like computational fluid dynamic and computational bio-informatics. In this case study, we apply component software technology and web technology in the development of an "Engineering Computing Portal", a Web-Enabled Component-Based Architecture (WECBA) for simplifying the uses and managing the runtime of computational and engineering applications. The objectives of this case study were on designing and validating a WECBA for these applications in a large scale computing grid environment, selecting and validating component software technologies and web technologies for implementing such an architecture, and assessing the benefit of an "Engineering Computing Portal".

In the following sections, we describe and discuss our steps in meeting these objectives. First, we describe the specific characteristics of the portal and common business requirements of WECBA for all legacy applications from the enterprise viewpoint. Second, we describe the WECBA and its implementation from the computation, technology, and engineering viewpoints. Third we review some related work. Fourth, we assess our design and implementation and provide some lessons learned. And finally we outline some future directions.

11.2 Characteristics of Engineering Computing Portal and Common Business Requirements of WECBA for Legacy Applications

11.2.1 Characteristics of Engineering Computing Portal

Scientific and engineering applications are often computationally intensive. These applications are generally hosted on powerful servers, often in multi-processor or cluster configurations, such as those from SGI, Sun and IBM. An application may partition its work in multiple jobs and they may run in parallel on different processors or different machines. Engineers typically login to these servers and launch these applications through shell commands or scripts. When multiple engineering applications need to run in a design-experiment flow, a complicated script in languages like PERL is needed. For example, a computational fluid dynamic application may reside on a multi-processor SGI server. Some applications of this type may take days or even weeks to complete the computation of a single specific problem. The user must frequently check job status to learn when the computation is complete and results can be accessed, especially for long-running jobs. Furthermore, special software is needed for a user to remotely login to the computation servers and the user must know on which machine an application resides.

The business requirements from the top level are very simple: simplify the process for using and managing these applications and bring the data and services from these applications regardless where they are and how they are implemented to the end users through a simple Web interface; at the same time, reduce the needs for multiple instances of high-end computing resources and thereby reduce cost.

With the maturity of Web technologies like Web Portals, Java Applets (applet), Java Server Pages (JSP), and Java Servlets (servlet), a web-enabled system for scientific and engineering applications would greatly reduce complexity, increase usability, and improve efficiency for users. A user of a web-enabled system would be able to launch a computation job from anywhere on the network with a web browser and receive notification of job completion, perhaps asynchronously. Web technologies by themselves are not enough, however. This is due to several reasons. First, computation server platforms (such as SGI servers, Sun servers, Linux PC clusters) and application implementation languages (such as Fortran, C/C++) are quite diverse in such environments. It would be difficult for a web server to interact with these diverse systems directly. Second, computation resources may be dynamic in their capability and availability. It may be difficult for a web server to locate resources, launch computation jobs, and manage computation states. This is also a problem that grid computing research aims to solve. Third, a job may be long-running (from several hours to days or even weeks) and a complex application may require a coordinated execution flow of multiple jobs. It would be inefficient for the web server to manage such jobs.

To deal with these issues, the key is to combine component software technology (CST) in the middle and backend tiers utilizing component-based application server and integration servers. Thus the technical aim is to design and validate a Web-Enabled Component-Based Architecture (WECBA) to effectively web-enable legacy applications (e.g., scientific and engineering applications).

11.2.2 Common Business Requirements of WECBA for Legacy Applications

The characteristics of engineering computing portal described in Section 11.2.1 are not unique. WECBA for legacy applications shares common business requirements. These requirements include:

– *Web-based access*: a web browser should be all the software needed on the end-user workstation. Graphical user interface capabilities may be downloaded as Java Applets if needed.
– *Security*: users must have security contexts to use any applications. A web single sign-on is required to establish security contexts and security contexts should be propagated in subsequent interactions.
– *Location transparency*: users need not know where applications are located or where they are running.
– *No change to computational applications*: applications should not be forced to change just for this Web-enabled system. They are executable modules and are used "as is".
– *Event-based notification*: asynchronous communications to deal with long-running jobs and maximize resource utilization.
– *Minimize overheads*: middleware should add as minimal overhead as possible. Computation performance is important.
– *Effective resource utilization*: the system should locate appropriate computation servers for job execution.
– *Persistent data as required*: store output data in persistent files so that they can be retrieved later.

Application domains may have additional requirements for WECBA. For example, the engineering computing portal requires supporting design to analysis cycle by coordinating sequences of engineering tasks from design to analysis automatically.

11.3 Web-Enabled Component-Based Architecture (WECBA)

To meet the business requirements, a number of technology choices and common services on web technologies and component technologies will be needed. Based on these requirements, Figure 11.1 shows a WECBA design of an "engineering computing portal" for scientific and engineering applications. This architecture is equally applicable to web-enabling any legacy applications. In the remaining of this article, we focus specifically on the case study for web-enabling engineering applications.

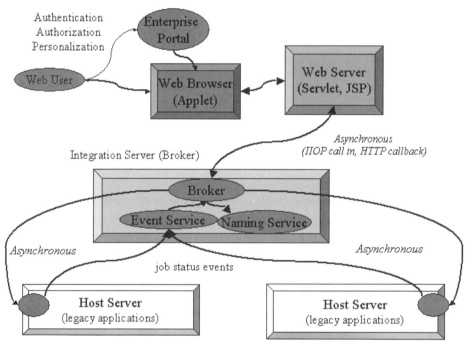

Figure 11.1: WECBA for Engineering Computing Portal: Architecture Design of Web-Enabled Engineering Applications

In this architecture, a user is first authenticated by an enterprise web portal, then presented with authorized list of applications that are authorized for access. The user interacts with application-specific interfaces provided by the engineering computing portal web server in Applets. The user does not need to know where a particular application is located or where it will run in terms of physical machine address. The user constructs input data required by the application for a job run. When a job run request is submitted by the user, the responsible servlet on the web server will submit the request to the integration server, the broker of the engineering computing portal, along with other data that may be required by the application (independent of any individual job run). The interaction between the servlet and the broker is asynchronous. After a job is submitted, the servlet returns without waiting for the completion of the job. A unique identifier is assigned to each job request so that when a job completes, the identifier can be used to match job status reports and output data with a particular user and the associated job run request.

The broker is responsible for locating computation resources, initiating a job run for an application, monitoring job status events, maintaining job status, coordinating sequences of job runs, and notifying job completion (successful or abnormal) to the user via a servlet on the web server. The user will receive a message (an email in our prototype), which includes a JSP link to output job data. A JSP on the web server assembles related data for a particular computational application so that the user can view computation results in desired format. The broker relies on a naming service (e.g., CORBA Naming service [OMG (1997n)]) to locate a resource and an event service (e.g., CORBA Event service [OMG (1997e)]) to monitor job status changes. The broker may initiate subsequent job runs automatically in a sequence when triggered by completion events of preceding jobs. Note that the broker is the center of the architecture. It must respond quickly to job requests from multiple web servers and notifications of many job status events from host servers. Therefore, the broker must be efficient and lightweight so that it adds as little overhead as possible to computation jobs. The Event service and Naming service are part of the broker for efficiency.

Recall that the computationally intensive scientific and engineering applications on host servers are written in several languages such as Fortran, C, and C++. They are executable modules, usually on Unix-based multi-processor servers or Linux-based clusters. Furthermore, some of these applications have security protections to prevent unauthorized runs. The host servers may also be geographically distributed and owned by multiple organizations. While it is possible to use a machine specific remote login procedure for the broker to login to these machines and launch applications, this approach has a number of drawbacks. First, security control would be hard to implement. Second, it requires a machine-specific login procedure and method of application launches. Third, it cannot deal with dynamic situations where host server resource availability changes independently from the broker. Last but not least, host servers would not have a uniform mechanism to notify the broker asynchronously about job status. A superior implementation alternative is to have a lightweight high performance object-oriented middleware on a host server.

The availability of lightweight high performance object-oriented middleware capabilities on a host server makes a standard interaction interface between the broker and host servers possible. It bridges the gap between passive procedural executables and active objects. In fact, these executables are considered as servants in CORBA and can be managed by a single CORBA object. Figure 11.1 shows (as a circle) an object-oriented Computation Manager on each host server. The broker launches a job on a host server by invoking a method of the CORBA object in the host server, which in turn launches one of its servants. The servant is identified by a parameter (the application name) of the method. The broker returns immediately without waiting for job completion. When a job completes (successfully or abnormally), the host server will send a job status event to the Event service, which pushes such events to the broker.

In the next section (Section 11.4), we discuss the rationale for using lightweight high performance CORBA for the broker and on host servers. We also describe system implementation issues for the WECBA in the next section.

11.4 Technology Choices and System Implementation of the WECBA

11.4.1 Lightweight High Performance CORBA

Middleware is fundamental to system integration from in-the-small (e.g., embedded systems) to in-the-large (e.g., open-ended web services). Middleware provides runtime management of components and distributed communications between components. Platforms like CORBA, J2EE, and .Net provide feature-packed middleware for integration needs. However, not all of these features are used by many applications and in fact, many applications don't need large portions of these features at all. Furthermore, some computing hardware platforms have resource constraints in terms of space and time. A full sized middleware runtime environment may not provide the needed performance and fit in given space on such hardware platforms especially when it has to share resources with other applications. Finally, from a cost perspective, it doesn't make sense to buy and deploy full middleware and expensive machines if many of the middleware features are not needed by these applications.

Lightweight high performance middleware is an alternative with only some essential communication and integration features, featuring a small memory footprint, efficient object management, low overhead in distributed communications comparable to raw socket. OMG's minimum CORBA specification [OMG (1998m)] is one such middleware specification. The minimum CORBA Specification is a subset profile of the full CORBA 2.2 specification. It supports all CORBA IDL constructs, retains essential features, and omits other features (especially dynamic aspect of CORBA like dynamic invocation interface). Since it is a pure subset, it is fully interoperable with full CORBA. If necessary, a group of minimum CORBA-based middleware can work together with a full CORBA deployed on a strategic node in the enterprise network. Several vendors have products implementing the minimum CORBA standard including Objective Interfaces' ORB Express, Vertel's e*ORB, and Iona's Orbix/E.

Lightweight high performance CORBA Object Request Broker (ORB) based on minimum CORBA has a small memory footprint, provides efficient object management, and requires low communication overhead. For example, a client can be as small as 90KB and a server can be built as small as 130KB in terms of memory footprint, in comparison with several megabytes for full CORBA. In terms of communication overhead, IIOP in these ORBs adds only about 20% overhead over raw socket TCP/IP communications, in comparison with double (200%) or triple (300%) overhead when using a full CORBA ORB product. For example, a simple test shows that latency for roundtrip calls with no parameter in IIOP is only 0.14ms in Orbix/E v1.01 for Java in comparison with 1.42ms for OrbixWeb 3.0 (a full CORBA ORB). It takes 0.08ms for raw socket TCP/IP in the same situation. The test environment is J2SDK1.3, Pentium 850MHz CPU, 384M memory. Furthermore, a lightweight high performance ORB has efficient runtime object management and improved system efficiency because it doesn't have to support many features not needed by applications in this domain.

A key question is of course whether such lightweight middleware is adequate for applications in this domain such as the integration of mathematically sophisticated applications. If so, where is lightweight middleware suited and where it is not (the type of applications where other features of the middleware are required) should be clearly understood. The idea is to use lightweight middleware for domain-specific integration needs, but to integrate it with full-featured middleware in a strategic enterprise integration broker. We intend to answer this question in our implementation and assessment of the WECBA.

11.4.2 *Implementing Broker and Computation Manager based on Lightweight High Performance CORBA*

CORBA is well known to make systems in heterogeneous platforms and languages interoperable. Due to resource constraints and performance requirements, lightweight high performance CORBA is essential. Objective Interfaces' ORB Express, Vertel's e*ORB, and Iona's Orbix/E are three products that implement the minimum CORBA specification. After evaluation, Iona's Orbix/E for Java is chosen for implementing the integration broker (see Figure 1). Orbix/E includes efficient Naming service and Event service.

Host servers include platforms like Unix-based machines from SGI and Linux-based clusters. For some of these platforms, no commercial CORBA products are available. The TAO ORB developed at Washington University, St. Louis, can be compiled for minimum CORBA configuration and it supports these platforms although it only supports C++ language. Therefore, TAO in minimum CORBA configuration is used for the implementation of object-oriented computation managers on our host servers.

Once lightweight high performance ORBs are selected, the implementation of the broker and the computation manager is straightforward. Books like [Vogel A., Duddy K. (1997)] [Henning M., Vinoski S. (2000)] have documented Java/C++ programming with (full) CORBA well. We'll describe our lessons learned with using lightweight high performance CORBA later in this chapter.

11.4.3 *Interactions between Web Server, Integration Broker, and Computation Manager*

Figure 11.2 shows a collaboration diagram detailing the components of the Engineering Computing Portal prototype implementation. The user-facing tier includes a standard web HTTP server, supplemented by portal capabilities, an applet repository, and a servlet engine providing the front-end job request mechanism. The middle tier comprises a light-weight broker capability incorporating a CORBA Event service. The back-end computation tier is represented by a computation manager service and the host native application runtime where our computationally-intensive jobs are actually executed. The system is supported by some typical enterprise infrastructure elements, a generic SMTP email server and an NFS/SMB-capable shared file service. The end user is assumed to have access to a web browser and email client on a standard PC or X-terminal workstation.

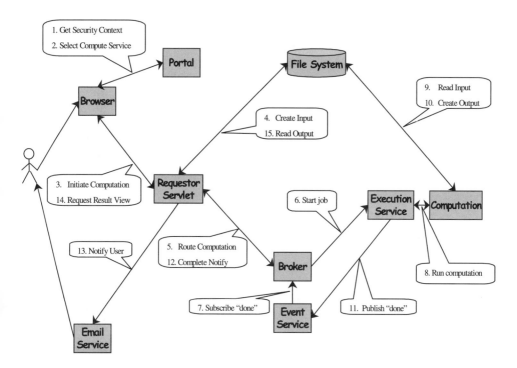

Figure 11.2: Collaboration Diagram: Components for Web-Enabling Scientific Applications

In an error-free, happy-path user interaction and job execution scenario, the user is first authenticated via a web-based security mechanism provided by a standard web portal facility. The portal authentication mechanism is part of a secure directory infrastructure provided in any enterprise, and is not examined further in this discussion. Once authenticated, the portal user is presented with a web page that offers links to application capabilities for which he/she is authorized. A link will perform an applet download, which in turn permits the user to interact with a graphically-oriented Java applet to define and collect many input parameters. Once the user hits the start button (a job requested is submitted), input parameters together with job-independent input data if any will be collected by a job requestor servlet.

The job requestor servlet exploits a command design paradigm that responds to a very small set of orders that it receives via HTTP GET or POST: (1) submit job, (2) notify user, and (3) display result. When a job submission order is received via HTTP POST from the user, it assigns a unique ID to the job request. It finds an appropriate workspace on a shared file server and creates input files necessary for the job being submitted. It then invokes the CORBA job execution request method on the Broker. Note that the job requestor servlet will return immediately after making this one-way asynchronous CORBA invocation and it does not maintain any session information with the user (information like application name, job id, and user contact information). Such information is sent to the Broker alone with all other information necessary to initiate the actual run. It includes the unique job ID assigned by the requestor servlet, along with the name of the requested application and the location of the working directory on the shared file server (for input/output data files). In addition, since its interaction with the Broker is asynchronous (IIOP call-in and HTTP call-back), it also passes a callback URL of a servlet responsible for formatting results and notifying the user to the Broker. The Broker maintains job status information including all information it received from the requestor servlet. Figure 11.2 illustrates the interaction sequences.

Upon receiving the job execution method invocation from the requestor servlet, the Broker locates an execution service on a computing resource that hosts a copy of the requested application. The execution service is a small CORBA server running as a daemon. The execution service receives a copy of the information received from the requestor. In an appropriate working directory, it forks a running instance of the requested application, then synchronously monitors the progress of the run and waits for its completion. The application is responsible for reading input data from the shared file system and produces its output in the same working directory. Upon successful completion of the job, control is returned to the execution service, which publishes a "done" event to the event service. This event contains status information (normal/abnormal status, location of data, and related information) together with any job identification information it received from the Broker at invocation.

As mentioned earlier, the Broker maintains job status information in a repository. It is subscribed to job status events published by the execution services. When it receives one, it updates its status repository and parses out status information, location of the computation results, and job identification information. This information is passed back to the servlet of the call-back URL in HTTP POST protocol, so that it can in turn construct a JSP page containing the computation's results and send an email notification to the user containing the

JSP link. Note that a job completion event will lead the Broker to change job status in its repository, which may in turn trigger pending job runs.

In our implementation, the user receives the job completion notification as a regular email, containing an informative message and a JSP link. When clicked or pasted into a browser, this link displays the results in the end user's browser window.

Table 11.1 summarizes the salient characteristics, operational requirements, and the communication and method invocation protocols used by the principal components of our implementation. The purpose of the "Platform" row in the table is largely to demonstrate the diverse types of platforms.

Table 11.1: Deployment Characteristics

	Requestor Servlet	Broker with Naming & Event Service	Execution Service	Engineering Applications	File Service
Role, Function	Formulate Input Submit Request, Format Output, Notify User, Display Result	Locate Resource, Initiate Job, Maintain Job Status, Coordinate Computation Steps	Object-Process Bridge, Local Job Management	Computation	Input/ Output Data, Script and Template
Platform	Sun Solaris	Dell Windows2000	SGI Origin IRIX	SGI Origin IRIX	Sun Solaris
Runtime Environment	Oracle J2EE container	Orbix/E CORBA	TAO C++ minimum CORBA	C/C++ native	
Protocols	HTTP IIOP	IIOP HTTP	IIOP	Native	NFS SMB

The distribution of functions among components as shown in Table 11.1 renders the Engineering Computing Portal architecture very flexible. For example, it is very easy to introduce new capabilities into the design, and in many cases modifications may be made without disrupting a deployed and functioning system of services. In particular, the system is designed to support the introduction of new scientific and engineering applications without requiring any running services to be modified or paused, and without requiring knowledge of either CORBA application development or Java servlet creation on the part of the application maintainer. The asynchronous interactions between the three tiers enable effective resource utilization and flexible configuration.

11.5 Related Work

Recent activities of the Global Grid Forum (GGF) [Global Grid Forum (2002)] aimed to build software frameworks for distributing computation of scientific applications among computing nodes. A computing grid [Foster I., Kesselman C., Tuecke S. (2001)] [Foster I., Kesselman C., Nick J., Tuecke S. (2002)] [Grid Computing Environments (2002)] is an infrastructure enabling integrated, collaborative use of high-end computers, networks, databases, and scientific instruments owned and managed by multiple organizations. The same general considerations that motivated the development of our Engineering Computing Portal architecture is being addressed in a slightly different manner by projects such as the Grid Portal Toolkit (GridPort) [GridPort (2002)] and the National Partnership for Advanced Computational Infrastructure (NPACI) Hotpage [NPACI Hotpage (2002)]. GridPort is designed to aid in the development of science portals on computational grids and Hotpage has the more specific, user-oriented goal of making computational science processes easier for scientists, engineers, and researchers. In the grid paradigm, features like resource management and load balancing in an open dynamic environment are important and the WECBA would benefit from such features.

Most of the differences between our WECBA and the GridPort lie in programming paradigms and the selection of specific web, security and metacomputing technologies. Our engineering computing portal employs an object-oriented interaction and development paradigm while GridPort is more a process-oriented interaction and development paradigm. Where we have employed CORBA capabilities to expose object-oriented security and directory interfaces to applications, GridPort exploits the Globus [Foster I., Kesselman C. (1997)] [Globus (2002)] toolkit security infrastructure and metadirectory capabilities to enable interactions with computational resources. Where our user-facing tier is constructed from Java and J2EE elements, the GridPort web pages are built using HTML and JavaScript elements that activate server-side Perl/CGI scripts. Both implementation architectures exhibit the key feature of resource availability form "any" web browser from any location on the network.

Recent efforts of the Grid community are focusing on mechanisms for exposing Globus-enabled computational facilities and other devices through a service-oriented architecture [Foster I., Kesselman C., Nick J., Tuecke S. (2002)]. The developers of the Globus toolkit are working to re-factor all of the toolkit capabilities to function in a service-oriented paradigm and to make them interoperable with SOAP and Web Services. The thrust of this strategy is to make capabilities available through ubiquitous, commodity protocols and APIs, thus enhancing the ability of individuals and organizations to accelerate their adoption of grid middleware. This strategy affords an unfortunate opportunity to add an additional layer of complexity to the framework. A portal in such a scenario might handle SOAP messages, perhaps carried on top of an HTTP protocol, and manage computational processes in a request/response paradigm. A scalable and conceptually less complex approach would incorporate a broker facility such as the one exemplified in our engineering computing portal.

Design tools presented in [Holmes V., Linebarger J., Miller D., Poore C., Vandwart R. (2000)] are used for distributing computing tasks on multiple host machines in a simulation type of applications. However, it is a two-tier architecture where coordination is based on an active object-oriented database. Events are sent to the database and actions may be triggered by coming events. The interface and the distributed communication between a host server and the database are based on CORBA. There is no broker facility in its architecture. The Broker in our engineering computing portal enables a location transparent and flexible architecture. Furthermore, we use lightweight high performance CORBA, which gives us lower overhead in computation management.

11.6 WECBA Design and Implementation Assessment, Lessons Learned

Components in the implementation of the WECBA are based on component models of J2EE and CORBA. The implementation has validated the design of the WECBA. As long as the interfaces between the layers of the architecture remain stable, any change or addition in one layer will not affect other layers. For example, addition of an application on a host server or change of an application from one server to another will not force the Broker layer and the Web layer to change as long as the application is registered or re-registered with the Naming service. The WECBA design has met our business requirements stated in Section 11.2.

The granularity of components in the "engineering computing portal" (see Figure 11.1 and Figure 11.2) based on the WECBA varies from small to medium. The Servlets on the web server (see Figure 11.1) are small grain components. They have simple roles and functions. The Broker (see Figure 11.1) is a medium grain component. It has an extensive role and some complex functions. It is further decomposed into multiple smaller components for these functions in its implementation. The Computation Manager on host servers (see also Figure 11.1) is a medium grain component as well, although not as large as the Broker component.   The Computation Manager consists of an Execution Service responsible for launching applications and monitoring objects for reporting job status events.   The roles and functions of these components are summarized in Table 11.1 (in Section 11.4).

The "engineering computing portal" based on the WECBA clearly demonstrates the benefit of combining component software technology and web technology to integrate, manage, and deliver data and services to end-users. The utilization of standard common services like Event service and Naming service also enables a flexible and extensible system. The portal brings convenience, usability, and productivity to end-users.

An Integration Broker may be implemented in a number of platforms including CORBA, J2EE, and .Net. For a particular application domain, however, some are more efficient in terms of resources and performance and more cost effective than others. With regard to the choice of using lightweight high performance CORBA to implement our integration broker (see Figure 11.1), lessons learned can be summarized as the following.

• Lightweight high performance CORBA is useful and effective for providing object runtime management and distributed object communications in environments with resource and performance constraints. It provides adequate features for integrating applications such as math and engineering applications with the web. Environments with resource constraints include not only small computation devices or embedded systems, but also hosts that require resource sharing between multiple applications.

• Lightweight CORBA is fully interoperable with full CORBA. In our experiments, Orbix/E is interoperable with Sun J2SDK1.3 ORB, TAO C++ ORB with/without minimum configuration.

• Lightweight CORBA can be deployed to an environment where any of the following characteristics is true:

– It has limited computational resources (CPU, Memory), e.g., embedded devices.

– It has to share computational resources with other applications, e.g, laptops, desktops.

– The features in the minimum CORBA specification are sufficient, e.g., simple brokers and gateways.

– It has to improve performance by reducing object runtime management overhead and communication overhead, e.g., in math/engineering computational applications.

– It requires back and forth object interactions in peer-to-peer collaboration among a large number of nodes.

• Lightweight CORBA is not suitable for applications where the ORB has to be directly involved in complex services like Transaction Service. However, it can always work together with a full CORBA that provides such services.

• It makes sense to combine J2EE technology and lightweight high performance CORBA technology to integrate heterogeneous systems in multiple languages and bring them to the web as web services.

It is clear that Component Software Technology must be used together with Web Technology and infrastructure technologies like Computing Grid and Networking to solve challenging large scale distributed scientific and business problems.

11.7 Conclusions and Future Work

Component software technology has dramatically improved our ability to architect large scale distributed systems and build systems from components. Component-based application servers and integration servers have simplified the development and integration of enterprise distributed systems. To effectively deliver data and services from backend enterprise information and computing systems to the end-users, it is necessary to combine component software technology with web technology for a web-enabled component-based architecture. In this case study, we designed and validated such an architecture for simplifying the uses and managing the runtime of computational and engineering applications. We discussed its implementation issues and validated the usefulness and adequacy of lightweight high performance CORBA for integration requirements in the broker and host servers layers of the architecture. Lightweight high performance CORBA plays an important role in the integration of systems with heterogeneous platforms and multiple languages. A combination of J2EE and lightweight CORBA offers a good technology solution to such integration problems.

Future work is planned for integrating our architecture and implementation of engineering computing portal with grid computing platforms like Globus. In particular, we plan to integrate the scheduling, security, and data management features of Globus within our architecture and implementation. These features will enable the portal to automatically schedule job runs, dynamically manage resources and move large volume of data in a large-scale and secure computing grid.

Acknowledgments

This article is based on a paper presented at the 6th international Enterprise Distributed Object Computing conference at Lausanne, Switzerland, 17-20 September 2002. We would like to thank our colleagues in the Mathematics and Engineering Analysis group for helpful discussions and valuable comments. We especially want to thank Yichi Pierce, Hong Tat, Abe Askari, Thomas Tosch, and Ping Xue for helping clarify application scenarios described in this article.

References

Atkinson C., et al (2001). Component Based Product-Line Engineering with UML. Addison-Wesley.

D'Sousa D., Wills A. (1998). Catalysis: Objects, Frameworks, and Components in UML, Addison-Wesley.

Foster I., Kesselman C. (1997). "Globus: A Metacomputing Infrastructure Toolkit", *International Journal Supercomputer Applications*, No.2, pp. 115-128.

Foster I., Kesselman C., Tuecke S. (2001). "The Anatomy of the Grid, Enabling Scalable Virtual Organizations", *International Journal Supercomputer Applications*, No. 3, pp. 200-222.

Foster I., Kesselman C., Nick J., Tuecke S. (2002). "The Physiology of the Grid, An Open Grid Services Architecture for Distributed Systems Integration", 2002 Global Grid Forum, Toronto, http://www.globus.org/research/papers/ogsa.pdf

Grid Computing Environments (2002). http://www.computingportals.org/papers.html

Global Grid Forum (2002). http://www.globalgridforum.org/

Globus (2002). http://www.globus.org/

GridPort (2002). https://gridport.npaci.edu/

Henning M., Vinoski S. (2000). Advanced CORBA Programming with C++, Addison Wesley.

Holmes V., Linebarger J., Miller D., Poore C., Vandwart R. (2000). "Distributed Design Tools: mapping Targeted Design Tools onto a Web-based Distributed Architecture for High Performance Computing", *Proceedings of the 2000 International Conference on Web-based Modeling and Simulation*, pp. 34-39.

J2EE (2002). Java 2 Enterprise Edition (J2EE), http://java.sun.com/j2ee

.Net (2002). Microsoft .Net, http://www.microsoft.com/net/

NPACI Hotpage (2002). https://hotpage.paci.org/

OMG (1998m). Object Management Group, "minimum CORBA" specification.

OMG (1997e). Object Management Group, "Event Service" specification.

OMG (1997n). Object Management Group, "Naming" specification.

OMG (1999c). Object Management Group, "CORBA Component Model" specification.

Vogel A., Duddy K. (1997). Java Programming with CORBA, John Wiley.

Wang G., Ungar L., and Klawitter D. (1999). "Component Assembly for Object-Oriented Distributed Systems," *IEEE Computer*, 7, pp. 71–78.

Wang G., Cone G. (2001). "A Method to Reduce Risks in Building Distributed Enterprise Systems", *Proceedings of the Fifth IEEE International Enterprise Distributed Object Computing Conference*, IEEE CS Press, pp. 164-168.

Szyperski C. (2002). Component Software: Beyond Object-Oriented Programming, Addison Wesley Longman.

Chapter 12

Component-based Problem Solving Environments for Computational Science

MAOZHEN LI

Dept. of Electronic and Computer Engineering, Brunel University
Kingston Lane, Uxbridge, Middlesex UB8 3PH, U.K.

OMER F. RANA, DAVID W. WALKER, MATTHEW SHIELDS and YAN HUANG

Department of Computer Science, Cardiff University
Queen's Buildings, Newport Road, PO Box 916, Cardiff CF24 3XF, U.K.
`O.F.Rana@cs.cardiff.ac.uk`

Abstract. A Problem Solving Environment (PSE) should aim to hide implementation and systems details from application developers, to enable a scientist or engineer to concentrate on the science. A PSE must also enable the construction of new applications, or enable the integration of existing software or application codes (in various programming languages, or as executable binaries) in a uniform way. Most importantly, a PSE must be intuitive to use, and should support the sharing of good practice within a given application domain.

After providing an overview of existing PSEs, common themes that must be present in PSEs are outlined. A domain independent infrastructure for a PSE is then described, followed by the description of case studies that make use of our PSE infrastructure. The case studies include Molecular Dynamics, Boundary Element codes and Fluid Dynamics. Lessons learned from utilising component based approaches in scientific computing are then outlined.

12.1 Introduction and Motivation

A Problem Solving Environment (PSE) is a complete, integrated computing environment for composing, compiling, and running applications in a specific area [Gallopoulos *et al.* (1994)]. PSEs have been available for several years for certain specific domains – and multi-disciplinary PSEs (M-PSEs) have only recently become popular (such as Cactus [Cactus (2003)], WebFlow/Gateway [Fox *et al.* (1999)] and Arcade [Chen *et al.* (2001)]). Extensions to current scientific programs such as Matlab, Maple, and Mathematica are also examples of PSEs, albeit in a very limited context. The emphasis in PSEs is to enable re-use of existing software libraries (such as mathematical and visualisation

281

routines, and resource management systems) and the facility to enable existing software to
be invoked remotely. PSEs are particularly relevant in the context of Grid Computing, allowing scientists and engineers at remote sites to interact using standard software interfaces
– some of which are being ratified within the Global Grid Forum [GGF (2003)]. Component based development is an important implementation technology for PSEs, as it enables
existing scientific codes (many of which have been hand tuned) to be used in new ways.
Re-writing existing codes in a new language is often not a possibility, and wrapping codes
as components often is the only viable option.

PSEs have the potential to greatly improve the productivity of scientists and engineers,
particularly through the use of distributed object technologies, such as CORBA and Java.
Existing tools for building specific types of PSEs include PDELab [Weerawarana (1994)],
a system for building PSEs for solving PDEs, and PSEWare [PSEWARE (2003)], a toolkit
for building PSEs for symbolic computations. More generic infrastructure for building
PSEs is also under development, ranging from fairly simple RPC-based tools for controlling remote execution to more ambitious and sophisticated systems such as Globus [Foster
and Kesselman (1997)] and Legion [Grimshaw (1997)] for integrating geographically distributed computational and information resources. However, most of these PSEs lack the
ability to build up scientific applications by connecting and plugging software components
together, and do not yet provide an intuitive way to construct scientific applications. The
tools necessary to construct applications in a PSE should be domain independent – such as
work flow engines, component models etc – although existing work has generally focused
on building application specific PSEs.

12.1.1 *Component Model*

A component in the context of our PSE is a self-contained program, and may be a sequential code developed in C, Fortran or Java, or may contain internal parallelism using MPI
or PVM libraries. A component has an interface, which defines how it may be invoked
from another component, and what results it will return once it has completed operation.
A component interface therefore defines the datatypes and return types associated with it,
and an execution model which outlines all the libraries that must be supported to enable its
execution. Components in our PSE are self-documenting, with their interfaces defined in
XML, which enables a user to search for components suitable for a particular application,
enables a component to be configured when instantiated, enables each component to register with an event listener and facilitates the sharing of components between repositories.
Components are subsequently connected together into a data flow graph, also encoded in
XML, and sent to a resource manager for executing the application on a workstation cluster, or a heterogeneous environment made of workstations and high performance parallel
machines. Components can also be hierarchic, i.e. a component can be composed of a
number of other component task graphs – called "compound" components in our PSE. A
detailed description of the data model associated with our component model (in XML), can
be found in [Rana *et al.* (1999)].

Depending on the execution environment used, a component may access a range of different available services, such as an event service (to co-ordinate activities between components), a naming service (to locate other components), a security service (to ensure that access to a particular component can only be made from an authenticated component owner). These additional services are currently provided through the Globus toolkit, but are also available in distributed object systems such as CORBA.

There are four component types used in our PSE, and include the *compute components*, which undertake computational work such as performing a matrix multiplication or a Fast Fourier Transform. *Template components* require one or more components to be inserted into them in order to become fully functional. Template components can be used to embody commonly used algorithmic design patterns. This allows a developer to experiment with different numerical methods or model physics. Thus, in a partial differential equation solver a template might require a pre-conditioner to be inserted. Template components can also be used to introduce control constructs such as `loops` and conditionals into a higher-level component. For example, for a simple `for` loop the initial and final values of the loop control variable, and its increment, must be specified, together with a component that represents the body of the loop. For an `if-then-else` construct a Boolean expression, and a component for each branch of the conditional must be given. A template component can be viewed as a compute component in which one or more of the inputs is a component. *Data management components* are used to read and convert between the different types of data format that are held in files and Internet data repositories. The intention of this type of component is to be able to (1) sample data from various archives, especially if there is a large quantity of data to be handled, (2) convert between different data formats, (3) support specialised transports between components if large quantities of data needs to be migrated across a network, (4) undertake data normalisation, and in certain cases also generate SQL or similar queries to read data from structured databases. The fourth type of common component is the *user interface component* which allows a user to control an application through a graphical user interface, and plays a key role in supporting application composition, and for specialised scenarios such as computational steering (which involves a close coupling between a component wrapping a simulation, and a component providing visualisation to a user. A user is able to specify simulation parameters through the visual interface, and these should be passed to the simulation in real-time, and the outcome reflected on the visualisation interface within a particular time period).

A component is therefore the basic element within a work flow – and represents one of the four types described above. We also allow components to be combined into *Compound Components*, which can integrate/group commonly used components. This hierarchic organisation enables resource managers to co-schedule components which are likely to be used often. Each Compound Component is given a separate name from its constituents.

12.1.2 *What should a PSE Contain?*

A PSE must contain: (1) application development tools that enable an end user to construct new applications, or integrate libraries from existing applications, (2) development tools that enable the execution of the application on a set of resources. In this definition, a PSE must include resource management tools, in addition to application construction tools, albeit in an integrated way. Component based implementation technologies provide a useful way of achieving this objective, and have been the focus of research in PSE infrastructure Based on the types of tools supported within a PSE, we can identify two types of users: (1) application scientists/engineers interested primarily in using the PSE to solve a particular problem (or domain of problems), (2) programmers and software vendors who contribute components to help achieve the objectives of the category (1) users. The PSE infrastructure must support both types of users, and enable integration of third party products, in addition to application specific libraries.

Many of these requirements are quite ambitious, and existing PSE projects handle them to varying extents. The component paradigm has proven to be a useful abstraction, and has been adopted by many research projects. Although a useful abstraction for integration, performance issues when wrapping legacy codes in Fortran as components have not been addressed adequately. Automatic wrapper generators for legacy codes that can operate at varying degrees of granularity, and can wrap the entire code or sub-routines within codes automatically, are still not available – although some progress has been made towards achieving this, as outlined in Section 12.2. Part of the problem arises from translating data types between different implementation languages (such as complex numbers in Fortran), whereas other problems are related to software engineering support for translating monolithic codes into a class hierarchy. Existing tools such as Fortran to Java translators cannot adequately handle these specialised data types, and are inadequate for translating large application codes, such as the Lennard-Jones molecular dynamics application discussed in Section 12.3. For PSE infrastructure developers, integrating application codes provides one goal, the other being the resource management infrastructure to execute these codes. The latter of these can involve workstation clusters, or tightly coupled parallel machines. We therefore see a distinction between these two tiers of a PSE, (1) a component composition environment, (2) a resource management system. A loose coupling between these two aspects of a PSE will be useful where third party resource managers are being used, whereas a strong coupling is essential for computational steering or interactive simulations. A more detailed discussion of these issues can be found in [Walker *et al.* (1999)].

Existing PSE projects which utilise a component model include WebFlow/Gateway [Fox *et al.* (1999)], ARCADE [Chen *et al.* (2001)], the Component Architecture Toolkit [Gannon and Bramley (2000)], Netsolve [Casanova and Dongarra (1997)], and Parallel ELLPACK [Houstis *et al.* (2000)]. Most of these projects do not provide wrapping of existing scientific codes, and focus on either creating a data flow environment, or on allowing a user to write their own modules. Based on existing projects, a PSE must therefore: (1) allow a user to construct domain applications by plugging together independent components. Components may be written in different languages, placed at different locations, or exist on different platforms. Components may be created from scratch, or wrapped from legacy codes; (2) provide a visual application construction environment; (3) support web-based task submission; (4) employ an Intelligent Resource Management System to schedule and efficiently run the constructed applications; (5) make good use of industry standards such as middleware (CORBA), document tagging (XML); and (6) must be easy for users to extend within their domain.

12.2   PSE Infrastructure

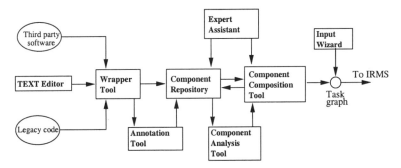

Fig. 12.1   *The software architecture of the Visual Component Construction Environment*

Figure 12.1 outlines the development process in our PSE. The Visual Component Composition Environment (VCCE) allows a user to construct an application by connecting together existing components. Components may be obtained from local or remote component repositories, and have interfaces defined in XML, based on a PSE-wide data model [Rana *et al.* (1999)]. Component repositories must be statically identified prior to launching the VCCE. A user can also register new components with the local repositories which contain instances of local or remote components.

Advice about the suitability of a component in a given situation, or about the types of components available, can be obtained via an Expert Advisor (EA). This is a knowledge based system (implemented with the Java Expert System Shell (JESS)) with rules that constrain the types of data a component can handle, the internal data distribution that is supported, and licensing requirements associated with components. Data types supported by a component, and execution constraints on it can be deduced from its interface. The EA is subsequently used by the Component Analysis Tool (CAT) to check the validity of the connectivity graph. After checking the connectivity graph it is then passed to the Component Evaluation/Execution Tool (CET) for the run-time stage of the application. The CET passes the task graph to the Intelligent Resource Management System (IRMS) to determine the computational resources to run the application. Using the IRMS, an application built in the VCCE may be scheduled onto single or multiple heterogeneous processor machines.

A complete legacy application may be wrapped as one object, or some object structure may be defined during the wrapping process. The granularity of a wrapped application is therefore dependent on how much is known about an application, whether the application can be successfully sub-divided, and whether constraints on the interfaces of components of a sub-divided applications can be derived. The use of hierarchy in the VCCE facilitates the sub-division and the use of wrappers. The VCCE also includes a text editor for creating a new component from scratch in some programming language. The Wrapper Tool can then be used to convert the new code into a CORBA-compliant component that can be placed in a CR, if required.

12.2.1 *Wrapper Tool*

Utilising existing codes (often in C and Fortran) is essential in scientific computing. Generally such codes are domain-specific, and written by various developers over many years – and therefore are often unstructured. Of the various conversion strategies for dealing with such legacy codes outlined in [Sneed and Majnar (1998)] re-engineering is often difficult (as few tools exist for scientific codes), and re-implementation of the entire code is very expensive. Wrapping the binary version of the application as a component, or wrapping I/O functions, is often the easiest option. Our wrapper generators can deal with both executable codes, and with source code.

We provide two wrapper generator tools – JACAW [Huang and Walker (2003)] is used when the source code is available, and WG [Shields *et al.* (2000)] when only the executable is available. JACAW allows an existing set of libraries to be converted to Java objects – utilising the Java Native Interface (JNI) libraries. The user must specify the header files to use, and JACAW automatically builds a class for each routine that may be invoked from Java. JACAW takes the C header files as input and automatically creates the corresponding Java and C files needed to make native calls. It also automatically builds the shared library that needs to be invoked from the Java wrapper. A particular focus of JACAW is the ability to deal with multi-dimensional arrays and pointers in languages such as C. JACAW uses pinning techniques to avoid excessive copying of array elements, and consequently reduce performance costs. Hence, when passing an array to a native method, pinning the array to a location that the native code can access and update means no copy is needed between Java memory and the C buffer. For multi-dimensional arrays this does not work however, as these are treated as object arrays in Java. To deal with multi-dimensional arrays, JACAW prevents any passing of object arrays to a native method (and only arrays of primitive types (such as ints, floats, doubles etc) are passed).

WG on the other hand is aimed at executable binaries, and allows these to be invoked remotely. WG adds a Listener and Publisher interface to a component, along with the XML definition defining its interface. To use WG, the developer must provide:

- the name of the component to be generated from the legacy code,
- the directory which is used to store all the files related to the component,
- the location and name of the legacy code,
- the name of the CORBA compiler used to generate the component (such as Visi-Broker),

- the language used by the legacy code (such as C or Fortran),
- the type of the legacy code, i.e. parallel (using MPI) or sequential, and the number of processors used if parallel
- the host name where the legacy code resides,
- the number of input parameters and their types. The WG supports seven types currently, *file*, *char*, *string*, *int*, *float*, *double*, and *long*,
- the number of output parameters and their types
- data file used to store results

After validating these parameters, the WG generates stubs and skeleton for the Listener and Publisher of the component. If there are no data input to the component, the generated Listener will automatically invoke the Body of the component once a request has been received. Otherwise, the generated Listener will first finish receiving data from another component, and then it invokes the Body of the component. Input data may either be streamed to the component, or read from a file. The Publisher is generated in a similar way to the Listener. The generation of the Body is completed by a Body template within WG, making use of the skeleton created by the IDL compiler. The main function of the Body is to invoke the legacy code wrapped inside it. After generating all the interfaces needed to wrap the legacy code as a component, the WG stores the component in the CR in XML for future use.

12.3   Applications using the PSE Infrastructure

We describe a molecular dynamics, a boundary element, and a computational fluid dynamics application that makes use of the generic component based PSE infrastructure described in Section 12.2 above.

12.3.1   *Molecular Dynamics*

The Molecular Dynamics (MD) application models a Lennard-Jones fluid. It is written in C, and was initially wrapped as a single CORBA object. A Java interface component is provided to the executable code which enables input from the user to be streamed to the executable, and subsequently to display output results to the user. The CORBA object makes use of an MPI runtime internally, and is distributed over a cluster of workstations. The intra-communication within the object is achieved via the MPI runtime, while the interaction between the client and the object is via the ORB. The interface to the code is specified by the PSE developer, and provided in Code Segment 1. In this case, an application developer does not need to know the details of how the code works, or how to distribute it over a workstation cluster. The wrapper therefore provides the abstraction needed to hide implementation details from an application user, requiring the developer to automatically handle exceptions generated from the CORBA and MPI system. The molecular dynamics code was subsequently sub-divided into four CORBA objects, to improve re-usability, and

```
module Simulation
{ interface Client{
 void displaySimulation(in unsigned long a,in float f1,in float f2, in float
                   f3,in float f4,in float f5); };
interface Wrapper{
 void startSimulation(in Client obj, in string SimulationParameter); };
};
```

Code Segment 1: The Molecular Dynamics code interface

included: (1) an `Initialization` object to calculate particle velocities and starting positions, (2) a `Moveout` object to handle communication arising from particle movement and "ghost" regions, (3) a `Force` object which calculates the force between molecules, and constitutes the main computational part of the code, (4) an `Output` object that generated simulation results for each time step. These four objects were managed by a `Controller` object, which coordinated the other four objects. Code Segment 2 provides part of the interface for the `Moveout` object. A user now has more control over component interaction,

```
...
import-data(in float rx, in float ry, in float rz,
      in float vx, in float vy, in float vz, in long head,
      in long list, in long map);
  void start-moveout();
  export-data(out float rx, out float ry, out float rz, out float vx,
      out float vy, out float vz, out long head, out long list,
      out long map);
```

Code Segment 2: The Moveout component interface

but still does not know how the MPI runtime is initialised and managed within each object. Figure 12.2 illustrates the invocation sequence for executing the molecular dynamics code, when wrapped as a single object. Hence, in this way, the application developer can construct a molecular dynamics application by connecting components together. Each component is self-documenting based on its XML interface, and component properties can be investigated using the Expert Advisor.

It is important to minimise performance overheads when using wrapped legacy codes as components for use in the PSE. As a critical criteria for usage in scientific computing is overall execution performance. In order to measure and compare performance between the wrapped CORBA component and the legacy code itself, we carried out a number of experiments running the MD CORBA component and the legacy code on a cluster of workstations and on a dedicated parallel machine (named *cspace*). The cluster runs Solaris2.7 and MPICH1.2.0, connected over an intranet (with shared file space) with 10Mb/s Ethernet. The parallel machine is a Sun E6500 with thirty 336MHz Ultra Sparc II processors, running Solaris2.7 and using MPI libraries from Sun Microsystems. We increased the number of molecules from 2048 to 256,000, using 8 workstations in the cluster and 8 processors in cspace. We use the Visibroker ORB from Inprise on both cspace and the workstation cluster. The results are illustrated in Figure 12.3. We find that there is almost no loss of

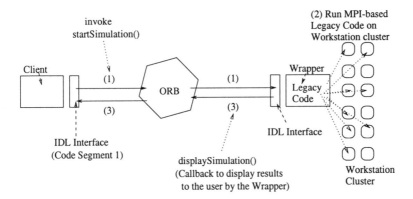

Fig. 12.2   *The invocation sequence of the Molecular Dynamics code*

performance between the CORBA component wrapped from the native code, and the native code itself. These results are observed on both the cluster of workstations, and on the dedicated parallel machine. We do however see a significant difference between execution speeds on cspace and the network of workstations when using CORBA.

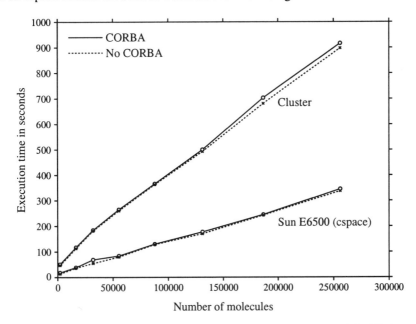

Fig. 12.3   Performance comparisons running the wrapped MD CORBA component and the MD legacy code itself on a cluster of workstations and on a dedicated parallel machine

Our results suggest that parallel CORBA components wrapped from parallel legacy codes using MPI can still maintain high performance. We attribute this to improved implementation of data management within the Visibroker ORB [VisiBroker (2002)], and the use of a shared file space in our experiments. We also reached a similar conclusion in a

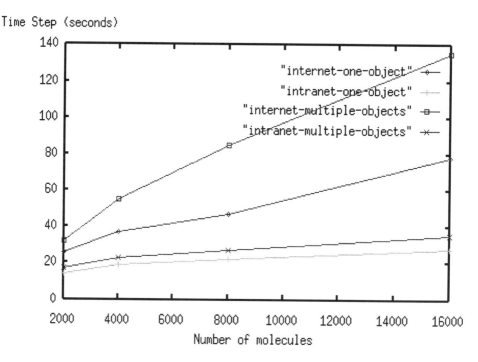

Fig. 12.4 *Performance comparison between wrapping the MD code as a single CORBA object and several different CORBA objects*

previous study where we have compared the performance of an MD code wrapped as a single CORBA component, versus the performance of the MD code divided into a collection of co-operating CORBA components [Rana *et al.* (2002)]. The performance results in these two situations are illustrated in Figure 12.4, and are presented for comparison on the same graph. The top curve on the graph, shown with the broken line, corresponds to communications over a distributed file system, and suggests a 150% decrease in performance compared to a similar set up over a shared file system. We find a similar reduction in performance when wrapping the MD code as a single object. When wrapping the MD code as separate CORBA objects, the communication costs between objects are significant, and with a shared file system represent a performance degradation of 23% with respect to wrapping the entire MD code as one object. When using the Internet with a distributed file system, the degradation in performance when wrapping the MD code as multiple objects is 33%, compared to wrapping the entire MD code as one object. These results correspond to 4000 molecules in the fluid. Our results therefore show that communication delays between CORBA objects with large amounts of data are significant (between different file systems), and using CORBA for communication between processes, in place of the MPI runtime is not recommended. Using CORBA in place of MPI to achieve parallelism, with standard CORBA ORBs can have significant performance degradation, unless the CORBA ORB is modified to support multi-threading or has specialised support for parallel processes. However, what we do recommend is the use of MPI clusters connected via CORBA, which will also enable multiple MPI run times to work together

12.3.2   *Boundary Element and Computational Electromagnetics*

The BE2D code is a 2D boundary element simulation code for the analysis of electro-magnetic wave scattering. The main inputs to the program are a closed 2D contour and a control file defining the characteristics of the incident wave. The original code was written in Fortran. To make the code easier to use within the PSE and also to provide runtime speed comparisons it was decided to convert the code into Java. The use of Fortran to Java converters was considered but abandoned fairly quickly because of the lack of support for complex numbers. Complex numbers caused a number of problems in converting the code, not least because of the fact that they are primitive types in Fortran, but are not directly supported in the standard Java API. A third party implementation of complex numbers for Java was found and used, from Visual Numerics called JNL [VN (1999)]. Complex number arithmetic proved to be more than just a straight translation from the Fortran code to its Java equivalent. As complex numbers in Java are objects, and Java does not yet support operator overloading, the complex number objects have to use their instance and class methods: add, multiply, subtract and divide. These methods are either unary or binary, taking a single input parameter which is used to modify the object calling the method or taking two input parameters on a static class method that creates a new result without any modification side effects. Thus calculations involving more than an arbitrary number of parameters become far more complicated in Java than their Fortran equivalents. The converted BE2D was subsequently used as a single component within the PSE. The solver is combined with a data component that generates co-ordinate pairs representing the 2D contour and a graph renderer, (JChart [Piola (1999)]) a third party component, which displays the resultant EM wave scattering result data. The output generated from the code is illustrated in Figure 12.5. When the complete BE2D solver is wrapped as a CORBA object, comprising a single Fortran executable unit, then the interface can be described as in Code Segment 3, which contains the name of the solver, and a single input file. If the data is to be streamed to the solver, a component that can convert a file (local or at a URL) into a stream is placed before the component.

The execution comparisons for the Java based BE2D code, against the original Fortran executable were: 0.99 seconds for Fortran and 15.1 seconds for Java. The initial version of the Java code took 24.3 seconds but the execution time was improved by modifying the execution process. By replacing the static binary complex number operators by the unary method wherever there was no side effect problem with modifying the original number we were able to improve the execution time by 9 seconds. This is almost entirely due to the fact that there are substantially less new operations in the code. Therefore, when incorporating legacy codes in Fortran as components in a PSE, it is important to consider data type conversions and their subsequent effects on performance. Much of the remaining difference between the Java and Fortran versions can be explained by the Java Virtual Machine

(JVM) start up overhead, running the BE2D code in an already running JVM would cut the difference even further. A direct conversion of existing legacy codes to components as Java or CORBA objects, without support for specialised data types encountered in scientific applications, may lead to the resulting application becoming unusable at worst, and slower at best.

```
module Be2dComponent {
    interface Run { string runBe2d(string inputsource); }; };
```

Code Segment 3: BE2D interface

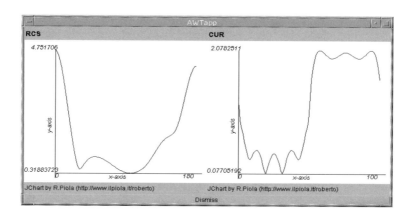

Fig. 12.5   *Output of the BE2D solver*

The BE3D code is a 3 dimensional boundary element simulation code, similar in functionality to BE2D. Like BE2D, BE3D is written in Fortran, however unlike BE2D, BE3D is parallel and makes use of MPI libraries. It is not realistic to convert BE3D to Java, as we did with BE2D, because it is a considerably larger piece of code and in addition we did not have access to the source code. Therefore BE3D was wrapped as a series of CORBA components. The increased complexity and size of the 3D code encouraged, allowed us to derive components with a smaller granularity – compared to the 2D version of the code. The input consists of two components: compute (1) the 3D Mesh representing the 3D contour, and (2) the incident wave properties data component. The solver is split into two components. One to compute the far-field boundary and the other to compute the cross section. Finally there are the output components which extract a 2D slice from the computed cross section and display the slice using the same graph renderer as BE2D. Each of the sub-components are wrapped as individual CORBA components and in this example all parameters are passed between the components as CORBA objects.

12.3.3 *Computational Fluid Dynamics*

The CFD code called PHI3D [Williams and Baker (1996)] written in Fortran is a finite element based computational fluid dynamics code for simulating incompressible Navier-Stokes flows, and may be used to model flows in the lung and upper respiratory system. Using a finite-element methodology, complex geometries can be easily simulated with PHI3D using unstructured grids. A time-accurate integration scheme allows the simulation of both transient and steady-state flows.

The legacy code PHI3D.x is a Fortran code making use of 1 processor. It has one input and twelve outputs: steps, inner steps, Mass, Uvel, Vvel, Wvel, Temp, PHI, Press, DeltaT, Time, Reyn. The IDL interface generated by the WG for the CFD legacy code is given in Code Segment 3.

```
module CFD
{
    interface CFDComponent{
        void Listener(in string ComponentID, in string inputs);
        void Body(in string parameters);
        void Publisher(out string ComponentID, out string outputs);
    }; };
```

Code Segment 3: The IDL for the CFD CORBA component

A user interface (Figure 12.6) is used to invoke the code through its Listener, which invokes the Body of the CFD component which in turn starts to execute the CFD legacy code using a command such as "PHI3D.x". When there is an output, the Body invokes the Publisher to make a callback to the UI component to display simulation results to the user. The implementation code for the CFD CORBA component generated by the WG is briefly described in Code Segment 4. An XML description of the CFD code is provided in Figure 12.7, and is based on the data model provided in [Rana *et al.* (1999)].

```
class CFDComponentImpl extends _CFDComponentImplBase
{
    public void Listener(String ComponentID, String inputs)
    {...
        if(ComponentID=="CFD")
            read parameters(inputs) from user interface component
        invoke Body of the Component
    }
    public void Body(String parameters)
    {...
        execute "PHI3D.x input.dat output.dat"
        send data(output.dat) to the Publisher of the component
        invoke the Publisher
    }
    public void Publisher(String ComponentID, String outputs)
    {...
```

read data(output.dat) from the Body of the component

ComponentID= "UIComponent"

invoke UI component with outputs

  }

}

Code Segment 4: The implementation code for the CFD CORBA component

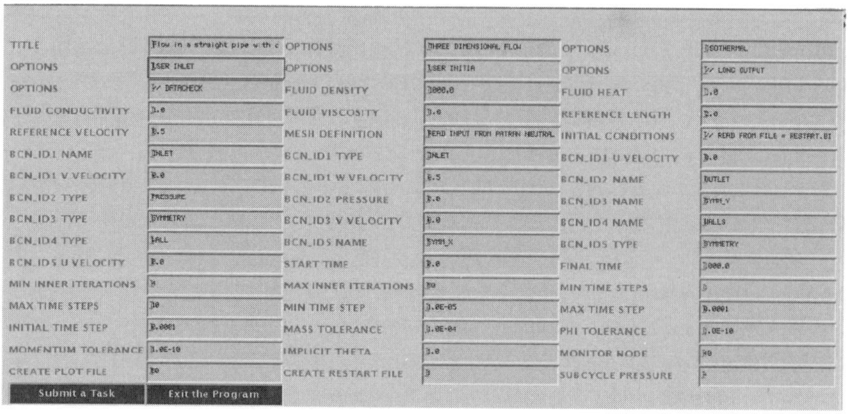

Fig. 12.6   A snapshot of the CFD user interaction. This interface supports interactions with a legacy code, wrapped as a component

12.4   Common Themes and Issues

Based on the case studies presented, various common themes arise. These include:

- **Performance**: In the context of scientific computing, performance is often a major concern. Often domain scientists and engineers are unwilling to adopt a component based approach if the performance is not comparable to their existing libraries. This has often been perceived as a major limitation of converting existing scientific libraries and codes to components. However, as we demonstrate in the Molecular Dynamics case study, provided data transfers are handled through efficient mechanisms, converting an existing code to components does not pose significant performance penalties. Performance issues are also related to whether the executable is being invoked through an interface – or whether a source code translation has been undertaken. Wrapping an executable is often likely to lead to comparable performance to the original – and is primarily constrained by the environment within which the wrapped code is now executed. For instance, constraints imposed by the Runtime.exec method in Java can constrain performance of wrapped C or Fortran codes. When a component has been derived by a source code translation, issues associated with data structures become significant – such as memory management issues associated with dealing with multi-dimensional ar-

```
<pse-def>
   <preface>
     <name alt="CFD" id="CFD"> CFDComponent</name>
     <pse-type>Computational Fluid Dynamics</pse-type>
     <component-directory>/home/wgen/Component</component-directory>
     <legacy-code>PHI3D.x</legacy-code>
     <language>fortran</language>
     <ORB-Compiler>idl2java</ORB-Compiler>
     <processors>1</processors>
     <host-name>sapphire.cs.cf.ac.uk</host-name>
   </preface>

  <ports>
    <inports>
    <inportnum> 1 </inportnum>
    <inport id="1"> file </inport>
    </inports>

    <outports>
    <outportnum> 12 </outportnum>
    <outport id="1"> int </outport>
    <outport id="2"> int </outport>
    <outport id="3"> float </outport>
    <outport id="4"> int </outport>
    <outport id="5"> int </outport> ...
    <outport id="9"> int </outport>
    <outport id="10"> float </outport> ...
    <outport id="12"> float </outport>

    <href name="file:/home/wgen/Component/output.data" value="output" />
    </outports>
  </ports>

  <execution id="platform">
    <type> Solaris 2.7 </type>
    <type> Sequential </type>
  </execution>

   <help context="instantiate">
     <href name="file:/home/pse/help/cfd.txt" value="NIL" />
   </help>
</pse-def>
```

Fig. 12.7   XML description of CFD legacy code

rays – and array copying and referencing for object arrays, compared with arrays of primitive types. A useful extension to a component model should be the ability to provide bounds on performance degradation likely to result as a consequence of wrapping a code.

- **Ownership**: Component models in scientific computing are also useful to invoke scientific codes remotely. This however raises important issues of ownership and security, as it is now necessary to transfer data sets to a remote location, and also store results temporarily at the remote site. Data ownership is an important concern for many domain scientists, and the underlying component framework should provide security support (such as SSL or similar encryption techniques). Ownership is also important when a number of components are used (in a work flow environment as proposed here, for instance) to construct a single application. Each component in this context may be separately owned, and the ownership of the combined application – or Compound Component – becomes an important concern. The underlying name service used to locate components should allow ownership issues to also be addressed.

- **Accuracy**: This issue becomes important when existing scientific codes (legacy codes) are wrapped as components. To enable data transfer between the legacy code and component interface wrapping the code, it is necessary to undertake data type conversions. Hence, a double precision number may need to be converted to enable another component in the work flow to receive results – and this may lead to inaccuracy in results. The component interface should therefore also identify if a conversion is to be undertaken – and should alert the user if a lower accuracy version is to be used. Alternatively, a user may tag a particular data type to use the IEEE 754 floating point format – although enforcing this across different components may not be practical.

- **User Interaction**: The complexity of user interactions can vary from a form based interface to more complex electronic notebooks. Should every component also support a separate interface for user interaction (along with an XML definition), or should generic interface components be defined that can read the XML description, and automatically create user entry capabilities? This is particularly relevant for Compound Components which can represent complete applications.

- **Configuration/Initialisation**: Initialising the PSE and the constituent components is an important concern. Should the components that wrap particular codes be constantly running, or should they be dynamically invoked at run time? In many existing scientific applications, it is assumed that a code is constantly running over the duration of the interaction with a user – generally as a daemon process. However, the use of "component factories" and dynamic launching mechanisms in component frameworks allows automatic initiation of components. This introduces important concerns in how work flow between components is to be managed, and how data transfers between components is to take place. Automatic launching also requires the recording of state of a particular interaction – in order to re-start the component at a later stage. Limited support is provided at present in component frameworks for supporting this.

- **Common Interfaces**: Ideally all components with a PSE (and across PSEs) should publish their interfaces using a common data model. No consensus at present exists on what these shared data model(s) should be. Although progress is being made towards identifying common formats in particular application communities – such as BioInformatics, and for wrapping common mathematical libraries (such as in the MONET [MONET (2002)] project) – the usage of these models is limited.

- **Usage Accounting**: An important requirement in using commercial components within a PSE is to measure the time for which a particular component has been used. Accounting mechanisms are therefore important to monitor usage of a particular component, and use this to support charging for use. Little infrastructure exists at present within commercial component frameworks for supporting usage accounting.

12.5   Conclusion and Future Work

Software engineering support for scientific computing has been lagging behind similar efforts in other domains. The reason has been the lack of tools and environments to enable sharing of existing scientific codes, and the ability to integrate these codes to compose applications. An infrastructure for a component based Problem Solving Environment is first outlined, followed by case studies to demonstrate how this can be used for interacting with particular scientific codes.

The emphasis in developing PSEs should be on creating an environment that is easy to use, and intuitive for an application/domain expert. A computational scientist should therefore not have to configure hardware resources in order to undertake molecular dynamics research, for instance. An important lesson learnt from our work is the necessity to understand the impact of specialised data structures on the usage and performance of legacy codes, when these are wrapped as components within a PSE. The Java programming language can be useful in integrating various components, but it still suffers from the absence of data structures that are essential for scientific codes. Current efforts are under way within the JavaGrande forum [JavaGrande (2003)] to address some of these issues, and the result of these efforts will be significant to future PSE infrastructure.

We have described various PSE projects currently under way, or nearing completion, and extracted common themes that must be supported in a PSE. Our system is similar in some ways to other projects in this area. For instance, the majority of projects use the dataflow paradigm together with a graphical component based composition tool with which to build meta-applications. Many are now using third party systems for the underlying communication, security and local resource management and scheduling, such as Globus [Foster and Kesselman (1997)].

References

Borland/Inprise (2002). The Visibroker ORB. http://www.borland.com/visibroker.

Bramley, R. (1998) Report of workshop on Problem-Solving Environments and Scientific IDEs for Knowledge, Information, and Computing (SIDEKIC 98). *Proceedings of SuperComputing97*, 1998. http://www.cs.indiana.edu/~bramley/Sidekic.html.

Bramley, R. and Gannon, D. (2003). PSEWare. http://www.extreme.indiana.edu/pseware.

Cactus Group (2003). The Cactus project. http://www.cactuscode.org/.

Casanova, H. and Dongarra, J. (1997) NetSolve: A Network Server for Solving Computational Science Problems. *International Journal of Supercomputer Applications and High Performance Computing*, 11(3):212–223, 1997.

Chen, Z., Maly, K., Mehrotra, P. and Zubair, M. (2001). Arcade: A Web-Java Based Framework for Distributed Computing. http://www.icase.edu:8080.

Darlington, J., Bunin, O. and Guo, Y. (2001). Design of Problem-Solving Environment for Contingent Claim Valuation. *Proceedings of Euro-Par: LNCS 2150*, 2001.

Foster, I. and Kesselman, C. (1997) Globus: A metacomputing infrastructure toolkit. *Int. Journal of Supercomputing Applications*, 11(2), 1997.

Fox, G., Haupt, T., Akarsu, E., Kalinichenko, A., Kim, K.-S., Sheethalnath, P. and Youn, C.-H. (1999). The Gateway System: Uniform Web Based Access to Remote Resources. *Proceedings of JavaGrande Conference*, 1999.

Gallopoulos, E., Houstis, E.N. and Rice, J.R. (1994). Computer as Thinker/Doer :Problem-Solving Environments for Computational Science. *IEEE Computational Science and Engineering*, 1(2), 1994.

Gannon, D. and Bramley, R. (2000). Component Architecture Toolkit. http://www.extreme.indiana.edu/cat/.

Global Grid Forum (2003). http://www.gridforum.org.

Grimshaw, A.S. (1997). Campus-Wide Computing: Early Results Using Legion at the University of Virginia. *Int. Journal of Supercomputing Applications*, 11(2), 1997.

Hariri, S., Topcuoglu, H., Furmanski, W., Kim, D., Kim, Y., Ra, I., Bing, X., Ye, B. and Valente, J. (1998). A Problem Solving Environment for Network Computing. In *Problem Solving Environments*, IEEE Computer Society, 1998. http://www.ece.arizona.edu/\~{}hpdc/projects/ADViCE/papers/bkch.html.

Houstis, E.N., Rice, J.R., Weerawarana, S., Catlin, A.C., Papachiou, P., Wang, K.-Y.and Gaitatzes, M. (2000). Parallel ELLPACK: A Problem Solving Environment for PDE Based Applications on Multicomputer Platforms. http://www.cs.purdue.edu/research/cse/pellpack/paper/pellpack-paper-1.html.

Huang, Y. and Walker, D.W. (2003). JACAW-A Java-C Automatic Wrapper Tool and its Benchmark. *Proceedings of IPDPS*, 2003.

JavaGrande Forum (2003). http://www.javagrande.org.

NAG (2002). MONET: Mathematics On the NET. http://monet.nag.co.uk/.

Piola, R. (1999). The JChart package. http://www.ilpiola.it/roberto/jchart/.

Rana, O.F., Li, M. and Walker, D.W. (2002). Wrapping MPI-Based Legacy Codes as Java/CORBA Components. *Future Generation Computer Systems(FGCS)*, 18:213–223, 2002.

Rana, O.F., Walker, D.W., Li, M. and Shields, M. (1999). An XML Based Component Model for Generating Scientific Applications and Performing Large Scale Simulations in a Metacomputing Environment. *Proceedings of Generative Component Based Software Engineering, Erfert, Germany*, September 1999.

Rice, J., Zhou, C., Catlin, A., Fleeter, S. and Houstis, E. (2000). GasTurbnLab: A Problem Solving Environment for Simulating Gas Turbines. *Proceedings of 16th IMACS World Congress*, (104-5), 2000.

Shields, M.S., Li, M., Rana, O.F. and Walker, D. (2000). A Wrapper Generator for Wrapping High Performance Legacy Codes as Java/CORBA Components. *Proceedings of SuperComputing*, 2000.

Sneed, H.M., and Majnar, R. (1998). A Case Study in Software Wrapping. *Proceedings of ICSM*, pages 86–93, 1998.

Szyperski, C. and Pfister, C. (1996). Why objects are not enough. *Proceedings of International Component Users Conference*, 1996.

Taylor, I. *et al.* (2003). Triana. http://www.triana.co.uk/.

Visual Numerics (1999). JNL: A numerical library for Java. http://www.vni.com/products/wpd/jnl/.

Walker, D., Li, M., Rana, O., Shields, M. and Huang, Y. (1999). The Software Architecture of a Distributed Problem Solving Environment. Technical report, Oak Ridge National Laboratory, Computer Science and Mathematics Division, PO Box 2008, Oak Ridge, TN 37831, USA, December 1999. Research report no. ORNL/TM-1999/321.

Weerawarana, S. (1994). PDELab. *Proceedings of the Second Annual Object-Oriented Numerics Conference*, 1994.

Williams, P.T. and Baker, A.J. (1996). Incompressible Computational Fluid Dynamics and the Continuity Constraint Method for the 3D Navier-Stokes Equations. *Numerical Heat Transfer, Part B Fundamentals*, (29):137–273, 1996.

Index